Beginning an Investment in Real Estate

ROBERT J. DONOHUE CCIM

THE REGENT SCHOOL PRESS

BEGINNING AN INVESTMENT IN REAL ESATATE

FIFTH EDITION

PUBLISHED BY

THE REGENT SCHOOL PRESS
26453 VERDUGO
MISSION VIEJO, CA 92692

EAN /ISBN 978 1-886654-10-5

TABLE OF CONTENTS

TABLE OF CONTENTS

Introduction to 5th Edition

The goal of all investing is the attainment and preservation of wealth.

This book is intended to provide an entry portal to investment real estate for the beginning investor as well as others who wish to diversify an existing portfolio not simply into other classes of stocks and bonds but into "hard assets" capable of responding to inflationary pressures. Most investors are aware of the need for asset diversification, but many lack sufficient knowledge and experience to invest safely and successfully in income-producing real estate.

The most immediate threats to both the attainment and preservation of wealth are the consequences of the staggering debt accumulated by federal and state governments and the manner in which governments seeks to manage the debt. The federal debt in 2015 exceeds $18.1 Trillion and the interest paid on this debt exceeds $238 Billion annually. This amount of debt is greater than 104% of U.S. GDP, the total value of all goods and services produced annually. Yet federal deficits continue to be added at a rate greater than $480 Billion per year. Debt is forecasted by the non-partisan CBO[1] to breach $20 Trillion within 1-2 years. State pension plans continue to be underfunded by $4.7 Trillion, a debt which in some states exceeds $25,000 per capita.

Both existing federal debt and new deficits have been financed by the Federal Reserve's purchase of Treasury notes, bonds and home mortgages while interest rates, which would normally rise in response to such demand, are artificially suppressed using a stratagem of "financial repression," by which central governments suppress interest rates in an inflationary environment. As a result, taxes are levied on inflating prices while the interest paid on outstanding obligations is held to a minimum. This tactic was employed following WWII by both the United States (when the debt to GDP ratio exceeded 122%) and the United Kingdom from 1945 to 1965. It has been estimated that it may take as long as 20 years to reduce the existing debt and return interest and growth rates to economically sustainable levels.

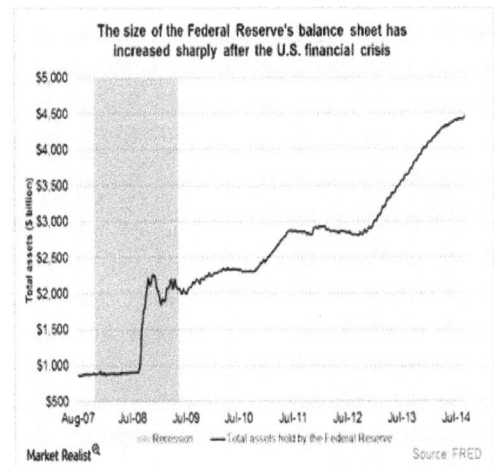

The size of the Federal Reserve's balance sheet has increased sharply after the U.S. financial crisis

The most damaging result of financial repression is that private savings accounts and pension funds as a source of investment funds are unable to achieve yields equal to the true inflation rate without incurring substantial risk. The real rate of return (nominal rate – inflation rate) turns negative and fails to preserve the purchasing power of the dollar. The accumulated wealth of the middle class which provides the bulk of investment funds is quietly but progressively eroded. Although middle income nominal wages have increased slightly, they have not kept pace with inflation and remain about equal to their purchasing power in 1964. Meanwhile both federal and most state pension funds have accrued unfunded liabilities

---

[1]   Congressional Budget Office. **www.cbo.gov**

which are now beyond reclamation by simply increasing taxes. Yet the structural reforms which are urgently needed are egregiously absent.

The course of action required of the "prudent man" is to assume as much control over his or her financial wealth as possible using investments which are responsive to the inflation that is almost certain to follow the debasement of the $US dollar.

James Rickards[2] refers to his study of families who, over many generations through wars, upheavals and revolutions, have been able to preserve their wealth through thick and thin. Rickards found that these families invest almost equally (1/3, 1/3, 1/3) in *art*, *precious metals* and *real estate*. Their knowledge of real estate investing is passed as a meme from one generation to the next. But for those not born to the manor, acquiring knowledge and skills in real estate is largely a post-graduate effort.

Gold (i.e. precious metals) and art are currently promoted as "hard assets" capable of hedging inflation. But neither delivers current income. Most investments in income properties, however, are unique in that they provide returns in the form of operating income, tax benefits (depreciation) and the potential for appreciation. In an inflationary environment real estate provides the opportunity to raise rents to preserve the purchasing power of the invested dollar.

This text is intended to provide the essential building blocks for an in-depth understanding of income-producing real estate as a means of acquiring and maintaining wealth. It covers basic ownership principles, property valuation, taxation, property selection, financing, leasing and disposition. Chapter 6 leads the reader step-by-step in the construction of an Excel-based 10-year, after-tax analysis program by which an income property's financial performance can be measured using many metrics. Although this program may lack the flowers and graphic flourishes of commercially available programs, it provides as much, if not more, actionable information to the prospective investor at a fraction of the cost.

Chapter 9 leads the income property owner step-by-step through the legalities, regulations and techniques of exchanging real estate under S.1031 of the Code. The ability to exchange real estate is one of its great advantages because it enables the reinvestment of capital before the payment of taxes. It is the Über capitalistic tool which preserves and leverages accumulated wealth for re-investment, jobs and growth. In Chapter 12 we have also provided guidelines for the safe investment in promissory notes secured by real estate.

I hope that you will enjoy and profit from this primer and that it will help you acquire assets which are not owned by somebody else.

Robert J, Donohue CCIM
Mission Viejo, CA 92692
robertdonohue@gmail.com
2015

---

[2] Author of "Currency Wars" and "The Death of Money."

• Robert J. Donohue CCIM
Professional Biography

Bob Donohue is the principal of The Donohue Company and is an accredited real estate investment specialist with more than 30 years experience in multiple investment-grade real properties. Bob earned his CCIM accreditation (Certified Commercial and Investment Member of the National Association of Realtors) in 1981 and has since represented scores of investors in the acquisition, disposition and exchange of a wide-range of property types including, self-storage, multi-family apartments, office, retail centers, as well as land for these kinds of investments. He maintains specialized skills in the marketing of long-term leasehold (ground-leased) interests as well as the leased-fee interest in these properties.

Bob's background includes senior marketing positions with three Fortune 500 companies. His initial business experience was in the pharmaceutical business with Upjohn where he began a career as a sales representative. At the time he left Upjohn he served as Senior Marketing Manager for the antibiotic group. Later he served as Vice-President, Marketing, for the pharmaceutical division of the Revlon Corporation (USV) and then as General Manager for a California-based pharmaceutical company.

Together with Carol Mullin Ph.D., Bob co-authored Professional Selling Skills, a program developed by Basic Systems Inc. and later sold to the Xerox Corporation which continues to market this distinctive sales skills program in a number of industries.

In addition to his marketing experience, Bob is an author and teacher. His text, Introduction to Cashflow Analysis, is a Referenced Text by the Certified Financial Planners Board of Standards, and has been widely used in universities in the training of financial planners. His second book, Beginning an Investment in Real Estate, is also used at the university level and is now used in the training program of commercial real estate companies

Bob was an instructor for more than 19 years at the University of California Irvine in the Professional Planning Program where he taught courses in finance and real estate investments. He has served as Vice-President and President of the Southern California CCIM Chapter as well as a Director of Lambda Alpha, an honorary world-wide professional land-economics society, and on the Business Development Committee for the City of Mission Viejo.

Bob is a graduate of the Catholic University of America and attended New York University for post-graduate studies in business and education. He lives in Southern California with his wife, Inga, and enjoys flying their Beech Bonanza.

His office is located in Mission Viejo, CA 92692

Tel. 949.235.1290

Email: robertdonohue@gmail.com

A cquiring an understanding of the fundamental concepts of property ownership is a vital pre-requisite to intelligent real estate investing. Investors who begin with only a fuzzy understanding of the basics find themselves continually hobbled throughout their investment careers. Lessons learned through trial and error may well be lasting, but are frustrating and often very expensive.

Chapter 1
Property,
Ownership,
Interests & Deeds

For example, many investors form or join a partnership to invest in real estate. Later, when the property has realized substantial appreciation, they seek to exchange their partnership interest under I.R.C. §1031 in order to defer capital gains taxes. It is only then they learn that an interest in a partnership is not an interest in real property but an interest in personal property, and as such is not eligible for an exchange into another real property. How they handle this issue can mean a successful exchange or a big tax bill.

There are additional reasons to acquire a basic understanding in this subject: law and taxes. In many important ways, the law handles issues related to real property much differently from personal property. The same is true for matters dealing with tax law. So it is important that we begin at the beginning.

In order to appreciate what it is that can be owned, we need first to understand the Classes of property.

Real Property vs. Personal Property

"Property" is defined as anything which can be owned; if we can own it, we can call it "property."

The basic distinction between real and personal property (there are only two kinds, but many gray areas) is one of *mobility*. Those items which are relatively immobile are usually classified in the law as real property, while those which are more easily moved or transported tend to be regarded as items of personal property. This is an important distinction.

The following table presents some examples of real and personal property:

Real Property	Personal Property
Land	Money, autos, gems
Trees, Landscape Plants, Standing Timber	Stocks, Bonds
Subterranean Oil, Gas & Minerals	Options - in both real and personal property
Easements	Partnership Interest
Stock in Mutual Water Company	Emblements[1]
Structures on the Land	Mortgages & Notes
Fixtures	Beneficial Interests In a Trust

Some of these items of personal and real property may not be entirely intuitive. "Stock in a mutual water company," ostensibly personal property, for example, is created when a developer in a new area drills a water well intended to supply a number of parcels owned by different parties. Each separate owner is granted a share of stock in the water company enabling the owner to share in the water supply. Under the law, this right is considered so *appurtenant* to the use of the property as to become real property. Upon transfer of the land served, the stock will transfer also. The same can also be said of an easement[2] which enables the owner of a property to gain ingress and egress to his land. Notice, too, that an option to acquire real property, or a mortgage on real property, is not equivalent to real property; both are examples of personal property.[3]

A Classical Definition

There is a "classical" definition which defines real property as –

> *... the land, all that it is above the land, all that is attached and appurtenant to the land, and all that is beneath the land...*

This definition postulates that ownership of real property extends from the borders of a parcel of land upward to infinity and downward to the center of the earth. In 1946 the U.S. Supreme Court[4] held that a landowner owns as much airspace as he or she can occupy or use in conjunction with the land, even though the owner does not take physical possession of the space.

IRS to Expand Definition of Real Property

In response to requests from REITs, the IRS is proposing to expand the definition of real estate assets to include inherently permanent structures such as broadcast towers, certain parking facilities, offshore drilling platforms, pipelines, transmission lines, stationary docks, bridges, railroad tracks and outdoor Sadvertising displays. The changes are expected in 2015.

MOG Rights

Oil and gas rights beneath a parcel of land, absent a prior transfer, are examples of real property which belong to the owner of the overlying dirt. In areas in which oil is found, parcels are often sold by a developer who *reserves* to himself the mineral, oil and gas rights (MOG rights) of all surrounding parcels. It is not

---

[1] Crops under cultivation which are intended to be harvested. Upon sale of the real property, title to these crops would <u>not automatically</u> pass to the new owner as real estate.

[2] An easement delivers the right to use another's real property but not the right to possess it.

[3] Mortgages, though personal property, are so intimately associated with real property that they are sometimes called *chattels real*. A chattel is an obsolete term for personal property

[4] U.S. vs. Causby

uncommon that oil derricks will be found interspersed among residential properties in these areas.

Here's a valuable distinction that has survived virtually unchanged for many, many years:

> "The term 'Land' in its broadest sense, includes not only all substances comprising part of the solid body of the earth, but all fluids and gases, metallic and non-metallic substances, located beneath the surface of the soil, as well as the soil and subsoil upon and immediately beneath the surface of the earth, and the erections on the surface, of a permanent and fixed character. The solid crystalline bodies, forming part of the substance of the earth and the liquids and gases, which do not possess a definite geometric form, that are put to commercial uses, because of their value to mankind are generally denominated "minerals," to distinguish them from the soil and subsoil and other elements of the term, 'land,' possessing no peculiar value. As long as such substances retain their place in the earth, they are included within the legal meaning of the term 'land' and are part of the realty and pass by a grant of the land, as such; but once such substances are severed from the soil in which they are naturally found, they lose their character as real estate and are considered personal property."
>
> *Christopher J. Tiedman*
> *The American Law of Real Property*
> ***July 1, 1892***

Fixtures

Probably no single issue in real estate has resulted in more lawsuits between buyer and seller than a dispute over fixtures. A fixture was once an item of personal property which has since become so intimately attached to real property as to become real property. For example, in the purchase of an apartment house with a pool, the pool pump and filtering system would no doubt be regarded as real property since they are firmly attached to the land and are an integral part of the pool system.

The poolside furniture, however, may be a different matter. A seller may contend that these are items not "affixed" to the land, are easily moved, and are items of personal property not to be included in a sale. The solution, as is so often the case, is to specify in the sale/purchase agreement which items of personal property are to be included in the sale of the real property and which are not, thus eliminating all ambiguity (as well as lawsuits).

Appurtenances & Easements

Appurtenances are not three-dimensional items as are fixtures, but rather intangible rights which are deemed necessary for the use of the property as intended. The examples cited above, easements and water rights (stock in water company) are appurtenances and, as real property, would transfer with the sale of the real property.

An easement is the right to use another's property but with no right to possess it.[5] Certain easements are *appurtenant* easements; for example, if it is necessary to traverse another's property in order to gain access, an appurtenant easement will typically be granted to the owner of the property by the seller of the land which created the landlocked situation.[6] The property which benefits from the easement is known as the *dominant tenement*, while the property over which the easement is located is known as the *servient* property.

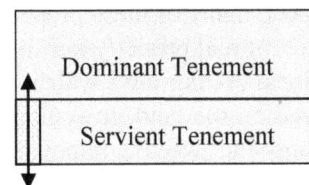

Dominant Tenement

Servient Tenement

---

[5]   No right to construct an improvement on the easement.
[6]   Parcels are sometimes land locked and require a court-ordered "easement by necessity."

In other cases, an easement may be granted to a person or entity rather than attached to a particular parcel of land. These *easements in gross* are typical of the kind of easement obtained by utility companies in order to maintain gas, water and electric lines serving the property. Almost all developed property will be burdened by easements in gross since a utility company will not supply the utility without the access necessary to maintain it. An easement granted to a hunter to enter upon the land to fish or hunt is another example of an easement *in gross*. This kind of personal easement is not defined by borders, as is an appurtenant easement.

Note: Allowing individuals to use one's land continuously and openly for five or more years without specific permission places the landowner at risk for a *prescriptive easement* which can be obtained against the landowner's interest. Granting permission, or "posting the property"[7] however, blocks a prescriptive easement.

Appurtenant easements are typically recorded but they do not appear in a deed even though, as real property, they transfer with the deed. Recorded easements, however, will be contained in a Report on the Condition of Title.[8]

Ownership as a Bundle of Rights

A very useful working definition of real property is to regard that which is owned as a collection or *bundle of rights* to the property.

This definition has a great deal of utility and practical value since any property right that can be identified may also be separated – then bought, sold, leased or exchanged.

BUNDLE of RIGHTS
♦ **Right to use**
♦ **Right to possess**
♦ **Right to encumber**
♦ **Right to demise**
♦ **Right to sell**
♦ **Right to partition**
♦ **Right to develop**
♦ **Right to MOG deposits**
♦ **Right to do nothing**

For example, in separating out the Rights to Use and Possess real property, its owner may sell - for a limited time - these Rights to a tenant under a lease or rental agreement. The owner who pledges his Right to Sell the property as collateral for a loan, or grants an easement, exercises his Right to Encumber[9] the property.

As mentioned above, an owner may also sell all of the Rights to the real property but reserve to himself the Mineral, Oil and Gas (MOG) Rights[10] underlying the land[11] below a specified depth. As you may suspect, many of these property rights are attenuated by regulations and local law. For example, while the owner of real property may have the right to develop the property, this right is often defined and restricted by local zoning laws which specify the type, use, size and position of the improvement[12] which may be placed on the land. In some jurisdictions even the Right to Do Nothing is conditioned upon the owner's cutting the weeds, removing accumulated trash and preventing the development of an "attractive nuisance." So while ownership of real property conveys many important and valuable Rights, these Rights are often far from absolute.

---

[7]   Placing signs such as "No Trespassing" on the border of the property at proscribed intervals.

[8]   Title Report

[9]   An encumbrance is said to *burden* a title by lowering its value or restricting its use.

[10] "The meek shall inherit the earth… but not its mineral rights." J. Paul Getty

[11] But does not necessarily acquire the right to enter upon the land to recover these deposits. Hence, slant drilling from a nearby parcel.

[12] An "improvement" is any structure or permanent covering placed on the land. Even the surfacing of a parking lot is a kind of improvement to raw land.

Interests in Real Property

An interest in real property is called an "estate." When we own all the Rights to real property, we are said to own an estate in *fee-simple*. The word *fee* is a corruption of the Old English word *fief*, which takes us back to feudal times and to our roots in feudal England and English common law.[13] A fief, during the Middle Ages, pertained to an interest in real property over which a feudal lord exercised control as reward for his pledge of fidelity and service to a sovereign. More importantly, perhaps, a fief represented an inheritable interest in the land. This interest was held by a *freeman*, and came to be known as a *freehold estate*. Anything less than a freehold estate was known as a less-than-freehold estate, which has elided to *leasehold*.

Therefore we are left with two classes of estates: freehold estates and leasehold estates.
The essential difference between the two is that freehold estates are inheritable and of an indefinite duration, while leasehold interests are for a limited or determinable period of time and are not inheritable. The accompanying table lists the various kinds of freehold and less-than-freehold estates which can be held in real property:

Freehold Estate	Less-than-Freehold (Leasehold) Estates
Fee-Simple (aka Fee-Simple Absolute)	Estate for Years
Fee-Simple Qualified	Estate from Period to Period
Life Estate Estate in Reversion Estate in Remainder	Estate at Will
	Estate at Sufferance

The Freehold Estates

Fee-Simple (aka Fee-simple Absolute)

This interest in real property is equivalent to ownership of <u>all</u> the rights to a property.
It is the highest and best form of real property ownership.

Fee-simple Qualified

This interest in real property is sometimes called Fee-Simple *Defeasible* since it is capable of being 'defeated,' invalidated or revoked. This interest in property may be encumbered by covenants, conditions and/or restrictions (CC&Rs).

Covenants are agreements to do or not to do a certain thing. A deed to vacant land may contain a covenant that the new owner will build a house of not less than a certain floor area. If a covenant is violated, the transferor of the property may be able to recover damages.

A *restriction* is a kind of covenant that limits the owner's use or development of the property. Many communities have extensive restrictions which attach to the ownership and govern the size and placement of signs, building colors, landscaping, set-backs, etc. These documents are sometimes referred to as

---

13   A body of law, originally English, which has evolved as the result of judicial decisions. Now the basis of law in every state except Louisiana whose law is based on the Napoleonic Code.

SLURs (Special Land Use Restrictions) and are used to impose limitations on the property which are often more strict than local zoning or building code.[14]

Conditions, on the other hand, are much more serious since the violation of a condition written in the deed may result in loss of ownership. In this case the deed is conveyed to the new owner subject to conditions, which are classified either as 1) *conditions precedent*, or 2) *conditions subsequent*, or 3) *special limitations.*

For example, one may choose to deed a property to the city for use as a park on condition that the city first establish within the next budget year a fund in the amount of $100,000 for perpetual upkeep and maintenance. If the city fails to do so, the deed becomes null and void. This type of condition is known as a *condition precedent* since its terms must be satisfied before the transfer of title (ownership by the city) becomes effective.

A second type condition is a *condition subsequent.* A parent may choose to deed a parcel of land to a daughter on the condition that she not marry before age 25. This deed becomes effective immediately but is revocable at the option of the grantor (the parent) if the daughter marries before age 25. If the daughter does not marry before age 25, her interest in the property converts to a fee-simple estate.

The third type of condition is a *special limitation.* The King Ranch in Texas once deeded a portion of the ranch to its employees for the purpose of providing homesites on the condition that alcoholic beverages never be sold in the town. The residents received and kept fee title to the land *so long as* alcoholic beverages were never sold there. If this special limitation were violated, the grantor had the option of reentering and repossessing title to the land (and all that was on the land, i.e. the house).

This same kind of special limitation can be used to restrict the type or size improvement placed on land. For example, you may own a large parcel of land which affords a panoramic vista of the surroundings. You may divide the parcel creating a new building lot to be sold for the construction of a home. To ensure that your view not be compromised, you could place a condition in the deed which places a *special limitation* on the height of any building to be built on the lot. If the buyer of the lot, or any subsequent owner,[15] later erected a structure which impaired your view, you would have the right to reenter and repossess the property.

These examples are of real property interests that are fee-interests because their duration is not determinable and because they are inheritable, but that might be upset by failing to meet a condition contained in the deed, hence defeasible.

Life Estates

A life estate consists of a fee interest in the property, but the duration of this interest is conditioned upon the length of someone's life. It is a fee interest because the length of the life of the party whose life controls the estate is indeterminable.

For example, an individual may wish to convey title to another for as long as either he (the grantor), or the grantee, or some third party, may live.

The deed conveying the life estate will specify that upon the death of the person whose life controls the estate, the property will either revert to the grantor or, if the grantor is deceased, to the grantor's heirs, or

---

[14] When a property is subject to both zoning law and restrictions in the deed, the more limiting applies.

[15] Special limitations *"run with the land."*

be conveyed to some third party. During the lifetime of the person whose life controls the estate, the grantee holds a life estate in the property, while the heirs would hold an *estate in reversion*, or the third party would hold an *estate in remainder*.

During the lifetime of the person whose life controls the estate, the grantee may possess and use, encumber, exchange, demise, lease and even sell or exchange the property. But upon the death of the person whose life controls the estate, all interest in the property conveyed to the grantee or to the grantee's successor-in-interest ceases *immediately*, and title to the property transfers at the moment of death to the heirs of the grantor, or to the holders of the estate in remainder. Any sale, lease or demise which may have been made by the original life grantee is immediately null and void.[16]

In a society which is experiencing a 50% divorce rate, a life estate is often used to vest fee title in either of the surviving spouses for as long as the surviving spouse lives. Upon the demise of the surviving spouse the interest in the property often reverts to the heirs of the spouse first to die.

Life estates are used much more frequently in Europe (especially England), but are much less commonly used in the United States. An owner may sell the property but reserve to himself or herself a life estate in the property which enables the seller to continue residency on the property for the life of the seller. The market value of these life estates varies according the life expectancy of the seller.

The Leasehold Estates

An *Estate for Years* is a misnomer. This kind of estate refers to an interest in real property for <u>any</u> definite, determinable time period, and not necessarily 'for years.' This interest is created by a contract called a *lease*. Although a lease conveys an interest in real property it is not real property; current law regards a lease as personal property. Because of its close association with realty, however, a lease is often referred to as a *chattel real*.[17]

Under the lease contract, the lessor conveys the rights to *use* and *possess* the property to the lessee in exchange for good or valuable consideration.[18] In some instances, the rights to use, possess and *develop* the property are conveyed. This type lease is known as a *ground lease*.

Whenever a property is leased, two derivative interests in real property are created: a *leasehold interest* held by the tenant and the residual *leased-fee* interest retained and held by the landlord.

All leases are rental agreements, but not all rental agreements are leases. The distinguishing characteristic of a lease is that it has a definite termination date specified in the lease document.

This distinction is not simply an academic one; many of the rights and obligations of the parties to a lease, the lessor and lessee, are defined by law. For example, a lessor is not required by law to give a lessee forewarning that the lease will terminate on such and such a date. The termination date is written in the lease and anyone, including the lessee, may determine that date by a careful reading of the document.[19]

A second important difference is that in executing a lease, the lessee obligates himself for the <u>entire amount of rent due under the lease</u>, even though the lease may specify that the obligation may be paid in

---

[16] A Life Estate may be sold or willed at any time prior to the death of the party whose life controls the estate.

[17] A chattel is an item of personal property; *real* refers to property (once) owned by the king.

[18] 'Good consideration' is money. 'Valuable consideration' is something other than money, perhaps services. A lease is a contract, and contracts must involve good or valuable consideration.

[19] A tenant occupying under a lease may be contractually required to give advanced notice if the tenant intends to vacate the property at the termination of the lease.

periodic installments; for example, monthly. In some cases a lessee is free to vacate the property but nonetheless remains committed to meet the lease payments as specified. In some commercial leases involving a shopping center, however, a major anchor retailer, such as a supermarket or department store, may be required to keep the premises lighted and open for business during the business day, often with certain minimum *shelf-stocking* requirements.

A third important feature of a lease is that the rent to be paid over the entire term of the lease is either specifically stated or scheduled (stipulated), or a method of determining the rent is clearly described. For example, a lease may state a specific dollar amount of rent for defined periods of the lease, or it may tie future rent to an inflation index, such as the Consumer Price Index (CPI), or to a defined percentage increase in retail volume per year. In any case, the lessor is not required to give the lessee advanced notice regarding a change in rent; it is written down in the lease for all to read.

Most residential leases contain a clause stating that if the lessee continues to possess and use the property beyond the original term of the lease, the interest in the real property will convert to a *month-to-month agreement*. A month-to-month agreement is an *Estate from Period to Period*, also known as a *Periodic Tenancy*. If a property is sold with a tenant in possession, the rental agreement or lease transfers with and continues to encumber the title, binding the new owner in the same way it bound the former owner.

An *Estate from Period to Period* differs from an Estate for Years in that no specific or pre-determinable ending date exists. The period of the rental may be weekly, monthly, quarterly, annually or for any regular period,[20] but no ending date is stated or determinable. These agreements are evidenced by Rental Agreements rather than Leases, although the terminology is often interchanged and loosely applied.

Occupancy under a rental agreement creates different obligations for both the landlord and tenant. For example, a notice to vacate by either party must be given over a period at least equal to the period for which rent is paid. If rent is paid monthly, the landlord must give the tenant at least one month's advance notice to vacate.[21] Conversely, a tenant must give a landlord at least one period's advance notice of an intent to vacate.
In contrast to a lease, a tenant under a monthly rental agreement is liable only for the current month's rent (to include rent owing for the advance notice period), and not for any rent beyond this period.

An *Estate at Will* pertains to a rental agreement which specifies no period of the tenancy and no specific period over which rent is to be paid. It may be terminated by either party at any time. This kind of Estate has caused so many legal complications and lawsuits that most states have modified it to resemble an Estate from Period to Period (periodic tenancy).

An *Estate at Sufferance* is the last leasehold estate and the most curious interest in real property. This interest is created when a tenant enters upon a property lawfully, but remains in possession of the property beyond the term of the rental agreement but does not pay rent. He is not a trespasser.[22]

For example, you may rent a vacation cottage to a tenant for the month of September, but the tenant remains in possession during October. Since the tenant has obvious Possession and Use of the property – even though he does not pay rent – he holds an interest (Estate) in the property. But since s/he remains

---

[20] But generally not less than 1 week.
[21] In some jurisdictions if a rent increase exceeds 10% in any one year a 60-day notice is required to raise rents.
[22] *Trespass* is the illegal or wrongful entry upon property belonging to someone else.

without the landlord's approval, and without paying rent, s/he does not occupy under either an oral or written agreement.

An Estate at Sufferance is the weakest interest which one can hold in real property since it can be readily terminated.[23] But it is, nevertheless, an interest in real property. This is one reason a construction lender will not lend money on a new project without first inspecting the property to assure itself that no one is currently in possession.

A License Conveys No Real Property Interest

Occupancy of a hotel or motel room is not enabled by either a lease or a rental agreement, but rather by a *license*. A license conveys neither possessory nor usage rights in the real estate; a license conveys the right to use and possess the property for a specific period of time. For example, a hotel guest buys the right to possess and use a certain room for a specific period of time but never acquires possessory or usage rights in the underlying real property. In many municipalities the occupancy time is required to be posted on the rear of the door to the room.

How Real Property Interests Can Be Owned

Interests in real property may be owned either by real or by legal persons. By *real*, we mean humans; by *legal* we mean entities created by law such as corporations, partnerships, limited liability companies (LLC), and trusts. The legal entities have almost all the rights accorded to humans, but not all. Corporations, for example, may not own real property as a joint tenant since the outcome is certain that the corporation will eventually own the entire property. (More about this in a moment.) Small business corporations (Sub-chapter S Corporations) may not own real estate if more than 25% of the S-Corporation's total gross income is derived from rents (characterized as passive income).

Minors may own real property, and often do, as the result of a gift or by inheritance . But they may not buy, convey an interest in, lease, manage or sell real property since they lack the *legal capacity* to enter into contracts until they reach the age of majority, which in most states is 18 years of age.[24]

In general, property may be owned in *severalty*, or in co-ownership with others. The word severalty does not mean several, many or a few. In law *severalty* means cut off from, or separate from, others. Therefore property held in severalty is property held by one individual or by one single legal entity apart from anyone else. The following table shows the various entities which may own real estate in severalty or in co-ownership with others.

In Severalty	Forms of Co-Ownership
Individual	Joint Tenancy
Partnership	Tenants-in-Common
Corporation	Community Property
Trust[25]	Tenants in the Entirety

---

23 In practice, it may require months before a tenant in possession can be evicted.

24 In Alabama, Alaska, Nebraska and Wyoming the age is 19. In Mississippi, Pennsylvania and Puerto Rico the age is 21. Some military bases have lowered the age to 18 for on-base consumption.

25 The trustee of the trust owns the *naked legal title* while the beneficiaries enjoy the benefits of the trust.

Ownership in Severalty

It's quite natural to think of a property owned by a partnership as one collectively owned by a number of individual partners. So it may come as a surprise to learn that property owned by a partnership is owned in *severalty*, since the partnership is a single legal entity and is the single owning entity of the interest held.[26]   The interest held by the individual partners is an interest in the partnership, and not a direct interest in the real property owned by the partnership.

For this reason, a partner's interest in a partnership which owns real estate is not exchangeable (under S.1031) for real property since a partnership interest is personal property and an exchange of real property for personal property is not a "like-kind" exchange as required by the tax code. A partnership may, however, exchange its real property for other real property whether the replacement property is held by an individual, by another partnership, by a corporation or LLC.[27] In each of these cases, it is the partner**ship** which does the exchanging, and not the individual partners.

Similarly, a corporation is a separate legal entity which may directly own real estate. The shareholders of the corporation own *shares* (personal property) in the corporation and not in the real property owned by the corporation; the beneficiaries of a Trust own *beneficial interests* (personal property) in the Trust and not direct interests in the real property owned by the Trustee.

When entering into an agreement to buy real property from a partnership, a corporation or a trust, it is important to verify at the outset that the individual with whom you are dealing has the legal <u>capacity</u> to sell the property. In the case of a partnership, request a copy of the partnership agreement authorizing the General Partner[28] to sell the property. In the case of a corporation, a resolution by the Board of Directors authorizing a corporate officer to sell should be obtained. Some states permit the buyer to rely upon a statement signed by an officer of the corporation with signatory rights.[29] The same pre-caution should be observed when dealing with a property owned in a Trust. An escrow agent will not transfer title to a new buyer without a copy of the Trust and evidence that the trustee has the power to sell the owned property.

The determination that the individual with whom you are dealing has the legal capacity to transfer title should not wait until after a great deal of time, money and effort has been expended in negotiations, inspections and agreement writing.

Co-Ownership of Real Property

The forms of co-ownership are those listed in the table above.

Two or more individuals may own real property as **Joint Tenants.** In order to hold title in this form, four conditions must be met. These conditions are known as the *Four Unities*.

---

[26]   A partnership may be a co-owner with others, but the interest owned by the partnership is held by the partnership as a separate, single entity.

[27]   Limited Liability Corporation

[28]   Only a General Partner can actively manage the partnership business. A limited partner may not conduct business in the name of the partnership without risking the loss of his or her limited liability protection. Nevertheless, the GP may be required to have the consent of the limited partners in order to sell.

[29]   Many vice-presidents are vice-presidents in name only and do not have the power to bind the corporation to an enforceable contract. "Do you have signatory rights?" is a good question to ask, and a declaration that the officer asserts such a right should be noted *in writing* on the signature page of the agreement.

To be considered Joint Tenants the owners must:

1. acquire title at the same **T**ime
2. acquire title by the same instrument of **T**itle
3. each have an equal, undivided **I**nterest in the entire property, and
4. each have the right of **P**ossession to the entire property.
   Time, **T**itle, **I**nterest and **P**ossession (**TTIP**) are the Four Unities

An example best illustrates this important method of ownership.

Inheriting the Family Farm

Four siblings inherit the family farm upon the death of their parent. The will which conveys title specifically states that the farm shall be held by the heirs as Joint Tenants. Under this circumstance, the first two requirements of Joint Tenancy are satisfied: the farm has been transferred to each heir at the same Time (at the moment of the parent's death), and by the same instrument of Title (the will).

Because the will specifies that the siblings shall hold title as "Joint Tenants," each holds an equal, <u>un</u>divided interest in the entire property. They do <u>not</u> each hold a separate 25% interest in the property. Further, each is entitled to possess and use the entire property without restriction. Therefore the requirements of the Four Unities have been met: same Time, same instrument of Title, same Interest and equal Possession.

The essence of Joint Tenancy is the Right of Survivorship which provides that upon the death of a Joint Tenant, the interest owned by the deceased passes immediately at the moment of death and by operation of law,[30] to the remaining Joint Tenants. Furthermore, this interest transfers to the surviving Joint Tenants <u>free of all liens</u>[31] <u>and encumbrances</u>. Although it is necessary to state in the instrument that creates the Joint Tenancy (deed, will) that the property is to be held in Joint Tenancy (or as Joint Tenants), it is redundant to add the words "with the Right of Survivorship," since this Right is implicit in the concept of Joint Tenancy.

Continuing with the example, let's assume that heir D decides to sell his interest in the farm to E.

A – B – C – D	A, B, C and D are Joint Tenants (JTs). Each owns an equal, undivided interest in the entire property.
A – B – C * E	D sells his (25%) undivided interest to E. This sale breaks the joint tenancy with A, B & C, but not among A, B & C. E is now a Tenant-in-Common with A, B & C. A, B and C own a 75% undivided interest as JTs; E owns a 25% undivided interest as a Tenant-in-Common
A – B * E	C dies. His 25% interest transfers immediately to A and B who now each own a 37.5% undivided interest between them as JTs. E owns 25% as a Tenant-in-Common.
A * E	B dies. A now owns a 75% undivided interest with E who continues to hold a 25% interest. The relationship between the two is now Tenants-in-Common.

[30] "Operation of law" means that no further legal action is required to bring about the result.
[31] Except tax liens.

A number of points are worth noting:

- ✓ A JT interest can be sold or exchanged, but it cannot be willed. Upon the death of a JT, the interest transfers immediately to the remaining JTs. Therefore there is no legal opportunity for a will to take effect; a JT interest is never subject to a will (avoids probate).
- ✓ Selling a JT interest breaks the Joint Tenancy between the selling JT owner and the remaining JTs. The new owner becomes a Tenant-in-Common with the remaining JTs. The JT relationship between or among the remaining JTs is unaltered.
- ✓ In a JT ownership one of the JTs will eventually own all of the JT interests, provided that no other JT has sold his or her interest. This is the reason that a corporation cannot hold title to real property as a Joint Tenant. The corporation, which never dies[32] would always become sole owner.

There are a few additional points which are not obvious from this example:

- ✓ A single JT interest can be mortgaged. But at the instant of death, the interest transfers to the remaining JTs free of all liens and encumbrances. This is the basic reason that a single JT interest is rarely (if ever) used as collateral for a loan. Upon the death of the JT, the lender's security for his loan would vanish.[33] If a joint tenant seeks a mortgage, all JTs are generally required to post their interest in the property as security for the loan.
- ✓ Each JT enjoys the right to possess and use the entire property, although a JT may lease his share to one or more of the other JTs.
- ✓ If a property is to be held in Joint Tenancy, the shares of ownership <u>must</u> be equal.
- ✓ Investment property held by two or more unrelated investors is almost never held in Joint Tenancy. Upon his/her death, the investor's share would transfer to the remaining JT owners and not to the investor's heirs.
- ✓ Upon the death of a JT, the Basis[34] of his interest only is "stepped up" to its fair market value at the time of death if at least 50% of the FMV of his interest in the property is included in the estate of the decedent.[35] The Basis of the remaining JTs, however, is not affected.

<u>Tenancy-in-Common</u>

This form of co-ownership with others does not require that the owners take title at the same time, nor by the same instrument of title, nor in an equal share. It does, however, require equal Right of Possession. There are a number of advantages to holding property as a Tenant-in-Common (TIC): Shares held may be equal or unequal (28-72%, 42-58%, 30-40%, 10-20%, etc.)

- ✓ A TIC owns a direct, fractional Interest in the entire property, but does not own 100% of the property with an undivided interest as does a JT.
- ✓ A TIC interest may be sold, exchanged or transferred by will.
- ✓ A TIC interest may be used as collateral for a loan. In the event of a default and foreclosure, the lender would assume a position as a TIC with the other owners.
- ✓ Upon the death of a TIC his ownership in the property does not automatically pass to the other TICs. Instead, it passes to his heirs.
- ✓ A TIC interest does not involve the automatic Right of Survivorship.
- ✓ A TIC interest is subject to probate.

---

[32] Though it may be dissolved.

[33] The promissory note would remain, but as an unsecured note greatly diminishing its value.

[34] The value of a property for the purpose of determining taxable gains and losses.

[35] See the chapter on taxation for additional details.

…and there may be a few disadvantages to a TIC form of ownership:

✓ With respect to investment property, ownership as a TIC raises the vital question of management: "Who will have the right and responsibility to make decisions regarding the operation of the property?" Lacking a management agreement, ownership of real property as a TIC can result in a great many disputes and headaches. A management agreement is absolutely essential.

✓ Ownership in an investment property as a TIC is subject to a will, and therefore in the event of the death of a TIC, the remaining owners of the property may have to await the outcome of probate to learn who will be their new co-owner. The waiting period may delay the sale of the property for a considerable time.

> See Chapter 9 for additional information about exchanging TIC interests.

✓ Acquiring a property interest from a TIC does not usually require the approval of other TICs, but there may be a pre-existing agreement among the TICs which gives the remaining TICs the first right to acquire the interest.[36]

Community Property

Community property laws are based on the presumption that all property (including earnings) acquired by a married couple during their marriage, and which is acquired using community funds, is property equally owned by both spouses.

There are nine states which provide Community Property vesting:[37] These states include Washington, California, Nevada, Arizona, New Mexico, Texas, Idaho, Wisconsin and Louisiana. Alaska enacted a 'community property' law in 1998, provided the husband and wife have made a written agreement. Property excluded from classification as Community Property includes:

✓ Property which was acquired by either party prior to marriage.
✓ Property which was inherited or received as a gift as separate property.
✓ Property which was acquired by either spouse during marriage using separate funds.
✓ Funds flowing from the ownership of a property which was either separately inherited or acquired with separate funds.

If, however, separate property is commingled with community property, perhaps by paying real estate taxes or property bills from a joint bank account, the separate property may unwittingly be converted to community property owned equally by both husband and wife.

Debts incurred during marriage are considered to be the debts of both, therefore a judgment rendered against one spouse may apply to the interests of both as community property. Further, although a sale of the property requires the signature of both spouses, either spouse may will his or her share of community property to a third party. In 2001 California enacted a law which enables married couples to hold property as *Community Property with the Right of Survivorship* which prevents a spouse from willing his or her share to a third-party. Many states have since followed suit.

For investors, there is an important tax advantage to community property vesting. Upon the death of a spouse, the entire property owned as community property receives a stepped-up Basis[38] equal to its Fair Market Value (FMV) .

---

[36] "First Right of Refusal"
[37] Refers to the manner in which title is held by the owner(s).
[38] Basis is the value of an investment for tax purposes such as determining gains and losses.

For example, John and Mary, husband and wife, hold community real property with a FMV of $1,000,000. Their Adjusted Basis in the property immediately before John's death is $400,000. If at least half the FMV of the property is included in John's gross estate, Mary's share of the property, as well as the share she inherits from John, will received a Basis stepped-up to FMV ($500,000 each). Therefore Mary would inherit the property with a total Basis of $1,000,000. If Mary were to sell the property immediately following John's death for $1,000,000, there would be no recognized (taxable) gain.

Part of the American Taxpayer Relief Act of 2012 made the federal estate tax exclusion[39] permanent and raised the exclusion amount for 2014 to $5.34M for singles and $10.68M for married couples. It also made this amount subject to annual adjustments due to inflation (using the CPI). A new feature of the estate tax law is the portability (transfer) of a deceased spouse's unused estate tax exclusion amount to the surviving spouse tax free. Upon the death of the surviving spouse, the value of the estate in excess of the excluded amount will be taxable. The tax on amounts in excess of the exclusion amount was raised form 35% to 40%.

Vesting Errors

It is very common to find that couples residing in a community property state have taken title to their property as Joint Tenants thereby foregoing the benefit of a stepped-up Basis. In most cases these couples were advised by a real estate agent or an escrow officer as to "the best way to hold title." The long-term tax consequences of a mistake in the method of holding title are so important that the advice of a competent real estate attorney should be sought.

Tenancy by the Entirety

The most common method for married couples to hold property in the United States is as Tenants-in-Common. In some states that are not community property states a couple may hold property as Tenants by the Entirety. This vesting method, as is true for Joint Tenancy, requires that the couple meet all Four Unities and that they be legally married at the time of acquisition.

Unfortunately, real property held by married couples either as Joint Tenants or as Tenants by the Entirety does not receive a step-up in Basis equal to that of property held as Community Property. Upon the death of a spouse who held a qualified joint interest,[40] the Basis of the property in the hands of the surviving spouse is equal to the original Basis of the surviving spouse's half-share plus one-half the Fair Market Value of the property at the time of the decedent's death. In other words, there is no full step-up in Basis to FMV for the surviving spouse's share.[41]

In acquiring property held as Tenants by the Entirety, neither spouse has the right to sell or transfer the property without the other spouse's concurrence. This concurrence requires the signature of both parties on all documents relating to the disposition of the property.

---

[39] An individual is entitled at death to an exclusion from the estate tax and gift tax (now Unified tax).

[40] Property held as Tenants by the Entirety, or by Joint Tenants who are married, provided there are no other Joint Tenants.

[41] If a property was acquired by married JTs or TICs prior to 1977, the surviving spouse may be able to elect to have 100% of the FMV included in decedent's gross estate thereby obtaining a step-up in Basis similar to community property. Refer to IRS Code § 2040.

Condominiums and Co-ops

Condominium ownership is a system of ownership by an individual owner in a separate unit of a multi-unit property. Ownership in a condominium consists of ownership of an individual unit (usually as a fee-simple interest) combined with a Tenant-in-Common interest in shared (common) areas, such as parking areas, walkways, halls, community buildings, etc. Ownership of a condominium interest consists of ownership of the interior space of a particular unit bounded by its walls, ceilings and floors. The structural elements are owned by the Condominium Association (typically a corporation) which is responsible for the maintenance of these elements and the common areas.

Any property can be condominiumized but residences are most common, followed by an occasional office property.

"Co-op" refers to co-operatively owned units which are generally of two types: *Stock co-ops* are properties owned in severalty by a corporation. The buyer of a stock co-op unit buys a share in the corporation which carries with it the right to exclusive use and possession of a designated unit. The owner receives an easement to use common areas.

Co-ops are also found as *Tenant-in-Common* interests. Under this system each TIC owner holds a percentage share of direct ownership in the entire real property, again with the exclusive right to use and possess a certain unit and a non-exclusive right to use the common areas.

A **"Townhouse"** is not a particular form of ownership but rather a distinct architectural style, as would be a Ranch style, or Tudor style, or a Cape Cod style. Townhouses are semi-detached, stacked units. This distinction is often missed by the popular press which equates *townhouse* to *condominium*.

How Real Property May Be Transferred

Real Property may transfer from one owner to the next in any of five different ways:

- By deed,
- By inheritance,
- By gift,
- By accession and
- By adverse possession.

By Deed

The most common way that investment properties transfer is by deed. The following language would constitute a legal transfer of title by a grant deed:

> *...the undersigned hereby grants to John Doe that certain real property located at 123 Main Street, Anytown, U.S.A.*
> *(s) John Smith*

A valid and effective grant deed must:

- Be in writing
- Contain a granting clause or phrase
- Contain the name of the grantee

- ♦ Contain an unambiguous identification of the property
- ♦ Be signed by the grantor.
- ♦ Be delivered to and accepted by the grantee to be effective

Although this brief deed is sufficient to convey legal title, it is not recordable. In order to be recordable the deed must also:
- ♦ Contain a legal description of the property[42]
- ♦ Be acknowledged by the grantor before a notary.

The deed need not contain a date when executed because the recording official will attach a date to it at the exact time of recording. Therefore the maker of the deed (grantor) ought not date it.

The purpose of recording a deed is to give public notice of a change in ownership. This type of notice is called *constructive notice*[43] since it affords anyone who is interested the means to determine who owns the property. A retained deed which is not recorded by the grantee exposes the grantee to the risk that the property may be subsequently re-sold or transferred to another who would record the trasnsfer. Prompt recording of a deed is vital since the law regards the "first to record as the first in right."

Types of Deeds

There are many types of deeds generally reflecting the circumstances under which the deed is granted. In general, Grant Deeds and Warranty Deeds are used.

- ♦ Warranty Deeds are used to convey title together with representations by the seller as to the quality of the title. Warranty Deeds appear in one of two forms:
  - ▪ General Warranty Deeds contain assurances by the seller that a *good and marketable* title is being conveyed. *Good* implies that the title being conveyed is free from liens other than those declared by the seller, and from lawsuits and other defects. *Marketable* implies that the property is free from reasonable doubts or objections from a third party.
  - ▪ Special Warranty Deeds contain assurances by the grantor that the title is free from defects only during the time the grantor owned the property. It conveys no assurances that the property is free from defects originating prior to the time the seller owned the property.
- ♦ Grant Deeds are similar to Special Warranty Deeds in that they contain no express[44] warranties, only the implied warranties that
  - ▪ The grantor has the legal capacity to deliver title, and
  - ▪ The grantor has not encumbered the property except as declared.
- ♦ Quitclaim Deeds are used principally to clear title. By using this deed the grantor does not claim any interest in the property but conveys whatever interest may indeed be held. In effect, the quitclaim grantor says: "I hereby convey whatever interest I may own, but I make no claim or assertion that I have any interest in the property."

---

[42] Using either of three methods of describing property: U.S. Geodetic Survey; Lot, Block and Tract; or Metes and Bounds.

[43] In contrast to "actual notice' whereby an individual is directly informed of the change in title.

[44] *Express* = written or specified

By Gift

The Gift deed transfers title to the property in the form of a gift. What is important to the investor is that property received by the donee carries with it the same tax Basis that existed in the hands of the donor. Therefore when a gift property is later sold the amount of gain is determined by reference to the Basis in the hands of the donor, not to its value at the time it was received. Properties received as gifts carry reduced depreciation benefits. A property which has been fully depreciated in the hands of a donor may not be re-depreciated in the hands of a donee.

By Inheritance

Property may also be acquired through inheritance which may result from a will or, in the absence of a will, through the operation of law governing *intestate*[45] succession in the state in which the property is located.

By Accession

Real property may also transfer to a new owner as the result of a physical addition to the property, whether made intentionally or as the result of a mistake.

For example, any additions or improvements made to a property by a tenant become the property of the owner of the property at the termination of a lease. Property used in a trade or business (*tools of the trade*) is excepted, providing the tenant repairs damages and restores the owner's property to its original condition, normal wear and tear excepted. You may also accede to the title of a fence built on your land by an adjoining neighbor. (Generally, local law allows for the repositioning of the fence within a reasonable time.)

An owner may also gain or lose real property as the result of its physical relocation following a flood, earthquake, landslide, or by the eroding force of water against land abutting a stream or river.

Adverse Possession

Under common law in most states an individual may take ownership of real property under a claim of adverse possession, sometimes called *title by possession*. Adverse possession differs from *prescriptive easement* (which only conveys the right of Use) in that additional requirements are made. In addition to the conditions required for a prescriptive easement,[46] the claimant must possess the property continuously for 5 years and pay the real estate taxes.[47]

Title Insurance

It is easy to see that the quality of title passed is only is good as the grantor's word or prior knowledge. Therefore all transfers of title today should be accompanied by a policy of title insurance. The role of the title insurer is to research the condition of the title and then to deliver to the buyer an insurance policy which guarantees a good and marketable title. If an undetected defect is later uncovered, the title company will undertake a legal defense of the title. If the defense fails, the company will reimburse the insured for the face value of the policy - which is generally the amount of the purchase price.

---

[45] Lacking a legal will.

[46] The right to use another's property by actions which are *open, notorious, hostile* to the true owner's interest, and are carried on *continuously* for a statutory period of time (usually five years).

[47] It is possible to rent the property and still claim possession as a landlord.

Three basic types of title insurance are now available, although there are countless variations of each type depending on the underwriter and the state in which the policy is issued:

♦ A "standard," or "owner's" policy insures the purchaser against any defect in the title which can be uncovered by a search of the public records as well as forgery, impersonation and a lack of the grantor's legal capacity.

♦ An "extended," or "lender's" policy[48] insures against any defects which can be uncovered by a search of the public records as well as any defect which could be uncovered by a physical inspection of the property, including the rights of persons in possession.

♦ In some states a combination (standard + extended) policy is now available to owners of 1-4 units. This policy contains maximums payable under certain categories of coverages and small deductibles payable by the insured. This policy makes available protection against certain risks that conventionally were available only to lenders and then only by endorsement.

Lenders who provide mortgage money to the borrower will always require the extended type policy in the amount of the loan. If a buyer obtains only a lender's policy and later encounters defects in the title he will be insured only to the amount of the lender's policy, and this cash will have been pre-assigned to the lender. Therefore it is wise not only to obtain a standard policy in the full amount of the purchase price, but even in cases in which the property is purchased for all cash, prudent to obtain an extended (lender's) policy as well.

The Preliminary Title Report

The preliminary title report (PTR) is a report of matters that affect a designated property issued and furnished to a buyer or mortgagor (lender) in connection with an application to purchase title insurance. It is not an insurance policy.

Every offer made for the purchase or exchange of real property should be made contingent upon the receipt and approval by the buyer, within a reasonable time period (5-10 days), of a current preliminary title report furnished by a reputable title company.

Be very careful not to assume that the preliminary title report is a guarantee that there are no unacceptable encumbrances against the title. The title company issuing the preliminary report has no responsibility or liability until a final title insurance policy is issued. Furthermore, there may be changes in the condition of the title which occur between the date of a sale-purchase agreement and the date of final closing. Before the transaction has ended, the title company will update the PTR and bring to the insured's attention any matter which has changed, such as a partial sale or an additional lien recently placed against the title.

The PTR is generally issued in two or more parts. Part A describes the interest owned by the seller, a legal description of the property, the date of the report and other standard information. Part B will list *exceptions* to the proposed coverage. It is in this section that the buyer will find encumbrances, judgments, easements, mechanic's liens, trust deeds, conditions, covenants, restrictions in the deed, as well as any legal notices (e.g. Lis Pendens[49]) of actions which may affect ownership. These exceptions will be in addition to the "standard"[50] exceptions contained in the pre-printed part of the policy. If the

---

[48] Also known as an ALTA policy. American Land Title Association. This type policy is required by lenders not only for the extra protection afforded, but also because it provides a consistent policy nationally.

[49] Literally, a thing pending. A public notice recorded on the title that a legal action has been undertaken which may affect ownership or the condition of the title. It is a red flag to a buyer to proceed only with great caution.

[50] Nothing in real estate should be considered "standard."

buyer accepts these exceptions, the buyer will not be insured against any of the items listed as exceptions or arising from these exceptions. Therefore it is critical that the buyer read and understand the PTR before approving it. If any item is not understood a few dollars spent for competent professional advice is a very sound investment.

The PTR tells the buyer what kind of interest he/she is buying, from whom, the condition of the title regarding easements, covenants, conditions and restrictions, trust deeds or mortgages, and a host of other matters that will affect the buyer's decision and subsequent use of the property. Wherever appropriate information in the PTR should be cross-checked with information in the purchase agreement. Discrepancies are cause to suspend approval of the report.

Visit City Hall

Unfortunately, the PTR will <u>not</u> tell the buyer about the zoning of the property and the permitted uses allowed under that zoning. It will <u>not</u> tell the buyer about required building codes, required land dedications, pending zone changes or assessments, parking requirements and property line set-backs. It will <u>not</u> tell the buyer if any additions or improvements to the property have been made without required permits. These kinds of information are available from the local government (city, county or state). Many local agencies now maintain electronic address files which contain all the information the agency knows about the property.

And....

In this chapter we have only touched upon some of the basic concepts dealing with real property. Hopefully the beginning investor now has a broader frame into which additional information can be fitted. Certainly a course in real estate Principles, offered at most community colleges, is an excellent investment of time and resources for those new to real estate.

There are also many excellent texts devoted to real estate Principles, especially those which narrow the focus to matters relevant to the particular state or states in which you will be investing. In many states the Department of Real Estate publishes a reference manual which provides a wealth of information of interest to the local investor. One of these texts should be your first real estate investment.

CONCURRENT CO-OWNERSHIP OF PROPERTY INTERESTS

	Tenancy In Common (TIC)	Joint Tenancy (JT)	Community Property (CP)
Parties	Any number of persons - (including husband and wife)	Any number can be JTs (including husband and wife)	Only husband and wife are eligible
Division	Ownership can be divided into *equal or unequal* shares	Ownership interests *must be equal*. (TTIP)	Ownership interest are equal
Title	Each owner has separate title	There is only one title to whole property (one instrument conveyed title to all)	Only one title, but each co-owner has separate, undivided interest
Possession	Each owner has right to possess his or her undivided interest	Equal right of possession (separate but undivided interest)	Equal right of management and control *except* in case of personal property used in business
Conveyance	Interest may be conveyed apart from other owners	Conveyance of interest by JT breaks the Joint Tenancy between the conveying JT and other JTs, but not between or among remaining JTs	Interest cannot be conveyed separately. Both must join in conveyance of real property. Either owner may transfer personal property
Purchaser's Status	Becomes a tenant-in-common with other tenants-in-common	Purchaser becomes a TIC with remaining JTs (who remain JTs among themselves)	Purchaser or devisee cannot acquire one co-owner's interest and hold title with remaining spouse as community property
Death	On death, passes to devisees or heirs. Also subject to laws pertaining to *intestate* succession.	On death of JT, deceased interest passes *immediately by operation of law* to remaining JTs. Interest *cannot be willed* and is therefore not subject to probate	In absence of will. 1/2 to spouse in severalty, 1/2 to one child, if any. If more than 1 child, 1/3 to spouse, 2/3rds to all remaining children If a will, to devisees as stated.
Successor's Status	Devisee(s) or heir(s) become tenant-in-common with remaining TICs	Last surviving JT owns the entire property in severalty (alone)	If interest is willed, devisee(s) becomes a TIC with surviving spouse.[1]
Creditor's Rights	Debtor's interest may be sold by execution sale. Creditor becomes a TIC with others	JT's interest may be pledged as security for a loan. On foreclosure creditor becomes TIC with remaining JT(s). (Lenders rarely lend on JT interest)	Community property is liable for debts of either party if contracted during marriage. Entire property available to satisfy creditor
Presumption	Favored in doubtful cases, except husband and wife	Must be expressly stated. Not favored. (TTIP)	Strong presumption that property acquired during marriage is community property

1   Some CP states now enable a CP interest to be held with "the right of survivorship" which prevents a spouse from willing his/her interest to a third party.

Nothing could be more important to the real estate investor than to understand how real estate delivers cash returns and how these future returns determine the financial value of the investment property.

If you have recently begun to explore investment real estate you probably have already heard terms such as 'gross rent multiplier,' 'capitalization rate,' 'cash-on-cash' and other financial jargon pertaining to valuation. Yet the very best method of determining real estate value (as well as any other type of investment) is to calculate the total *present worth* of all future income you can reasonably expect to receive during your period of ownership, when *discounted* at an acceptable rate. The future income from real estate includes the net income derived from operating the property on a year-to-year basis as well as the net income to be received on sale (the *reversionary* income).

How Discounting Works

Discounting is a method of converting a sum of cash to be received at some time in the future to its value today. For example, we may ask: "If you were to receive $1,000 one year from today, what is it worth to you now?" The answer depends on the rate of return you could earn if you had the money to invest today.[1]

For example, if you could put capital to work in a similar-risk investment to earn 10%, today's value of $1,000 in one year can be represented by this simple expression:

$$PV = \frac{FV}{(1 + i)^n} \quad \text{Where:}$$

PV = Present Value

FV = Future Value

i = discount rate

n = number of periods

---

[1] Your 'opportunity cost of money.'

Therefore its Present Value today is:

$$PV = \frac{\$1,000}{(1.10)^1} = \$909.09$$

If a sum of $1,000 were not to be received until <u>2</u> years (periods) in the future, its Present Value would be:

$$PV = \frac{\$1,000}{(1.10)^2} = \$826.45$$

> Note the change in the exponent. The PV is controlled by both the discount rate and the time to receipt.

(Investing $826.45 for 2 periods @ 10% interest per period yields [$826.45 * (1.10)*(1.10)] = $1,000.)

This technique of converting the value of the future receipt of money into a *Present Value* is known as *Discounting.* It is a technique fundamental to the valuation of <u>all</u> investments, including real estate. Here are some points to consider:

- An *interest rate* carries a Present Value forward in time to deliver its Future Value.
- A *discount rate* carries a Future Value backward in time to express its Present Value.
- A discount rate and an interest rate are opposite sides of the very same coin.
- The farther in time the receipt of cash, the lower its Present Value.
- The higher the discount rate, the lower the Present Value.

Why the Discount Rate is an Important Number

When you discount the future receipts from a real estate investment by a selected discount rate, <u>that rate will also be your intended yield, or expected rate of return on your investment</u>. The result you obtain is the *Present Value*, or *Present Worth*, of the investment today.

Therefore the investment value of any income-producing property is the sum of the Present Values of all the future cashflows which the owner can reasonably expect to receive over the holding period. The discount rate used to create these Present Values is also the owner's expected rate of return (yield) on his invested cash.[2]

Three Sources of Returns from Real Estate

The annual cash amount that flows from a real estate investment is its Net Operating Income (NOI). It is the collected, or *operating*, income[3] less the required operating expenses. Take note that NOI does not include any deduction for mortgage expense since debt service is an *ownership* expense, and not an *operating* expense. This is so because the decision to leverage the investment by borrowing money is a decision made by a particular owner. The same owner could buy the same property using all cash; whether it carries a mortgage or not, the investment will deliver the same NOI in the same set of hands. Mortgaging the investment simply determines how the net operating income is to be shared between the equity owner and the lender.

In addition to the NOI, the owner also looks forward to the disposition of the property at an appreciated price. Therefore, a second leg of his total return will be in the form of *net proceeds* from the final sale. By

---

2   Return on Equity, ROE.
3   Income after adjustments for vacancies and credit losses.

net proceeds, we mean the cash proceeds after payment of all sales costs, mortgages, liens, state, local and federal taxes. The net proceeds amount is equal to the amount received following the satisfaction of all ownership liabilities.

There is, however, a third cashflow arising from a real estate investment that distinguishes it from an investment in stocks or bonds. That cashflow arises from depreciation deductions from income that the owner may take to compensate for the wearing out of his income-producing asset. Deductions for depreciation are not cash deductions and do not reduce the owner's cashflow. They are non-cash deductions from otherwise taxable income that reduce, or 'shelter' a portion of the investor's ordinary income from immediate taxation.[4] The third cashflow is the amount of tax saved by 'sheltering' some of the NOI from immediate taxation.

Mix of Cashflow Returns, the Original Three-legged Stool

Imagine these three sources of returns - net operating income, tax benefits and appreciation – to be three legs on an investment stool. Taken together as percentages, they amount to the total yield from the real estate investment. The investment stool at the left has three legs of equal length, suggesting that these sources of cashflow returns are equal and that the investment offers stability and evenly diversified risk. But real estate properties rarely, if ever, deliver cashflow returns from these sources evenly. The amount derived from each leg can vary according to current interest rates, tax law and product demand. But regardless of the mix, the total yield from all cashflow sources must add up to satisfy the investor's yield requirements. If this were not so, real estate would fail to attract investment capital.

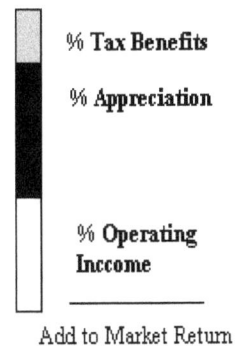

% Tax Benefits

% Appreciation

% Operating Income

Add to Market Return

For example, prior to 1987 when tax law permitted the depreciation of property over a very short span of 15 years, prices were marked up so high that many properties returned relatively little taxable cashflow from normal operations. The depreciation benefits were so large that many limited partnerships were formed in which some partners were assigned all the depreciation benefits – but little or no cash – because these high tax-bracket investors could convert depreciation deductions into *cash-saved* at a very high marginal rate.[5] Beginning in 1987, these depreciation benefits were sharply reduced and the focus became intensified asset management in order to increase operating income. At that point, real estate became far less oriented to tax benefits and remains so in 2015. Some of these limited partner interests from the early eighties are still available for purchase at drastically reduced prices.

This relationship among the three sources of cashflow may be viewed as:

$$\frac{\text{Tax Benefits} + \text{Appreciation} + \text{Oper. Income}}{\text{Total Cash Invested}} = \text{Yield}$$

---

[4] The concept behind tax shelters is that a depreciation deduction shelters income from current taxation at Ordinary tax rates. Under 2014 tax law, all depreciation taken is now recovered (taxed) at sale time at the 25% fixed rate paid by all taxpayers regardless of their tax bracket.

[5] 50% at that time. Therefore $10,000 in depreciation sheltered $10,000 of ordinary income which otherwise would be taxed at 50%, resulting in a tax savings of $5,000.

Note that an investment in vacant and un-leased land provides neither tax benefits nor operating income. As such, its yield depends upon one single source of return: Appreciation. It is because of this dependence on only one source of return that *an investment in raw land is real estate's riskiest investment.*

Value and the Principle of Anticipation

Although the real estate market is reasonably efficient in responding to changing economic conditions, it is not so efficient that vigilant investors cannot anticipate a change in the mix of cashflow returns by buying and selling real estate before trends become widely recognized. The acquisition of well-located properties based on sound operating income just prior to a period of inflation can return excellent yields. In the same way, property disposed of prior to an economic slump, lower rents and higher vacancy factors can preserve wealth attained.

In either case, the key is a prospective assessment of future performance, and has much less to do with past performance than many investors believe. In fact, one of the hallmarks that distinguishes the neophyte from the experienced investor is what they see when they examine the same dilapidated property on a very busy corner: The neophyte looks at the existing improvement on the property and says, "I would never buy a wreck like that!"
Meanwhile, the seasoned investor muses to himself –
"Now if I tear down that wreck, I could build a......... on this site!"
Months later, the neophyte passes by the now-redeveloped site and exclaims,
"Now why didn't I think of that!"

The more one becomes experienced in real estate investments the more one appreciates that value has to do with the *Principle of Anticipation* and much, much less to do with history. Property renovators understand this very well, and the beginning investor would do well to tear one or two pages from their playbook that has to do with adding future value to existing real estate.

Equity Return Rate Declines

There is another important distinction between investing in stocks and in real estate. Dividends from stocks can usually be reinvested in additional shares to keep all capital working at an acceptable rate of return.[6] Annual returns from real estate, however, are generally not so large that they can serve as a down payment sufficient to acquire another comparable real estate investment. The increase in equity in a real estate property tends to accumulate and lie fallow like a cache buried in the backyard that silently grows larger each year. For this reason real estate investments typically experience a steadily *declining* rate of return on pre-tax equity (ROE) often starting with the very first year of ownership.
In many cases 'buy and hold' real estate investors reach a rate of return on currently invested capital (ROE) which is substantially below the rates they could otherwise achieve from more passive and less risky investments, such as fixed-rate securities. This situation can develop rapidly, especially when rents are rising rapidly.

As time passes, increased annual net operating income translates into a higher property value and this amount of appreciation gets inserted into the bottom line of our rate of return (yield) formula. But the cash value of appreciation is not available to the equity owner until he either refinances or sells the property.

---

[6]   Direct Reinvestment Plans (DRIPs) enable the stock investor to buy fractional shares on a regular basis.

$$\frac{\text{Tax Benefits} + \text{Appreciation} + \text{Oper Income}}{\text{Original Cash Invested} + \textbf{Appreciation}} = \text{Current Return Rate}$$

Since real estate trades at a multiple of its net operating income, a property that delivers a 6% capitalization rate[7] will insert $16.67 into **Appreciation** for every $1.00 increase in net operating income.[8] The lower the current market cap rate, the greater the appreciation value of each new dollar of net operating income.

If the property carries an amortizing mortgage, the portion of the monthly loan payment dedicated to reducing the principal (*loan paydown*) is also equity, and it too is added to total investor equity. This is not a very significant amount during the first few years of the typical mortgage term, but eventually the portion of the total payment devoted to loan paydown begins to grow.

$$\frac{\text{Tax Benefits} + \text{Operating Income}}{\text{Original Cash Invested} + \text{Appreciation} + \textbf{Loan Paydown}} = \text{Return Rate (ROE)}$$

Purchasing Power is the Name of the Game

It comes as a surprise to many investors that the Equity Return Rate is usually at its peak near the very inception of the investment but begins to decline thereafter. How far the investor allows the rate to decline before taking financial action is a critical factor in long-term investment success. If the objective of the investment is not just a profit but also the accumulation of wealth then a very important index of real estate performance is the *annual* ROE which measures *current* dollars returned for dollars *currently invested*. Investors are frequently misled by advertising that estimates the cashflow from a future year measured against the *original* investment amount. This is a metric both useless and grossly misleading.

The goal is to maintain a *current* ROE greater than the current inflation rate. It is not sufficient that the ROE be positive; the ROE may show a positive nominal rate of return but be less than the rate of inflation. In this event, the investor will lose purchasing power even though income increases. It is only when the ROE exceeds the inflation rate that the investor can be said to be adding to his wealth by increasing the *purchasing power* of accumulated dollars.
Purchasing Power is the name of the game.

After-tax Cashflows

It helps a great deal to understand how real estate generates pre-tax and after-tax income. The essence of the operating statement for an income-producing property is simply this: ⟶

Collected Rent
− Operating Expenses
= Net Operating Income (NOI)

The real estate "operating statement" is different from the one an accountant might prepare for a business in that it does not include as expenses deductions for mortgage interest, income taxes, depreciation or amortization costs. It is, in fact, a *cashflow*, or EBITDA,[9] statement.

The **NOI** is the starting point for calculating both the annual After-tax Cashflow and Taxable Income.

---

[7]   The ratio of NOI to Fair Market Value
[8]   Dividing the NOI by 0.06 is equivalent to multiplying it by 16.67.
[9]   EBITDA = Earnings Before Interest, (Income) Taxes, Depreciation and Amortization

	After-tax Cashflow	vs.	Taxable Income
1	Net Operating Income		Net Operating Income
2	Less Mortgage Interest		Less Mortgage Interest
3	Less Mortgage Paydown	- - - - - - - ▶	(not tax deductible)
4	= Cashflow Before Tax [10]		Less Depreciation
5	Less Tax Payable		Less Amortization[11]
6	= Cashflow After-Tax (CFAT)		= Taxable Income
7			x Marginal Tax Rate[12]
8			= Tax Payable

We are taking some tax accounting liberties here since Cashflow Before Tax (line 4) is classified as Ordinary income and would be moved over to the individual taxpayer's Form 1040 as additional taxable income. The annual tax resulting from ownership of the property would be the incremental tax amount attributable to this extra income. The most accurate way to determine the amount of tax attributable to the real estate investment is to calculate the tax with and without the real estate data. The difference will be the tax resulting from the property. We assume here that the added income would not increase the taxpayer's incremental tax rate, but it well might.

The number on line 6, CFAT, is the number we require to estimate investment value since it is the cash that we can bank after all expenses of operation, after paying the mortgage and after paying the taxes due on the annual income realized.

Valuing a Series of Future CFATs

The Present Value, or Present Worth, of the investment depends on the value of the future after-tax cashflows, discounted at a rate acceptable to the individual investor. These future cashflows must be forecasted in the same way and with an understanding of the same limitations that would apply to any other business plan or financial model. All forecasts are best estimates about the future performance of the business using a line-by-line analysis of revenue and expenses. The farther out in time one goes with these forecasts, the greater the margin of error. Some investors, pointing out this potential for error, prefer not to address this issue at all. If, however, they were in the business of manufacturing widgets, one has to wonder how they would anticipate and plan to meet the future need for raw materials, labor and capital without a valid attempt to forecast future revenue and expenses. Real Estate is no different: **real estate ownership is a business.**

The Pro-forma, a Look into the Future

The construction of a pro-forma results in a series of annual Cashflows After Tax (CFATs) linked together by a series of assumptions or forecasts. The total present value of these cashflows is the summation of each future cashflow, discounted at an acceptable rate.[13] Once the future estimates of the CFATs are

---

[10] Sometimes called "Spendable Income"

[11] Typically, the recovery of points and fees paid for a loan.

[12] The rate at which the next dollar of ordinary income would be taxed.

[13] Discounted Cashflow Analysis, or DCF

determined, any price paid above the calculated present value (PV) will result in a lower yield to the investor; conversely, if he/she can negotiate a lower market price, the yield will increase.

$$PV = \frac{CFAT_1}{(1+i)^1} + \frac{CFAT_2}{(1+i)^2} + \frac{CFAT_3}{(1+i)^3} + \frac{CFAT_4}{(1+i)^4} + \cdots\cdots\cdots \frac{CFAT_n}{(1+i)^n}$$

The last cashflow, $\frac{CFAT_n}{(1+i)^n}$, includes not only the operating income for the last year, but also the net after-tax proceeds from the disposition/sale of the property at the end of the nth year. This net proceeds number is the final sales price, net of the mortgage balance, sales costs, commissions, depreciation recapture and state and federal capital gains taxes. This *reversion value* is the same as the amount of the check in the investor's hand as he/she exits the escrow office, having paid all expenses of sale and final tax bills.

Using Multiple Discount Rates

In the formula line above, the exponent in the denominator increases to adjust the Present Value for *time to receipt*. Even in the case of a fixed cashflow, the Present Value of the each successive cashflow diminishes because of the lengthening time until it is received. This is the essence of the concept called the Time Value of Money.

But the discount rate (**i**) applied is the same for each future period. However, using the same discount rate is at odds with common experience. A review of an investment opportunity may indicate that the first few years of an investment may be the most uncertain, calling for a higher risk premium and therefore a higher discount rate. Once the investment stabilizes and risk decreases, it may be appropriate to reduce the risk premium and therefore the discount rate. Or the reverse may be true: the risk of the investment may increase with time which should call for an increase in the discount rate. None of the common algorithms in financial calculators or computer spreadsheet functions, such as Present Value, Net Present Value or Internal Rate of Return provide for this flexibility. However, periodic changes in the discount rate can be easily handled manually in a computer spreadsheet. The Present Value total of all future CFATs so determined will equal the financial value of the investment. QED.

A Caveat: Investment Value vs. Market Price

The calculated PV number is the investment (financial) value of the property *to a particular investor*, but it is not necessarily the market price of the property. The investment value is the maximum price a particular investor can pay in order to realize the yield (discount rate or rates) used in arriving at the Present Value. The market price, however, is the price other informed investors,[14] not acting under duress, will pay for the same property. This differential sets up market competition among potential buyers. Those using a higher discount rate (i.e. require a higher yield) will pay less for the property, while those using a lower discount rate will pay more.[15]

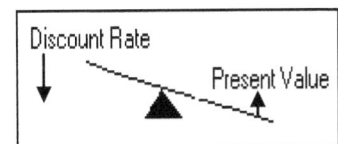

The differential is intensified when real estate prices are changing. When your barber or hairdresser tells you that this is the time to buy real estate, it is probably too late. And when they tell you that this is not the time to invest in real estate, it is probably a time to invest. Warren Buffet has opined that: ".. you pay

---

[14] Wide variation here.
[15] The market price varies inversely to the discount rate.

a high price (in the stock market) for a cheery consensus." And, of course, Baron Rothschild, who made his first fortune buying in the financial panic that followed Napoleon's defeat at Waterloo, said: "The time to buy is when there is blood in the streets." The point is that the capable investor must be his/her own arbiter of market value and to that end must have reasonable skills in determining value apart from the value estimate of the ovine crowd.

Yield Capitalization and the IRR

When the investor works to determine the investment value, he designates the desired yield and uses it as a discount rate to convert future cashflows to a Present (Investment) Value. But often the task is to determine the discount rate (yield) which will convert forecasted cashflows to a pre-established Asking Price. Compare the difference in these two approaches:

$$(1) \text{ Investment Value} = \frac{CFAT_1}{(1+i)^1} + \frac{CFAT_2}{(1+i)^2} + \frac{CFAT_3}{(1+i)^3} + \frac{CFAT_4}{(1+i)^4} + ... \frac{CFAT_n}{(1+i)^n}$$

$$(2) \text{ Asking Price} = \frac{CFAT_1}{(1+x)^1} + \frac{CFAT_2}{(1+x)^2} + \frac{CFAT_3}{(1+x)^3} + \frac{CFAT_4}{(1+x)^4} + ... \frac{CFAT_n}{(1+x)^n}$$

In the first formula line, the value of **i** is known; it is the investor's desired yield from the investment. It results in an investment (present) value for the particular investor who selected **i**.

On the second formula line, the Asking Price is known and the value of **x** (the yield) is unknown. The value of **x** is the discount rate that will convert the present value total of all future CFAT values to a sum exactly equal to the pre-specified Asking Price. This value of **x** is known as the Internal Rate of Return. The IRR is both a discount rate and a yield. This valuation technique is also known as *Yield Capitalization*.

It helps to understand the IRR by assuming that you have already held the investment for a number of years and that it has performed as recorded in your pro-forma log. A fair question might be: "Considering all the annual cashflows and the final net proceeds I received from this investment, at what *overall* rate did my original investment (wealth) grow each year?" The IRR tells you the rate at which cash *remaining in the investment* grew per year over the entire holding period.

The IRR is an overall assessment of the investment, while the ROE is a quick snapshot of how well the investment is returning cash on *currently invested* cash (equity) at a particular point in time. The IRR will tell you the rate at which the investment grew overall, but it will not tell you the specific rate at which it grew in any single period. The best use of the Equity Return Rate is to measure it together with the IRR because the ROE can decline for a number of periods before the decline begins to be noticeable in the IRR.

Limitations to the IRR

There are two limitations sometimes cited in the use of the IRR as a valuation metric:
1. There may be multiple solutions to the determination of the IRR.
2. The IRR depends upon the rate at which cash flowing from the investment is reinvested.

The first of these is true. Descartes' Rule for Polynomials states that there are as many discrete solutions as there are changes in the sign of the values. Academes who seek to demonstrate this point are required to construct cashflows whose *net present values*[16] (NPV) swing from positive to negative during the holding period. However, this is seldom a practical matter in judging most real estate investments, new construction and renovated property excepted.

The second of these is entirely false, though repeated all too frequently in otherwise reputable finance textbooks. The yield realized from a particular investment has absolutely nothing to do with the rate at which its cash proceeds may be reinvested in a subsequent, separate investment. To assert otherwise is tantamount to asserting that a high-yielding investment opportunity should be rejected because a subsequent investment at a comparable return rate is unavailable.

A more complete explanation of this perceived limitation and its probable origin is available to those interested.[17]

Constructing a Discount Rate

There are important advantages in constructing your own discount rate because in doing so you retain control over the inflation and risk rates which are components of the discount rate.

A discount rate is a built-up rate consisting of at least two, and sometimes four, sub-rates. The four potential rates for a depreciating real estate asset are:

1. The *basic* Safe Rate for money.
2. An allowance for future inflation.
3. A Rate of Return *of* invested capital.
4. A Premium to compensate for Risk.

> These two sub-rates are combined in the yield of a standard Treasury Bond of comparable Duration and Maturity

The *basic* **Safe Rate** for money in the United States is published every day as the yield on U.S. Treasury Inflation-Protected Securities (TIPS). This rate can be found on the bond page of most financial newspapers and on the Web[18]. The yield on TIPS does not include an allowance for inflation. Therefore when the yield on TIPS serves as the basic safe rate one's own estimate of future inflation should (can) be added.

However, the yield on *standard* **U.S. Treasury** bonds does contain an allowance for inflation. If the current yield on a standard Treasury bond is used as the safe rate for money, the user indicates acceptance of the market's estimate of inflation and no additional adjustment is indicated.

If the current yield on Standard Treasury bonds (of similar Duration and maturity) is subtracted from the current TIPS yield the result should be a very close approximation of the current inflation rate.

TIPs Yield – Standard Treasury Yield = Inflation Rate

Although this is a handy method to determine the current inflation rate it suffers from continuing government interference is the manipulation of the CPI and in the artificial suppression of market interest rates. Suppressing the CPI restrains interest rates and government expenses tied to the CPI,[19] but also collaterally reduces the amount by which a TIPS bond should be increased. Other stratagems such as

---

[16] The Net Present Value is simply the Present Value minus the original investment amount.
[17] See Introduction to Cashflow Analysis, (Regent School Press, 2012), EAN 978-1-886654-09-9 via Amazon
[18] http://www.bloomberg.com/markets/rates-bonds/government-bonds/us/
[19] Such as interest on the debt, government payrolls, pensions and social security payments.

Quantitative Easing (QE) and Financial Repression limit interest rates on bonds, including U.S.Treasury securities.

For the time being, it seems prudent to avoid using the TIPS yield as the Basic Rate for money. The apparent inflation rate can be subtracted from the Standard Treasury yield and the result increased by one's own estimate of the inflation rate.[20]

A **Rate for the Return of Capital** is included when, as in the case of a leasehold investment, ownership of the improvement typically reverts to the ground lessor at the end of the lease. In these cases, the ground lessee cannot recover his original cash investment by selling the property since title reverts to the ground lessor at lease expiry. Instead, he must recover his original cash during (over) the holding period.

For example, a ground lease with 40 years remaining must recapture originally invested capital at the rate of 100%/40 = 2.5% per year. A leasehold with a much shorter remaining life, say 20 years, must return invested capital at the rate of 5% per year. When this higher rate is added to the other sub-rates, the resulting higher discount rate lowers the Present Value of the leasehold investment. In the case of a fee-simple property, it is unnecessary to add a rate for return of the investment since the originally invested cash is usually recovered in the final sales price.

In those cases in which payments under a <u>lease</u> are purchased, an annual rate for the recovery of the total acquisition cost of the lease should be added to the safe rate together with the inflation rate and a risk premium.

Ah, Risk

A Risk Rate is a premium added to reflect the chance of not collecting the Scheduled Income for the contemplated holding period. It is not a rate to compensate for inflation. As such, it varies according to the quality of the individual tenant and the tenant's capacity to continue to pay the rent.[21] When multiple tenants are involved, as with office and multi-family residential properties, the risk premium is a weighted risk for the tenants as a group. Office buildings are designated "Class A" not only because they are more attractive and of higher quality but also because they attract quality tenants with "Class A" Balance Statements who represent lower risk.

Risk also varies according to the duration of the rent stream; rent collected from a highly rated *credit* tenant [22] under a long term lease will add a smaller risk premium to the discount rate and therefore will result in a higher market value. Lower risk also reduces loan costs.

Risk, like beauty, is in the eye of the beholder. One investor may regard a property leased to General Electric or Microsoft for 20 years to be a very low-risk situation. As such he will require a low risk premium. This low risk premium added to the other sub-rates results in a lower discount rate and therefore, a higher price for the property. The Present Value and Discount rate vary inversely.

The same investor may judge the very same property leased to Heretodayandgonetomorrow.com Inc. to be a very risky situation possibly presaging months of future vacancy and loss of income. In this situation

---

[20]   See John Williams, www.shadowstats.com

[21]   As reflected in the tenant's credit history and Balance Statement.

[22]   A tenant whose Balance Statement gives reasonable assurance that the tenant will be capable of paying the rent for the entire term of the lease.

he will add a higher Risk Premium and utilize a higher discount rate and bid a lower offering price. This fact underscores the importance of selecting quality tenants.

Valuing the Aging Property

A property has value "as improved" and as "unimproved." When the unimproved value of the underlying land exceeds the value of the property "as improved," it is time for redevelopment. There are times, however, when this does not occur. Many older properties sit on land which has increased so much in value that the income from its aging improvement is insufficient to provide an adequate return on the value of the underlying land alone. These properties ought not to be valued according to current income, but rather from the potential income which could source from an appropriate new improvement.[23] Unfortunately local zoning laws, General Plan restrictions and environmental concerns often block the construction of a suitable new improvement. This is especially true of littoral properties and others in highly regulated locations. The net effect is to put upward pressure on the rents from the existing improvements. Prior to acquiring this kind of property it is crucially important to investigate current and proposed zoning laws and regulations, especially as they pertain to a contemplated replacement.

Adding all these sub-rates together results in the discount rate required by a particular investor, and this discount rate, applied to future after-tax cashflows, will yield the Present Value of the anticipated after-tax cash returns. This Present Value is the Investment Value of the property *to that investor.*

Capitalization Rates

Although discounting anticipated future income is the preferred method of valuation by almost all institutional investors, it is not the method used by the majority of private investors. The most commonly used method by individuals is to capitalize Net Operating Income by a single "cap rate." By *capitalize* we mean to assign a capital value to the *current* income stream. This technique is known as *Direct Capitalization* in contrast to *Yield Capitalization* (DCF).

Re-consider the formula for determining the Present Value of a constant cashflow:

$$PV = \frac{NOI}{(1+i)^1} + \frac{NOI}{(1+i)^2} + \frac{NOI}{(1+i)^3} + \ldots \frac{NOI_n}{(1+i)^n}$$

In this format, the cashflow (NOI) remains constant over the holding period. If, however, the series is extended to infinity, the formula for the Present Value (PV) of the infinite series of cashflows reduces to a simple expression: $PV = \dfrac{NOI}{i}$.

Then Let NOI = C. $\longrightarrow$

Therefore, Direct Capitalization refers to a valuation process in which:
  1) the income is assumed to remain constant, and
  2) the cash flow is assumed to continue forever.

Derivation of Present Value of a Perpetual Ordinary Annuity

Let $a = C$; let $x = \dfrac{1}{(1+i)^1}$ then,

$PV = ax + ax^2 + ax^2 + ax^3 + ax^4 + ax^5 \ldots \infty$

Multiplying each side by x we have,

$PVx = ax^2 + ax^3 + ax^4 + ax^5 \ldots \infty$

Subtracting the second equation from the first we have,

$PV - PVx = ax$

$PV(1 - \dfrac{1}{(1+i)^1}) = \dfrac{C}{(1+i)^1}$

$PV = \dfrac{C}{i}$ **The Capitalization formula.**

---

23 Properties need not be old to be an under-improvement.

Why Direct Capitalization Remains a Popular Method

The Direct Capitalization of income method owes the bulk of its popularity to its simplicity, even though most individual investors are unaware of the two very improbable assumptions that are implicit in this method.

There is also a third consideration. The most frequent means of determining Direct Capitalization rates is to gather market data on properties that have sold recently. Ideally, these properties should be very similar to the subject property in terms of location, quality of construction, age, condition, quality of tenant, similarity of rent levels, etc. When the Net Operating Income and the sales price of a comparable property have been obtained, its Net Operating Income can be divided by its Price to deliver the *overall* [24] capitalization rate.

For example, market research may reveal the recent sale of a very comparable property for $1,000,000 whose NOI was $95,000. The capitalization rate becomes:

$$\text{"Cap Rate"} = \frac{\text{Net Operating Income}}{\text{Fair Market Value}} = \frac{\$95,000}{\$1,000,000} = 0.095 = 9.5\%.$$

This rate, 9.5%, could be applied to a very similar property with a current NOI of $125,000 to estimate its value:

$$\text{Fair Market Value} = \frac{\$125,000}{0.95} = \$1,315,789$$

The limitation of cap rates obtained from historic data is that these data are *retro*spective, not *pro*spective. Therefore, when interest rates are declining the use of last year's higher cap rate may undervalue a property in today's market by dividing the NOI by too high a number. If interest rates are rising, last year's lower cap rate may overvalue the property by dividing by too low a number. Investors need to be prospective and not retrospective: history is history.

Timing the Capitalization of Income

The Direct Capitalization method of determining value may be applied to either the end of the current year or to the end of the next year of operation.

This variation in applicability sometimes creates confusion and controversy when it comes to valuing an income property for sale. If the property is submitted to a formal appraisal in which a well-trained appraiser utilizes the *income to value approach* method,[25] the annual income will be taken as of the time of the appraisal. The appraiser will typically not extend income and expense trends beyond the current year. Following a transfer, future income belongs to the buyer and not to the seller. Once the property is in the hands of the new owner, however, it is customary to determine the income which will be in place at the end of the first year of operation. Many income properties listed for sale quote a capitalization rate determined by using next year's NOI even though the seller has not guaranteed this income.

---

[24] "Overall" since the rate includes both the equity and debt components of the price.

[25] The most common method of appraising income-producing property.

Adjusting the Direct Cap Rate for Constant Growth in NOI

Unlike discount rates, 'cap' rates do not contain an allowance for inflation. But cap rates can be adjusted to reflect steady growth in the NOI by subtracting from **i** an allowance for the rate of growth (g):

$$PV = \frac{NOI}{i - g}$$

If NOI is projected to increase at a 2% annual rate *indefinitely*, this growth factor will affect value:

$$Fair\ Market\ Value = \frac{\$125,000}{0.10 - 0.02} = \$1,562,500$$

Growth may also be negative as the result of an excess of supply over demand, economic obsolescence of the market area,[26] or the growing functional obsolescence of the improvement itself. If NOI is forecasted to follow a steady 2% annual decline, the value becomes:

$$Fair\ Market\ Value = \frac{\$125,000}{0.10 - (-0.02)} = \$1,041,667$$

In adjusting the capitalization rate for either positive or negative growth in the NOI, the assumption always remains that this adjustment will never change and that it will continue forever.

When low cap rates are encountered in the marketplace, it is frequently an indication that sellers expect prices to rise and want to be paid extra for an appreciating asset. There is nothing wrong with this, except that prices do not rise forever. But a constant growth subtraction from the capitalization rate (resulting in a lower cap rate and a higher price) implies they will.

Varying the Discount Rate

Properties do not continue to operate under the same market conditions. One great advantage in using Yield Capitalization,[27] as opposed to Direct Capitalization to arrive at property value, is that Yield Capitalization permits changes in the discount rate to meet anticipated changes in economic conditions that could affect the Risk Premium, the Inflation Rate, or both.

For example, there may be a shortage of available office space in a certain market which is expected to prevail for 2-4 years. As a result, office rents are anticipated to rise and the risk associated with vacancies to decrease. If, however, the market is able to create an additional supply of office space, rents are then likely to stabilize and the future vacancy rate may thereafter increase.[28]

The risk associated with these changing economic conditions justifies a change in the discount rates for the affected years. Stewart Myers[29] points out that the early years of an unproven project are often the riskiest, justifying a higher initial discount rate. Once the project has stabilized, however, the discount rate

---

[26] Deterioration of the physical surroundings or supporting systems.

[27] DCF = Discounted Cash Flow = Yield Capitalization Think Detroit.

[28] The risk of vacancy should be accounted for in the operating income pro-forma. The risk of never receiving the rent should be reflected in the risk premium.

[29] Principles of Corporate Finance, Richard Bealey, Stewart Myers, McGraw Hill Inc. **ISBN:** 0073286982. (Dr. Myers is Professor of Finance at the Massachusetts Institute of Technology.)

may be lowered. Direct Capitalization cannot reflect these changes because the assumptions implicit in this method of valuation are based on no changes.
Never. Ever.

Net Present Value

Some investors prefer to use the Net Present Value (NPV) method to value an investment. This method is a simple variant of Yield Capitalization.
The NPV is the Present Value of the investment minus the amount of the initial investment. Therefore, if the discounted value of all future cashflows is equal to $500,000 and the initial investment is $450,000, the NPV would be stated as +$50,000. If the initial investment were $550,000 the NPV would be −$50,000.

A negative NPV does not necessarily mean that the investment would lose money; it does mean, however, that the investment will not return the discount rate used to produce the PV. If the NPV is positive, it means that the IRR of the project will be greater than the discount rate used to calculate the PV. If the discount rate used produces a PV exactly equal to the initial investment, the resulting NPV will be zero, and that discount rate will be the Internal Rate of Return. (This is why the IRR is alternately defined as that discount rate which produces an NPV of zero.)

Provide a Discount Rate or Ask For One?

But the significance of the use of the NPV instead of the IRR lies elsewhere.

In determining the IRR, the investor provides both the initial investment and estimates of the future cashflows, and then asks the calculator or computer to determine (force) the discount rate (IRR). In utilizing the NPV method, the investor supplies the same data but also proposes a selected discount rate. This discount rate may be either the investor's opportunity cost of funds or a "hurdle" rate determined as the result of an evaluation of the safe rate and a suitable premium for risk. Quite frequently, the hurdle rate chosen will be the cost of capital on the theory that the investor should receive a rate of return at least equal to his lender who typically is lower on the risk-exposure pole.

If the NPV is positive it indicates that the Present Value of the investment, discounted at the supplied rate, is greater than the amount of the initial investment. This may indicate a "good to go" decision. If the NPV is negative, however, and the hurdle rate is a firm number, the project may be rejected if it cannot be modified to meet the minimum.
Many financial analysts show a strong preference for the NPV metric because it allows for the selection of a discount rate using different rate components. Institutions which favor the Internal Rate of Return also *partition* the IRR to determine the proportion of the total return flowing from operating income, from depreciation and from appreciation (the three legs of the investment stool). Partitioning the IRR helps identify component risks.

NPV Error in Excel®

All financial calculators and computer spreadsheets offer NPV functions. But the function in Microsoft's Excel® which is labeled **=NPV(rate,value1**,value2, ...) does not return the actual NPV of a cashflow series. The **PV** function in Excel delivers the Present Value of

To access any Excel function type the desired function and then press *Control+Shift+A*. E.g.
=NPV *control+shift+A*
Excel will display
NPV(rate,value1,value2, ...)
for you. Replace the names of the variables with their values.

a cashflow series in which all the cashflows are *equal,* both in sign and amount; however, the **N̲PV** function in Excel delivers the **PV** of a series of *unequal* cashflows only. If the NPV is desired, the initial investment amount must be removed from the series and subtracted from the result.

If the pull-down menu for the NPV function in Excel is used, it directs the analyst to insert the original investment as a negative number, but cautions that it will be calculated as occurring at the end of the first period. This is contrary to common practice because original investments are always negative and occur at the beginning of the first period, not at the end.

The following formula inserted directly into an Excel cell will deliver the correct NPV. Note that the *rate* must be entered as a decimal amount per period: e.g. (0.10/12 to use 10% monthly.)

$$NPV = (rate, CF_1, CF_2, CF_3 ... CF_n) - \text{Initial Investment}$$

If the first cashflow occurs at the beginning of the first period (as in a lease) do not discount the first cashflow. Instead, remove it from the series and add its value to the result of the function:

$$NPV = (rate, CF_2, CF_3 ... CF_n) - \text{Initial Investment} + \textbf{CF}_1,$$

Cash-on-Cash & Gross Rent Multipliers

Two other single-period investment yardsticks are in popular use: Cash-on-Cash, and the Gross Rent Multiplier.[30] The latter index, the Gross Rent Multiplier (GRM), is simply the quotient resulting from the division of a property's Fair Market Value by its Gross Scheduled Income:[31]

$$\frac{\text{Fair Market Value}}{\text{Annual Gross Scheduled Income}} = \text{Annual Gross Rent Multiplier}[32]$$

If it can be ascertained that a local property which recently sold for $1 million had a Gross Scheduled Income (GSI) of $125,000, then its "gross multiplier" would be:

$$\frac{\$1,000,000}{\$125,000} = 8.0 = GRM$$

Therefore, a nearby property of very similar characteristics showing a Gross Scheduled Income of $150,000 could be expected to have a market value of approximately:

$$\$150,000 \times 8.0 = \$1,200,000$$

The **GRM** is widely used in the marketing of smaller, multi-family residential units, probably because operating expenses submitted by many owners of these units are notoriously unreliable.[33] Understated or unreported expenses will inflate the Net Operating Income resulting in an inflated market value. Therefore many small-property investors choose to disregard any seller-reported expenses and apply expense data from their own or other verifiable sources.

The GRM is best used as a screening tool only, since it measures nothing below the level of Scheduled rental income. It certainly provides no indication of a property's operating income after vacancy and

---

[30]　The Annual Property Operating Dataform in Chapter 4 may help clarify this section.
[31]　Sometimes described as Gross Potential Income.
[32]　The Gross Rent Multiplier can be expressed either as an annual or monthly figure.
[33]　Frequently as the result of poor record keeping and poor management, but sometimes as the result of guile.

credit losses, no gauge of operating expenses, nor of future cashflows. But it is precisely future cashflows which the informed investor is buying.

The **Cash-on-Cash** index is a useful, single-period measurement of value because it looks beyond vacancy, beyond operating expenses and beyond net operating income to income remaining after debt service (mortgage payments). It is the relationship of the Spendable Income (income after debt service, but before taxes)[34] to the cash initially invested in the property, or:

$$\frac{\text{Cash Remainng After Debt Service}}{\text{Cash Initially Invested in the Property}}$$

It, too, may be faulted in that it does not encourage a look at the potential for future income. But it does give a rather good indication of the cash return the investor can expect in relation to his total cash investment at the end of the **first period** of ownership. Since it measures cash after operating expenses and after the costs of servicing the debt, it is also a reflection of the 'mortgageability' of the property and the potential for leverage.

Investors who rely upon the Cash-on-Cash index operate on the assumption that if the property can perform to a reasonable standard in its first year of operation, it should, in the absence of any unforeseen problems, continue to perform well. This is akin to saying that if your automobile runs trouble-free for the first 50,000 miles, it will run trouble-free for the next 50,000 miles. Sometimes it does, oftentimes it does not.

ROE and Cash-on-Cash Misrepresentations

Some unethical, inexperienced or untrained real estate promoters project future cashflow and then compare it to the original cash invested. This is a rank misuse of this metric. If the investor wishes to use cash-on-cash, the nominator should always be the **current** cash from operations and the denominator should always be the amount of total net equity **currently invested** in the property.[35] Any other measurement is misleading and fallacious.

In Summary:

What we hope you will glean from this chapter is that:

1. The value of any real estate investment is always equal to the discounted value of all the future cashflows which the owner can reasonably expect to realize over the intended holding period.
2. These cashflows are converted to a present-day value estimate by the use of a *discount rate,* which summarizes the TIPS safe rate for money, a rate to compensate for risk and a rate to reflect inflation.
3. The use of capitalization rates to determine value is more convenient but the method carries with it tacit assumptions which will probably not be true over the typical holding period.
4. Gross Rent Multipliers should be used only as screening tools, not as value estimates.
5. Cash-on-cash calculations give a better indication of a return rate but should be confined to the first year of ownership.

---

[34] Cash-on-Cash *after* taxes is also, but less frequently, measured.
[35] Which is also the amount of net proceeds the owner would realize on sale.

6. We anticipate that the beginning investor also recognizes that valuation is a subjective process and because of this subjectivity, two different investors, given the same data, can come to measurable differences about the value of the very same property.

Chapter 3
Taxes & the
Investment
Property

The U.S. taxpayer's challenge to understand the tax code is analogous to the never-ending task which faced Sisyphus, the mythical king of Corinth, who was punished by the Greek gods by having to push a huge boulder to the top of a hill in Hades. When it reached the top the boulder rolled down to the bottom and Sisyphus was required to perform the task over again for all eternity.

The income tax law under which we now operate was first passed in 1913 and required a book 400 pages long to contain its rules and regulations. By 1939, the book had grown to 504 pages; by 1945 to 8,200 pages. In 2013 the U.S. tax code required 73,954 of the same size pages. It has become so complex that fewer than 50% of U.S. taxpayers can now prepare their own taxes – including a recent Secretary of the Treasury who must now use a proprietary computer program to prepare his return. Despite repeated calls for tax simplification, the code continues to grow larger, more complex and more burdensome.

This chapter will cover *some* of the essentials in the code which affect real estate investments, firm in the understanding that, like Sisyphus, we will soon be fated to do it all over again. In this regulatory morass it would be naive to expect the average real estate investor to master all the nuances of the current IRS code as it affects real estate. What is, perhaps, a more realistic and doable goal is for the investor to develop a degree of tax awareness that will alert him or her to changes in tax law that may apply to real estate owned. Then...

Get Competent Guidance

There are now more than 1.2 million professionals in the United States whose primary job is furnishing tax preparation, advice and guidance. The I.R.S. reports receiving more than 100 million telephone calls each year of which it is unable to answer approximately 25%. Of the balance answered, 29% of the answers have been found to be incorrect, but the agency disclaims any responsibility for incorrect information it dispenses. The reader is cautioned to rely neither on the information in this text nor on the IRS, but to consult experienced tax counsel for actionable guidance.

Categories of Business Assets

The Internal Revenue code (IRC) distinguishes three principal categories of business-related assets:

- ♦ Code Section 1231 includes both real and personal property used in a trade or business and held for more than one year.
- ♦ Code Section 1245 pertains specifically to gains and losses from the disposition of personal property used in a trade or business that is subject to depreciation, as well as to certain specialized types of real property such as petroleum storage tanks and single-purpose agricultural and horticultural buildings.
- ♦ Code Section 1250 pertains to gains from the disposition of real property used in a trade or business that is also subject to depreciation. This section of the code contains rules related to depreciation recapture (taxation) and the treatment of gains recognized when depreciable property is exchanged for vacant land.

Defining Capital and Non-capital Assets

An I.R.S. publication[1] defines a capital asset, as,

> *"...for the most part, everything you own and use for personal pleasure or investment."*

Capital assets include such things as your home, art and collectibles, your non-business-use auto, stocks, bonds, mortgages, promissory notes, gold and silver coins and jewelry.

Non-capital assets include property held primarily for sale (e.g. inventory) which is taxed as Ordinary income.

The significance of defining capital and non-capital assets is the rate at which gains are taxed and the limitation placed on the deductibility of losses.

Gains arising from the sale of a capital asset held for one year or less are taxed as Ordinary income. Gains from qualified assets held for more than one year are taxed at the applicable Long Term Capital Gains rate which, for many taxpayers, will be less than the tax on Ordinary income.

Recent Changes in Tax Rates

The Jobs and Growth Tax Relief and Reconciliation Act of 2003 (JGTRRA), reduced Ordinary tax rates from 27%, 30%, 35% and 39.6% to 25%, 28%, 33% and 35%, respectively. The American Taxpayer Relief Act of 2012 kept these rates unchanged for most taxpayers but reinstalled a maximum tax rate of 39.6% for single filers with Adjusted Gross Income (AGI) above $400,000 and married couples filing jointly with AGI above $450,000.[2]

In 2013, taxpayers in the 15% bracket (or lower) pay no tax on *qualified* dividends or long term gains (LTCGs). Those in the 25–35% brackets will continue to pay 15% tax on qualified dividends and LTCGs. Taxpayers in the 39.6% bracket will pay 20% on both qualified dividends and LTCGs. Unqualified dividends and gains will be treated as Ordinary income.

> *Qualified dividends* are those paid by a U.S. corporation or a qualified foreign corporation. In addition, a holding period for stocks requires that a stock paying qualified dividends must be held for more than 60 days during the 120 day period which begins 60 days before the ex-dividend date
> See IRS Pub. 550 for more information.

Medicare Surtax New in 2013

Two new taxes were added as amendments to the Affordable Care Act[3] in 2010 but were delayed by a challenge to the constitutionality of the Act, which has now been upheld. The first of these is a surtax on the existing Medicare tax. This new law calls for an additional 0.9% on employee wages in excess of $200,000 in a calendar year to be

---

[1]   IRS Publication 550.

[2]   See p. 3-26 for Tables and Rates. Tax brackets are now subject to adjustments for inflation.

[3]   ACA, aka Obamacare

withheld automatically by the employer beginning in Jan. 2013. This additional tax is not applicable to estates or trusts.

Although the employer is required to withhold an additional 0.9% on wages paid in excess of $200,000, the taxpayer may not be liable for this additional tax if the taxpayer's income is below the relevant threshold amount (listed below). If the taxpayer is not liable for this additional tax, a claim may be entered for any Additional Medicare Tax against the total tax liability shown on the individual's Form 1040 return.

The Net Investment Income Tax

Section 1411 Of the Health Care and Reconciliation Act of 2010 which amended the Patient Protections and Affordable Care Act outlines a second "Medicare" tax, the Net Investment Income tax, which became effective Jan. 1, 2013. The tax is applicable <u>only if the NII is above zero</u>.

This 3.8% tax applies to the <u>lesser</u> of (1) the NII or (2) the amount by which the MAGI exceeds the *threshold* allowance. A comparative test must be made to determine which income amount is subject to the additional tax. If the NII is the lesser amount, then the tax is applied to the NII; if the excess of the MAGI over the threshold amount is the lesser amount, then the tax is applied to the excess. The thresholds listed below apply:

<u>Net Investment Income</u> includes (but is not limited to) interest, dividends, capital gains, <u>rental</u> and royalty income, non-qualified annuities, income from trading financial instruments or commodities, and businesses that are passive activities to the taxpayer. The added tax is applicable to **S**-Corporations or partnerships to the extent that the taxpayer was a passive owner. Otherwise, the tax is not applicable to corporations. Certain expenses associated with these income sources are deductible from the NII total. The tax on NII does not apply to any gross income that is excluded from gross income for regular income tax purposes: for example, income which is excluded under S.121[4] upon the sale of a personal residence. The tax is also deferred under S. 1031 (exchanges).

Filing Status	Threshold Amount
Married Filing Jointly	$250,000
Married filing separately	$125,000
Single	$200,000
Head of Household (with qualifying person)	$200,000
Qualifying window(er) with dependent child	$250,000

<u>Modified Adjustable Gross Income</u> is defined as wages, salaries, tips, taxable interest, certain dividends, business income, capital gains, and unemployment compensation, as well as annuities, Social Security payments and some pensions.

The tax on collectibles, which includes art, rugs, precious metals or gemstones, stamps or coins, fine wines and antiques, remains at 28% for all taxpayers.

The tax on "Real Estate Unrealized Gain" (Section 1250 property)[5] is 15% for filers in the 15% bracket or below, and 25% for all others. However, any depreciation previously taken in excess of the straight-line method will be taxed as ordinary income.

Ordinary and Capital Gains and Losses

Ordinary income is the type of income derived from a salary or service, from interest on savings or a promissory note, or from a bond, or from dividends paid on stock holdings. It is also the character of income derived from real property rents.

---

4   The exclusion of up to $250,000 (single) or $500,000 (joint return) from the sale of a qualified personal residence. A reduced exemption is available under certain circumstances. See S. 121. Amounts in excess of the excluded amount are included in taxable income.

5   Depreciation Recapture for most filers.

The sale of a capital asset usually results in a capital gain or capital loss. Gains from the sale of most assets held for **more than one year** are taxed at the long-term capital gains (LTCG) rate which is typically lower than the Ordinary Income rate. Gains arising from the sale of capital assets held one year or less are treated as short-term gains and are taxed as Ordinary income.

Losses arising from the sale of a capital asset held for personal (*non-business*) use, such as a residence or vacation home, are currently not deductible. Net losses for the individual taxpayer from the disposition of property not classified as S.1231 property, are deductible up to a limit of $3,000 per year.[6] Losses by an individual may not be used to offset prior years' gains, but they may be carried forward to succeeding tax periods, subject to the same $3,000 limitation, until depleted. Corporations, however, may "look back" three years and offset any reported gains with current losses, provided the adjustment does not result in negative income for the year adjusted. But corporations may carry losses forward for no more than five years.

Netting of Gains and Losses

When gains and losses occur in the same tax period, the short-term gains and short-term losses must be netted[7] together. Similarly, the long-term capital gains and losses are also netted. Then the results from the short term and long terms groups are again netted together. Surviving short-term gains are added to other Ordinary income and taxed at the indicated Ordinary income rate. Surviving losses (up to a maximum of $3,000 per year for individuals) are deductible from ordinary income until used.

If the netting of short-term gains and losses and the long-term gains and losses results in a surviving long-tem gain, the result is a Long Term Capital Gain taxed at the prevailing LTCG rate.

Netting of Section 1231 Losses

If a gain results from the sale of property used in a trade or business (Section 1231 property), and if the taxpayer reported losses in any of the previous 5 years, the gain is treated as an Ordinary gain and is netted against the losses reported in any of the previous 5 years up to the amount of the loss. In this way, losses greater than $3,000 may be used to offset Capital Gains in a single year.

For example, if the taxpayer reported a loss of $10,000 in one of the last 5 years, and a loss of $15,000 in another within the same time frame, then a S.1231 gain of $20,000 in the current year would be treated as an Ordinary gain and netted against the previous total loss of $25,000. The surviving loss of $5,000 would be carried forward (for an individual) until used. If, however, the offsetting results in a residual gain, the gain is treated as a LTCG.

Short-Term Capital Gains

Short-term capital gains, which generally refer to investments held less than a year (and therefore cannot be S.1231 losses,[8]) has experienced no tax reform, and will continue to be included with the taxpayer's other Ordinary income and taxed at the prevailing rate.

Estate Taxes

The estate tax exemption for singles for 2014 is $5.34 million. The exemption for future years is to be indexed to inflation. This exemption is *per spouse* and is portable: if one spouse passes away in 2014 the surviving spouse can claim the exclusion resulting in a total exclusion of $10.68 million. Amounts above the excluded amount are to be taxed at 40%.

---

[6] $1,500 if married and filing separately

[7] Added together observing the signs.

[8] Section 1231 losses and gains must originate from property held more than one year.

Unrecaptured S. 1250 Depreciation Tax Rate

In years prior to 1987, owners of real estate had the option of depreciating the improvement on accelerated schedules which were shorter than a straight-line schedule. These "accelerated" methods resulted in "excess" deprecation.[9] When the property is sold this excess depreciation, regardless of the holding period, must now be "recaptured" (taxed) as <u>Ordinary</u> income. If no excess depreciation has been taken, the straight-line depreciation taken over the entire holding period is referred to as *Unrecaptured S.1250 Deprecation*. Depreciation taken on all real estate acquired after 1986 is straight-line depreciation because accelerated methods have not been available to the real estate investor since that year. This straight-line depreciation is recaptured at the time of sale at a fixed 25% rate, except for those in the 15% bracket for whom the tax is currently 15%.

For example, assume that you acquired a residential income property for a total cost of $1,000,000 and allocated $800,000 to the value of the depreciable improvement. Over a ten-year holding period you deducted straight-line depreciation in the amount of $288,485[10] resulting in an Adjusted Basis of $711,515 at the time of sale. Your selling price, net of sales commissions and costs, is $2,200,000. The portions of your gain[11] will be taxed as follows:

		Tax Rate	Tax Payable	Total Tax
Net Sales Price[12]	$2,200,000			
Less Adjusted Basis	-711,515			
= Recognized gain	1,488,485			
Less S.1250 Deprec.	-288,485	@ 25%	$72,121	
= Remaining L.T Gain	$1,200,000	@ 23.8%[13]	$286,560	$358,6s81

Determining Holding Periods

Purchased Property

For the purpose of determining the length of time an asset is held, start counting on the day following the acquisition of title. The same date in each subsequent month is counted as a month, regardless of the number of days in the preceding month. The long-term capital holding period begins one day following the 12th month.

For example, for property acquired on June 1, 2013 the first day of the holding period is June 2, 2013. June 2, 2014 marks the 12th month. If the property were sold on June 2, 2014 the gain would be taxed as Ordinary income. If the property were sold on June 3, 2014, the holding period, which includes the day of disposition, becomes one year and one day and the gain would be taxed as LTCG.

Inherited Property

If you inherit property you are considered to have held the property more than one year, regardless of how long you have actually held it.

Gift Property

If you obtain a property by gift, your holding period includes the time the property was held by the donor.

Exchange Property

If you acquire a property using a S.1031 exchange and your Basis in the new property is determined, in whole or in part, by consideration of the Basis in the relinquished property, your holding period begins on the day you first

---

[9]   Defined in the code as amounts in excess of the straight line amount.
[10] Includes allowances for mid-month convention.
[11] Assumes no offsetting losses.
[12] Net of sales commissions and selling expenses.
[13] For taxpayers subject to the 3.8% "Medicare Tax."

acquired the relinquished (exchanged) property. If the relinquished property was also acquired using an exchange, the holding period reverts back to the date of the original acquisition.

Installment Sale Note

If you sell a property and take back a promissory note as part of the purchase price, thereby qualifying for the installment method of reporting the gain, the holding period for each subsequent payment of principal is determined by the original holding period of the property sold. This period does not extend into the repayment period of the note.

Repossessed Property

If you sell property and take back a promissory note secured by the property, and then later repossess the property as the result of a foreclosure, your holding period includes both the time you formerly owned the property and the time you owned the property after repossession until subsequent sale. It does not include the time the buyer held title.

Basis of Property

Basis is defined as the amount of investment[14] you have in a property for the purpose of determining taxable gains and losses. Basis is important to the investor since it is the starting point for the determination of Adjusted Basis which, when subtracted from the net sales price, typically determines the amount of taxable gain (or loss).

Purchased Property

With only a few exceptions, the Basis of property which is acquired by purchase is the sum total of all the costs proper and necessary to place title in the hands of the owner. Therefore, in most instances, the original Basis will be greater than the purchase price and may include the following if paid by the buyer:

Legal and escrow fees	Surveys
Transfer taxes	Sales commissions
Installing utilities	Toxic waste reports
Pest control reports	Back Taxes
Repairs ordered by seller	Appraisal (if not required by lender)

Costs which represent future operating costs, however, should not be added to Basis. These costs should be included in the first year's operating expenses where they will act to reduce taxable income.

Charges incurred in obtaining a mortgage are not added to Basis but rather are grouped separately and recovered by *amortizing* these costs over the duration of the loan.[15] These charges may include:

Loan Points	Appraisal fees (if
Mortgage Insurance premiums	required by lender)
	Loan assumption fees
Cost of credit report	Refinancing fees
All other loan –connected fees	

Note that points on a mortgage obtained on property held for investment are not deductible as prepaid interest in the year paid as they are on the acquisition of a first-time home mortgage.[16]

---

[14]   Debt plus equity
[15]   Duration is the scheduled life of the loan, not its amortization schedule.
[16]   Points and fees paid to refinance a residence must also be amortized.

Inherited Property

If you inherit property your Basis will be stepped-up to its Fair Market Value (FMV) on the date of the decedent's death. If the personal representative (executor) of the estate chooses to use the alternate valuation date,[17] your Basis will be the FMV on the alternate date of the valuation. This rule does not apply in a situation in which you inherit property from a decedent to whom you, or your spouse, had gifted the property to the same decedent within one year of the decedent's death. If that is the case, your Basis will be the decedent's Adjusted Basis immediately preceding the decedent's death, and not its FMV. There will be no step-up in Basis

Community Property

If you live in a community property state,[18] and either spouse dies, the total Basis in the hands of the surviving spouse is stepped-up to FMV on the date of death. In order for this rule to apply, however, at least ½ the value of the property must be included in the decedent's gross estate, whether or not the estate must file an estate return. Following the Supreme Court Decision in 2013,[19] the Federal Government now affords same-sex couples who are married, or who are registered domestic partners and who reside in a community property state, the right to file federal tax returns as married, community-property taxpayers regardless of the state in which they were married. This issue and others related to same-sex marriages are still being adjudicated in a number of states.

Basis of a Surviving Spousal Joint Tenant

In the case of two *spousal joint tenants*, one of whom dies after Dec. 31, 1981, the determination of the Basis of the property in the hands of the surviving tenant is limited to 50% of the FMV of the property at the time of death, provided that 50% of the FMV was included in the decedent's estate. This rule applies only to joint tenancies held as *qualified joint interests*. A qualified joint interest is either:

♦ an interest held by Tenants-in-the-Entirety, or
♦ a joint tenancy interest if the only joint tenants are husband and wife.

When the interest held by the tenants is a qualified joint interest, only 50% of the FMV is includable in the decedent's taxable estate. This amount would be covered by the federal marital tax deduction.

An exception to this rule applies when the property owned by spouses was acquired prior to Jan. 1, 1977 and when the deceased joint tenant died after Dec. 31, 1981. Where it can be shown that the first to die contributed more than 50% of the cost of the acquired property, that amount may be included in the estate of the decedent. The total amount so contributed is also subject to the federal marital tax exclusion. If the qualified joint interest were created before 1977,[20] the tax court and two appeals courts have allowed a 100% step-up in Basis to the surviving spouse. In 2001 the I.R.S. acquiesced to this ruling and announced that it would abide by the courts' decisions.[21]

Basis of a Surviving Non-Spousal Joint Tenant

The Basis of a non-spousal surviving joint tenant is determined by the "Consideration Furnished" rule. The Basis in the hands of the surviving joint tenant is the sum of the interest originally furnished by the surviving tenant plus the decedent's proportionate share of the FMV of the property at the time of the decedent's death. If depreciation has been taken then the sum of the Basis in the hands of the survivor is reduced by ½ the depreciation taken.

---

[17] Six months following death.
[18] See Chapter 1, p.1-15.
[19] United States vs. Windsor
[20] Between 1977 and 1982 property owned by husband and wife was not subject to federal gift tax unless so reported as a gift tax return timely filed,
[21] Therese Hahn v. Commissioner, 110 T.C. 140 (1998) T.C. Dkt. No. 17210-96

For example, assume that a property was originally purchased at a cost of $120,000, with co-tenant A contributing 40% and co-tenant B contributing 60%. At the time of tenant B's death $20,000 in depreciation had been taken and the property had a FMV of $180,000. Surviving tenant A's Basis is calculated as indicted in the adjacent table.

Tenant A's contributed cost (40%)	$48,000
Interest received from tenant B, 60% of FMV of $180,000	$108,000
Total	$156,000
Less ½ Depreciation taken previous to tenant B's death22	-10,000
Basis in tenant A's hands	$146,000

If tenant A had not contributed to the purchase price,[23] the Basis would be:

Interest Received from tenant B,	180,000
Less ½ Depreciation taken previous to tenant B's death	-10,000
Basis in tenant A's hands	$170,000

Property Converted to a Rental

If a residence is converted to a rental property, the Basis at the time of conversion is the *lower* of:

- the FMV of the property at the time of conversion, or
- the Adjusted Basis at the time of conversion.

If the property is re-converted to use as a residence at a later date, any depreciation taken during the rental period will be recaptured at the time of sale.

Property Transferred in a Divorce

The Basis of real property received in a divorce, or incident to a divorce, is the same as the Adjusted Basis in the hands of the transferor.

Adjusted Basis

Once the Basis has been established it may be increased or decreased over the holding period in a variety of ways to result in the *Adjusted Basis*. The major reduction in Basis is usually the total of the depreciation deductions taken, or which could have been taken, over the holding period.

If, for example, you convert a residence into a rental property but fail to take depreciation over a five year holding period, the I.R.S. has the right to estimate the depreciation allowance which you could have, and should have taken, but did not. This estimated depreciation will be deducted from your Basis in the property at the time of sale, thereby increasing your taxable gain. Since you, as an individual, cannot amend a tax return older than three years, you will have had 2 years deprecation allowance deducted from your Basis for which you received no tax benefit. Moral: Take depreciation deductions when available. See IRS Form 4797, Line 22)

Capital Additions and Improvements

In general the cost of additions and improvements made to the property which extend its economic life more than one year, or which adapt it to a different use, must be capitalized and added to Basis. Repairing a roof, for example can be treated as an operating expense in the year of the repair, but the cost of replacing an entire roof is a capital addition and must be added to Basis. Re-wiring or re-plumbing the property would also be examples of capital improvements the cost of which must be capitalized and depreciated over the required number of years.

---

[22] The deduction for depreciation taken is ½ the total, and disregards the "Consideration Furnished" ratio.

[23] In which case the full FMV of the property would be included in the decedent's estate.

Assessments

If the municipality assesses you for street improvements, such as widening or paving a road, or adding sidewalks, these costs must be added to Basis. The cost is depreciable. But if the cost of their maintenance is separately billed to you, the maintenance is deductible as an ordinary expense.

Casualty Losses

Any casualty loss which is currently deductible and not covered by insurance must be deducted from your Basis.

Easement Fee

If you accept a fee for the use of an easement[24] you grant, the amount of the fee must be deducted from your Basis. If the deduction will reduce your Basis below zero, the excess is reportable as Ordinary Income in the year received.

Section 179 Property

The purpose of code Section 179 is to enable the cost of eligible *personal* property used in a trade or business to be expensed[25] rather than to be capitalized and depreciated over time. By expensing the cost, the tax payer reduces his current taxable income, resulting in tax savings. Any S.179 expense taken must be subtracted from the Basis of the property.

S.179 property is generally limited to tangible, depreciable, personal property acquired by purchase for use in a trade or business. The personal property may be new or used. Buildings and their structural components are not eligible. Section 179 has very limited application for owners of investment properties except when the owner's principal trade or business is rental real estate.

The amount that can be expensed has been decreased from $125,000 in 2013 to $25,000 in 2014. This deduction amount is decreased, dollar for dollar, by the amount of purchases in excess of $200,000. Therefore, a taxpayer who purchased $220,000 of new equipment would be required to reduce the $25,000 deduction under S.179 to $5,000: ($25,000 – ($220,000–200,000)).[26] The amount of the deduction is also capped by the amount of annual taxable income earned by the business.

50% Bonus Depreciation

No longer available for properties placed in service after Dec. 31, 2014 with the exception of certain assets requiring long production periods (LPPP), such as aircraft.

Tenant Improvement Allowances

Cash or rent abatement given to a lessee to improve non-residential property (only) is not considered income to the lessee unless the amount of cash or rental abatement exceeds the cost of the improvements made. In both short-term leases (15 years or less) and longer-term leases the value of the improvements allowed to the lessee may be added to the landlord's Basis as improvements to real property. If, however, the improvements are made to qualified non-residential, retail or restaurant property, the costs may be expensed under S.179 as outlined above.

Exchanges

In a S.1031 tax-deferred exchange, the value of any unlike property received (which is called 'Boot') increases the Basis of the replacement property. Boot received will be taxed in the year of the exchange.[27] Costs of the exchange (commissions, transactions costs, etc.) are not deductible in the current year but are added to the Basis of the replacement (received) property.

---

[24] The right for someone else to use, but not possess, your property.
[25] To be deducted from current income.
[26] S. 179 is intended to assist small businesses and not corporations.
[27] The increase in Basis means that the recognized gain at the time of subsequent sale will be reduced.

Subdivided Land

If you sell land which you have subdivided, you must allocate the Basis between the property sold and the property retained according to their Fair Market Values at the time of the sale. The Basis of the sold properties is subtracted from the original Basis of all properties.

Multiple Properties Acquired in a Single Transaction

If multiple, separate properties are acquired in a single transaction, and the FMV of each property is not identified, then the Basis of each property must be allocated by the application of a fraction, the numerator of which is the FMV of each separate parcel at the time of acquisition, and the denominator of which is the total acquisition cost.

Allocation of Basis

Once the Basis of a property has been determined, a portion of the Basis must be allocated to the depreciable improvements on the property (if any) and the remaining amount to the non-depreciable land. Land is not depreciable because its economic life cannot be quantified. This allocation results in the Depreciable Basis of the property.

Unfortunately there are no published guidelines to help the investor in deciding this allocation. The I.R.S. will generally accept the ratio of improvement to total property value used by the local tax assessor. If this is not suitable, a formal appraisal may be in order, although most investors proceed on the basis of an informed guesstimate.

Note that a low allocation of total property value to the improvement results in a low Depreciable Basis and therefore exposes more of the rental income to taxation at Ordinary rates in the current year. A higher allocation raises the Depreciable Basis and "shelters" more net operating income from immediate taxation. But remember, too, that all unrecaptured depreciation[28] taken is recaptured at the time of sale at the rate of 25%.

Depreciation

The original concept associated with a depreciation deduction was to permit the owner of an asset used in business to recover the cost of the asset over its remaining useful life. Much legislative water has gone under the bridge, however, and the rules for depreciating real property are now highly codified and regulated and bear little or no resemblance to the original concept or to the condition or age of the property. A 75-year old apartment building must follow the same rules as are applicable to a brand new building.

For the purpose of classifying real property as residential or non-residential, a residential property is one from which at least 80% of the collected (not scheduled) income is derived from the rental of dwelling units. This collected rent may include the rental value of any part of the property occupied by the owner. If a newly constructed property is mixed-use (residential + non-residential uses), the non-residential depreciation rate must be used until the income from the residential rentals equals or exceeds 80% of the collected rent. At that time, the shorter residential depreciation schedule may be used. This is one of the rare times that a schedule, once initiated, may be changed without prior I.R.S. approval.

In the schedules specified by the I.R.S. in MACRS[29] residential real estate placed in service after Dec. 31, 1986, is depreciated over 27.5 years, regardless of its age. All real property which is not residential is classified as non-residential. For non-residential property placed in service after May 12, 1993 the recovery period is 39 years.[30]

---

[28] Not previously taxed

[29] Modified Accelerated Cost Recovery System

[30] For non-residential property placed in service after Dec. 31, 1986 but prior to May 13, 1993, the recovery period is 31.5 years. A transition rule applies for property contracted for (buy or build) prior to May 13, 1993 and placed in service before 1994.

Mid-Month Convention

Real estate is subject to a "mid-month" convention, which requires that, regardless of the day in the month in which the property is placed in service, only ½ month's depreciation is allowable for that month. Therefore if a property were placed in service on any day in January of a calendar year, approximately 11.5 months worth of deprecation would be recoverable in that year.

The same convention applies in the year of the sale: only ½ month's depreciation is allowable in the month in which the property is disposed, regardless of the day in the month on which it is disposed.[31]

The table on page 3-24 lists the percentages of the <u>Depreciable</u> Basis which may be deducted in a calendar year based on the month in which the property is first placed in service.[32] Note that in the table for residential property the allowance varies after year 9.

For example, if a residential property were acquired with a Depreciable Basis of $1,500,000, and placed in service in March, the first year's depreciation would be 2.879% * $1,500,000 = $43,185. The allowance for the 2nd (full) year would be 3.636% * $1,500,000 = $54,540.

Mid-Year Convention

Any personal property must also be depreciated according to its class life. Most items of personal property which would be installed in a residential rental property, such as refrigerators, washers, microwaves, furniture, exercise equipment etc., have a 7-year 'class life.'

This class of property is subject to a mid-<u>year</u> convention which requires that any personal property placed into service at any time in the taxable year will be regarded as having been placed into service at mid-year regardless of the actual date it is placed in service; similarly, ½ year's depreciation is allowed in the year of the sale, regardless of the date of the sale.

The deduction in the 8th year allows for the recovery of depreciation not allowed in the 1st year.

Mid-Quarter Convention

If however, the taxpayer places into service in the last quarter of a taxable year property which has a Basis which exceeds 40% of the Basis of all the property placed into service in the same taxable year, the mid-quarter convention must be followed. The total does not include the Basis for either residential or non-residential S.1250 real property placed in service that same year.

MACRS Tables are on p. 3-22

Depreciation Recapture

You may have already noticed in the example given on page 5 of this chapter, that the total gain was segmented into two parts: 1) the portion due to the depreciation taken over the holding period and 2) the remainder of the total gain.

Under current rules the "Unrecaptured S.1250 depreciation" is recaptured (taxed) at the time of sale. The current (2013, 2014, 2015) rate on this portion of the gain is fixed at 15% for taxpayers in the 15% or lower tax bracket while the rate on the remainder of the gain is determined by the tax bracket: taxpayers in the 15% bracket pay no additional LTCG tax. Those in the 25-35% brackets are taxed at the 15% LTCG rate and those in the 39.6% bracket pay 20%. Taxpayers whose NII or MAGI is above $200,000 ($250,000 married) are subject to the additional 3.8% tax as described above.

---

[31] Buyers like to close on the 31st; sellers like to close on the 1st.

[32] Placed in service = offered for rent.

How Depreciation Shelters Income

Depreciation taken during the holding period acts to "shelter' ordinary income from taxation at the ordinary rates because, in arriving at annual taxable income, annual depreciation allowances are deducted from current net operating income, even though they are non-cash deductions. The reduced taxable income is taxed at the investor's marginal rate.[33] The portion of the annual income sheltered by depreciation is not tax-free because depreciation taken will eventually be recaptured at the time of sale.

Passive Activity Rules

In the early 1980s, depreciation benefits were so liberal that 100% of the depreciation benefits could be recovered in as little as 15 years. As a result, limited partnerships were formed which allocated to high-income limited partners all or nearly all of the depreciation benefits. These non-cash deductions from income acted as a tax shelter even for these individuals who could not be actively engaged in the business of owning, managing or renting the property.

Beginning in 1987, Congress took steps to curb these deductions by passing a 'passive activity' law which was intended to discourage tax-shelter investments. The law extends not only to tax shelters but covers all real estate investors as well as "silent partners"[34] who are not actively engaged in the business. The essence of the law is that losses from a passive activity are deductible only from taxable income derived from passive activities. Owning rental real estate is defined as a passive activity.

This law also prevents taxpayers whose Adjusted Gross Income (AGI) exceeds $100,000 from deducting part or all of their losses from rental real estate. The law makes an exception for real estate professionals, defined as those whose activities are regular, continuous, and substantial, and who spend more than 750 hours[35] or more per year and more than half their working hours in developing, managing, developing, constructing, renting and/or selling real estate. Individual taxpayers with Adjusted Gross Income (AGI) of $100,000 or less may be able to deduct up to $25,000 in net losses[36] from rental real estate in which they "actively participate." The first requirement is that the taxpayer must own at least 10% of the property.

For amounts of AGI over $100,000, 50% of the excess amount is deducted from the $25,000 limitation. Therefore a qualified taxpayer whose annual AGI is $135,000 is able to deduct up to $7,500 ($150,000 − $135,000 x 50%)) of an operating loss. Investors whose current AGI exceeds $150,000 are unable to deduct any passive activity loss in the current tax year but may carry these losses forward as *suspended losses* until they do become deductible in a later year.

Tests for Material Participation

There are 7 tests[37] which the I.R.S. has devised to determine whether participation is material participation in a business. If you meet ANY of these 7 requirements, you have materially participated for the year. These tests are:

♦   You participated in the activity for more than 500 hours during the tax year.
♦   You were substantially the only participant in the activity during the year.

---

[33]   The rate at which the next dollar of ordinary income would be taxed·
[34]   Limited partners are 'silent partners" because they may not take an active role in the management of the partnership without losing their limited liability status.
[35]   Real estate professionals who manage rentals of properties rented for 1 week or less may not use time in this activity to apply to the 750 hour requirement. (Bailey TC Summ. Op,2011-22).
[36]   The limitation is reduced to $12,500 if you are married but lived apart from your spouse for 1 year and file a separate return.
[37]   These tests do not apply to C corporations. Consult your tax advisor.

♦ You participated in the activity for more than 100 hours in the tax year, which was at least as much as any other participant, including employees and independent contractors, such as property managers.
♦ You are involved in a number of activities but each activity does not qualify as a material participation. Nonetheless, if you spend at least 100 hours in each activity and the total time spent exceeds 500 hours, you are treated as a material participant in each activity. (the "significant participation" test.)
♦ You materially participated in any 5 of the preceding 10 tax years.
♦ The activity is a personal service activity in which you materially participated for any three prior tax years. A personal service activity is one that involves services in the fields of health, law, engineering, architecture, accounting, actuarial science, performing arts, consulting, or any trade or business in which capital is not a material income-producing factor.
♦ Based on all the facts and circumstances, you participated in the activity on a regular, continuous basis during the year, and you participated for more than 100 hours. Your participation in management will not count toward this test if anyone else was a paid manager or spent more hours than you in managing the business.

Suspended Passive Activity Losses

A qualified investor who experiences Passive Activity Losses (PAL) may be unable to deduct all or some of these losses because:
♦ there is no passive activity income[38] from which to deduct these losses, and/or
♦ the investor's Adjusted Gross Income (AGI) for the current tax year is equal to or greater than $150,000.

If either of these circumstances exists, the taxpayer must "suspend" the deduction of these losses until he/she has passive activity income from which to deduct the losses and/or until a lower AGI permits the deduction of the loss.

Any passive activity income (all net rents are passive activity income) may be reduced by all or part of the suspended losses being carried forward from prior years. If the suspended losses exceed the current passive activity income, the excess of the loss over the income must be suspended and continued to the next tax year. If, however, the taxpayer qualifies for a deduction of PAL up to $25,000, these losses may be recognized in the current year and applied against other ordinary gains.

Income derived from investments in securities (stocks, bonds, promissory notes etc.) is <u>not</u> classified as Passive Activity Income but rather as "portfolio income." Therefore PAL may not be used to directly offset income from these investments.

Significance of PAL

Passive Activity Rules were of greater significance during the years when deprecation benefits were recaptured over 15, 18 or 19 years rather than the 27.5 and 39-year standards now in place. In 1986, just prior to the enactment of the law, a Depreciable Basis of $1,000,000 for non-residential property yielded an annual depreciation write-off of $66,667. The same non-residential Depreciable Basis in 2014 yields only $25,641. So it was once much more common for a property to show a taxable loss for as many as 4-5 or more years, depending on the Net Operating Income. Today, most depreciable income-producing properties may not show taxable losses for more than 1-3 years.[39]

The loss limitation of $25,000 is also quite low in terms of inflation-adjusted (constant) dollars. Had the $25,000 limitation been adjusted for inflation, it would have reached more than $57,000 in 2014. As it is, taxable rents have increased but the constant value of the $25,000 loss limitation of 1987 remains and is now equivalent to less than

---

[38] The property does not produce taxable income
[39] This depends on the capitalization rate. Properties acquired at low cap rates carry higher depreciation write-off amounts (due to higher values) in relation to NOI.

$11,000 in 1987 dollars.[40] Therefore while the investor should be aware of the Passive Loss Limitations, they are of relatively minor significance in most situations today.

The Installment Sale

There are many instances in which the seller of an investment property accepts a promissory note as part of the purchase price. The installment method of reporting the gain permits the seller to pay tax on his gain in the years in which it is received rather than in the year of the sale.

An installment sale is a sale of property whereby at least one payment is to be received after the tax year in which the sale occurs. Any payment on the selling price which is received in the year following the sale *automatically* creates an installment sale. If the taxpayer does not wish to have the gain reported as an installment sale he must "elect out" by reporting the entire gain for the taxable year of the sale. "Electing out" in subsequent years may not be made without prior approval of the I.R.S.

If the investor has taxable losses which could offset capital gains, utilizing the installment method of reporting the gain may not be to the taxpayer's advantage since the capital gains can be netted with losses. If, however, the losses are later denied on audit, the capital gains may become all due and payable since the I.R.S. may interpret any request for a reversion to the installment method as an attempt to avoid taxes.

Note that the installment method is not available to those holding trade or inventory property such as developers, brokers and those whose principal business is buying and selling real estate. As a general rule this method is not available to any sale which would be characterized as the sale of trade or inventory property and therefore one subject to tax as Ordinary income.

S.1250 Depreciation Immediately Recaptured

One of the most important considerations in contemplation of an installment sale is to bear in mind that all Unrecaptured S.1250 depreciation which has been taken will be recognized (taxed) in the year of the sale, and is not subject to reporting on the installment basis. This tax will be in addition to any tax payable on the cash (including down payment) received in the year of the sale. This is an important consideration because it affects the amount of cash down payment the seller must receive in order to cover his or her costs and immediate tax liabilities.

Automatically Qualifying for the Installment Method

Consider the investor who has depreciated a $500,000 apartment property with an original depreciable Basis of $400,000 over 15 years. Accumulated depreciation in this example would be approximately $216,970 ($400,000/27.5 * 15 years less 2 x ½ month's depreciation).[41]

Assume the property sold for $1,000,000 with a down payment of $200,000, with the balance of the sales price in the form of a note in favor of the seller in the amount of $800,000 payable monthly in the amount of $6,713.57, including fixed interest at the annual rate of 9%,[42] scheduled over 25 years, but all due and payable in 10 years. The first payment is due next year. Assume also that total costs of sale are $60,000 and that the property is now free and clear of debt. Since he will receive part of the sales price in the year(s) following the sale, this transaction automatically qualifies for the installment method of reporting the gain.

---

[40] The government is adept at levying hidden taxes.

[41] Due to the mid-month convention, ½ month depreciation is lost on acquisition and ½ on disposition.

[42] Holding the payment constant, it may be advantageous to use the lowest permissible interest rate to minimize the amount recognized as Ordinary income.

Calculating the Installment Sales Basis & Gross Profit Ratio

The applicable fraction, or gross profit ratio, of each partial payment to be considered receipt of gain is the ratio of the gain to the contract price. The numerator of this fraction is the gross sales price less the *Installment Sales Basis*.

For the purpose of determining gross profit ratio, the *Installment Sales Basis* is the sum of the usual <u>Adjusted Basis</u>, the <u>costs of sale</u> and the amount of <u>depreciation recapture</u> realized in the year of the sale. The resulting total is subtracted from the Gross Sales Price to yield the nominator of the applicable fraction. The denominator is the contract price, which is equal to the sales price less the amount of any mortgages assumed or taken *subject to*[43] by the buyer plus any amount by which the transferred mortgage exceeds the Installment Sales Basis.

Line #	Description	Entry
6	Less Mortgage Assumed	0
7	Line 5 - Line 6	1,000,000
8	Original Cost	500,000
9	Less Depreciation Taken	216,970
10	Adjusted Basis[44] (8–9)	283,030
5	Sales Price	$1,000,000
11	Commissions & Costs	60,000
12	Depreciation Recaptured	216,970
13	Installment Sales Basis[45]	560,000
14	Line 13	440,000
15	Homeowner's Exclusion	0
16	Gross profit	440,000
17	Mortgage over Basis	0
18	Contract price	1,000,000
19	Gross Profit Ratio 16÷18	44.0%

The adjacent computation follows I.R.S. Form 6252 which is used to report the Installment Sale Income. The line numbers also correspond to the line numbers on IRS Form 6252.

The gross profit ratio in this example is 44.0%. Therefore 44.0% of the cash received in the year of the sale and 44.0% of the *principal portion* of each payment received on the note will be recognized as taxable gain in the year received. However, <u>all</u> of the depreciation taken, $216,970, is subject to recapture @ 25% in the year of the sale, resulting in an immediate tax liability of $54,243. In addition to this amount, the down payment of $200,000 @ 44.0%, or $88,000, is also taxable in the year of the sale at the prevailing long-term capital gains rate.

Calculation of Gain After Depreciation Recapture

Each dollar of principal subsequently recovered under the note is composed partly of gain and partly of Adjusted Basis. Of the portion of the principal payment recovered, 44% will be taxable gain while the remainder of the principal is considered recovery of Adjusted Basis and is not taxable. All interest received under this amortizing note, however, will be taxed as Ordinary income. Note that in this case, the amount of taxable LTCG increases each year while the amount of taxable interest declines. The following table shows the amount of interest and the amount of principal payable.

\Year	1	2	3	4	5	6	7	8	9	10
Interest	71,638	70,801	69,885	68,883	67,787	66,589	65,278	63,844	62,276	60,561
Principal	8,925	9,762	10,678	1,1680	12,775	13,974	15,285	16,718	18,287	20,002
44% Taxable	3,927	4,295	4,698	5,139	5,621	6,148	6,725	7,356	8,046	8,801
LTCG Tax @23.8%	935	1,022	1,118	1,223	1,338	1,463	1,601	1,751	1,915	2,095

---

[43] Mortgages which remain on the property and for which the new buyer will be responsible.
[44] Original cost less adjusted Basis
[45] The sum of the three immediately preceding lines.

Taxes paid (exclusive of tax on $667,542 in interest over10 years received from the note)[46] will be:

Source	Amount	Gain (44%)	Tax @ 23.8%
Total Principal over 10 yrs.	$138,086	$60,758	$14,460
Remaining Bal.10 yrs.	661,914	291,242	$69,316
Down payment	200,000	88,000	$20,944
		Sub-total	$104,720
Depreciation Recapture	$216,970	Taxed @ 25%	54,243
		Tax Paid	$158,963

Notice that, with this conventionally written promissory note, the largest portion of the taxable gain, $291,242, occurs at term, at 10 years. Consideration may be given to scheduling periodic paydowns of principal in order to spread the balance of the loan, and therefore the tax owing, over a number of years.

When Mortgages Transfer to Buyer

When a buyer assumes or takes the property with existing mortgages intact, the amount by which the mortgage exceeds the Installment Sales Basis is considered cash received by the seller in the year of the sale. In addition, if you pledge as security for a loan a note received as part of an installment sale of property which sold for more than $150,000, the net loan proceeds will be counted as receipt of payment on the installment obligation. The receipt of instruments which are "readily tradable" by the seller, such as registered bonds, debentures‚ stocks and other instruments which are readily tradable, will also be counted as the receipt of their FMV in the year of the sale by the holder of the installment obligation.

Mortgage Over Basis

Line	Description	Entry
5	Sales Price	$1,000,000
6	Less Mortg .Assumed	600,000
7	Line 5 - Line 6	400,000
8	Original Cost	500,000
9	Depreciation Taken	216,970
10	Adjusted Basis47 (8–9)	283,030
11	Commissions & Costs	60,000
12	Deprec. .Recaptured	216,970
13	Installment Sales Basis	**560,000**
14	Line 5 – Line 13 = Gain	440,000
15	Homeowner's Exclusion	0
16	14 - 15 = Gross profit	440,000
17	6 – 13 = Mortg. over Basis	40,000
18	7+17 = Contract price	440,000
19	Gr. Profit Ratio =16 ÷18	100%
20	17 = Mortg. Over Basis	40,000
21	Down Payment (20%)	200,000
22	Amt. Rec'd in Yr. of Sale	$240,000

An often overlooked factor in an installment sale occurs when the existing mortgage exceeds the "Installment Sales Basis" of the property. The amount by which it exceeds the Installment Sales Basis is also counted as cash received in the year of the sale. The following example illustrates this point.

We have added a $600,000 mortgage to be assumed by the buyer. Again, the line numbers correspond to I.R.S. Form 6252. In the year of the sale $240,000 of long-term gain will be recognized at the long-term capital gains rate. In addition, all the depreciation taken, $216,970, will be recaptured at the 25% rate. In the ensuing years, 100% of the principal payments received on the note will be recognized as long-term capital gain. The interest on the note, as before, will be ordinary income subject to the seller's ordinary tax rate in the year received

---

[46] The tax on interest will be at the taxpayer's Ordinary rate.
[47] Original cost less Adjusted Basis.

Adequate Interest Required on Installment Notes

In the case in which no interest is stated in the buyer's promissory note, or in those cases in which the amount of interest is below minimum federal standards, then the amount of "unstated taxable interest" must be determined.

An installment sale contract generally provides for adequate stated interest if the contract's principal amount is at least equal to the sum of the present values of all principal and interest payments called for under the contract.

In application, the test for unstated interest is carried out by identifying all the payments due under the schedule of the loan. In the next step, all the payments are discounted by the applicable AFR (see below). The result is the Present Value of the payments. This total is subtracted from the principal of the note to yield the *unstated* taxable interest.

Consider a note in the principal amount of $1,000,000, payable monthly in the amount of $15,472.35 with final payment of $500,000 at the end of 36 months. The interest rate on this note is easily calculated:

The resulting interest rate is 0.21...% per month, which indicates an annual rate of 2.50%. Assume that the discount rate required under the Applicable Federal Rate is presently 0.32% per month. Under the first scenario the total interest payable on the note is $57,004.80. But when all future payments are discounted at the applicable federal rate (e.g., 0.32% per month) the PV of future payments is

n	i	PV	PMT	FV
36	?	-1,000,000	15,472.35	500,000
	0.21.			

n	i	PV	PMT	FV
36	0.32	?	15,472.35	500,000
		-971,001.91		

$971,001.91. The *unstated taxable interest* is the difference between the principal amount of $1,000,000 and the discounted Present Value of $971,001.91, or $28,998.09. Therefore the total taxable interest for this note will be $88,002.81 ($57,004.80 + $28,998.01). This adjustment will lower the buyer's Basis (increasing the LTCG on sale) and raise the tax which the seller must pay on Ordinary income.

The Applicable Federal Rate (AFR)

The applicable AFR is the discount rate published monthly by the I.R.S. It is the test rate which must be applied to an installment note to determine any unstated taxable interest. This rate is available for notes payable monthly, quarterly and semi-annually and varies according to the maturity of the promissory note. Three AFRs are published monthly in the I.R.S. *Bulletin*:

◆ Short-term AFR – applicable to a note of 3 years or less.
◆ Mid-term AFR – applicable to a note longer than 3 years but not over 9 years.
◆ Long-term AFR – applicable to a note longer than 9 years.

Period for Compounding (Oct. 2013)			
Annual	Semiannual	Quarterly	Monthly
Short-Term			
.32%	.32%	.32%	.32%
Mid-Term			
1.93%	1.93%	1.93%	1.93%
Long-Term			
3.50%	3.50%	3.50%	3.50%

When seller financing does not exceed $5,339,300 the test rate cannot exceed 9.0%, compounded semi-annually. But for seller financing which exceeds $5,339,300 the test rate is 100% of the AFR.

Land Transfers Between Related Parties

The rules of S.483 also apply to debt instruments issued in a land sale between related persons to the extent the sum of the following amounts does not exceed $500,000:

♦ The stated principal of the note issued in the sale or exchange

♦ The total stated principal of any other debt instruments for prior land sales between these parties during the calendar year. In this case the test rate cannot exceed 6.0%, compounded semi-annually.

For land sales in which the debt instruments exceed $500,000, or in which a non-resident alien is involved, S.1274 rules apply which permit test rates of 100% of the AFR.

Disposition of Property by Related Parties

When an investment property is sold to a related party,[48] and the related party disposes of the property in a second disposition, the owner of the property under the first disposition may be forced to recognize the proceeds of the second sale as gain received in the same year.

Recognition is not applicable if the disposition of the property by the related party was more than 2 years after the date of the first disposition. In addition, recognition is not applicable if the second disposition occurs after the death of either the first seller or the buyer of the property, or if the second disposition was as the result of an involuntary conversion.

Sale of Multiple Parcels of Subdivided Land

Dealers in real estate are not entitled to long-term capital gains treatment on the sale of property held as inventory. Gains on their sales are taxed at Ordinary rates. So the question arises as to whether or not a private individual (or S Corporation) who subdivides real property and sells or exchanges lots or parcels becomes a dealer.

If the taxpayer is not a dealer then at least part of the gain on the sale of subdivided land may be treated as a long-term capital gain. But to qualify for such treatment, these conditions must be met:

♦ The taxpayer must not have previously held the parcel or any portion of it as inventory for sale in the usual course of business.

♦ The taxpayer does not hold any other real property as inventory in the year of the sale

♦ No 'substantial improvements' have been made during the time the property was held by the taxpayer, or are to be made pursuant to a condition of the sales contract.

♦ The property has been held for at least *five* years except if it were acquired by inheritance, in which case there is no minimum holding period other than that required qualifying for LTCG treatment.

♦ A plat map and list of improvements made must be submitted with the taxpayer's return applicable to the year of the sale.

The first two requirements effectively eliminate dealers in real estate.

There is an exception to the 'substantial improvement' requirement above. Certain improvements such as roads, culverts, water and drainage facilities will not be considered 'substantial improvements' if the property has been held at least ten years, if the taxpayer elects not to add their cost to the Basis of the property (or deduct costs as expenses) and if the improvements were necessary to achieve the price at which the parcels were marketed.

---

[48] As defined in S.267(b)

Five Parcel Limit Rule

If the conditions are met, gains from the sale or exchange of the first 5 parcels of the same tract may be treated as long-term capital gains. However, in the year in which the 6th parcel is sold, and in every subsequent year, the first 5% of the sales price of each and every parcel sold will be treated as ordinary income. The balance will be treated as long-term capital gains income.

For example, an owner who had held a tract for more than the minimum required for LTCG treatment, subdivided the tract into 10 parcels and sold 3 parcels in the same year. In the following year he sold an additional 4 parcels from the same tract. The entire gain on the first three parcels would be treated as LTCG.

In the second year the gain on each of the 4 parcels sold would be subject to ordinary income tax to the extent of 5% of the sales price because all 4 parcels were sold in the year in which the 6th parcel was sold. The remainder of the gain would receive LTCG treatment. If the remaining 3 parcels were sold or exchanged within 5 years of the last sale, the gain realized would be subject to ordinary income tax to the extent of 5% of the sales price. If the remaining 3 parcels were sold later than 5 years following the sale of the last parcel sold or exchanged, then the gain from all 3 parcels would be LTCG.

When any portion of the gain is taxed as ordinary income, the costs of the sale are deducted first from the ordinary income amount. Any excess cost is deducted from the remaining LTCG portion.

Tax-Deferred Exchanges Using S. 1031

Because exchanging real estate is so important a wealth-building strategy to the investor, the subject is covered in a separate chapter.

Caveat Taxpayer

Tax law and regulations are in a constant state of flux. Some of the subjects discussed in this chapter are not complete in all details and some matters important to your individual situation may not be covered here at all. Therefore, you are encouraged to consult a competent tax advisor prior to any tax-related decision.

MACRS TABLES:
The use of these tables is mandatory.

Year	Month 1	2	3	4	5	6	7	8	9	10	11	12
				Residential Real Estate Placed in Service After December 31, 1986								
					Month Placed in Service in Taxable Year							
1	3.485%	3.182%	2.879%	2.576%	2.273%	1.970%	1.667%	1.364%	1.061%	0.758%	0.455%	0.152%
2-9	3.636	3.636	3.636	3.636	3.636	3.636	3.636	3.636	3.636	3.636	3.636	3.636
10	3.367	3.367	3.367	3.367	3.367	3.367	3.367	3.367	3.367	3.367	3.367	3.367
11	3.636	3.636	3.636	3.636	3.636	3.636	3.636	3.636	3.636	3.636	3.636	3.636
12	3.367	3.367	3.367	3.367	3.367	3.367	3.367	3.367	3.367	3.367	3.367	3.367
13	3.636	3.636	3.636	3.636	3.636	3.636	3.636	3.636	3.636	3.636	3.636	3.636
14	3.367	3.367	3.367	3.367	3.367	3.367	3.367	3.367	3.367	3.367	3.367	3.367
15	3.636	3.636	3.636	3.636	3.636	3.636	3.636	3.636	3.636	3.636	3.636	3.636
16	3.367	3.367	3.367	3.367	3.367	3.367	3.367	3.367	3.367	3.367	3.367	3.367
17	3.636	3.636	3.636	3.636	3.636	3.636	3.636	3.636	3.636	3.636	3.636	3.636

Year	Month 1	2	3	4	5	6	7	8	9	10	11	12
			Non-residential Real Estate Placed in Service After May 13, 1993									
1	2.461%	2.247%	2.033%	1.819%	1.605%	1.391%	1.177%	0.963%	0.749%	0.535%	0.321%	0.107%
2-39	2.56%	2.56%	2.56%	2.56%	2.56%	2.56%	2.56%	2.56%	2.56%	2.56%	2.56%	2.56%

	MACRS Depreciation Rates for 7-Year Property				
Year	Half-Year Convention	← Mid-quarter Convention →			
		1 Q	2 Q	3 Q	4 Q
1	14.29%	25.00%	17.85%	10.71%	3.57%
2	24.49	21.43	23.47	25.51	27.55
3	17.49	15.31	16.76	18.22	19.68
4	12.49	10.93	11.97	13.02	14.06
5	8.93	8.75	8.87	9.30	10.04
6	8.92	8.74	8.87	8.85	8.73
7	8.93	8.75	8.87	8.86	8.73
8	4.46	1.09	3.33	5.53	7.64

Tax Tables 2014.

Year 2014 –Adj. for Inflation at Various Rates

Tax Rate	Single	Married Filing Joint	Married Filing Separate	Head of Household
10%	Up to $9,075	Up to $18,150	Up to $9,075	Up to $12,950
15%	$9,076 – $36,900	$18,151 – $73,800	$9,076 – $36,900	$12,951 – $49,400
25%	$36,901 – $89,350	$73,801 – $148,850	$36,901 – $74,425	$49,401 – $127,550
28%	$89,351 – $186,350	$148,851 – $226,850	$74,426 – $113,425	$127,551 – $206,600
33%	$186,351 – $405,100	$226,851 – $405,100	$113,426 – $202,550	$206,601 – $405,100
35%	$405,101 – $406,750	$405,101 – $457,600	$202,551 – $228,800	$405,101 – $432,200
39.6%	Over $406,750	Over $457,600	Over $228,800	Over $432,200

2014 Alternate Minimum Tax	
Filing Status	**Exemption Amount**
Single	$52,800
Married Filing Jointly	$82,100
Married Filing Separately	$41,050
Head of Household	$52,800

2014 Standard Deduction and Personal Exemption	
Filing Status	**Exemption Amount**
Single	$6,200
Married Filing Jointly	$12,400
Married Filing Separately	$6,200
Head of Household	$9.100
Personal Exemption	$3,950

2014 Personal Exemption Phase-Out		
Filing Status	**Phase-Out Begins**	**Phase-Out Complete**
Single	$254,200	$376,700
Married Filing Jointly	$305,050	427,550
Married Filing Separately	$152,525	152,525
Head of Household	$279,650	$402150

Tax Tables 2015.
Year 2015 –Adj. for Inflation at Various Rates

Tax Rate	Single	Married Filing Jointly	Married Filing Separate	Head of Household
10%	Up to $9,225	Up to $18,450	Up to $9,225	Up to $13,150
15%	$9,225 – 37,450	$18,451 – $74,900	$9,225 – 37,450	$13,151 – $50,200
25%	$37,451 – 90,750	$74,901 – $151,200	$37,451 – 75,600	$50,201 – $129,600
28%	$90,751 – 189,300	$151,201 – $230,450	$75,601 – 115,225	$129,601 – $209,850
33%	$189,301 – 411,500	$230,451 – $411,500	$115,226 – 205,750	$209,851 – $411,500
35%	$411,501 – 413,200	$411,501 – $464,850	$205,751 – 232,425	$411,501 – $439,000
39.6%	Over $413,200	Over $464,850	Over $232,425	Over $439,000

2015 Alternate Minimum Tax	
Filing Status	Exemption Amount
Single	$53,600
Married Filing Jointly	$83,400
Married Filing Separately	$41,700
Head of Household	$53,600

2015 Standard Deduction and Personal Exemption	
Filing Status	Exemption Amount
Single	$6,300
Married Filing Jointly	$12,600
Married Filing Separately	$6,300
Head of Household	$9.250
Personal Exemption	$4,000

2015 Personal Exemption Phase-Out		
Filing Status	Phase-Out Begins	Phase-Out Complete
Single	$258,250	$380,750
Married Filing Jointly	$309.900	$432,400
Head of Household	$284,050	$406,550

A frequently quoted maxim among real estate professionals is that "there an investor for every property and a property for every investor." This may be so, but in the experience of many seasoned investors finding a good investment property is a major challenge.

Chapter 4
Selecting
The Investment
Property

For some, a "good" property means a property in prime condition in a prime location. For others, the objective is a property with remediable issues which, when resolved at reasonable cost, can add a great deal to market value. But in the end, a "good" property is one which fulfills the needs and wants of a particular investor, and this is a subjective call.

Where to Buy

Before you begin to investigate *what* to buy, you should first consider *where* you should buy. The question of *where* to buy involves not only the conditions of the intended market but also the practical consideration of the distance from your home or office. Acquiring your first income-producing property reasonably close to home, i.e. within 1/2 - 3/4 hour driving time is a prudent decision. If your first improved property is not able to support professional management, you will need to make a number of trips to deal with tenants and their problems, and perhaps even do a few small repairs. Traveling to and from a distant property will consume far more of your free time than you anticipate. Many owners of smaller investment properties cite travel time and their need to escape the weekend chores of ownership as a major reason for selling the investment.

A second reason is that you will find it much easier to stay abreast of market conditions in a location closer to home than you would be for a property located many miles away. Local market conditions, supply and demand trends, rents, vacancy rates and new competition will be critical factors in future decisions. Even if you are acquiring a property large enough to bear the cost of third-party management, or if you are investing with others, proximity to your property will enable you to independently monitor the property to assess its performance, the local investment scene and the performance of your manager.

When to Buy

"Buy when everyone else is selling and sell when everyone else is buying." This John Paul Getty advice runs counter to the ovine instinct that most investors follow.

Many owners whose properties have appreciated tend not to want to sell them, and the same owners tend to shun buying when the market is in a trough. "If I sell now, what can I buy" is a song sung frequently by many. The answer is "...you may not want to buy anything until prices (in relation to income) decline." "Why would I ever want to buy when the market is so bad" is also heard.. "Because when the market is bad prices are low. Why would you want to buy when prices are high?"

Advice given by stockbrokers to ignore the ups and downs of stock prices and to keep investing through good times and bad is not consistent with the investment strategy of most successful stock investors, nor with the facts. Those who sell *near* the top and buy *near* the bottom have been shown to do much better than those who muddle through both these times equally. If an asset priced at $100 falls 25% in value, it requires a 33 1/3% increase to regain the lost territory. The first rule of investing for many is " Never lose money."

The real estate market is not equivalent to the stock market in many ways, but successful real estate investors tend to follow the same strategy of selling near the top and buying near the bottom. They are not traders but rather buy, sell and exchange their real estate investments at times that appear to be contrary to the market activities of other investors.

What to Buy

The kind of property that the beginning investor can buy is a function of available cash, current mortgage rates and prices in a particular locality. An investor with $250,000 to invest in apartment units will be very limited if available units are selling for $250,000 per unit. If this investor is willing to leverage his investment 75%, his cash will act as a 25% down payment on a $1,000,000 property ($250,000/0.25), which will buy four units.

If he has $500,000 to invest and is interested in a convenience (strip) center[1] which sells in that locality for $175 per sq. ft. he can probably leverage not more than 65%. Therefore, his $500,000 down payment will control a small center worth about $1,400,000, or about 8,000 sq. ft., or about 5-6 stores.[2] If the same investor had $750,000 for apartments, or $2,500,000 for a shopping center, he might be able to acquire a 12-unit apartment building or a 40,000 sq. ft. neighborhood retail center.

Since property values per unit and per sq. ft. vary considerably throughout the country, the size of the property is a function of the price per unit, the investor's available cash and the mortgage which the rents will support. The type property, however, needs to be decided not solely by the available cash, but by the supply and demand factors in a defined market area. Acquiring an investment property at a low cost is desirable but not necessarily predictive of a good investment.

---

[1] A convenience center may be a neighborhood center with 2-10 retail stores, but no major tenant.
[2] Shop sizes vary, of course, but a common small size is about 1,200 -1,500 sq. ft.

What is the Strategy?

No doubt your goal is to increase your wealth, but what is your strategy? If you have neither the time nor the patience to deal with tenants, you may wish to consider investing in an equity Real Estate Investment Trust (REIT). Buying stock in a REIT is <u>not</u> a direct investment in real estate since stocks (equities) are objects of personal property. But such an investment is an <u>indirect</u> way to benefit from real estate which would ordinarily be beyond the financial reach of most private investors.

A REIT typically invests in only one or two genres of real estate and offers the advantage of specialization with few or no management chores for stockholders. Investments in regional malls, shopping centers, office buildings, self-storage facilities, health-care and timber properties are commonplace. Some REITs invest in residential and/or commercial mortgages (viz. *mortgage REITs*); a few invest in both real properties and mortgages and are referred to as *Hybrids*. Recently a number of REITs have been formed specifically to acquire foreclosed single-family houses to be held as rentals.

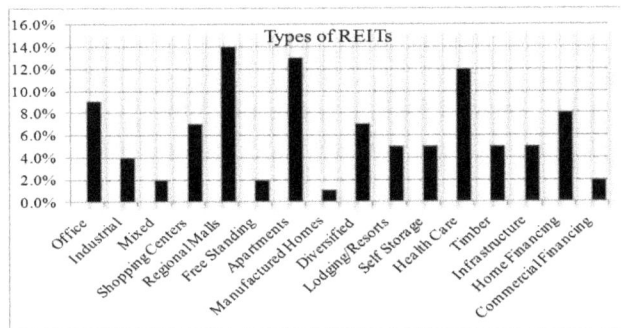

There are also ETFs[3] and Mutual Funds that invest in assorted types of REITS thereby enabling portfolio diversification. The chart at the left displays the percentage of total REITs held by each type in 2013.

Because REITs are legally required to distribute 90% of their annual earnings (dividends and realized capital gains), they may be very good sources of regular income. In fact, many REITs distribute 100% of their earnings to avoid the higher corporate tax rate on retained earnings.

The most conspicuous disadvantage of a REIT is that the dividends are not taxed at the (current) 15% rate,[4] as are qualified dividends. Dividend cash received from a REIT is plain-vanilla Ordinary income and taxed at the investor's marginal rate. Nor can income from a REIT be used to absorb *passive losses* from other real estate owned directly. A REIT, unlike a partnership, may not pass through any losses to shareholders.

The second disadvantage is that stock in a REIT is not exchangeable under S.1031. Therefore accumulated gains cannot be exchanged for a subsequent direct interest in other real estate because shares do not qualify as *like-kind* property. They also cannot be exchanged for shares in another REIT since the I.R. Code specifically bars the exchange of stocks, bonds and beneficial interests in a trust. Investment in a REIT is a definite strategic commitment.

There are currently more than 250 SEC-registered REITs but probably more than 1,100 in operation. REIT.com and Greenstreetadvisors.com are excellent sources of information concerning this type of investment.

---

3   Exchange Traded Funds
4   For investors in the 25-35% marginal bracket.

Vacant Land

A second kind of real estate that requires minimal attention is vacant land. Vacant land generates no positive cashflows – but it does require the payment of property taxes and insurance, and occasional maintenance fees for weed and trash control. There are also no tax benefits since there is no depreciable improvement. Therefore, the only path to wealth in owning vacant land is through price appreciation. This single leg on the investment milk stool renders vacant land the riskiest path to achieving wealth in real estate. If the land does not appreciate, or fails to appreciate sufficiently, losses can be substantial.

The essential skill in acquiring vacant land is the ability to forecast the "path of progress." Communities undergoing expansion and growth do not usually grow in all directions equally and simultaneously. There always seems to be a "better part of town." Vacant land in the "wrong" direction may lie fallow for many years and may never rise in price sufficient to deliver a reasonable return on investment. If, for example, improved properties in the same locale are returning a 9.0% annual ROE as the result of the combination of operating income, tax benefits and appreciation, a vacant parcel must appreciate $\cong 30\%$ in value over 3 years just to keep pace.

Developers, of course, are usually very interested in acquiring developable land, but are most often interested in land they can develop "yesterday." Buying and holding land for future development is an alluring trap for all too many developers, many of whom have declared bankruptcy sitting on land for which demand never materialized.

The formula for the valuation of vacant land illustrates the problem: although the land may increase in value over a long holding period, the increase must offset the loss in the diminishing present value of the land due to the time value of money:

$$PV = \frac{\$0_1}{(1+i)^1} + \frac{0_2}{(1+i)^2} + \frac{0_3}{(1+i)^3} + \frac{0_4}{(1+i)^4} + \ldots\ldots \frac{Sales\,Price_n}{(1+i)^n}$$

For this reason, an investment in vacant land is a bet solely on its future value. If it appreciates enough and fast enough, you may be well rewarded. But if you guess wrong you may be left with an investment which can only be left to your heirs.

Acquiring Foreclosed Properties

The foreclosure of 7.5M condominiums and single family properties since 2007 suggests the possibility of acquiring one or more of these properties as an entry into the investment market.

The root causes of the collapse of the housing market beginning in 2007-8 encompass political, financial, social and economic factors. These factors are reasonably well understood by most investors but they are not well understood by most first-time homebuyers and some wannabe real estate investors. What is key for some investors is an assessment of the potential to realize long-term investment gains from participation in a market which has resulted from this real estate debacle.

REO Properties

Many of these properties are still on the books of lenders and held as REO[5] properties. But the market has changed greatly from the years 2005-2007 when a single family house could be bought using low-interest rate loans, re-carpeted, re-painted and re-sold in a matter of months at a large profit.[6] In January 2014 an estimated 1.7M properties remained on the balance sheets of lenders as Tier 3 assets.[7] This is more than twice the number of foreclosed homes held by lenders in 2007. The same source estimates that as many as 2 million more homes will face foreclosure during the 2012-2015 period. This "shadow inventory" held by lenders hangs like a pall over both the new home and resale markets. The days of 'fix and flip' are gone.

Commercial (non-residential) properties have not been spared. A host of commercial properties were financed in the years 2005-2008 with relatively short-term (3-7 year) loans at low interest rates.[8] As these loans become due, owners find that much more stringent underwriting guidelines and reduced operating income due to a recession have made it impossible to obtain replacement financing sufficient to retire the maturing loan.

In those cases in which the non-residential owner was incapable of servicing the existing loan (or a modification of the loan) the lender foreclosed. But in those cases in which the owner remained capable of servicing the existing debt, the lender usually followed a policy of "pretend and extend."[9] An admixture of commercial properties resulted consisting of properties in technical default but still in the hands of the owner and vacant foreclosed properties held on the balance sheet of the lender as REO properties.

Pursuing the Bargain Foreclosure

A group of agents has emerged who specialize in selling these foreclosed and "pre-foreclosure" properties. The "pre-foreclosure" properties are those on which a Notice of Default (NOD)[10] has already been recorded signaling an impending foreclosure by the lender. Residential foreclosure and pre-foreclosure properties are heavily marketed to first-time homebuyers and first-time investors alike. If the potential buyer is one who seeks to buy and occupy as a residence, all may be well and good; many of these properties can be acquired at prices substantially (20-40%) below current market values. But buyers who acquire a foreclosure with the intent of renting and holding until the market recovers need to be especially cautious since a foreclosed property tends to suppress the appraised value of nearby properties.

Acquiring a Short-Sale Property

Many owners who have received a Notice of Default, indicating an imminent foreclosure, are soon approached by a real estate agent who suggests a "short sale." A short sale involves listing the property for an amount below the current balance of the existing mortgage on the property.[11] These agents

---

5   Carried on the balance statement of the lender as "Real Estate Owned,"
6   By refurbishers, not investors.
7   A bank asset whose price cannot be accurately determined.
8   Some of which were payable interest-only.
9   Pretend that a default has not occurred and extend the maturity date of the existing loan.
10   The initial step in the foreclosure process.
11   First Trust Deed or Mortgage loan only. Junior liens will be expunged.

rationalize that if the property proceeds to foreclosure the owner will receive no cash but will suffer a blemish on his/her credit for..x.. numbers of future years. The agent posits that the property can be sold at current *market value*[12] with the approval and cooperation of the lender. The owner will still not receive any cash from the sale but he will avoid tarnishing his credit report.

The property is listed by the current owner at a price below the current balance on the existing loan. The owner has no special interest in negotiating a higher price since he will receive no cash on sale. The agent is incentivized to value the property low enough to attract a large number of bargain-hunting buyers. When a number of offers have been received the agent presents one or more to the lender and suggests that the lender choose the best offer.

Lenders prefer not to foreclose on property because it involves not only the expense of the foreclosure but also the risk that the property may suffer vandalization if left unoccupied.[13] If the best offer is within a margin of loss the lender can accept, the transaction is completed. If not, the lender will direct the agent to try again at a higher price.

It is for this reason that participating short-sale buyers often experience long waiting periods before they know the result of their bid. This waiting period can extend into months. It is also understandable that many bidders will overbid the asking price.

Buyers who enter bids in this market need to appreciate the dynamics of this arrangement and prepare to be disappointed before being rewarded.

Upside-down Properties

Investors should be aware that the sale of a foreclosed property usually has an immediate effect on the appraised value of similar properties in the same neighborhood. As a result, nearby homeowners, though current on their debt, experience a reduction in the market value of their homes, often to the extent that they become "upside down" in their properties; i.e. they owe more on their property than its current market value. In 2014 it is estimated that approximately 9.7 million homeowners nationally are "upside down." In addition, 9.3 million more would have no equity after sales costs. This deterioration has not been mitigated by government programs, such as HARP and HAMP,[14] designed to restore health to the housing market. It is likely that the return to a "normal" market will take 3-5 years, or longer.

Buying into this market is not something the beginning investor should undertake lightly. Success with these properties depends upon the ability to lease the properties for rents which will cover all operating costs[15] and to hold these properties until the local market stabilizes. Even then, satisfactory yields are heavily dependent upon appreciating home prices.

---

[12] As defined by the agent.
[13] The value of a foreclosed property is also carried on the lender's books as a non-performing asset which increases the lender's reserve requirements but not the lender's capacity to make new loans.
[14] HARP = Home Affordable Refinance Program; HAMP = Home Affordable Modification Program
[15] A vacancy of only 1 month per year results in a loss of 8.3% of annual gross revenue.

Non-Residential Properties

Non-residential properties on the books of lenders are there because the former owner either could not lease the property or could not lease the property at rents adequate to service the debt. Las Vegas is now notorious as the country's second leading house foreclosure market. In 2013 one in every 46 houses was in active foreclosure. But the Clark County NV market is also replete with foreclosed commercial properties that can be purchased at prices substantially below replacement cost. They are of investment value to the buyer who will occupy the property (a "user") or to the investor who has a tenant-in-waiting.

The fact is that the real estate market now requires the investor to be very, very selective in the property he acquires. It needs to be located in a healthy rental market.

Profiling a Healthy Market

The level of employment in a regional market and the amount of job growth are the very best macro-indicators of an area's economic health and therefore of its real estate health. Growth and stability in the number of jobs reflects the soundness of an area's *economic base*, the basic economic wellspring from which a region draws its primary income.[16] In the optimum situation, a region's economic base is well-diversified and not dependent upon one industry alone, but instead enjoys income from diverse business sectors. This diversification provides financial health insurance to communities in the event of an economic downturn and helps to maintain stable real estate markets.

New companies and industries entering an area expand its economic base and create new job opportunities that support the needs of an expanding population. The United States has an employable work force of approximately 146 million[17] which supports a population in excess of 318 million[18]. Therefore each new job will support the addition of approximately 2.2 consumers to the average community. Seventy-one percent of the U.S. economy is supported by consumer spending. When jobs leave a community, the number of consumers lost is approximately twice the number of jobs lost and the impact over a broad array of real properties in the area can be severe.

New job opportunities create demand not only for office and industrial space but also for single family homes and apartments, for retail space to service local merchants, food outlets, and space for service providers such as doctors, lawyers, accountants, plumbers, electricians etc. If this growth is healthy and sustainable, you can expect a healthy real estate market. If the growth is not a sustainable expansion, then the real estate markets may be headed for contraction troubles in the form of higher vacancies, lower rents, and possibly numerous foreclosures. Communities rarely remain static for very long.

Follow the Trend in Rents

The health of industrial, office, retail and apartment markets can be measured by indicators such as the trend in rents, the vacancy rate for apartment units, or the square feet of industrial and office properties leased and recently leased. But apartment vacancy rates and the number of square feet of office or industrial space leased are not by themselves sufficiently reliable indicators. The number of square feet recently leased in a market may be declining as the result of a temporary shortfall in supply; vacancy rates

---

[16]   As opposed to doctors, lawyers, plumbers, etc. who generate secondary or service income.

[17]   As of April, 2014. These data can be obtained from www.bls.gov.

[18]   As of 1Q 2014

may currently be high because of new supply which has recently entered the market and has not yet been absorbed. All three indicators must be followed together.

If one were forced to rely on one indicator alone, it would be the trend in rents. The level and trend in rents is a lagging but accurate indicator of supply and demand forces currently at work in the community. Whether rents will continue to rise or fall, however, must be gauged by the underlying economic conditions and whether these conditions are stable or temporary. Expansion in some markets is often transitory.

For instance, the notorious hyperinflation in rents in California's Silicon Valley in the 1997-1999 period offers a classic example: rental demand for office and industrial space was spurred by the overnight formation of dot.com companies which, flush with IPO[19] cash, rented every available space in town. Many industrial spaces that had stood vacant for years were gobbled up for conversion to nouveau-tech spaces at rents that were double and triple the rents for 'Class A' office buildings downtown. The demand for space became so intense that many landlords were offered warrants and stock options in the start-up company as an inducement to lease. All this ended with the bursting of the bubble and the collapse of the dot.coms in March, 2000.[20] The demand for industrial, office, retail and apartment space plummeted 15-40%.

In the end, a determination of whether or not a realty trend is reality-based and will continue is a matter of careful inquiry, experience, judgment and common sense.

Gathering Market Information

Information available via the computer affords the diligent investor the opportunity to obtain data, information and knowledge once accessible to only a few, and even then quite expensively. The computer, the Internet and the world-wide web (www) have revolutionized real estate. State, regional and local economic conditions which were once remote and difficult to obtain are now readily available at little or no cost. Conditions in markets in other states and communities can now be accessed and downloaded in minutes.

State population and employment statistics are available for all Metropolitan Statistical Areas (MSAs).[21] In many cases one can access via the Web a newspaper in a particular community to follow local economic trends, market developments, and new construction. Even current rents for industrial, retail, office properties and apartments can be obtained by reading on-line a newspaper's classified and display ads. And all this can be done at minimal cost.

Web Portals

There are a very large number of Web sites of value to the beginning investor.

The **Beige Book**, published 8 times a year by the Federal Reserve Bank's Open Market Committee (FOMC), provides both summary and detailed descriptions of regional market conditions in each of the 12 Federal Reserve Districts throughout the country.

---

[19] Initial Public Offering
[20] The NASDAQ closed 14 years later in May, 2014 at 4127, still 18% below the peak level of 5,018 in March, 2000.
[21] Areas linked together by economic ties and not necessarily linked to a central city or area.

These reports, though anecdotal, are gathered from a wide range of businesses and regional information sources. The reports include current information about salaries and wages, retail trade, services and manufacturing, as well as agriculture and other resource-related industries. They also include an overview of current conditions in the residential, commercial and construction real estate markets. A 5-year history of these reports is maintained at the site, www.federalreserve.gov/FOMC/BeigeBook.

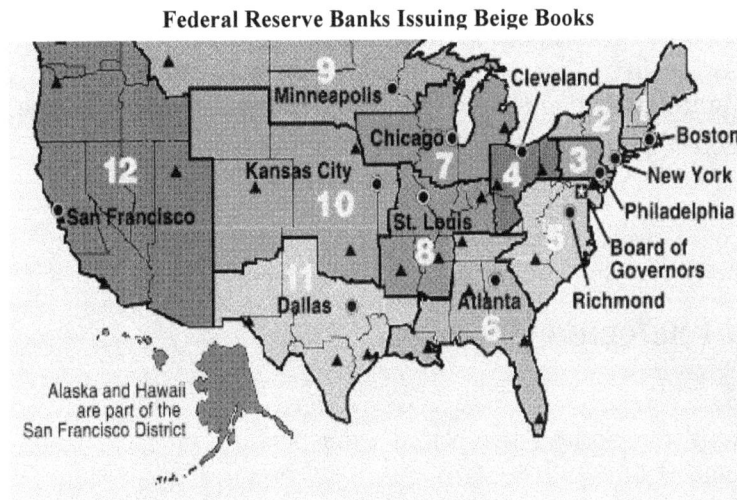

Federal Reserve Banks Issuing Beige Books

The site maintained by the **Bureau of Labor Statistics** is another valuable portal to a vast array of information about national, regional, state and metropolitan economic and market conditions. The site is located at www.bls.gov. Other kinds of information are available through myriad professional and trade organizations. Search engines, particularly www.google.com, are excellent means to find information on almost any subject related to real estate.

Sites such as www.loopnet.com, co-star.com, showcase.com and www.Realtor.com provide information about available investment properties.

Commercial real estate agents can also be valuable sources of information about local markets, especially if they are associated with companies that maintain research departments which gather leasing, sales, vacancy and financing data.

Converting a Residence to a Rental

Many beginning investors launch their investment career in real estate by converting a house or condominium to a rental. In all but a few cases (FHA and VA loans[22]), the owner may convert a residence to a rental without the permission of, or interference from, the lender. In terms of 'knowing your market,' the owner should know quite well the local market and local rents having lived there. But there are other considerations in converting a residence to a rental.

> **Note**: A residence is converted to rental (investment property) on the day when it is first offered for rent, and when the owner begins to treat it as a rental by deducting certain expenses and taking depreciation allowances. It is not necessary that the property be rented before the owner can begin to accumulate tax-deductible expenses and take depreciation allowances.

Basis of Converted Property

The Basis of a converted property, for the purpose of establishing a Depreciable Basis, is its fair market value _or_ the owner's Adjusted Basis at the time of conversion, whichever is lower. If the property is

---

[22] These properties may be converted by the resident-owner after they have been "seasoned".

converted, this Basis must be allocated between the improvement value and the land value in order to determine a beginning Depreciable Basis.

If the property has been owned a number of years, this Basis may be quite low. A low Basis restricts the amount of depreciation available to shelter income and it may make better financial sense to sell the property as a residence, enjoy the LTCG exemption currently available to homeowners under IRS S.121, pay the tax and reinvest the cash.[23] Carrying along a low Basis in a residence into an investment property simply carries along the unrecognized tax liability which may be avoided by homeowners, in part or in whole, under current (2014) tax law. If the converted property is held for more than 3 years, the owner will lose the valuable exemptions available under S.121 since the owner must have lived in the property for at least 24 months of *the last 60* months to qualify.

Further, if the property is refinanced prior to its conversion to an investment property, the new mortgage, which may be higher than the Basis, may present problems later on in the form of Net Mortgage Relief [24] if the owner wishes to exchange in order to defer tax recognition.

Therefore a residential property which has been owned for years is often a better candidate for an outright sale as a residence than converting the property into an investment and assuming these burdens.

Investment Characteristics of Selected Properties

Apartments: Multi-Family Units

In 2011-2013 the high rate of single-family foreclosures has placed extra pressure on multi-family properties to house new tenants who are unable to buy. Very few lower-cost, new 1-4 unit residential properties have been built since 2008 because developers also have difficulty in spreading the dramatic increase in building fees and permit costs over a smaller number of units; they strongly prefer to build 100 or more units.

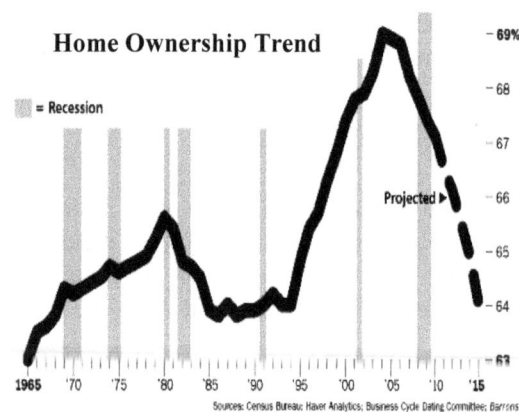

Home Ownership Trend

To complicate matters, there is a sharp decline in home ownership in the 24-35 age group which has historically been the prime home-buying cohort. This decline forces more individuals and families into rentals. In 2011, sixty-seven percent of all Americans lived in their own homes, but 33% rented. By 2015 it is anticipated that fewer than 64% will be home owners and more than 36% will be renters. This may seem like a small decrease but 3% of 154,000,000 U.S. households means that more than 4,600,000 families who formerly would have been homeowners will be seeking rental units. This increase in rental demand is now accompanied by an increase in market rents. In 2014-2015 multi-family apartments remains the brightest section of the real estate market.

Apartments: Lower-Income

Units targeted to the lower-income group are best located proximate to job centers, large shopping malls, public transportation and easy access to freeways. The cost of gasoline has made it economically

---

[23] $250,000 exempted from LTCG for singles and $500,000 for married taxpayers. Other requirements apply.

[24] Acquiring a replacement property in a S.1031 exchange with a mortgage less than the balance of the mortgage on the relinquished property.

impossible for many workers to travel long distances to work. In-fill and redevelopment projects close to job centers now experience increased demand, and rising rents.

"Bread and butter" units in a less attractive part of town are frequently offered to the beginning investor because of a lower cost per unit. These units are often occupied by a high number of occupants per room. High *occupancy density* results in greater wear and tear, more frequent repairs and higher operating costs, especially if the owner remains responsible for one or more utilities.

High occupancy density also seems to correlate with higher crime rates, higher operating costs and a lower price/unit. In lower socio-economic areas tenants will often double - and triple-up. In some urban areas it is not unusual to find as many as 10 persons occupying a 2-bedroom apartment, despite local zoning, health law restrictions and lease clauses to the contrary. These properties experience much greater wear and tear, higher utility and service costs, especially water and waste collection. A rough gauge of the income group of the tenants in a particular property can be had by driving the property's parking area and observing the models and ages of cars and trucks parked there. These properties are usually management intensive.

Section 8 Housing

Some low-income individuals and families, the elderly and some veterans may qualify for rental assistance through affordable housing programs such as Section 8.[25]. Under the Housing Voucher Program of Section 8, a subsidy is assigned to a qualified tenant who is free to live anywhere in the U.S.A. in an approved apartment unit or house. Although the Voucher attaches to the tenant and not the housing unit, the local Public Housing Authority (PHA) makes payment directly to the landlord to cover up to 70% of the cost of rent and utilities. The tenant remains responsible for up to 30% of the rent.

In recent years developers of multi-family properties have been required to set aside from 10-20% of the units for subsidized renters. Therefore many apartment houses built in the last 10-15 years will have Voucher tenants in place. Voucher tenants initially occupy under a one-year lease which may then be extended by the landlord or converted to a month-to-month tenancy. The waiting list for a Voucher can extend into the thousands and the waiting time for some tenants to obtain a Voucher can vary from 3 to 5 years. Therefore these tenants are very infrequently involved in activities which could result in their eviction and the resulting revocation of their Voucher.

Maximum rents paid are determined annually by Housing and Urban Development (HUD) as Fair Market Rents (FMR)[26] and are based on the costs of housing in the area. Rents are rarely reduced even during periods of high vacancy.

For additional information see: http://portal.hud.gov/hudportal/HUD?src=/program_office

Apartments: Section 42 (Low Income Housing Tax Credits)

Section 42 of the Tax Code was added in 1986 to provide private developers a way to deliver affordable housing units to individuals and families whose household income does not exceed 50-60% of an area's median income.

Under S.42, a developer applies for tax credits provided by the federal government but administered by the state government. These *credits* provide for a direct deduction from federal income tax due rather than a deduction from taxable income. They are invariably sold by the developer in the secondary market for

---

[25]   Of the United States Housing Act of 1937, amended many times over.

[26]   For Fair Market Rents in any state go to http://www.huduser.org/portal/datasets/fmr.html

amounts close to 75-85% of their nominal value. The proceeds, together with a standard mortgage or municipal bond financing, provide funds for the construction of affordable housing units. The purchasers of the credits apply them over a period of 10 years.

More than 2 million apartment units have been newly constructed or renovated using S. 42 tax credits and the program now far outstrips Section 8 as a provider of housing for lower-income families. Although credits have been available for the development of apartment properties as small as 20 units,[27] most development projects now involve properties consisting of 100 or more units and ownership by syndications and corporations. Owners of S.42 properties must continue to offer affordable units to low-income families for 15 years. Because of the size of these properties they are seldom acquired by individual investors.

Apartments: Suburban

In the middle arena are the typical suburban-type multi-family properties ranging in size from 10-12 units and greater. This tends to be a very competitive market and occupancy is sensitive to a large number of market variables:

Proximity to transportation	On-site amenities	Attractive landscaping
Patios and decks	Covered parking	Security
Modern kitchen appliances	On-site management	Spas & pools
Proximity to schools	Physical size of units	Crime-free area

In most suburban multi-family properties, the 2-bedroom, 2-bath and 2-bedroom, 1-bath units predominate in the mix of units. The unit mix generally provides for fewer one-bedroom and "studio" units accommodating one or two persons. These smaller units rent for prices somewhat higher per square foot than the larger units but tend to have a higher turnover rate. Three bedroom units, if included in the mix at all, are relatively scarce since the rent for these units will often support a mortgage or rent on a small house. Nevertheless, 3-bedroom units, when available, are often fully rented.

Senior and Student Housing

Housing for seniors is a highly specialized segment of the rental market. Properties in demand are those which offer extensive support services and are located within walking distance to a shopping center and close to major hospitals. Some properties are composed of an assortment of free standing units, duplexes, triplexes and fourplexes situated on a campus or park-like site. When the building is greater than a single story in height, elevator service is essential.

Seniors are very security conscious and will choose apartments located in gated or highly securitized complexes over those offering less security, even at a lower rent.

Many thousands of senior-only (≥55-62 years old) residences have been built in recent years. Demand is likely to increase as more than 75.4 million of the U.S. population are now older than 65 and enter retirement. An increasing number of younger seniors shed their empty-nest homes and migrate back to the center of town or to a dedicated community where they can enjoy easy shopping and other cultural events nearby. Due to the many supporting services often

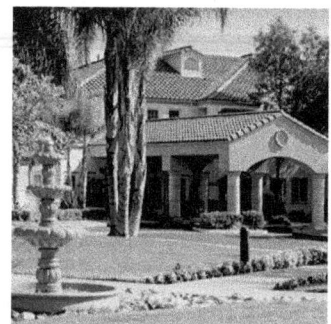

---

[27]   The minimum size of eligible projects is determined by individual states.

included, these properties are typically quite large (>100-150 units) and are rarely owned directly by individual investors. High fixed operating costs also reduce operating leverage making it difficult to proportionately increase net operating income by raising rents.

Demand for housing close to colleges and universities is constant. But renting to students is demanding and the wear and tear on a property can sometimes be unbelievable. It is not for the faint of heart. Owners may also find themselves in competition with on-campus units.

Multi-tenant Industrial Properties

When smaller companies grow, or when larger companies establish a physical presence in a community, they create a direct need for industrial, technical, warehouse, distribution, and office space, as well as a need for space to house suppliers, sub-contractors and professional service providers.

Setting aside the very large properties, an expanding local economy also presents good opportunities to invest in the smaller business properties that are created. Many of these are built by local developers who typically have little interest in retaining these properties on a long-term basis; they prefer to build, lease and sell – then to build again. Investors should be alert to this type of new construction opportunity.

Among the more popular of these properties is the multi-tenant industrial property housing a mixture of smaller businesses that require a blend of office and unimproved 'shop' space. Leases on these properties often do not extend more than 1-3 years, making them quite management intensive. Their attraction to many investors is that they tend to maintain good occupancy rates. They are full in a rising economy and, in contrast to large industrial properties which can remain vacant for years, rarely stand empty in a falling one. As one multi-tenant owner put it: "They're great - because I catch them on the way up and on the way down."

In acquiring a property with multiple tenants it should be your inviolable rule to obtain and <u>read a copy of every lease</u>. Do not accept as an excuse for not providing a copy of each lease an agent's assertion that "they are all the same and when you've seen one, you've seen them all." Experience shows that almost every lease will be different, not only in the amount of rent to be paid, but also in other important ways which will affect the value of the investment. Some tenants may have a number of options to renew a lease on terms very favorable to the tenant but unfavorable to the landlord. Other tenants may have negotiated an escape clause allowing them to vacate without penalty upon the happening of this or that event. Leases to the United States Post Office are an excellent example: the credit of the tenant may be great,[28] but the lease usually allows the Post Office to cancel the lease at its sole discretion without penalty on relatively short notice. Additional information on leases is available in Chapter 10, q.v.

Sale-Leasebacks

Many businesses which become well-established in a community eventually want to own their own property in order to stabilize location and overhead. If the business is owned by an individual or by a closely-held corporation,[29] the property is often acquired by the owner of the business as a personal investment in order to avoid the double taxation to which a corporation and its dividends are subject.[30] These owners frequently acquire the business property and then sell it to an investor under a *sale-*

---

[28] The U.S. Post Office was near bankruptcy in mid-2014.
[29] A non-public corporation which has a small number of shareholders.
[30] Some, but not all, states permit one- person S Corporations

leaseback arrangement using a Net lease. In this way, they not only recover the purchase capital for re-investment in the primary business, but also remove long-term mortgage debt from the company's balance sheet.[31] Since the sale is always conditioned upon the buyer's acceptance of the lease, they also have an opportunity to control the rent, future rent escalations, duration of the lease and the tenant's obligations under the lease.

In acquiring a sale-leaseback property the buyer must negotiate not only the price of the property but also the occupancy lease. <u>The key to these transactions is the financial health of the entity which will guarantee the lease payments.</u> The financial condition of the entity or person who will guarantee the rent is the first order of negotiations, even before discussion of price. If the seller is incorporated and files SEC reports, these reports can be examined to determine the seller/lessee's financial health. In the more likely case that the business is closely held, an offer to buy should be made subject to an inspection by the buyer's accountant of the most recent 3 years of financial statements and tax returns. The lease can be guaranteed by anyone with a good financial statement. It is also prudent to check the guarantor's credit reports and, perhaps, the Dun & Bradstreet reports. Sale-leaseback properties are often marketed by owners whose primary business is in financial difficulty. These businesses may find it difficult to make the payments due under the lease.

Retail Properties

Retail properties can range in size from the regional mall, to the anchored neighborhood center, to the unanchored neighborhood center, to the local convenience 'strip' of 2-10 stores, one of which may or may not be a well-branded business, to the stand-alone specialty property (fast-foods, electronics and drugstores). The keys to the success of a smaller retail center for the beginning investor are the location and street visibility of the center, the amount of consumer traffic, the mix of tenants, the ease of ingress and egress and the adequacy of parking spaces.

Of all these factors, the location and visibility of the stores are the most important. Location alone is not sufficient; the shops must have line-of-sight visibility by a passing driver. If the stores in a center are not readably visible at eye-level from the street, the retailer must spend a larger amount of its operating budget on awareness advertising and less on rent, since without market awareness nothing happens.

The *mix* of tenants is also important. Retail strips which concentrate similar tenants in the same property are *destination specialty centers* and attract shoppers because of the larger number of choices available in the same class of merchandise. Examples include furniture and clothing marts, auto malls, jewelry and design centers, factory outlets, et al. But unless there are sufficient numbers of similar tenants to establish the center as a destination specialty center, the duplication of tenants is usually fatal to one or both.

In order to prevent this duplication, retail tenants will insist on an *exclusivity clause* in their leases barring a directly competitive business from tenancy in the same center. These exclusivity clauses may also prohibit a current retailer, major anchor tenants excepted, from adding a line of competitive products in the same location. Tenancy in the destination specialty centers is limited by the savvy landlord to businesses offering the same general merchandise category.

---

[31] As of March. 2014, the FASB is still considering changes in lease accounting which will require bringing all capital leases longer than 1 year onto the balance sheet.

One red flag to be noted in a center is the presence of tenants in ground locations whose businesses contribute little or very little to consumer traffic. The best example is a 'store-front' church or gym, but others include uses which are devoted to assemblage, inventory storage and other types of small businesses which do not draw, and therefore do not interact with, shoppers. When you see retail stores with frosted windows, you are generally in a failing center.[32]

Some small centers are two-storied with the second floor typically devoted to specialized service businesses, e.g. loan brokers, dentists, counseling services, trade schools etc. Unless this center in located in an area hard-pressed for space, you will find these suites much more difficult to lease (indicating the need for greater vacancy allowances) and that the rents are less than both ground-level shops and nearby dedicated office space. Most lenders and many investors will heavily discount scheduled income from these retail spaces in arriving at total property value. Some lenders will ignore entirely income from these spaces in configuring a loan amount.

Retail: Category Killers

Downtown retailers and many suburban retailers have been driven from business by the entry of large discount stores which have entered the local market. When these large retailers focus on a single line of related merchandise (food, electronics, toys, bed and linen goods, hardware and home improvements, sports equipment, and the like) they tend to *kill-off* the viability of these product lines in smaller, mixed-retail businesses.

It is common for "food" clubs such as Costco and Sam's Club, for example, to do an annual volume equal to $1,000-2,000 per sq. foot of floor space per year in contrast to the smaller retailer's $150 - $200 per sq. ft. Each foot of discount space may displace 10 times as many feet of traditional retail space. A discount warehouse of 60,000–80,000 sq. ft. entering a community can take the place of 600,000 – 800,000 sq. ft. of traditional retail space,[33] enough to wreck a downtown market or to decimate a small town's entire downtown shopping area. Some smaller towns and cities have enacted zoning limitations on the size of "big-box" retailers to prevent this type of competition.

Retail: Free-Standing NNN Properties

Many retailers prefer to buy a street-facing pad in an anchored shopping center and construct a building which follows a branded architectural design. Examples include highly visible and recognizable fast-food restaurants such as Applebees, MacDonald's, Carls Junior, Burger King, Taco Bell, KFChicken, etc. Other popular stand-alones include Best Buy, Walgreens, Rite-Aide, CVS, Quick-lube shops, banks and retailers who prefer to design their own outlets and write their own leases.

These retailers will usually acquire the land, construct their branded improvement and then write a long-term net lease to themselves which becomes active upon sale of the entire property to an investor. The length of the lease is often 15, 20 or 25 years with a number of 5-year options to renew under defined terms and rent. The completed property is then offered for sale to investors subject to the pre-written lease. There are, however, times when the improvement is built on land leased to the retailer. This is a fundamentally different investment from one in which the investor acquires the fee interest to the property (subject to the occupancy lease). See Chapter 10 for additional information.

---

[32] Because these uses pay low rent.

[33] Two hundred to 400 stores of 1,500 – 2,000 sq. ft. in size.

Many investors are attracted to these properties because the NNN lease is guaranteed by a major corporation,[34] spans a long period of time and is virtually management-free. These properties pose as annuities. Whether they are good investments, however, depends upon the terms of the lease. Most frequently the cash-on-cash return for the first year of the lease is attractive. But increases in rent are subsequently scheduled every 5-7 years, very commonly at 10%.[35]

The penalty is that a 10% increase every five years equates to a 1.92% compounded increase per year. Domestic inflation has varied considerably, but over a long period of time inflation has historically averaged close to 3.0% per year. By the end of the fifth year when inflation–adjusted rent should increase by 15.9%, the pre-scheduled rent increases by only 10.0%. By the end of the 20th year, when the rent should be 1.8 times the initial rent, the contract rent is only 1.46 times the starting rent. The investor has had a steady and secured income but has lost 19% of the purchasing power of his rental dollar.

When this property is re-offered for sale by the investor, the fair value is a function of a below-market rent which may continue for a number of years and a number of future options periods.[36] The result is a significant reduction in market value. These properties can be very attractive but the investor needs to be careful to consider only those properties which offer some semblance of control over future increases in contract rent.

Office Properties; General Office

Office buildings are categorized as "A," "B," and "C" properties according to their location, attractiveness and age.

"A" properties are those designed and built to attract high-end, image-conscious tenants for whom a successful image is very important. These properties are frequently located in the central business districts (CBD) of cities and appeal to well-established law, accountancy, investment, brokerage and banking firms who may occupy thousands of square feet or multiple floors in the building. Rents paid for these spaces will set the highest rents for the local MSA.

"B" properties are those not quite as distinguished as are "A" properties but are nevertheless well-located, attractive and well-maintained. Rents for these properties are closer to the median office rent for the MSA in which they are located. They house a wide variety of tenants who pay a wide range of rents.

"C" properties are those which are not especially well-located, are typically older and appeal to smaller-sized tenants who often require small spaces. The average rents for these properties will be the lowest in the MSA and will house tenants on shorter-term leases or month-to-month rental agreements. Turnover and vacancy in these properties are usually higher than average.

---

[34] Caveat: Some retailers are franchisees licensed to use a branded name but whose lease obligations are not guaranteed by a the franchisor.

[35] Many Walgreen leases, for example, provide zero increases in rent for 25 years!

[36] These properties are often advertised as properties with "upside potential."

Specialized Properties

<u>Medical Facilities</u>

Office spaces dedicated to use by physicians and dentists require much more elaborate plumbing, electrical services and structural components and are therefore more costly to build, equip and maintain. These uses also require larger parking ratios, typically 6 sq. ft. of parking area for each sq. ft. of office space.[37] Accordingly, rents are much higher than median rents for comparably sized office space.[38] Smaller medical buildings ranging in size from 5,000 to 50,000 sq. ft. are often owned by practitioners who restrict occupancy to like-kind medical and dental professionals. As medical practitioners continue to consolidate to spread costs, fewer and fewer of these properties are being built in favor of multi-floor medical centers located close to or allied with a local hospital. Investors attracted to the smaller properties need to be alert to any plans[39] to develop large medical office buildings close to the hospital; when these newer building become available the smaller properties can empty out rapidly leaving specialized vacant space releasable only at lower rents.

<u>Executive Office Space</u>

Executive office space located in a well-located and attractive office building may fill a well-defined market need. This space can be occupied by a building tenant whose principal business is the operation of this type of business. But at other times the executive office space has been segregated by the present owner of the entire building who operates the business under a separate DBA.[40] When the building is offered for sale some of these owners will improperly include the income from the business as income from the building. Since executive office space rent is always higher than comparable rent in the same building, the re-characterization of the business income as real estate income exaggerates the building's market value.

The author has encountered an instance in which the owner of the building combined income from the executive space business, which he also owned, with regular tenant income and sold the building to an uninformed foreign investor who later defaulted on his loan when the executive office business collapsed. The seller of the property was convicted of fraud and sentenced to jail.
Every tenant should be represented by a current lease. Caveat lessor.

Self-Storage Facilities

When these properties were first developed they were called "mini-warehouses," an inaccurate moniker to which today's owners of self-storage facilities (SSFs) strongly and properly object.[41]

These properties were originally developed under a strategy which posited that land in the "path of progress" would become more valuable as a community's growth pattern expanded and "ran over" the land site. Therefore the early SSFs were typically located on the edge of town on less expensive (and less convenient) land and were often considered a "land play."

---

37 6:1 parking vs. perhaps 3:1 for standard office space.
38 Larger lots require additional rent to maintain acceptable yields.
39 A visit to the local planning department can provide this kind of information.
40 DBA = "doing business as." A business name. An alias.
41 There are important legal differences between SSFs and warehouses.

Since then, the entire premise of SSFs has evolved. Fostering this change has been the reduction in the size of apartments and the reduction in the size of building lots large enough on which "stuff" could once be stored. The early SSFs were constructed of less expensive building materials (galvanized steel frames and corrugated steel panels) which could partition indoor space into separate storage areas that could be isolated and secured.

Over time, SSFs have returned to the more densely occupied areas of the community, even into the heart of the city, designed as multi-storied, air-conditioned, fire-proof, highly secure buildings catering to both industrial and residential tenants. They no longer represent a strategic *land play* but instead are full-fledged dedicated businesses providing an important type of business real estate in the community.

The return to the city and to high land prices has, however, resulted in higher development costs, so rental rates per sq. ft. now often exceed rates for nearby apartments. It is also a fairly unsophisticated type of development which can attract new operators capable of overbuilding the area. A pre-buy competitive market analysis (CMA) is essential, as is a visit to the local municipal Planning Department.

Today's SSF requires competent on-site management in the form of trained managers responsive to the needs of the tenant and the business. Most SSFs today provide an on-site residence for trained manager-couples. Additional information and education can be obtained at http://www.selfstorage.org. A well-located SSF with a wide "moat"[42] can be a very fine long-term investment for the informed investor.

Interest Rates Presage Real Estate Prices

The "trick" in selling near the top or buying near the bottom is in the ability to discern an impending turn in interest rates because real estate values are very sensitive to current interest rates. As interest rates decline so do capitalization rates and declining "cap" rates presage higher prices. The reverse is also true: as interest rates increase, cap rates also increase and prices – for the same level of rents – decline. Therefore the best barometer to watch is the trend in interest rates, not because of the cost of borrowing, although that is important too, but rather because of their effect on direct capitalization rates and, therefore, on market prices.

An obvious disadvantage to buying when interest rates, and therefore capitalization rates, are high is that high loan rates restrict the amount of mortgage that an income property can support. For this reason, more cash must be invested to acquire a property. When the trend reverses and rates fall, the investor can refinance the property to obtain a tax-free extraction of equity[43] and better leverage at lower rates. It is very unusual, however, that owners of desirable properties will trade them at every turn in interest rates. The cost of trading real estate is much more costly than trading equities.

In Summary...

Locating and investigating a new real estate investment property is a demanding task. But today's nvestor has many tools and more information at hand than ever before.
Using them well pays great dividends.

---

[42] Wide threshold of entry.

[43] Refinancing a property is not a taxable event.

Chapter 5
Financing the
Investment
Property

The ability to secure adequate financing with favorable terms is important to most real estate investors. There are only a few investors who prefer to own income-producing real estate without using borrowed funds. These investors have no worries about meeting a mortgage payment or a refinancing deadline, but the lack of leverage greatly diminishes the yield which they can reasonably expect from their invested dollars.

For all other investors, adequate financing under favorable terms is an important part of the yield equation. The extent to which a property is financeable determines the amount of downpayment required to control it. The lower the percent downpayment in relation to the price, the greater the value of the property that can be controlled; the greater the value of the property, the more the investor stands to gain from depreciation and appreciation.

In our discussion of financing we will concentrate on what the investor needs to know to acquire a sound and workable loan for his investment property. We want to emphasize the fundamentals and, in keeping with a theme of this book, rely on the individual investor's initiative and industry to expand his or her working knowledge of mortgages in this rapidly changing market. Let's begin by looking at the subject of Leverage.

Leveraging the Investment

Leverage can be defined simply as the *use of borrowed money to control an investment*. When a great deal of other people's money is used to acquire the investment, the investment can be said to be "highly leveraged." The advantage of financial leverage sources from three important facts:

1. Money borrowed at a rate lower than the rate at which the investment earns income (its "cap rate") results in increased cashflow to the owner during the holding period.

2. Any increase in property value usually belongs solely to the owner of the investment. Therefore the more valuable the investment, the greater the potential gain from appreciation.

3. Higher-valued properties furnish greater amounts of depreciation allowances thereby reducing taxes.

The Polarity of Leverage

We know from previous discussion that the rate at which a real property throws off Net Operating Income (NOI) in relation to its market value is its *capitalization rate*. The property produces this NOI ignorant of how much or how little of someone else's money may be invested in it. Therefore a property acquired at a capitalization rate of 10% will cast off $10.00 in NOI for each $100.00 invested in it, without regard to its capital structure.[1]

Give me a place to stand and I will move the world
Archimedes

♦ If $50.00 of invested capital represents borrowed funds, and the lender charges 10% for the use of these funds, then the owner pays a rate for the use of money exactly equal to the rate (10%) at which the borrowed funds earn income. This is a situation of *neutral* leverage.

♦ If, however, the lender requires 11% for the use of $50 ($5.50 interest), then the owner pays a premium equal to 1% of the total amount borrowed; hence, 1% of $50, or $0.50. The borrowed $50 earns $5.00 but costs $5.50. The difference comes from the owner's pocket. This is a position of *negative* leverage.

♦ If the lender requires only 9% for the use of $50 ($4.50 interest), the owner earns a premium on every dollar borrowed equal to 1% of the amount borrowed; hence 1% of $50 = $0.50. The borrowed $50 earns $5.00 but costs only $4.50. This is a position of *positive* leverage.

Therefore positive leverage occurs whenever the yield from the investment exceeds the interest rate on borrowed funds. Negative leverage occurs when the interest rate on borrowed funds exceeds the capitalization rate of the investment.[2] Neutral leverage occurs when the yield is equal to the interest rate on borrowed funds, in which case the investor neither makes nor loses money on these borrowed funds.

Whenever the investor borrows money at a rate less than the interest charged for the use of the funds, he is in a position to enhance his investment yield.

Leverage and Appreciation

If it were not for appreciation, it would make no financial sense at all to borrow money when prevailing interest rates equal or exceed the yield rate on an investment. But a leveraged property carries on its day-to-day production of NOI entirely unaware of its capital structure.

In the case of real estate, market value is tied to rents; when these rents increase market value also increases. When it does, the entire amount of the increase accrues to the equity owner.[3] The greater the value of the property controlled, the greater the amount of appreciation accruing to the benefit of the owner. This is the fact that justifies negative leverage during times of inflation when interest rates may exceed capitalization rates creating negative leverage.

---

[1] The amounts and sources of capital used to control a property.
[2] The capitalization rate is one expression of the investor's yield.
[3] There are exceptions, such as a participation loan when a lender shares in the proceeds of the investment.

The Risks of Leverage

The same high leverage which can be a wealth generator during inflationary periods can turn into a howling beast during times of deflation. These are times when property rents, and therefore NOIs, are declining, either as a result of vacancies or as the result of rent reductions required to fill vacant space. The property owner who is highly leveraged sends a greater and greater share of the NOI to his lender, until – in terminal cases – the entire property, equity and all, is delivered to the lender via foreclosure.

Leverage is the original two-edged sword. Handle With Care.

Consider this capital structure of an investment property purchased for $1,000,000 and on which a lender has made a 75% loan[4] with an interest rate of 9%, amortized over 25 years. The buyer has also secured a secondary mortgage from the seller who is carrying back 10% of the purchase price in a short-term *straight note*[5] at 10% annual interest. Assume that the property was purchased at a 9% capitalization rate:

Net Operating Income	$90,000
Annual Pmt. on 1st Mortgage	-75,527
Annual Pmt. on 2nd Mortgage	-10,000
Pre-tax Spendable Cash	$4,473

This property, leveraged to a total of 85% of its value, is perilously close to a negative income. If the property has a number of tenants, the loss of only one non-credit tenant[6] or the bankruptcy of a major credit tenant could force the owner to supplement the income from his own funds in order to service the existing debt. In a serious economic downturn resulting in the loss of a number of such tenants, both the owner and the carrier of the 2nd mortgage could be in jeopardy of losing their entire investments through foreclosure.

You can readily see why many lenders will not permit secondary (junior) financing on fully leveraged property. Without secondary financing the investor is compelled to add more equity dollars to the investment. Lenders point out that the owner who has a larger equity stake in the investment is less likely to walk away from the property if problems develop.

There is also the investment "risk" of too little leverage. The investor who buys income property all-cash limits his initial pre-tax rate of return on his invested capital. He is never at risk of losing his property through loan foreclosure, but he is also "at risk" of never achieving a rate of return commensurate with the risk of owning and operating income real estate.

Effect of Leverage on IRR

The IRR - the owner's overall yield on invested cash - is extremely sensitive to the amount of the initial investment. The lower the initial investment amount required to capture future cashflows, the higher will be the IRR (because the IRR is a discount rate; a higher discount rate is required to convert future cashflows to a smaller initial investment).

---

[4]   The Loan-to-Value ratio. Seventy-five percent of established value.

[5]   A note which pays interest only and does not provide for periodic reduction of principal.

[6]   A credit tenant will continue to pay rent even if the tenant vacates the property.

But when more and more operating cash goes to service debt, the income component of the IRR derived from annual operations declines steeply while the IRR component attributable to reversionary (resale) value rises steeply. This is simply another way of saying that if an asset is highly leveraged, most of the return will derive from the net sales proceeds at the end of the holding period and less from cash returns during the holding period. This "wait to see" effect of high leverage is the essence of the increased risk which almost always accompanies high IRRs.

Leverage in Relation to Investment Strategy

The amount of leverage to employ is a function of the investment strategy and this strategy changes from one investor to another. The most common objective of younger and more aggressive investors is the accumulation of new wealth, while the most common objective of the older investor is the preservation of attained wealth. Younger investors can afford to take riskier positions because they have time to replace capital lost; older investors do not usually take risky positions because they know that they could not readily replace capital lost.[7] Along the continuum of high leverage to low leverage should be a position comfortable to every investor, even if the position is at one end of the leverage spectrum.

A Loan is an Annuity, not a Favor

Many beginning investors enter the lending arena with the assumption that a lender is doing them a favor to lend money on a good property. Nothing could be farther from the truth. Lenders understand that loans have a nutritional value for them: if they don't make them they don't eat. So the lender is anxious to make a good loan; but he is also quite averse to making a bad one.

It helps to look upon a mortgage as the sale and purchase of an ordinary *annuity*. When a lender lends money he is actually buying an annuity from the property owner. The lender pays the present value (PV) of the loan for the right to receive from the owner-borrower a specified number of future payments, payable at regular intervals, including interest at a certain rate.

The borrower is really the seller of the same annuity. He receives a lump sum of cash (the amount of the loan) in return for his promise to return a stipulated number of payments on time and in the amount required to reduce its balance to zero.

It makes sense to look upon a mortgage as a bilateral contract, because that is exactly what it is: an annuity contract. No matter how friendly the lender may be, the two parties to the loan contract do not sit on the same side of the negotiating table. The lender's objective is to buy the lowest risk annuity at the highest return, which means he seeks the highest payback (payment) for cash extended and risk taken. The borrower's objective is to sell the annuity for the lowest payments over the same amortization schedule. This is not necessarily to suggest that the borrower and lender are declared adversaries, but it does emphasize that the lender's goal in lending money at the highest possible rate is antithetical to that of the borrower, which is to borrow money at the lowest possible cost. Therefore it follows that all loans should be diligently shopped among a number of potential lenders and skillfully negotiated.

Negotiability of Loans

When dealing directly with a lender of funds, it is more the rule than the exception that residential (1-4 units) loans are not very negotiable. It's true that the modern "house" lender presents a kaleidoscopic array of loan terms, shaken together with different interest rates, loan points and loan fees. The borrower

---

[7]   And also because they don't need to.

has the option of choosing from among a variety of loan "plans," but regardless of the payment plan selected, the cost of the loan to the borrower, as measured by its Annual Percentage Rate (APR),[8] doesn't vary very much.

For example, consider this array of actual terms from a major, national home lender for a $200,000 loan, amortized over 30 years, all due and payable in 7 years:

Rate	Points	Fees	APR
6.75%	2.375	$1,297	7.03%
6.88%	1.75	$1,314	7.09%
7.10%	1.00	$1,331	7.14%
7.13%	0.50	$1,347	7.22%
7.25%	0.125	$1,364	7.31%

Notice that as the interest rate increases, the points decrease, while loan fees[9] stay essentially the same. The last column, the Annual Percentage Rate (APR), tells the consumer the yield which the lender will realize on this loan including points and fees.. The yield to the lender[10] is the same as the cost to the borrower. Despite the variety of options, the true cost of any choice varies less than *3 tenths* of one percent.

However, this is not the case when it comes to a loan on income-producing properties, units 1–4 excepted.[11] Except for the very largest lenders, the ebb and flow of cash available to the lender is not constant. During times when the bank has lots of money to "get out," the loan officers and underwriters will be anxious to see you and the total cost of the loan may be low; but when money is sparse you will find them picky, parsimonious and pinchfisted.

Insurance companies, for example, are often much better sources of investment loans in the first part of their fiscal year than in the last part. These institutions often make loans to cover guaranteed investment contracts (GICs) they enter into with pension fund and trust managers; they accept pension funds and contract to provide a guaranteed return to the fund. They make loans to investors at a higher rate and profit from the margin, or spread, between the rate paid and the rate received. Once these contracts are covered for the year and the amount budgeted for real estate loans has been reached, insurance lenders become reluctant brides and may put off a suitor until the next budget year.

Because the tide of available cash ebbs and flows, it pays to shop around. Although you should first consider your present bank or lending institution, shopping for a loan can save you thousands of dollars in points, fees and random charges. In presenting your loan application, it's important to present a complete loan "package" of information which reflects your knowledge of what the lender requires. If this is not your hidden skill, consider the services of a reputable, experienced and well-established mortgage broker who has a relationship with a number of primary lenders.

---

[8] Under the Truth in Lending Act, Reg. Z, the APR is required information to be provided to the home buyer, 1-4 units only.
[9] Ostensibly, fixed charges.
[10] The lender's IRR on the loan.
[11] These loans are underwritten using the lender's guidelines for single-family loans.

How the Lender Looks at the Loan

There is a sharp line which divides investment property loans. The line is drawn not especially between residential income properties vs. commercial properties, but rather between residential properties of 1–4 units, on the one hand, and residential properties of 5 or more units and commercial properties on the other.

The smaller duplex-triplex–fourplex loans are generally originated by Savings Associations and "thrift" lenders who are limited by law to the amount of their loan portfolio that can be apportioned to commercial loans. Banks, insurance companies and institutional lenders focus on the larger residential and commercial loans. It is not uncommon for a smaller bank or institutional lender to limit its loan portfolio to a few types of properties. They simply may not have legal or administrative staff experienced in the type property for which you are seeking a loan.

When a potential buyer of a home applies for a loan, the lender looks primarily to the ability of the borrower to repay the loan. But when the investor applies for a loan on 5 units or more, or on non-residential property, the lender looks *primarily* to the ability of the property to repay the loan. Since the primary source of repayment for the investor's loan is the property's net income, the lender's focus is on the NOI and all the factors which produce and affect it. A lender's checklist will include:

- the quality, quantity and duration of the leases
- property location
- quality of construction
- age and condition of the major improvements, parking area and support structures
- local economic and market conditions
- supply and demand factors for similar properties
- potential for new competing construction
- desirability[12]
- present and potential uses (utility and adaptability)
- future marketability
- presence or absence of toxic materials and hazardous wastes on, under and around the property
- estoppel certificates (certification of lease terms by tenant)
- location near geological faults or within a potential flood plain

Important Lender Considerations

The quantity, quality and duration of the leases refer to:

1. the amount (quantity) of rent being paid
2. the credit-worthiness (quality) of the entity paying (guarantying) the rent
3. the length (duration) of the lease.

Common sense tells us that a credit-worthy tenant, signed to a well-written lease and committed for many years, will be just as attractive to a lender as to a property owner. Most buyers will pay a premium for

---

[12] Value is a function of Desirability, Utility, Scarcity and Transferability

such an investment and most lenders will lend a little more on such a property, often at their best interest rate.

The key to understanding the myriad requests for data and information which the lender asks of the borrower is exactly this: the lender understands that he might become the owner. Most lenders do not want to become owners via foreclosure, but since foreclosure is a lender's last resort to protect its investment, it typically asks itself:

> *"If I have to market this property because I become its owner, how likely is it that I can retrieve my capital investment in a reasonable time?"*

The lender is interested in all the factors which influence the safety as well as the profitability of the loan. The underwriter of the loan needs this information in order to assign a *risk premium* to his basic loan rate. The more uncomfortable the underwriter becomes with these factors, the higher the risk premium and the higher the total interest rate. The discomfort may become so great that the lender may not be interested in underwriting the loan at any rate.

In a secondary (but not minor) position of importance is the loan applicant: who he is; whether he has a prior business relationship with the lender; whether he *could have* a business relationship with the lender; his ability, as measured by his liquidity, to repay or guarantee the loan; his credit history (does he pay his debts on time); and his prior experience in owning and managing this type property.

Recourse and Non-Recourse Loans

Some lenders, however, will not only require that property be pledged as security for the loan, but also that the borrower make a personal pledge of assets to guarantee repayment. Loans by these credit lenders are known as *recourse loans* because the lender has the option of foreclosing on the mortgage and pursuing the borrower to recover any deficiencies that remain.[13]

Lenders issue non-recourse loans as a competitive marketing tool, but they are really quite uncomfortable with them. Over time, most lenders have made various exceptions to their "non-recourse" loans which enables the lender to pursue a borrower upon the violation of a "carve out" provision. These carve-outs among lenders are sometimes referred to as "bad boy" provisions alluding to actions by borrowers which threaten the security of the lender's loan.

The following list enumerates some of the more common loan bad-boy activities which may prompt a lender's foreclosure action:

- Losses for fraud or intentional misrepresentation
- Losses for committing waste
- Losses for misappropriation of tenant security deposits or rents
- Specific performance of the loan documents
- To enforce any guaranty
- To enforce any indemnity
- To enforce any environmental indemnity
- To enforce any release of liability
- To obtain a receiver

---

[13] Many states, but not all, have laws which prevent the lender from simultaneously pursuing both claims for debt recovery under the "one cause of action" provision in their civil codes.

- ♦ To enforce the assignment of leases and rents
- ♦ Losses regarding required insurance of the collateral
- ♦ Losses from the failure to pay over insurance proceeds
- ♦ Losses from the failure to pay over condemnation awards
- ♦ Voluntary bankruptcy or insolvency
- ♦ Involuntary bankruptcy or insolvency

These carve-outs have become so commonplace that very few truly "non-recourse" loans remain.

Additional Lender Safeguards

In addition to gathering the usual financial information about the tenant and the borrower, the lender will order a formal appraisal of the property to ascertain its Fair Market Value (FMV). As the result of the Dodd-Frank legislation of 2010 appraisals may no longer be done "in house" by a resident appraiser. Appraisals must now be done by licensed appraisers who are independent of, unaffiliated with or otherwise owned, controlled or influenced by the lender.

The lender will also require a preliminary hazardous and toxic waste survey from a licensed inspector, as well as a preliminary report on the condition of the title, and will often visit the site to inspect the condition of the property and its environs. In fact, a prudent lender will do all those things that a prudent buyer ought to do.

Determining the Amount of the Loan

The methods by which lenders determine the amount of some loans on income property are in a state of transition. Loans on 1-4 residential units are still handled by loan originators and certain mortgage banks[14] using the guidelines established by Fannie Mae and Freddie Mac. Fannie and Freddie, "government sponsored entities" (GSEs),[15] do not make loans but they do buy them and the purchasing guidelines which they publish for these loans are the guidelines used by most originators who offer 1-4 unit loans.

Underwriting criteria for small residential units focus heavily on the ability of the owner to repay the loan. Income from property operations remains an important consideration but lenders who originate loans on duplexes, triplexes and fourplexes recognize that income from these units can be highly volatile and the safety of the loan may ultimately rest on the owner's ability to continue the payments.

Originators who make loans on 5 or more residential units as well as other non-residential properties have traditionally focused on the amount of Net Operating Income (NOI) produced. The ability of the borrower to continue debt payments is a strong consideration, but it is not the primary consideration. Let's consider the first of these metrics.

Debt Coverage Ratio (DCR)

The DCR is the ratio of the property's annual Net Operating Income (NOI) to (divided by) the annual payment on the loan. For example, a lender may require a 1.20 DCR for multi-family residential properties of 5 or more units. Therefore the loan he will advance is that amount which can be serviced

---

[14] Banks which do not accept deposits but exist solely to buy loans for resale to others.

[15] Both Fannie and Freddie collapsed and were taken over by the Federal government on Sept. 8, 2008 having lost billions of dollars.

by $\dfrac{NOI}{1.20}$. If the NOI is \$100,000 per year, the annual cost of servicing the debt should not exceed \$83,333.33 (\$100,000 ÷ 1.20).

Just how large a loan this annual cash amount will buy depends upon the negotiated interest rate and on the amortization schedule. If the interest rate is 9% and the schedule is 25 years (payable monthly over 300 months), the <u>amount</u> of the loan (its PV) can easily be determined using Excel© or any financial calculator:

On Excel insert the following formula in any cell then replace the variables with the relevant values:[16]

=PV(rate, nper, PMT, FV, type)   or,

=PV(.09/12,300,**100000**/1.20/12,0,0) = –827,511.26

> Use commas in Excel to separate variables, never to format numbers.

Using a financial Calculator:

n	i	PV	PMT	FV
300	9/12	?	83,333.33/12	0
	Solving →	–827,511.26		

Therefore by one parameter, the DCR, the lender could lend as much as \$827,511, payable \$6,944.44 per month (\$83,333/12/yr.). But the lender will also be guided by the appraisal amount. If his underwriting guidelines restrict him to a loan of not more than 75% of the appraised value, and if the appraised value were delivered at \$1,060,000, the lender would not exceed a loan of \$795,000 (\$1,060,000*75%). Since this loan amount, determined with reference to the appraised value, is less than the amount determined by the DCR (\$827,500, rounded), the lender will offer only the lower amount. The analysis spreadsheet which we will construct in the following chapter is designed to determine the loan amount using three mortgage underwriting criteria - and to choose the lesser amount.

DCRs Vary with Risk

Lenders maintain a range of DCRs in their guidance to a maximum loan amount according to the intended use of the property. The most common DCR range for retail, office and industrial properties falls between 1.20 and 1.30. Multi-family residential properties vary from 1.15 to 1.25, while a specialized property such as a self-storage facility, a bank building or other single-purpose structure,[17] may indicate a DCR of 1.30 – 1.50, or greater.

The percent of the NOI which the lender will permit to be devoted to loan service is the reciprocal of the DCR. Therefore a DCR of 1.40 indicates that the lender will restrict the size of the loan to that which can be serviced by approximately 71% (1/1.40) of the NOI. A DCR of 1.53 corresponds to a leverage of approximately 65%.

---

[16] The "**type**" position enables adjustment for PMTs made at the beginning or end of the period. Insert **1** for beginning of the period and **0** for end of period. Default = 0. Almost all loans call for end of period payments.

[17] Which may be difficult and expensive to adapt to an alternate use

The theoretical maximum leverage an income-producing real property can support depends on the cost of money. In terms of property operations, we can say that the maximum supportable debt occurs when:

$$Net\ Operating\ Income = Cost\ of\ Debt\ Service,\ or$$

$$Value\ x\ Capitalization\ rate = Loan\ Amt.\ x\ Loan\ constant,\ [18]\ or$$

$$\frac{Loan\ Amt.}{Value} = \frac{Capitalization\ Rate}{Loan\ Constant}$$

$$Leverage = \frac{Capitalization\ Rate}{Loan\ Constant}$$

Commercial lenders, however, are quite sensitive to the advantages and disadvantages of leverage and will not permit 100% of the NOI to be used for debt service. They require a safety cushion in the form of the Debt Coverage Ratio. Therefore:

$$Max.\ Loan\ Amt. = \frac{Capitalization\ Rate}{Loan\ Constant\ x\ \textbf{DCR}}$$

For example, a property with a capitalization rate of 10%, employing a loan whose annual constant[19] is 0.1053, with a DCR of 1.25, could be leveraged:

$$Maximum\ Leverage = \frac{0.10}{0.1053*1.25} = 0.76 = 76\%$$

The borrower can arrive at a workable estimate for the potential amount of loan by asking the lender for his DCR for the property type, the current interest rate and the applicable amortization schedule. The lender is not likely to give an exact answer, but a range for these values should be sufficient for a preliminary screen of lenders as well as a preliminary financial screen of the property.

The Debt Yield Ratio

Note that the maximum loan amount is a function of the loan constant, which, in turn, is a function of the interest rate and the amortization schedule. As the interest rate drops, the loan constant declines and the amount of the loan increases. This is what happened in the 2003-2007 period as the Fed lowered interest rates. One would have hoped that the LTV ratio would have put a safety cap on the loan amount, but this did not happen. Appraisers *accommodated* both lenders and buyers by raising the appraised value. By 3Q08 income properties were trading at very high prices and carried large loans. As the market collapsed, interest rates rose and the short-term (3-5 years) loans carried by many properties could not be refinanced.

As a result, many lenders, especially those involved in the CMBS[20] market, have begun to utilize a third lending metric: the **Debt Yield Ratio**, which is unrelated to interest rates.

---

[18] The annualized periodic payment necessary to amortize $1.00 of loan principal over the number of months in the schedule of the loan.

[19] An annual loan constant is the annual amount of PMT necessary to amortize $1.00 of loan at a certain interest rate and amortization schedule. Frequently expressed as Pmt/$1,000. Annual loan constants for loans payable monthly differ from annual constants for loans paid annually.

[20] Collateralized Mortgage Backed Securities involving Conduit lenders.

The DYR is simply the ratio of the NOI to the maximum amount of loan. Contrast these two ratios:

$$\frac{NOI}{\textbf{Annual \textit{Cost} of Loan}} = \textbf{DCR} \qquad \frac{NOI}{\textbf{\textit{Amt.} of Loan}} = \textbf{DYR}$$

In the case of the DCR the ratio delivers the amount of cash that can be used to service debt; in the case of the DYR the ratio delivers the actual amount of the loan. The DYR is not determined by the current interest rate or the amortization schedule. It measures the Net Operating Income in relation to the actual amount of the loan and is, therefore, independent of the appraised value.

For example: consider a property delivering $240,000 in trailing NOI. The lender offers a 6.0% annual interest on a loan amortized and payable over 300 months. Current DCR for this type of property is 1.25, while the lender sets a DYR at 10%.

Amt. of Loan by DCR

$$\text{Annual Debt Service Amt} = \frac{NOI}{DCR} = \frac{\$240,000}{1.25} = \$192,000$$

This amount of annual cash payable monthly would buy a loan in the amount of :

n	i	PV	PMT	FV
300	6/12	?	192,000/12	0
	Solving…	-2,483,310		

Amt. of Loan by DYR

$$\text{Amt. of Loan} = \frac{\$240,000.}{0.10} = \$2,400,000$$

The monthly payment is determined by the monthly loan constant.[21]

Loan amount x monthly loan constant = monthly payment.

$$\$2,400,000 \times 0.006443 = \$15,463.23$$

Expressed in terms of the DCR:

$$DCR = \frac{\$240,000}{\$15,463.23 \times 12} = \textbf{1.29} \text{…}$$

The use of the DYR provides the lender with an index to the riskiness of his loan. If he judges the risk of the loan to be less he can lower the DYR to 9.0% which would provide a higher loan amount. Major lenders continue to use all three metrics to determine the amount of loan: Loan-to-Value (LTV), DCR and DYR.

---

[21] The monthly loan constant is not equal to the annual constant/12. It is that calculated monthly payment which will amortize $1.00 of loan principal over the monthly amortization schedule at a given interest rate.

Borrower Liquidity

In addition to these lending standards, an increasing number of lenders are requiring a certain degree of borrower liquidity. The amount of liquidity is expressed as a percentage of the requested loan amount and can vary from 5% to 50% of the loan amount. This approach places more emphasis on the quality of the of the borrower's balance statement as a potential source of loan repayment.

Types of Loans

There are basically only two types of mortgage loans: those that amortize and those that don't.
As you already know, the term "a morte" means "to the death." Amortizing loans are those whose balances will eventually be "killed off" if the required periodic payments are timely made over the full amortization schedule. Loans whose payments provide for no amortization of the principal are known as *straight notes.* [22]

Fixed-rate amortizing loans involve interest rates which do not change; therefore the payment remains constant over the scheduled life of the loan.

Adjustable-rate amortizing (mortgages) loans (ARMs) are those in which the interest rate is linked to an outside base rate - such as the prime rate or the current LIBOR rate[23], or more commonly, a U.S. Treasury security (Note or Bond) whose maturity is closely matched to the maturity date, not the amortization schedule, of the loan. The payment for this type loan will change from time to time according to the amount necessary to continue to reduce the loan to a zero balance over the original amortization schedule of the loan.

Determining the Payment Using Excel®

In order to determine the payment required to amortize a fixed-rate loan you must first have the interest rate, the amortization schedule and the amount of the loan.

Excel has a loan payment function which is very convenient and simple to use. Enter in any cell the following formula: **=Pmt(rate, nper, PV, FV, type)** where:

    rate   is the interest rate *per period*, expressed as a decimal
    nper   is the number of payment periods in the amortization schedule
    PV   is the principal amount of the loan (entered as a negative number)
    FV   is the remaining balance of the loan at the end of the last scheduled payment
    type   is the timing of the payment: (0) = end of period, (1) = beginning of period.

In the case of a loan which uses a fully amortizing schedule, the FV will always be zero. If the loan has a call date <u>do not</u> enter the call amount in FV. The payment on the loan will generally be determined by its amortization schedule, and not when it becomes all due and payable.

Take care not to use commas in the formula to express large numbers; the computer will interpret the numerals which follow a comma as the next variable in the function. Be sure that if the loan is to be paid monthly, the rate and nper are also expressed as monthly numbers

---

[22]   See Chapter 12 for additional types of notes.
[23]   London Interbank Offered Rate for inter-bank dollar deposits in 5 London-based banks.

For example, the formula for the payment of a $1,250,000 loan, payable on a 25-year fully-amortizing schedule, using monthly payments which include fixed interest at the annual rate of 8.0% would read: = **Pmt(.08/12, 300, –1250000, 0).** If no value is entered for **type**, the computer defaults to zero.

When you press ENTER Excel will return the monthly payment required to amortize the loan: $9,647.70. (Had you used -$1.00 for the loan amount you would have determined the monthly loan constant, 0.007718. Multiplying the loan amount by this factor will deliver the same monthly payment.)

The amount of principal, $1,250,000, is entered in the formula as a negative number in order that the payment will be expressed as a positive number. If the negative sign is omitted, the payment will still be correct but will read out as a negative number.

Generating an Amortization Schedule for a Fixed–Rate Loan

An amortization schedule is simply a numerical record of the progress an amortizing loan makes as it marches toward an ending balance of zero. The schedule typically shows the required payment, the starting and ending balances, together with the interest paid and equity buildup (loan paydown) of the loan per period. These schedules come in handy whenever it is necessary to calculate the interest paid over a number of consecutive payments, or the amount of loan reduction which takes place over an interval of time, or the remaining balance of a loan after a specified number of payments have been made.

For example, you may need to know how much tax-deductible interest you have paid on the loan over the last tax year. Or you may need to know how much principal reduction will occur in a certain mortgage over the next three years. Or you may want to know what the balance of your mortgage will be in five years when you intend to sell the property or refinance the loan. An amortization table will answer these questions.

One important fact about the typical amortizing mortgage is that the interest is paid in arrears. This means that the payment for the use of the money during the month is paid at the end of the month – not in advance at the beginning of the month as is rent under a lease. Therefore a mortgage note commencing March 1 will call for its first payment on April 1.

Let's consider the amortization schedule for the first two months of a loan. Let's also assume that the loan is in the original amount of $1,250,000, payable monthly over 25 years and bearing interest at the rate of 8% per annum. We calculated the required payment on page 5-13.

Period	Beginning Balance	Payment	Interest	Paydown (Equity)	Remaining Balance
A	B	C	D	E	F
1	$1,250,000	9,647.70	8,333.33	1,314.37	1,248,685.63
2	$1,248,685.63	9,647.50	8,324.57	1,323.13	1,247,362.50

Here's how these numbers are determined: the Interest for the first period is equal to $1,250,000 x (.08 ÷ 12.) = $8,333.33. This amount is subtracted from the calculated Payment ($9,647.70) to yield the amount of the Paydown, $1,314.37 (the equity portion of the payment). The paydown is subtracted from the Beginning Balance to yield the Remaining Balance at the end of the first period. Make the Beginning

Balance of the loan for the second period equal to the Remaining Balance at the end of the first period by using an equal sign + cell reference: **B2(=F1).**

After you have completed two rows, simply highlight the entire second row (only) and drag down for the required number of periods. The result will be an amortization schedule showing the interest, paydown and remaining balance for each period formatted.

You may wish to insert a blank row at the end of every 12th year. This will not alter the computations which follow, but it will provide a blank line on which you can sum up the annual interest paid over the preceding 12 months.

Amortizing ARMs

In the case of the adjustable rate mortgage, the lender establishes a spread, or margin, over a base rate, so that regardless of the rise or fall in the base rate he is always guaranteed his margin of gross profit. As the base rate changes, the payment changes in order to keep the loan on its path to a zero balance over the original amortization schedule. Because ARMs transfer future interest rate risk to the borrower, they are typically offered at rates somewhat lower than fixed-payment loans in which the lender bears the entire risk of rising rates.

Construct an amortization schedule for an ARM in exactly the same way as for a fixed-rate loan. In the month in which the interest rate changes enter the corresponding Payment cell and rewrite the formula for the Payment observing these changes:

> **rate** is the new interest rate per period
> **nper** is the *remaining months* in the original schedule
> **PV**   is the Beginning Balance of the loan for the period in which the change is made
> **FV**   is still zero

Fill in the following line manually, and then highlight all cells in the (new) second line and drag down for the next number of periods.

"Fully amortized" commercial loans are not common except on multi-family residential properties where both the amortization schedule and the due date are often the full 30 years. Otherwise, the amortization schedule can vary from 15 years to 20 or 25 years. But most amortizing non-residential loans, though structured and scheduled as though they would continue for 20 or 25 years, are due and payable in 3-15 years. Shorter due dates usually mean lower risk to the lender and therefore lower interest rates.

Hybrid Loans

A hybrid loan is one which combines the characteristics of a fixed-rate loan and an ARM. These loans offer an initial number of years during which the interest rate is fixed; at the end of the fixed-rate period the loan converts to an Adjustable Rate. These loans became very popular around 2003-2007. Lenders offered lower starting fixed rates in exchange for the right to convert the loan to an ARM. In this way the lender hedged against a significant future increase in interest rates. At that time, many borrowers who were attracted to the lower starting rates planned to sell the property before the loan converted to an ARM. These loans offered a degree of safety to the lender but represented a very substantial risk to the borrower.

By 2009 many of the 3 and 5-year maturity loans issued in 2003 and after began to convert to ARMs. Unfortunately by that time the recession of 2008-2009 and the "subprime" crisis were in full bloom and lenders became very reluctant to refinance many of these loans. Debt coverage Ratios advanced from 1.20 to 1.30 /1.35 and LTV ratios declined from 80% to 60%, and less. At the same time, vacancies in properties, especially in office and retail properties, advanced well above 12% in many markets. The lower net operating income of these properties proved insufficient to fund a replacement loan and foreclosures ensued.

The table which follows illustrates loan terms in 2Q09 from a major FHA wholesale lender for multi-family loans :

Program	Start Rate	Points	Index	Margin	Floor	Amort.	Maturity	Prepay	Caps
3 Yr. Fixed	6.25	0.500	1Yr.T-Bill	2.875%	Start Rate	30-Yr.	30-Yr.	3-2-1	2% Period, 6% Life
3 Yr. Fixed	6.50	0.000	1Yr.T-Bill	2.875%	Start Rate	30-Yr.	30-Yr.	3-2-2	2% Period, 6% Life
5 Yr. Fixed	7.25	0.500	1Yr.T-Bill	2.875%	Start Rate	30-Yr.	30-Yr.	3-2-3	2% Period, 6% Life
5 Yr. Fixed	7.50	0.000	1Yr.T-Bill	2.875%	Start Rate	30-Yr.	30-Yr.	3-2-4	2% Period, 6% Life
15 Yr. Fixed	7.50	0.500	N/A	N/A	N/A	15 Yr.	15 Yr.	5-4-3-2-1	N/A
15 Yr. Fixed	8.99	0.000	N/A	N/A	N/A	15 Yr.	15 Yr.	5-4-3-2-1	N/A

These loans were made available at a maximum 60% LTV ratio and required a 1.30 DCR. In addition, loans which offered a 3-5 year fixed rate provided for "lifetime" caps on the ARM interest rate equal to the start rate plus 6%. In most cases, these conversion rates can reach the 12% -13% range, levels almost certain to doom many commercial properties.

Caveat

Borrowers contemplating the use of a hybrid loan should bear in mind the likelihood of a significant increase in market rates due to inflation. The Federal Reserve Bank in 2009 began a series of "quantitative easings" which is a euphemism for the inflation of the currency. The extraordinary amount of new dollars placed into circulation using "quantitative easing" and under various stimulus plans will eventually surface in the form of a debased dollar and severe monetary inflation. In the history of every fiat[24] currency, the debasement of the currency has <u>always</u> been followed by marked inflation.

The picture at the left shows a fraulein burning German Reichmarks for fuel during the post-WWI period when Germany was struggling with the inflation of the Weimar regime and war reparations. The currency had been so badly debased by the Weimar government that it was cheaper to burn the paper money than to use it to buy firewood for the stove.

All fiat currencies eventually collapse.

---

24   Paper money not backed by any tangible asset.

Value of an Amortizing Loan

The significance of an amortizing loan for the investor is twofold:

1. Each payment contains an equity portion which will be used to reduce the balance of the loan. If the investor's strategy is maximum wealth accumulation over the distance run, this increase in cash lying fallow in the property reduces the rate at which he is building wealth (the efficiency of the investment). This subject is discussed later in this chapter, but as you can see from the graph that follows, this equity build-up becomes pronounced in the latter half of the amortization schedule. Many investors do not monitor their Return on Equity (ROE) and therefore own properties whose ROE has quietly slipped below acceptable return rates. If, on the other hand, the investor's strategy is no longer wealth accumulation but rather preservation of capital and a steady income, this equity buildup reduces risk.

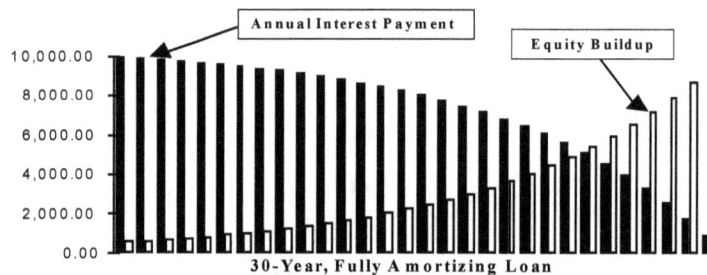

2. The payment on both fixed-rate and adjustable-rate loans which have been in place for a number of years begins to contribute a higher and higher percentage of the total payment to equity. Therefore assuming a maturing loan is equivalent to depositing more and more cash (in the form of paid-in equity) in the owner's bank and less in the lender's bank.

The counterpoint to assuming such a loan is that as the balance of the loan decreases, the owner's equity increases and a larger down payment is required. This problem may sometimes be solved by using secondary financing, though secondary financing is more expensive and may offset the financial benefits of assuming a lower rate loan.

Yield-Maintenance, Defeasance and Lock-in Clauses

A very large percentage of commercial loans over the past 20 years have been sold to REMICs, Real Estate Mortgage Investment Conduits. REMICs are special U.S. tax vehicles for collateralized mortgage-backed securities (CMBS) – the capital market innovation developed in 1983 to redistribute the prepayment and interest rate risks associated with Mortgage-Backed Securities among investors with specifically defined investment needs.

Once a primary loan originator conveys its loan to a REMIC, a pre-payment of the loan by the original borrower removes the source of interest and principal payments for the issued bonds. Therefore these loans contain *lock-in* clauses which prohibit pre-payment within the first two years measured from the date it is conveyed to the REMIC (but not more than three years from the origination date of the mortgage note). After that time, the loan may be pre-paid but the REMIC is required to substitute other qualified mortgages or bonds to securitize and fund those it has issued.

If the interest rate for the bonds to be substituted is less than the interest rate payable on the mortgage, the lender will require from the borrower either a cash penalty sufficient to make up the difference or will require the conveyance to the REMIC Treasury bonds whose principal and interest payments will cover the REMICs obligation on the issued bonds.

Yield Maintenance Clause

A cash penalty may be provided by a *yield-maintenance* clause. For example, a lender may insert a clause in its promissory note which requires the borrower to pay a single lump sum which, when invested at the then-current Treasury yield, will deliver the same monthly payments necessary to reduce the current balance of the note to the balance which was anticipated on the defined maturity date (e.g.10 years).

Calculating the Yield Maintenance Penalty

Consider a $4,560,000 note containing a yield maintenance clause. The note is payable monthly including interest at the annual rate of 7.63%, amortized over 30 years but all due and payable in 10 years. The required monthly payment is:

n	i	PV	PMT	FV
360	7.63/12	-4,560,000	?	0
		Solving⟶	32,291.08	

The balance of the original note at the end of 120 months (maturity) will be:

n	i	PV	PMT	FV
120	7.63/12	-4,560,000	32,291.08	?
			Solving...	**3,969,104.46**

If the borrower seeks to pre-pay the loan at the end of its 3rd year (36 mos.), the REMIC must invest a sum which, over the remaining 84 months to term, will deliver monthly payments of $32,291.08 and a final 7-year reversion amount of $3,969,104.46 when invested at the current Treasury rate (say, 5%) for securities of comparable maturity. That sum can be calculated:

n	i	PV	PMT	FV
84	5/12	?	32,291.08	3,969,104.46
	Solving...	-5,083,668.41		

But at the end of only 36 months, the balance of the original note will be:

n	i	PV	PMT	FV
36	7.63/12	-4,560,000	32,291.08	?
			Solving...	4,427,094.08

Therefore the borrower must pay a total of $5,083,668.41 against an expected balance of $4,427,094.08, or a penalty equal to the difference, $656,574.33.

Be especially cautious in contracting for a loan whose promissory note contains a yield maintenance clause when interest rates on federal securities are anticipated to decline.[25] Consider the previous example but under conditions in which the 7-year Treasury is not 5.0% but 2.0% (circa 2015):

n	i	PV	PMT	FV
84	2/12	?	32,291.08	3,969,104.46
	Solving…	**–5,980,150.99**		

In this case the borrower must pay a total of 5,980,150.99 against an expected balance of $4,427,094.08, or a penalty equal to the difference, $1,553,056.91. If neither the seller nor the buyer is willing to pay this penalty the property become virtually unmarketable.

Defeasance Clauses

If the mortgage note contains a *defeasance* clause, the borrower must buy and convey to the REMIC a sufficient dollar value of Treasury bonds such that the interest and payments from these instruments will timely cover the interest and principal payments from the mortgage to be pre-paid.

It is considerably more complex to determine the exact cost of a defeasance pre-payment amount since the amount necessary to fund the penalty is determined by the cost of acquiring a bond ladder[26] to provide the corresponding annual payments. The cost will depend upon the spread between current Treasury securities of similar maturity and the interest rate of the mortgage. The higher the mortgage interest rate over the T-bond rate, the greater the cost. Although defeasance calculators are available on the Web, they should be used with great caution since yields on bonds vary daily. It is far better to consult one of the established firms specializing in arranging a defeasance payoff.

If the yield on T-bonds rises above the mortgage's interest rate, however, there may be no defeasance penalty[27] and the lender will generally accept a cash settlement to retire the loan.

Why Borrow From a Conduit Lender?

Conduit lenders may offer the investor a small reduction in interest rates and perhaps a lower DCR thereby providing a larger loan amount in comparison to a non-conduit lender. But the borrower must be alert to the potential problem of a large pre-payment penalty in the event interest rates decline.

If a sale or exchange is contemplated any penalty due needs to be paid either by the seller or the buyer. In either case, large penalty payments undercut net sales proceeds or can contribute to the difficulty of finding a ready buyer willing to assume the existing loan, especially when the remaining balance is low and the mortgage note prohibits a second mortgage on the property. These penalties may become so severe that the property becomes virtually unmarketable at its fair market value.

---

[25] A difficult call since long-term interest rates have become more under the control of the Federal Reserve rather than the market.

[26] A series of bonds arranged according to date of maturity.

[27] Most CMBS loans carry a pre-payment penalty even when the current Treasury rates are above mortgage rates.

Mezzanine Loans

To an architect, a mezzanine floor in a building is a low story placed between an upper story and a lower story. To a commercial lender, a mezzanine loan is a loan which occupies the position between a primary mortgage and the owner's equity in the property.

Conduit lenders have always been uncomfortable about second financing placed on a property on which they hold the primary (senior) mortgage. When those on Wall Street who securitize mortgages began to downgrade properties with secondary financing, conduit lenders responded by prohibiting the placement of junior mortgages on their properties.

During periods of low interest rates – and therefore low capitalization rates – a certain NOI will indicate a market price much higher than would be indicated when interest rates return to higher levels. Under these conditions commercial lenders anticipate higher rates and, as a defensive step, lower the Loan-to-Value ratio which they use in determining their maximum loan amount.

During these times, lenders who once were comfortable with LTVs of 75% lower their maximum loan limits to 55-65% of appraised value. As a result, investors are required to invest 35-45% of the acquisition price in the form of equity. This increased equity requirement results in two negative consequences for some investors:

 ♦ higher down payments result in lower yields (ROEs and IRRs)
 ♦ higher down payments consume available cash limiting the ability to invest in additional properties.

For investors seeking to increase their leverage, a mezzanine loan acts to improve overall LTV, raising it from, say, 65% to as high as 75-90%. Mezzanine loan lenders often bypass the prohibition against secondary financing secured by the real property by making loans secured by the borrower's <u>ownership interest</u>[28] in the property. Since the owner's interest is an article of personal property (not real property) such a loan technically bypasses the prohibition of secondary financing secured by the real property.[29]

Mezzanine loans are an alternative to selling an equity position to a provider of new capital. Although mezzanine loans are more costly and more complex than typical secondary financing, they allow the owner to maintain an undiluted s equity position in the property and to retain all future profits. But because they are significantly more costly, mezzanine loans generally have short durations, perhaps 2-5 years.

The All-Inclusive – or Wraparound – Mortgage

The All-Inclusive Deed of Trust Mortgage (AITD), or "Wraparound Mortgage" as it is sometimes called, is a junior lien whose principal (PV) includes (or "wraps around") the principal of one or more senior notes.

The payments of an AITD also include the amount of the payment or payments necessary to service the senior obligations. An AITD can wrap around one, some, or all previous notes, including other AITDs,

---

[28] Usually in the form of an SPE, Special Purpose Entity.
[29] Many conduit lenders now include loan clauses which prohibit mezzanine loans secured by the owner's interest.

secured by the property. An AITD should never be structured to "wrap" notes which are recorded in a position junior to its own.

The principal use of the AITD is to preserve the economic benefit of one or more favorable senior mortgages, most frequently for the benefit of the seller. Although AITDs can also be of value to the borrower, they are not commonly structured primarily for the buyer's benefit.

How AITDs Come About

When a property is sold with an existing mortgage in place, the mortgage may either be "assumed" by the buyer or the property may be transferred to the buyer "subject to" the existing mortgage. Although these terms are sometimes carelessly interchanged, they ought not to be, because there is a difference between the two. This difference has major legal and financial implications for both seller and buyer, but especially for the buyer. (See below)

Consider a property offered for sale for $4,000,000: The title is encumbered by a first trust deed (mortgage) lien securing a promissory note whose current balance is $1,290,628. This original note bears interest at the attractive rate of 6% per annum, payable $14,328.62 per month. This loan will reach a zero balance exactly ten years from now.

Let's further assume that the seller of this property desires to carry-back the financing, enabling him to report his transaction as an installment sale. He requires a qualified buyer who is able to make an $800,000 down payment. Assume that Mortgages for a property such as this one now carry an 11% interest rate.

There are four ways in which the transaction might be structured for sale:
1. The buyer, with $800,000 in hand, could find a new mortgage for $3,200,000 and refuse the seller's carry-back offer. If the seller acquiesced, the buyer would pay the current 11% interest rate, plus the points and fees on a new mortgage. Mortgages on residential property (1-4 units) may not contain clauses which prevent a pre-payment of the loan.[30] This is not the case, however, with mortgages secured by residential properties greater than 4 units or by non-residential (commercial) properties.
2. The property could be sold "subject to" the balance of the existing mortgage, $1,290,628. The seller would carry-back the difference as a second trust deed note in the amount of $2,709,372.
3. The buyer could "assume" the existing mortgage and the seller would carry back the difference as a second trust deed note in the amount of $2,709,372.
4. The seller could accept the buyer's down payment and carry back an All-Inclusive (second) Deed of Trust (mortgage) in the amount of $3,200,000.

---

[30] Pre-payment penalties, however, are not illegal.

Let's compare these capital structures:

	#1 New Mortgage	#2 Subject to 1st TD	#3 Assume 1st TD	#4 AITD
Sales Price	$4,000,000	$4,000,000	$4,000,000	$4,000,000
Buyer's Equity	800,000	800,000	800,000	800,000
New Mortgage	3,200,000	-	-	-
Existing Loan	-	1,290,628	1,290,628	-
New 2nd TD	-	1,909,372	1,909,372	-
New AITD	-	-	-	3,200,000
Total Sales Price	$4,000,000	$4,000,000	$4,000,000	$4,000,000

As you can see, each arrangement results in the same equity position for the buyer and totals to the same sales price. There are important differences, however.

The New Mortgage option requires the buyer to apply for and secure a new $3,200,000 mortgage. At closing, the existing first trust deed will be expunged and the new first trust deed will be recorded against the title. The seller will have no further interest in the property.

If the property is taken "subject to" (#2) the existing mortgage, title will transfer without any contact with the present lender. The buyer takes full advantage of the low 6% interest rate and the fact that the loan has been paid down for a number of years. As a result, a greater portion of the buyer's future payments will be devoted to reducing the loan balance. The buyer will enter into a contract with the seller to make the payments on the existing loan on behalf of the seller. The seller will remain liable for the original loan.
In the event of a default by the buyer, the lender will foreclose against the seller, since it may be unaware of any transfer of title. The seller's second trust deed position may be wiped out unless he is willing to "step up" and cure the default on the first trust deed mortgage and then foreclose under the second which he holds.

Under the third option, a formal "assumption," (#3) the buyer is contractually obligated to present himself to the existing lender and seek to be placed in the legal shoes of the seller. If the lender approves the assumption of the loan, the seller *may* be relieved of all liability for the loan. Nevertheless, in the event of a default by the buyer on the first trust deed loan, the seller's second trust deed loan is still in jeopardy and must be defended, as above.

Under the AITD arrangement, the buyer signs a promissory note for an amount equal to the sales price less his down payment. This amount includes the amount due on the first trust deed note. The buyer pays the seller on the AITD loan at the interest rate specified in the AITD note. The seller (or fiduciary) removes from the buyer's monthly payment an amount necessary to service the underlying first trust deed note, sends this amount to the holder of the first trust deed note, and pockets the difference.

At close of escrow two trust deeds encumber the property: a first trust deed securing a note whose balance is approximately $$1,290,628 and a junior second deed of trust in the amount of $3,200,000. This second trust deed, however, legally must specify that it is an AITD and also stipulate the particulars regarding the underlying note or notes which it "wraps around." These stipulations put any person interested in the property on notice that the property is encumbered by an AITD and not by a conventional second mortgage.

For the purposes of the example, let's assume the seller offers a 10% interest rate to the buyer. This loan will be scheduled for 20 years, but all due and payable in 10 years.

Seller's Position	Principal	Mo. Payment	Seller's Account Annually
AITD Face Value	$3,200,000	$30,881	$370,572 Received
1st TD Loan Bal.	1,290,628	14,329	179,480 Paid Out
Net Position	1,909,372	16,552.	198,624 Retained

The seller appears to have lent $3,200,000, but $1,290,628 of this amount is the bank's funds in the form of the balance on the existing mortgage. His equity in the AITD loan is the difference, $1,909,372, the same equity he would have had in a note if either the "subject to" or "assume" options had been used to structure this sale.

But the seller, using an AITD, is earning $198,624 on a net equity of $1,909,628, indicating a true annual interest rate of approximately 10.4%.

This method of estimating the yield on an AITD is convenient and simple – but not entirely accurate because it ignores the actual paydown amount on both loans and the fact that the senior note now has a larger portion of its payment devoted to equity buildup which accrues to the benefit of the seller.

Calculating the Yield on an AITD Accurately

First, determine the payment amount (PMT) and then the remaining balance (FV) for the AITD note after ten years. We will do this in two steps: first calculating the PMT due under the note, and then the remaining balance, the FV, after 120 PMTs have been made.

n	i	PV	PMT	FV
240	10/12	-3,200,000	?	0
		Solving... ➤ 30,880.69		

Now we can determine the remaining balance after 120 PMTs (ten years) have been made. Do this by "writing over" the value in the **n** register. Then solve for FV:

n	i	PV	PMT	FV
120	10/12	-3,200,000	30,880.69	?
			Solving ➤ **2,336,778**	

Underlying First Trust Deed

We do not know the original amount of the underlying senior note, but we don't need to. We do know that its Present Value (current balance) is now $1,290,628, the loan PMT is $14,328.62 per month, and the interest rate, **i**, is 6% per annum. We need to know, however, what the remaining balance of this note will be in ten years (120 months). The calculator keystrokes to accomplish this are:

n	i	PV	PMT	FV
120	6/12	-1,290,628	14,328.62	?
			Solving...	$0.00

You can see that the seller has structured this note so that it will be completely retired at the end of 10 years. He has also inserted a balloon payment in the AITD note to coincide with this payoff date.

Constructing a table will help us visualize the AITD cashflows. Note that the payments and the interest rate on the senior note are specified, not calculated.

The rightmost column is the result of subtracting the cashflows in the middle column from the AITD cashflows on the left. The seller's net investment position is on the right. He invested $1,909,628, received payments of $198,624 each year for nine years and in the tenth year the same annual payment plus the remaining balance of $2,336,778 on the AITD note. Meanwhile the entire balance of the underlying 1st TD mortgage has been reduced to zero.

	AITD Note	Underlying 1st TD	Seller's Net Position
Year	<3,200,00>	<1,2909,628>	<1,909,628>
S1	370,572	171,948	198,624
2	370,572	171,948	198,624
3	370,572	171,948	198,624
4	370,572	171,948	198,624
5	370,572	171,948	198,624
6	370,572	171,948	198,624
7	370,572	171,948	198,624
8	370,572	171,948	198,624
9	370,572	171,948	198,624
10	370,572 + 2,336,778	171,948 + $0	198,624+ 2,336,778

His annual yield on this investment is easily calculated:

n	i	PV	PMT	FV
10	?	-1,909,628	198,624	2,336,778
Solving→	11.7			

Note that the FV of the Net Position column is greater than the PV of the same T-Bar. It says that, in addition to the payments received by the seller over a ten-year period of time, he will receive a loan payoff greater than the amount he originally lent. The difference is accounted for by the extra cash earned by the seller in the form of a faster equity buildup in the underlying senior loan. Since the seller remained responsible for the underlying first trust deed loan, he benefited from its reduced balance, although the buyer's cash funded all the payments.

AITDs can be very profitable investments for the holder. But notice too, that the Buyer of the property benefits by obtaining a 10% loan from the seller at a time when the market rate is 11%. The "loser" in this transaction is the lender on the first trust deed mortgage since his loan is continued at a very low interest rate (6%) at a time when market rates are much higher. You can readily appreciate why lenders are usually resolute in calling in below-market rate loans "due and payable" upon the transfer of the securing property.

Always Escrow AITD Payments

There have been a number of instances in which a seller accepts a down payment from the buyer and carries the balance of the purchase price in the form of an AITD, but then never makes the payments on the senior loans. Therefore no AITD payments should ever be made directly to the seller-holder of the AITD note. These payments should be made through an escrow account, or, preferably, the AITD note should be collected by a bank,[31] title company, or other reputable financial institution which will extract from the AITD payment the amounts necessary to service all the underlying loans. The remaining balance, less a small servicing fee, may then be forwarded to the AITD note holder.

What About the Deed?

In every discussion of AITDs someone always asks: "What About the Deed?!!" "When do I get my deed?!!"

The buyer receives a deed to the property at the close of the purchase escrow in exactly the same way he would had he bought all-cash or financed the acquisition with a new, conventional bank loan.

> There is no rational reason why any buyer should ever arrange to acquire property using a Land Contract, and no rational reason why a seller should arrange to sell property using a Land Contract. It is an archaism fraught with problems and difficulties for both parties.

Confusion about this probably arises from transactions in which a buyer enters into a *Contract for Deed*, sometimes called a *Land Contract*. Under this arrangement, the buyer (vendee) does not receive legal title to the property until he has made a specified number of payments to the seller (vendor). During this time, the vendor retains legal title, conferring only "possessory and use" rights to the vendee. These contracts call for the vendee to obtain a loan at some time in the future and to pay off the balance of the Contract held by the vendor. Only at that time does the vendee receive legal title to the property.

AITDs are not Land Contracts. They are a kind of Trust Deed (or mortgage). The buyer receives title to the property at the same time he would have had the financial structure not involved an All-Inclusive Note: It is legally impossible to execute a trust deed or mortgage to be recorded against property you do not own.

---

[31] Sometimes called a "lockbox" account

CAVEAT

There are times when the use of an AITD can be very beneficial to both buyer and seller in a real estate transaction. Today, however, the presence of due-on-sale clauses in almost all institutional loans has greatly reduced the opportunity to use AITDs in the capital structure. Even when there is no acceleration clause or due-on-sale clause in a senior note, the use of an AITD is not a simple financing exercise. It is strongly recommended that both buyer and seller consult an experienced real estate attorney familiar with the many pitfalls that await the unwary in the use of AITDs today.

The Actual/360 Amortizing Mortgage

Since the days of Noah's ark, a banker's month has consisted of 30 days, and a banker's year has consisted of 360 days. Interest charged in any month was $1/12^{th}$ the annual interest calculated on the balance at the beginning of the period, regardless of the number of days in any month.

Now that commercial loans are being packaged by 'conduit' lenders and used as collateral for bonds sold on Wall Street, the traditional 30-day month is going the way of the dodo. The Actual/360 loan – or as it is sometimes called, the 365/360 loan – has emerged as a means of squeezing a bit more interest from the borrower. This type loan is now used by most conduit lenders.

For the purposes of illustration only, the amortization period for a $1,000,000 loan (which follows) is compressed to one year. The loan is payable monthly including interest at the nominal rate of 10% per year. The note is dated January 1, but the first payment – as is customary – is not due until February 1.

The payment is calculated as it would be for a conventional loan and remains fixed for the term of the loan. The interest for the first period is calculated by multiplying the beginning balance ($1,000,000) times the annual interest rate (10%) and dividing this amount by 360. This produces the daily interest amount based on 360 days per year. The interest for the preceding month[32] is determined by multiplying the daily interest amount by the actual number of days in the month. The equity is the difference between the fixed monthly payment and the interest so determined.

This foreshortened example loan shows that the loan does not fully amortize over the original schedule (12 periods) because the payment was calculated in the conventional way while the interest was calculated using the 365/360 method. As a result, there is a balance at the end of the amortization schedule. This difference, $568.91 in one year, seems small but if this loan were set to amortize over 20 years (in the table which follows) the difference in extra interest would amount to $74,293.05, and this difference would be the balance remaining when, ordinarily, there would be none.

---

[32] Mortgages are Ordinary annuities which make payments at the end of the period.

Pmt #	Month	Days	Begin	PMT Amt.	Interest	Equity	Remain Bal.
	1-Jan	31					
1	1-Feb	**28**	1,000,000.00	87,915.89	8,611.11	79,304.78	920,695.22
2	1-Mar	31	920,695.22	87,915.89	7,160.96	80,754.92	839,940.30
3	1-Apr	30	839,940.30	87,915.89	7,232.82	80,683.07	759,257.23
4	1-May	31	759,257.23	87,915.89	6,327.14	81,588.74	677,668.49
5	1-Jun	30	677,668.49	87,915.89	5,835.48	82,080.41	595,588.08
6	1-Jul	31	595,588.08	87,915.89	4,963.23	82,952.65	512,635.43
7	1-Aug	31	512,635.43	87,915.89	4,414.36	83,501.53	429,133.90
8	1-Sep	30	429,133.90	87,915.89	3,695.32	84,220.57	344,913.33
9	1-Oct	31	344,913.33	87,915.89	2,874.28	85,041.61	259,871.72
10	1-Nov	30	259,871.72	87,915.89	2,237.78	85,678.10	174,193.62
11	1-Dec	31	174,193.62	87,915.89	1,451.61	86,464.27	87,729.35
12	1-Jan	31	87,729.35	87,915.89	755.45	87,160.44	**568.91**

Balance of 365/360 Loan at Maturity, 20 Years

	A	B	C	D	E	F	G	H
255	236	1-Sep	30	$118,259.20	$9,650.22	$1,018.34	$8,631.87	$109,627.32
256	237	1-Oct	31	$109,627.32	$9,650.22	$ 913.56	$8,736.66	$100,890.67
257	238	1-Nov	30	$100,890.67	$9,650.22	$ 868.78	$8,781.44	$92,109.23
258	239	1-Dec	31	$92,109.23	$9,650.22	$ 767.58	$8,882.64	$83,226.59
259	240	1-Jan	32	$83,226.59	$9,650.22	$ 716.67	$8,933.54	$74,293.05

These loans are becoming much more commonplace even among lenders who do not collateralize their loans or sell them to Wall Street. Lenders relish the idea of collecting more interest and like the notion that, if circumstances should arise, they have the option of selling these loans in the secondary market for a better return.

The lender's yield on the example 20-year loan is not the nominal 10%, but 10.14% before points and fees. These 14 extra basis points[33] on a Wall Street CMBS portfolio of $10 billion[34] amounts to $7,000,000 in extra interest, an amount the late Sen. Everett Dirksen was wont to call *serious money*.

Assuming a Loan vs. Taking "Subject To"

We have made a number of references to *assuming* an existing loan and taking a property *subject to* an existing loan. The difference is very important to the investor since there is a vital legal difference between the two.

In assuming a loan, the buyer of the property presents himself to the lender and applies for the formal transfer of the loan from the seller to the buyer. If approved, the buyer stands in the legal shoes of the original debtor. The approval of the new buyer is typically conditioned upon an assumption fee, an adjustment of the interest rate and a credit check.

---

[33] One basis point = one-one hundredth of 1%, i.e. 100 basis points = 1.0%

[34] CMBS issuance peaked in 2007 at $228 billion.

Assumption of the loan by the buyer, however, does not necessarily mean that the seller is automatically relieved of the responsibility for the loan. Lenders frequently attempt to keep the seller "secondarily liable" for the loan so that, in the event of a foreclosure, the seller may become additionally liable for any deficiency in the proceeds from a foreclosure sale. Sellers whose loans are assumed should stipulate that the lender absolves the seller from all future responsibility for the loan.

Taking a property "subject to" an existing loan means that the buyer never approaches the lender for permission to become the payor of the existing mortgage note. The obligation to make these payments is a contractual arrangement between buyer and seller, not between buyer and lender.

This situation often arises because the buyer wants to capture a favorable existing interest rate and also wants to avoid qualifying for an assumption. In this case the seller remains legally liable for the loan. In the event of a default by the buyer, the lender will foreclose against the seller (former owner). Lenders generally learn of an unauthorized transfer of title via the insurance company's cancellation of the seller's insurance policy.

The existence of a Due-on-Sale clause in a note effectively prevents the use of an All-Inclusive Trust Deed (wraparound) mortgage in which the seller alienates himself from his property . There are those who offer (for a fee) to circumvent this clause by transferring the property to a trust controlled by the seller, then re-designating the buyer as the new beneficiary of the trust. But most due-on-sale clauses will provide an option for the lender to accelerate the loan payments upon a transfer of title or beneficial interest in a trust. If the transfer is designed only to evade the clause, you can be sure the lender will exercise its option.

How to Calculate the APR on the Loan

Lenders on 1-4 unit residential properties are required under Regulation Z of the Truth in Lending Act to furnish the borrower with a good faith estimate of all loan costs and to calculate the Annual Percentage Rate (APR), sometimes referred to as the Annual Percentage Yield (APY).
This disclosure is not required, however, on loans for 5 or more residential units, nor for any type of commercial property.
But the APR is a valuable tool for the real estate investor to determine the true cost of a loan when all the loan charges, including interest rates, points, origination fees, processing fees and so-called "junk fees" are included in the lender's charges. The APR is really the lender's internal rate of return (IRR) on its loan, and —conversely - the true interest rate that the borrower is paying for the loan.

Example: Consider a fixed-rate commercial loan in the amount of $2,000,000, bearing interest at the annual rate of 6.0%, payable monthly, on an amortization schedule of 25 years, but all due and payable in 10 years. The lender requires a 1.0% origination fee and other miscellaneous loan charges totaling $4,500. These charges may include an appraisal fee, document fee, escrow fee, title fees, legal fees, processing fees, etc, etc, etc, ...

Using a financial calculator, the first step is to determine the required monthly payment on the loan:

n	i	PV	PMT	FV
300	6/12	-2,000,000	?	0
		Solving…	12,886.03	

Next, determine the remaining balance of the loan at term, in this case 10 years. Do this by placing 120 (months) in the **n** register. Solve for FV.

n	i	PV	PMT	FV
120	6/12	-2,000,000	12,886.03	?
				1,527,039.61

Now, total the cost of the points and fees. In this example the total will be $20,000 (1% of $2,000,000) *plus* other fees totaling $4,500, for a grand total of $24,500. Subtract this total from the loan amount to yield $1,975,500. Re-enter this number in the PV register as a negative number. Do not alter any other registers. Re-solve for **i**.

n	i	PV	PMT	FV
120	?	-1,975,500	12,886.03	1,527,039.61
	0.5151			

Since this loan compounds monthly determine the annual interest cost by investing $1.00 in an account which compounds the monthly rate 12 times per year. Solve for FV.

n	i	PV	PMT	FV
12	0.5151	-1.00	0	?
				1.0636

The true interest rate (APR) on this loan = 1.0636 – 1 x 100 = 6.36%.

Using the APR a borrower can compare a number of loan offerings with different points and other fees to determine the loan with the lowest cost. It almost goes without saying that the loan with the lowest cost may not necessarily be the best choice when other loan conditions (e.g. pre-payment penalties, carve-outs, etc.) are considered.

Other Loan Clauses to Study

If you invest in a state which uses the Mortgage system, a careful reading of the Mortgage document will include both the promissory note and the securitizing Mortgage since they are usually contained in the same document. But if you invest in an area which uses Trust Deeds to secure the promissory note, or in those cases in which the note and security agreement are drawn separately, you will need to read both documents. Be especially careful to read the fine print (boilerplate) in the security agreement (mortgage or trust deed) since this is where the lender spells out the conditions under which you may be deemed in default even though you may continue to make timely payments on the note.

Pay particular attention to these clauses:

ACCELERATION CLAUSE: This clause permits the lender to call, or accelerate, all the unpaid loan payments and accrued interest due and payable upon the happening of one or more events. The most frequent circumstance is the transfer of the property to a new owner without the lender's agreement. But there are other grounds for acceleration which you will find in the boilerplate of the securitizing document: failure to pay property taxes, failure to maintain adequate insurance, failure to properly maintain the property, permitting unlawful uses, committing waste upon the property, violation of zoning laws, etc.

DUE-ON-SALE CLAUSE. This clause is a specific kind of acceleration clause which allows the lender to call all the remaining payments due under the note immediately payable upon the transfer of ownership, or a beneficial interest in the property, to a new owner. This type clause is not operative in the case of a transfer to an heir upon the death of the debtor, but in most other cases it is. A due-on-sale clause, if present, is a major impediment to your acquiring a property "subject to an existing loan" (see below).

ASSUMPTION CLAUSE: This clause will describe the circumstances under which a new owner may assume the existing loan. This clause will describe some of the terms, if any, under which a prospective new owner may apply to take over the legal responsibility for the payments due under the note. This clause, together with the due-on-sale clause, is intended to prevent the transfer of a very favorable mortgage without conforming to the lender's current requirements. These requirements include the transferee's credit worthiness. The lender usually charges an assumption fee and may reserve the right to adjust the interest rate. A 1% loan fee applicable to either the original or remaining balance of the loan is a typical assumption fee. In effect, the new owner must apply for and be approved for a new loan in the amount of the balance on the existing loan. These fees are often negotiable.

PRE-PAYMENT AND LOCK-IN CLAUSES: (COVERED ABOVE, BUT BEARS REPEATING) Pre-payment clauses in commercial loan documents are very common. If loan documents forbid the pre-payment of the loan under any circumstances, these clauses are known as *lock-in* clauses. They are frequently found in loans issued by insurance companies and loans which are later packaged and sold as collateral for a security (bond). While lock-in clauses are illegal in residential home loans, they are not illegal in commercial loans or in loans on residential properties greater than 4 units.

Sometimes pre-payment clauses specify a declining percentage of the loan (e.g. 4%, 3%, 2%, 1%) as a penalty depending on the number of years to term. In other cases, the pre-payment amount will be a function of the amount necessary to maintain a certain yield to the lender. This type clause is known as a *yield-maintenance* clause and is often used by lenders who need to match the income from their loan to the interest under a contract issued to a depositor (e.g. pension or retirement fund).

SUBORDINATION CLAUSE: This type clause moves the security instrument for a loan from a senior position to a more junior position. They are found frequently in loan documents involving vacant land intended for later development.

For example, a seller of developable vacant land may carry back a substantial portion of the price in the form of a promissory note secured by a first trust deed or first mortgage on the property.. Lenders who make construction loans will rarely, if ever, agree to a trust deed loan or mortgage junior to a pre-existing (senior) security. A subordination clause inserted into the note of the seller of the property requires the seller to allow the construction loan to be recorded as a senior mortgage ahead of the seller's mortgage. Construction loans are risky loans and any mortgage subordinate to a construction loan is even riskier. It should be a hard and fast rule never to agree to a subordination clause in a carry-back note without the advice and help of an experienced real estate attorney. If a subordination clause is to be included in a promissory note, or its security instrument, there should always be a limit placed on the amount to be borrowed and on the interest rate of the senior debt. Without such a limit the protective equity which the seller enjoys in his carry-back note may be reduced to zero.

SUBROGATION CLAUSE: The right of a mortgage insurance company to file a suit to recover from the borrower sums it must pay out to a lender as a result of the borrower's default on a loan. This type clause may also require the borrower to allow the lender to pursue the insurance company in seeking full compensation for a loss payable to the borrower. The primary intent is to prevent the borrower from profiting from a default.

CARVE OUTS: Exceptions to non-recourse loans are very prevalent and can render a non-recourse loan the equivalent of a recourse Loan. Request an advanced copy of the promissory note and security instrument and have them reviewed by a competent real estate attorney. Many carve outs are negotiable.

In Conclusion...

Placing a loan on your investment property is a major ownership event. The consequences of the choice of loan are not limited to rate, points and term, but extend to important clauses which may affect the financial safety and future marketability of your property. Proceed with caution.

Chapter 6
Financial Analysis
Of the Investment
Property

T he financial analysis of an investment property under consideration for acquisition is somewhat analogous to test-driving a new car. A financial analysis affords the investor the opportunity to measure how the investment is likely to "handle" under a variety of future economic conditions. It is especially important to the real estate investor because a proper analysis helps identify potential risks and rewards and enables a better estimate of the likelihood of reaching a targeted investment goal. For an investment property already owned, a decision to continue to hold is financially equivalent to buying it again for the amount of equity currently invested in the property. The objective of this kind of proactive analysis is not past performance but rather whether or not a continued holding of the property is likely to achieve future investments goals.

In this chapter we will first explore the methods of analysis which lead to an acquire/no-acquire decision. In the following chapter we will address options available to the current owner of a property which are most likely to meet future investment needs.

Calculators and Spreadsheets – Tools of the Trade

Calculators are handy, but when it comes to the analysis of an income property the computer's spreadsheet can't be beat. Once the spreadsheet is correctly modeled, it can render nearly instantaneous answers to a change in any one of the large number of variables involved in property performance and the investment decision. It can also test the sensitivity of the result to changes in any variable which is important in weighing risk. Working backwards, the spreadsheet can accept a targeted goal and determine the required value of a specific variable, such as the acquisition price or rents needed to achieve the defined goal. And on top of all this, it can deliver a hard (printed) or file copy which can be shared with others or retained for future reference.

Among current spreadsheet programs Microsoft's Excel® has become the favorite of more than 90% of spreadsheet users and is now available as an owned program or as a cloud rental. Apple's Numbers is also excellent. Google's Docs contains a very capable spreadsheet and is free, although it is cloud-based only and requires a connection to the internet. But the reader can use any seasoned spreadsheet since they all accomplish the same result and most have only minor differences in basic financial functions. The examples given in this chapter, however, will be given in terms of Excel. Conversion to other spreadsheets should not be at all difficult.

Gathering the Inputs

Before data can be analyzed they must be assembled and organized. Some of the required information will be hard data available from recent records, while others will need to be reasoned guesstimates about the property's future performance. The hard data include a laundry list of financial facts about current operations but other data, such as real estate taxes and insurance costs which can change significantly with a change in ownership, will require some investigation.

Visit the Tax Assessor & Planning Departments

In many communities, a change of ownership will trigger a reassessment of the taxable (assessed) value of the property which may or may not be equivalent to its sales value at the time of transfer. Some states have enacted laws which permit the property to be reassessed only following a transfer of ownership; future tax increases are then capped by an annual percentage. Other jurisdictions are free to reassess the value of the property on a regular basis and are therefore free to adjust real property taxes.[1]

Real estate taxes typically comprise about 1/3 of total operating expenses. The tax collector's office will be able to tell you the status of current taxes and any other levies which are collected, but the place to obtain essential tax information is from the *assessor's* office in the county or city in which the property is located. The local assessor provides information regarding the method of assessment, the tax area code, the applicable tax rate and the timing of future reassessments, if any. Taxes of one sort or another may be imposed by the state, the county and/or the local municipality. A copy of the latest tax bill (which may also be available on the municipality's website) will also show any special taxes, improvement bonds[2] or assessments levied against the property which will survive a change of ownership. Assessments act as a deduction from the current owner's equity in the property.

The one source not to rely upon is a statement from the owner or promotional brochure from the sales agent as to current taxes and insurance costs. The seller and agent may be perfectly forthright in declaring current taxes, but it's the future tax in which you are interested.

A visit to the local planning department is also very important and can help determine any planned municipal improvements which may become an assessment, a lien or encumbrance which will impact future property value. While you are there, check on the current zoning since it will not be in the preliminary title report you will later receive from the title insurance company. Some properties may be legal under current zoning law but in the case of a fire or destruction may not be rebuilt with a similar improvement under previously enacted down-zoning.

---

[1] Texas, for example, does not provide the tax assessor with the sales price of a property. Therefore reassessments must be made periodically.

[2] Some property-specific improvement bonds are not deductible taxes but are collected by the tax collector as a convenience. Other assessments may be the result of costs for which the owner had the choice of paying or allowing the cost to "go to bond."

The planning department of many jurisdictions maintains property files for every parcel in town. If this is the case, ask to see the file and check carefully to ensure that the current improvement is legal, that the municipality's records conform to the description of the properly given to you and that no additions or changes have been made without required permits. A scheduled appointment with a Planner is very helpful and highly recommended.

Insurance

When you apply for a loan the lender will require that you carry adequate casualty and liability insurance naming the lender as "additionally insured." The amount of insurance required will depend upon the location, type and quality of the property, but in general you will be required to insure the structure for loss due to fire and, if the property is in a flood plain, damage due to flooding. Even if you were to acquire the property paying all-cash, adequate insurance is essential.

The amount of insurance must satisfy a minimum percentage of the cost of replacing the improvement but will not include the cost of foundations and other components which could be re-used in reconstruction. Most insurers adopt the position that unless you are insured for a minimum of 80-90% of replacement costs, you will be regarded as a *co-insurer* and will receive only a percentage of the replacement costs.

The most reliable method of arriving at the cost of adequate insurance is to obtain new quotes from insurers experienced in the same property type and in the geographic area where the property is located. Insurance carriers should be rated at least **B+** by A.M. Best Company, a service which rates the financial soundness of insurance companies. The Best Company's ratings rank insurance companies on their financial strength and ability to meet the claims of policyholders. The company maintains a web site at www.ambest.com which furnishes an explanation of ratings as well as a list of insurers who meet a specified rating.

It is never advisable to use the insurance costs of the current owner since he/she may have insured the property years ago for the minimum amount necessary to satisfy a lender's exposure. In other circumstances, the current owner's cost of insurance may be a part of a *blanket insurance policy* under which a number of properties are insured at rates which cannot be duplicated for a single property. In addition to liability insurance, consider loss of income insurance which will provide a cashflow adequate to pay taxes and debt service during a period of reconstruction. Lenders invariably require this type insurance.

Other Variable Expenses

Taxes and insurance are considered "fixed" expenses since they must be paid whether the property is occupied or not. Other expenses are termed "variable" since they tend to vary with the extent of occupancy. The Annual Property Operating & Mortgage Data form, which follows on the next page, serves as a good checklist for other expenses. Before stepping through this form, note that while Line 31 indicates Net Operating Income (NOI), this widely used format does not lead to the customary Net Operating Income you would expect from an accountant for a business operation. That's because the Operating Statement which an accountant prepares for a business is prepared primarily for the purpose of reporting taxable income. As such, accountants deduct non-cash expenses such as depreciation and the amortization of certain capitalized costs, such as loan fees. The form on the following page delivers a 'Net Operating Income' which is really EBITDA income: Earnings Before (loan) Interest, (income) Taxes, Depreciation and Amortization. It is a Cashflow statement.

Line Definitions & Notes

Line #   Application/Use

G & H   The total value of the property must be apportioned between the land and improvement(s). If personal property is included in the price of the real property it should be deducted from the total acquisition value and depreciated on a Personal Property MACRS schedule. Personal property can be depreciated over a shorter period than real property. Therefore it is advantageous to separate these two.

I   If the seller will not issue a Bill of Sale for the personal property, you may deduct up to 15% of the total purchase price for allocation to personal property. Amounts over this will require a separate Bill of Sale from the seller.

K   This is a non-legal way to identify the property according to its Assessor's Parcel Number. It is not a required legal description acceptable to the recorder of documents.[3]

1.   Potential Income pertains to the total income which could be realized if all units, offices or leasable space were rented. For example if an apartment property contains 24 units which are scheduled to rent @ $1,500 per unit per month, the annual Potential Rental Income would be $432,000 (24 * $1,500 * 12).

2   Income attributable to reimbursable Common Area Maintenance (CAM) charges or to ancillary income from garages, vending machines, washers and dryers etc.

3.   All property is subject to an adjustment for vacancy and/or credit losses. Even an industrial property leased to a single credit tenant for 10 years should reflect an allowance for vacancy. A property which stands vacant for only 6 months after a 10-year occupancy by a single tenant shows a 5% vacancy factor (6/120). If a vacancy factor is not included in the operating statement submitted to a potential lender, the lender will insert its own.

5.   Effective Rental Income is sometimes referred to as Gross Operating Income.

6.   This type income may source from a broadband antenna on the roof, or from payments from the use of an easement. Neither will change with changes in tenant occupancy and are not included in Potential Income.

7.   This line represents the base line (100%) for the percentage computation of all operating expenses which follow (lines 8-30).

9-10   The real property and personal property taxes which will apply for the next operating year in the hands of a new owner.

11.   Fire, casualty, liability and loss of income insurance. Premiums often cover three years but this number should reflect an annual expense. An accrual account may be set up to accumulate these expenses, but do not deduct more than a one year's amount on this statement.

12.   If the property supports offsite management, its cost is entered here. If free rent or some rent abatement is provided to an on-site manager or tenant its market value should be included in Line 1 and its adjusted value deducted here.

13-15   The total of compensation, payroll taxes and benefits paid to service providers who are employees and not independent contractors.

16   Estimated repairs and maintenance for the coming operating year which will not extend the economic life of the property beyond one year. Improvements which will extend its economic life, such as a new plumbing or electrical system, or a new roof, must be capitalized and should not be included here.

---

[3]   Recordable descriptions include Lot, Block and Tract; U.S. Geodetic Survey; Metes and Bounds.

ANNUAL OPERATING EXPENSES AND LOAN DATA

A	Trade Name				Date					
B	Location				Price					
C	Type of Property				Existing Loan					
D	Size of Improvement		Sq.Ft/Units		Equity					
E	Land Area (s.f. or ac.)									
F	Assessed Values	Value	% To Total		Existing	Balance	Payment	/Yr.	Interest	Term
G	Land				1st					
H	Improvements				2nd					
I	Personal Property				3rd					
J	Total Assd. Value				Potential					
K	Tax Area Code				1st					
L	Assessor's Parcel Number				2nd					

	All Figures Are Annual	Expense	% To Total	Notes
1	POTENTIAL RENTAL INCOME			
2	Plus: Other Income			
3	TOTAL POTENTIAL INCOME			
4	Less: Vacancy & Cr. Losses			
5	Effective Rental Income			
6	Plus income unaffected by vacancy			
7	GROSS OPERATING INCOME			
8	**OPERATING EXPENSES:**			
9	Real Estate Taxes			
10	Personal Property Taxes			
11	Fire & Extended Coverage Insurance			
12	Off Site Management			
13	Payroll			
14	Expenses/Benefits			
15	Taxes/Worker's Compensation			
16	Repairs and Maintenance			
17	Utilities:			
18	Gas			
19	Electric			
20	Water			
21	Trash			
22	Accounting and Legal			
23	Advertising/Licenses/Permits			
24	Supplies			
25	Miscellaneous			
26	Contract Services:			
27				
28				
29	Reserves			
30	**TOTAL OPER. EXPENSES**			
31	**NET OPERATING INCOME**			
32	Less: Annual Debt Service			
33	Less Leasing Commissions/Fees			
34	**CASH FLOW BEFORE TAXES**			

18-20   Utilities for which the owner is responsible. Apartment properties should have one meter for gas and one meter for electric service for each residential unit, plus one meter for 'house lighting.' Laundry facilities should be separately metered as well. Most properties have but one water meter, although systems[4] are now in place which allocate water costs to the tenant on the basis of the number of occupants or the size of the unit. If there are more tenants than meters, either the landlord is paying for the utilities or two tenants are sharing one meter, possibly indicating an illegal unit. Count the meters. Count the tenants.

21.   Landlords are typically responsible for trash service. When extra trash or specialized waste services are required, such as for the disposal of medical, dental or laboratory waste, the extra expense should be billed to the tenant as provided in the lease.

26.   A copy of all contracts which will survive the change of ownership should be required from the seller prior to closing. Multi-year contracts should contain a clause which permits cancellation in the event of a change of ownership. If not, your approval of contracts which will survive the change in ownership should be subject to your review and approval as a condition precedent (contingency) to your obligation to complete the purchase.

29.   Annual reserves to cover the cost of replacing major elements, such as a new roof, re-plumbing etc. This number should be included in any operating statement submitted to a prospective lender. If one is lacking, the lender will supply it.

31.   The difference between Line 7 and Line 30. This is the number used in capitalizing income to arrive at market value.

32.   The annual cost of new or assumed financing from Lines W & X above.

33.   Smaller apartment properties generally do not incur separate leasing fees since the rental of units is usually handled by on-site managers. The initial leasing commissions incurred for new industrial, retail and office properties are usually provided for in construction loan proceeds. In established properties the leasing fees may be recognized in the year paid or spread out over the term of the lease, and deducted from operating income. However, leasing fees are generally not included in operating statements drawn for the purposes of valuation since they are not predictable, recurring annual expenses.

34.   This Cashflow line is not used in setting market value by capitalization.

Standard Operating Expenses

It is fair to say that there are no "standard expenses" incurred in operating any real property. Every property is different, and the factors accounting for the difference are all too obvious: age, quality of construction, condition, location, availability and cost of labor, utility rates, availability and cost of contract services, etc. Operating expenses should never be estimated as a percentage of Gross Operating Income. It costs measurably more to operate an older property than a new one and a fixed percentage of the rents achieved is no indication of this.

Operating expenses provided by some sellers and agents strain credibility and cannot be used to arrive at a reliable estimate of expenses. Even if expenses are accurate they generally pertain to last year's expenses and not to the expenses for the coming operating year. Forecasting next year's operating expenses is equivalent to establishing a budget. Every business needs one.

Commercial brokers whose companies also provide management services are sometimes good sources of average operating expenses for local property. The investor may also find useful data available from the

---

4   RUB: Ratio Utility Billings systems allocate costs based on sq. footage or number of residents.

Institute of Real Estate Management (IREM) which collects operating data each year from its members (Certified Property Managers). These data are available for apartments (low-rise, mid-rise and high-rise), for retail centers, industrial properties and office buildings.

IREM also provides a variety of forms and inspection sheets useful in assessing the condition of the interior and exterior of buildings, as well as books and courses helpful in acquiring reliable information and relevant management skills. IREM maintains a web site @ http://www.irem.org.

Constructing Your Own Analysis Spreadsheet

There are great advantages to be realized and enjoyed in building your own analysis program. Perhaps the most important of these is that you will be able to determine the value of an investment opportunity based on your own forecasts of income, expenses and financing costs. But we would like to add a few others:

Versatility: Once constructed, you will be able to change any single variable and measure immediately its effect on pre-tax and after-tax cashflows.

Utility: This program will measure results in terms of Pre- and after-tax cashflows, the Internal Rate of Return, Return on Equity, Present Value and Net Present Value.

Flexibility: The program will reflect immediately any proposed changes in terms during the negotiating period to measure the impact on targeted price and yield.

Immediacy: Changes in personal tax status or governmental tax rates and regulations can be made quickly with no need to wait weeks for a commercial 'upgrade.'

Control: You will achieve a level of understanding and comprehension which few private investors enjoy, which will help you make better investment decisions.

Economy: The program will provide all the essential information needed to analyze an income property at the least possible cost.

The task is not simple, but the skills acquired in constructing the spreadsheets will be long-lasting. Commercially available analysis programs sell for many thousands of dollars, yet, shorn of their bells and whistles,[5] do not provide the range and depth of information which you will have upon completion of this program.

---

[5]   In the author's experience teaching this course at a university, almost all students made interesting and attractive changes to the spreadsheets' appearances.

TEN-YEAR AFTER-TAX ANALYSIS

	A	B	C	D	E	F	G	H	I	J	K	L
1	Multi-Family Real Estate Analysis											
2	Property Ident.	Dartmouth Apts.						Date	Today			
3	Residential (Y/N)	Y										
4	Number of Units	28	197,500	cost per unit								
5	Acquisition Price	5,530,000					**Loan by Leverage**				LTCG Tax Rates, Depreciation Recapture Tax	
6	Acquisition Costs @ 0.5%	27,650					1st TD Loan	**4,147,500**			LT Capital Gains Rate	15.0%
7	Total Acquisition Cost	5,557,650					Int. Rate	5.25%			CA State Tax	9.30%
8	% To Improvement	75.00%					Amort Schedule (Yrs)	30		1250 Depreciation Recapture		25.0%
9	Depr. Value of Improvement	4,168,238					Term (Yrs.)	10				
10	Estimated Expenses/Unit/Yr	5,600					Pmt/Month	22,903		Ordinary Income Rates		
11	Rent Inflator/Yr	3.00%					**Loan by DCR**				Federal	33.0%
12	Expense Inflator/Yr	3.00%					NOI	298,010			State (CA)	9.30%
13	Vacancy & Credit Loss	4.00%					Minimum DCR	1.25			Blended Rate	39.23%
14	Tax Area Code Rate	1.16%					Annual Loan Cost	238,408			NII Rate	3.8%
15	Tax Inflator/Yr	2.00%					Pmt/Month	19,867				
16	Owner's Ord. Tax Rate (Fed+CA)	39.23%					1st TD Loan	**3,597,822**				
17	Capitalization Rate In	5.39%					**Loan by DYR**			**Loan Points**	0.50	
18	Capitalization Rate Out	5.64%					Lender's DYR	9.000%		Other fees	6,622	
19	Leverage (vs. Acq. Price)	75.0%					Loan Amt	**3,311,218**		Total Loan fees	23,179	
20	Total Investment Base	$2,269,611										
21												
22		Year	1	2	3	4	5	6	7	8	9	10
23	Loan Progress	Beg. Bal.	3,311,218	3,264,528	3,215,327	3,163,480	3,108,844	3,051,270	2,990,600	2,926,666	2,859,295	2,788,299
24		Rate	5.25%	5.25%	5.25%	5.25%	5.25%	5.25%	5.25%	5.25%	5.25%	5.25%
25		Payment/Yr.	219,416	219,416	219,416	219,416	219,416	219,416	219,416	219,416	219,416	219,416
26		Interest	172,726	170,215	167,569	164,780	161,842	158,746	155,483	152,044	148,421	144,603
27		Paydown	46,690	49,201	51,847	54,636	57,574	60,670	63,933	67,372	70,995	74,813
28		Remain. Bal.	3,264,528	3,215,327	3,163,480	3,108,844	3,051,270	2,990,600	2,926,666	2,859,295	2,788,299	2,713,486
29		DCRatio	1.36	1.40	1.45	1.49	1.54	1.59	1.64	1.69	1.75	1.80
30	Income											
31	Potential Annual Rental Income		470,400	484,512	499,047	514,019	529,439	545,323	561,682	578,533	595,889	613,765
32	Other Occ. Depend Income		3,360	3,461	3,565	3,672	3,782	3,895	4,012	4,132	4,256	4,384
33	Total Potential Income		473,760	487,973	502,612	517,690	533,221	549,218	565,694	582,665	600,145	618,149
34	Vacancy/Credit Loss		18,950	19,519	20,104	20,708	21,329	21,969	22,628	23,307	24,006	24,726
35	Effective Rental Income		454,810	468,454	482,508	496,983	511,892	527,249	543,066	559,358	576,139	593,423
36	Non Vacancy-depend Income		0	0	0	0	0	0	0	0	0	0
37	Total Gross Operating Income		454,810	468,454	482,508	496,983	511,892	527,249	543,066	559,358	576,139	593,423
38	Expenses											
39	Oper Expenses < Taxes		92,652	95,432	98,295	101,243	104,281	107,409	110,631	113,950	117,369	120,890
40	RE Taxes		64,148	65,431	66,740	68,074	69,436	70,825	72,241	73,686	75,160	76,663
41	Total Operating Expenses		156,800	160,863	165,034	169,318	173,717	178,234	182,872	187,636	192,528	197,553
42	% Increase Tot. Expenses/Year		NA	2.59%	2.59%	2.60%	2.60%	2.60%	2.60%	2.60%	2.61%	2.61%
43	Percent Expenses to GOI		34.5%	34.3%	34.2%	34.1%	33.9%	33.8%	33.7%	33.5%	33.4%	33.3%
44	Net Operating Income		298,010	307,591	317,473	327,665	338,176	349,015	360,194	371,722	383,611	395,871

TEN-YEAR AFTER-TAX ANALYSIS

	A	B	C	D	E	F	G	H	I	J	K	L
45												
46	CashFlow Before Tax											
47	Net Operating Income		298,010	307,591	317,473	327,665	338,176	349,015	360,194	371,722	383,611	395,871
48	Annual Debt Service		219,416	219,416	219,416	219,416	219,416	219,416	219,416	219,416	219,416	219,416
49	Cash Flow < Taxes		78,594	88,175	98,057	108,249	118,760	129,599	140,778	152,306	164,195	176,455
50	Taxable Income, CFAT											
51	Net Operating Income		298,010	307,591	317,473	327,665	338,176	349,015	360,194	371,722	383,611	395,871
52	Less Interest		172,726	170,215	167,569	164,780	161,842	158,746	155,483	152,044	148,421	144,603
53	Less Depreciation		145,257	151,572	151,572	151,572	151,572	151,572	151,572	151,572	151,572	145,257
54	Less Amort. of Points		2,318	2,318	2,318	2,318	2,318	2,318	2,318	2,318	2,318	2,318
55	Total Deductibles		320,301	324,105	321,459	318,671	315,732	312,636	309,373	305,934	302,311	292,177
56	Total Taxable Income		-22,291	-16,514	-3,986	8,994	22,444	36,380	50,821	65,788	81,300	103,694
57	Passive Losses/Taxable Inc.											
58	Estimated AGI		150,000	140,000	135,000	145,000	125,000	110,000	130,000	125,000	137,000	140,008
59	Maximum Deductible Loss		0	-5,000	-7,500	-2,500	-12,500	-20,000	-10,000	-12,500	-6,500	-4,996
60	Suspended Loss + Taxable Income		-22,291	-38,805	-37,790	-21,296	3,648	36,380	50,821	65,788	81,300	103,694
61	Net Taxable Income (Loss)		0	-5,000	-7,500	-2,500	3,648	36,380	50,821	65,788	81,300	103,694
62	Incremental Tax Bracket	39.23%	39.23%	39.23%	39.23%	39.23%	39.23%	39.23%	39.23%	39.23%	39.23%	39.23%
63	Tax (Tax saved)		0	-1,962	-2,942	-981	1,431	14,272	19,938	25,809	31,895	40,680
64	Susp. Losses Carry Fwd	0	-22,291	-33,805	-30,290	-18,796	0	0	0	0	0	0
65	Cash Flow After Regular Tax		78,594	90,137	101,000	109,230	117,329	115,327	120,840	126,497	132,300	135,775
66	NII Tax											
67	Estimated NII		20,000	0	15,000	25,000	5,000	30,000	20,000	20,000	20,000	40,000
68	Estimated MAGI		260,000	265,000	255,000	260,000	200,000	260,000	235,000	210,000	240,000	310,000
69	Threshold		250,000	250,000	250,000	250,000	250,000	250,000	250,000	250,000	250,000	250,000
70	Taxable Amt		10,000	0	5,000	10,000	0	10,000	0	0	0	40,000
71	NII Tax		380	0	190	380	0	380	0	0	0	1,520
72	Net Cash Flow >NII Tax		78,214	90,137	100,810	108,850	117,329	114,947	120,840	126,497	132,300	134,255
73	Adjusted Basis & Indicated Gain.											
74	Total Acquisition Cost		5,557,650	5,557,650	5,557,650	5,557,650	5,557,650	5,557,650	5,557,650	5,557,650	5,557,650	5,557,650
75	Less Total Depreciation Taken		145,257	296,829	448,401	599,974	751,546	903,118	1,054,690	1,206,263	1,357,835	1,503,092
76	Plus R.E. Commission	3.00%	150,000	150,000	150,000	150,000	150,000	150,000	150,000	150,000	150,000	150,000
77	Plus Other Costs of Disposition	0.50%	26,424	27,274	28,150	29,054	29,986	30,947	31,938	32,960	34,014	35,101
78	Total Adjusted Basis		5,588,817	5,438,095	5,287,399	5,136,730	4,986,090	4,835,479	4,684,898	4,534,347	4,383,829	4,239,660
79	Gross Sales Price		5,284,831	5,454,752	5,629,997	5,810,733	5,997,127	6,189,354	6,387,595	6,592,034	6,802,862	7,020,277
80	Less Adjusted Basis		5,588,095	5,438,095	5,287,399	5,136,730	4,986,090	4,835,479	4,684,898	4,534,347	4,383,829	4,239,660
81	Indicated Pre-tax Gain		-303,987	16,657	342,599	674,003	1,011,037	1,353,876	1,702,697	2,057,686	2,419,033	2,780,617
82	Tax Computation on Sale											
83	Indicated Gain		-303,987	16,657	342,599	674,003	1,011,037	1,353,876	1,702,697	2,057,686	2,419,033	2,780,617
84	CA State Tax Payable	9.30%	0	1,549	31,862	62,682	94,026	125,910	158,351	191,365	224,970	258,597
85	Remaining Fed.Taxable Gain		0	15,108	310,737	611,320	917,011	1,227,965	1,544,346	1,866,321	2,194,063	2,522,019
86	Total Depreciation Taken		145,257	296,829	448,401	599,974	751,546	903,118	1,054,690	1,206,263	1,357,835	1,503,092
87	Recapturable Depreciation		0	15,108	310,737	599,974	751,546	903,118	1,054,690	1,206,263	1,357,835	1,503,092
88	Depreciation Recapture Tax @	25.00%	0	3,777	77,684	149,993	187,886	225,780	263,673	301,566	339,459	375,773
89	Remaining LTCG		0	0	0	11,347	165,465	324,847	489,656	660,059	836,228	1,018,928
90	Federal LTCG Tax @		0	0	0	1,702	24,820	48,727	97,931	132,012	167,246	203,786
91	Unamortized Loan Points		20,861	18,543	16,225	13,907	11,589	9,271	6,954	4,636	2,318	0
92	Total Suspended Losses		22,291	33,805	30,290	18,796	0	0	0	0	0	0
93	Total Susp. Losses + Points		43,152	52,348	46,515	32,703	11,589	9,271	6,954	4,636	2,318	0
94	Ord. Tax Credit from Points	39.23%	16,929	20,537	18,248	12,830	4,547	3,637	2,728	1,819	909	0
95	Total Tax on Sale		-16,929	-15,211	91,297	201,548	302,186	396,780	517,227	623,124	730,765	838,156

TEN-YEAR AFTER-TAX ANALYSIS

A	YEAR → B	1 C	2 D	3 E	4 F	5 G	6 H	7 I	8 J	9 K	10 L
Net Proceeds											
Sales Price		5,284,831	5,454,752	5,629,997	5,810,733	5,997,127	6,189,354	6,387,595	6,592,034	6,802,862	7,020,277
Less Costs of Sales		176,424	177,274	178,150	179,054	179,986	180,947	181,938	182,960	184,014	185,101
Less Mortgage Balance		3,264,528	3,215,327	3,163,480	3,108,844	3,051,270	2,990,600	2,926,666	2,859,295	2,788,299	2,713,486
Proceeds < Tax ($1031 Funds)		1,843,879	2,062,151	2,288,368	2,522,835	2,765,871	3,017,808	3,278,990	3,549,779	3,830,548	4,121,689
Less Total Tax on Sale		-16,929	-15,211	91,297	201,548	302,186	396,780	517,227	623,124	730,765	838,136
After Tax Proceeds		1,860,808	2,077,361	2,197,070	2,321,287	2,463,685	2,621,028	2,761,764	2,926,655	3,099,783	3,285,533

Internal Rate of Return

	Init. Invs tmnt.	1	2	3	4	5	6	7	8	9	10
1	-2,209,611	1,939,021									
2	-2,209,611	78,214	2,167,498								
3	-2,209,611	78,214	90,137	2,297,880							
4	-2,209,611	78,214	90,137	100,810	2,430,137						
5	-2,209,611	78,214	90,137	100,810	108,850	2,463,685					
6	-2,209,611	78,214	90,137	100,810	108,850	117,329	2,735,975				
7	-2,209,611	78,214	90,137	100,810	108,850	117,329	114,947	2,882,604			
8	-2,209,611	78,214	90,137	100,810	108,850	117,329	114,947	120,840	3,053,152		
9	-2,209,611	78,214	90,137	100,810	108,850	117,329	114,947	120,840	126,497	3,232,083	
10	-2,209,611	78,214	90,137	100,810	108,850	117,329	114,947	120,840	126,497	132,300	3,417,788
IRR =		-14.57%	-0.54%	2.91%	4.67%	4.94%	6.60%	7.02%	7.40%	7.68%	7.81%
ROE =		4.20%	4.34%	4.59%	4.69%	4.76%	4.39%	4.38%	4.32%	4.27%	4.09%

Performance Indices

Capitalization Rate In	5.39%			
Cash-on-Cash > Tax	3.43%			
Discount Rate				
Calculated Cap. Rate	5.39%			
Inflation Rate	3.00%			
Discount Rate	8.39%	Equity Value	Debt	Total Value
Present Value @	8.39%	2,182,670	3,311,218	5,493,888
NPV @ IRR.	7.81%	0		
Constructed Cap Rate				
Current Safe Rate	2.95%			
Return of Investment per Yr.	2.00%	→ 50 years estimated remaining economic life		
Risk Premium	1.00%			
Constructed Cap Rate	5.95%			
Value @ Constr. Cap Rate	5,008,565			
Listed Price	5,530,000			
Asking Premium	521,435			
Constructed Discount Rate				
Constructed Cap Rate	5.95%			
Add Inflation Factor	3.00%			
Constructed Discount Rate	8.95%	Equity Value	Debt	Total Value
PV at Discount Rate	8.95%	2,076,481	3,311,218	5,387,699
Asking Premium	142,301			

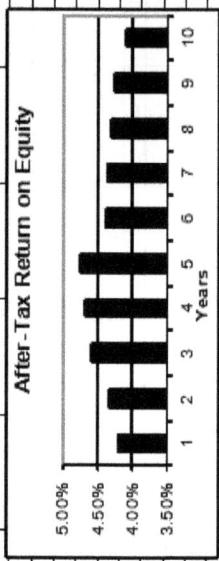

After-Tax Return on Equity

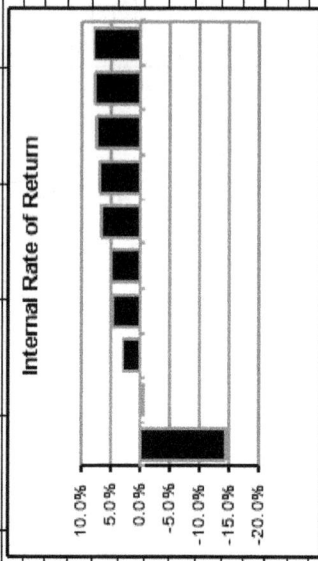

Internal Rate of Return

Structure of the Spreadsheet

The spreadsheet to be constructed delivers an after-tax analysis of the property for each year of a 10-year holding period. The holding period can be expanded or shortened as desired. The spreadsheet consists of three pages:

 ♦ The first page will contain most of the entered variables associated with price, ownership, mortgage and operating data. The upper middle and right sections of the first page show loan data and current tax rates.

 ♦ The second page will use these entered variables in developing a ten-year, pre-tax and after-tax forecast of income, expenses and profits.

 ♦ The third page is devoted to measuring the result employing all the commonly used indices of performance and value: Net Present Value, Internal Rate of Return and Return on Equity.

	A	B
1	Multi-Family Real Estate Analysis	
2	Property Ident.	Dartmouth Apts.
3	Residential (Y/N)	Y
4	Number of Units	28
5	Acquisition Price	5,530,000
6	Acquistion Costs @ 0.5%	27,650
7	Total Acquisition Cost	5,557,650
8	% To Improvement	75.00%
9	Depr. Value of Improvement	4,168,238
10	Estimated Expenses/Unit/Yr	5,600
11	Rent Inflator /Yr	3.00%
12	Expense Inflator/ Yr	3.00%
13	Vacancy & Credit Loss	4.00%
14	Tax Area Code Rate	1.16%
15	Tax Inflator /Yr	2.00%
16	Owner's Ord, Tax Rate (Fed+CA)	39.23%
17	Capitalization Rate In	5.39%
18	Capitalization Rate Out	5.64%
19	Leverage (vs. Acq. Price)	75.0%
20	Total Investment Base	$2,269,611

The reason for confining the variables to the top section of the program is that it obviates the need to enter each of the target cells and formulas in the body of the spreadsheet which perform the computations. Changing a variable produces instantaneous changes in every affected cell throughout the spreadsheet.

Entering Variables

The first section of the program may be entered in the upper left-hand corner of the sheet. This spreadsheet details the proposed acquisition of a 28-unit residential property, *Dartmouth Apartments*, acquired for $5,530,000. Cells 2-19 will contain most of the program variables. Cell B20 contains the Investment Base.

Cell # Explanation

B3   Entering either **Y** or **N** in this cell toggles the program between a residential and non-residential analysis. Depreciation allowance in (C53) is automatically converted to appropriate schedule and estimated expenses (B10) are alerted to show costs either as costs/s.f./year (non-residential) or as expenses per unit/year (residential). See Page 6-16 for formula.

B4   Number of rental units in the property (or if non-residential the leasable s.f.)

B5   Contemplated purchase price

B6   Acquisition costs (title, escrow, legal) exclusive of loan costs

B7   Purchase price plus estimated costs of acquisition.

B8   Percent of total acquisition cost allocated to the improvement.

B9   This number serves to establish the first year's Depreciable Basis.

B10   Estimated annual cost of operation per unit or per s.f. (B3 controls)

B11   Annual rent inflator. In this case it will serve as the inflator for the entire holding period, but this value can be changed by entering the income line (31) at any point in the 10-year analysis to either increase or decrease this value.

B12   Estimated annual expense inflator, which can be similarly changed.

B13   Vacancy estimate and loss due to credit problems.

B14   This property is located in a municipality which reassesses the property for taxes upon change of ownership. This is the tax rate per dollar of assessed value.

B15   Taxes in this state are limited by law to a 2% per year increase. Since this portion of the expense will inflate at a rate different from other expenses, it is handled separately.
        If taxes increase at the same rate as other expenses they can be inflated at the same rate as other expenses. (Cell B12)

B16   This is the combination of the owner's federal and state tax brackets. In this example, the federal rate is 33% while the state rate is 9.3% delivering an effective tax of 39.23%. (0.33*(1- 0.093) + 0.093). (The state taxes are deductible on federal return.)

B17   This is not an entered value but is calculated by the program by dividing the NOI (from line 44) by the Acquisition Price. Cell contains: **=C44 ÷ B5**.

B18   This value is used to capitalize the end-of-year income in order to estimate the sales price. It is equal to the capitalization rate at which the property is acquired plus 0.25%. This small percentage addition is a conservative step taken when capitalization rates are low. If capitalization rates are forecasted to increase, the 10th year sales price will be lowered. If capitalization rates are forecasted to decline, this rate may be lowered, resulting in a higher ending year sales value.

B19   This is the desired leverage (LTV) expressed as a percentage of the Acquisition Price (B5). Any percentage equal to or below the lender's loan-to-value maximum ratio is acceptable. The loan value in cell H6 is a product of the Acquisition Price x the Leverage percentage: **= (B5*B19)**

B20   This is the total *Investment Base* which the equity owner has initially invested in the property: Total Acquisition Cost (B7) – Loan Amt. (C23) + Total Loan Fees (K19). It will be used in the computation of the Internal Rate of Return. If the property is acquired by means of a S.1031 exchange, the amount of tax which would have otherwise been paid should be deducted from this value since part of the acquisition cost is financed by the deferred tax and not by the owner's direct cash investment.

Loan Computations

This program computes the amount of the loan in three different ways: the range of the spreadsheet located at H6:H10 determines the amount of the loan by multiplying the desired leverage (B19) by the Acquisition Price (B5). The result is located in cell H6. **(=B19*B5).**

The annual interest rate (%) is entered in **H7** while the amortization schedule (in years) is entered in **H8**. Cell **H9** contains the term, or maturity date, of the loan. This value is used to amortize the loan points over the <u>term</u> of the loan and results in a more rapid recovery of loan points than would be the case if the points were amortized over the full schedule of the loan.. The Pmt (**H10**) is determined using the Excel cell formula **=PMT(H7/12,H8*12,–H6,0)**

◄── Review this Excel function on page 5-9

At the same time, cells **H12:H16** configure the loan amount using the Debt Coverage Ratio (DCR). The annual cost of servicing the debt is the NOI (**C44**) divided by the DCR (**H13**), which delivers in (**H14**) the total annual cost of servicing the loan. Until there is an NOI value in cell C44, the computer will indicate an error. But pay no mind. Once cell C44 contains a calculated operating income value, the loan number will fall into place and the error sign will disappear.

The size of the loan in cell H16 (1st TD Loan) which can be supported by this annual payment amount is easily computed using the posted interest rate (H7) and the posted amortization schedule (H8). The formula in cell H16 is: **=PV(H7/12,H8*12,–H14/12,0)**

[**Note:** The values in both the PMT and PV formulas are entered as negative values so that the results will be rendered as positive values. This is a convention of both spreadsheets and hand-held calculators which requires there be at least one negative cashflow.]

This spreadsheet also calculates the amount of the loan using the lender's specified **Debt Yield Ratio** to determine the loan amount. **H19=(C44/H18)**. This metric is gaining increasing popularity, especially with those lenders who work with CMBS.[6] Review the formula for this calculation on page 5-11.

Selecting the Lowest of Three Potential Loan Amounts

Consistent with the lender's practice of lending the least loan amount, as determined by the Loan-to - Value ratio, the loan amount using the Debt Coverage Ratio and the Debt Yield Ratio, cell C23 selects the lowest of cells H6, H16 and H19 by means of the Excel function: **=Min(H6,H16,H19)**. This function returns $3,311,218, the lowest loan amount.

Amortizing the Loan

Cell C23, the lowest of the three possible loan amounts, serves as the beginning of the loan amortization table (lines 23 through 28) which will furnish the annual loan payment, the annual interest, the loan paydown amount (equity buildup) and the balance of the loan for each year of the 10-year analysis. We need these numbers to calculate not only the annual cashflow but also the annual taxable income.

The interest rate in cell C24 is referenced from cell H7. By referencing from cell H7 we need only change the value in H7 to have both loan computations change automatically. The amount of the loan in H19, however, is not determined using the interest rate.[7]

The Payment/yr. amount in C25 is re-calculated using the Beginning Balance in cell C23 (which could have been either loan amount) and the amortization schedule specified in cell H8: **=PMT(C24/12,$H$8*12,–C23)*12**. The resulting PMT is multiplied by 12 to express the annual cost of the debt for the loan selected.[8]

Determining the Interest Paid Per Year

There is no function in Excel which will deliver the total interest paid for an amortizing loan over a number of consecutive loan periods.[9] But there is a way to calculate this value.

If we determine the loan balance at the end of the year and subtract it from the loan balance at the beginning of the year we will always have the amount of the loan paydown. The interest paid will be the difference between the total loan payments for the year and the loan paydown for the year.[10]

---

[6] Collateralized Mortgage Backed Securities.

[7] Which is the lender's purpose in using the Debt Yield Ratio. Very low interest rates exaggerate the potential loan amount increasing lender's risk.

[8] The variable in cell H18 is converted to a fixed value by inserting dollar signs as shown. To do this, place the cursor between H and 8 and press key F4.

[9] The Excel function, **IPMT,** delivers the interest portion of the nth payment in a scheduled loan of nper payments. This is not what we need.

[10] This will be true for any amortizing loan using constant payments.

**The remaining balance of any fixed-payment, amortizing loan is always equal to the
Future Value of all the made payments.**

Therefore, cell C28 will be: **=FV(C24/12,12,C25/12,–C23)**. The loan paydown (or equity build-up) will be the difference between C23 and C28. This amount is entered into C27.

The total interest paid for the first 12 months, C26, will be the difference between the total payments made, C25, and the Paydown: C26: (**= C25-C27**). The beginning balance for the second year (cell D23) will be equal to the ending balance of the first year (**D23=C28**). Once this reference has been entered into D23, highlight cells C2<u>4</u>:C28 and drag right through column D. Then highlight cells D23:D28 and drag right to the 10th year. This will deliver the interest and remaining balance of the loan for each year of the analysis period.

Line 29 records the changing Debt Coverage Ratio (NOI ÷ Annual Debt Service) as the NOI increases. (=C44/C25). This may be of interest to a lender considering a loan on this property.

Configuring the Income and Expense Lines

It is reasonably certain that the income for the property will not grow at a constant rate, even though this is implied by the rent inflator entered in cell B11. It is much more likely that the rent will grow at an uneven rate over the next 10 years, and perhaps even decline at some point.

An alternate approach would be to insert a row above the income lines, and in this row enter the forecasted percent increase or decrease in rent for the corresponding year. The rent for that particular year would be equal to the previous year's rent * (1+ % forecast).

One addition that could be made to this spreadsheet would be to construct a separate worksheet within the same workbook that would tabulate all the rents from each individual tenant or unit per year. The total rent can be linked to the analysis worksheet so that changes in the income worksheet will be immediately reflected in the spreadsheet's income line. But for our purposes here, we will maintain the 3.0% rent inflator. In either case, the rent inflator is a critical assumption which will materially affect the total yield from the investment.

> [**Note:** A second worksheet[11] could also be used to tabulate annual expenses, either on a budgeted or actual basis. Totals from this expense sheet can also be transposed or, preferably, linked to the main spreadsheet. In this way, a change in any individual expense item will immediately flow through the entire spreadsheet. Consult your Excel Help file to see how data can be transferred from one worksheet to another.]

The Potential Rental Income for year 1 is an entered amount in cell C31. The rent for year 2, however, is the first year's income inflated by the inflator in B11. The formula in D31 is: **=C31*(1+$B$11).**[12] By dragging right, projections for the remaining years' income can be completed.

You may also enter any particular year's Potential Rental Income cell on line 31 and change the rent inflator to a new percent estimate of change or new dollar value. For example, you may judge that the

---

[11] A Workbook may contain a number of separate or linked Worksheets.
[12] The dollar signs entered into a cell location converts the value from a variable to a constant.

3.0% annual rent increase will be hard to maintain once new competition scheduled to come online in year 3 is completed. You judge that rent increases in year 3 and beyond will be limited to 2.5%. You can enter Cell E31 and enter the formula: **=D31*(1+.025)**. Once the change is made, highlight E31 and drag right to extend this formula for as many periods as you deem this rent rate will continue.

Other sources of income may be from services which are sensitive to vacancy and those which are not. Income from washers & dryers and other vending machines is an example of the first while income from a communications relay antenna on the roof would not be dependent upon occupancy. The spreadsheet provides for the first on line 32 and for the second on Line 36.

Expenses per unit for the first year are estimated to be $5,600 (B10), including property taxes. The total estimated annual expense number appearing in C41 is the product of **=B4*B10**. The real property taxes are entered in cell C40: (**=B5*B14**).[13] All other expenses, Cell C39, is the difference between C41 and C40. This split in expenses is necessary because tax increases in the example state, California, are limited to a statutory 2% per year, while other expenses will increase by the expense inflator in cell B12. This split accounts for the difference in the annual rate **(Line 42)** at which total expenses are increasing vs. the expense inflator in B11.

Net Operating Income.

The NOI for each year is computed by subtracting Total Operating Expenses (C41) from the Gross Operating Income (C37).

[**Note**: the determination of the loan amount using the DCR method (H12 to H15) depends upon the prior determination of the NOI. Therefore, the spreadsheet will not complete calculating the mortgage amount using the DCR until a value is entered into C44.]

Cashflow before Tax (CFBT)

The NOI is the starting point (**C47:L47**) for the determination of annual cashflow before tax and for the computation of taxable income. Cashflow before tax (CFBT) is computed on line 49 using the values on Lines 47 and 48. The values On Lines 47 and 48 are referenced, not entered, from lines 44 and 25 respectively.

Some investors use the **Cash-on-Cash ratio** (C49/B20) to value an investment. This metric is a pre-tax measurement and is valid for the first year only; it should not be used for subsequent years because it does not take into account the equity buildup created both by appreciation and loan paydown after year 1.

Cashflow after Taxes (CFAT)

In order to compute the cashflow after tax, the tax must first be determined. As indicated below, this computation involves the determination of the annual depreciation allowance, the annual interest on all loans, and the taxpayer's marginal tax bracket.

Note that the Paydown (Equity) portion of the loan payment is not a deduction from NOI in calculating the Taxable Income. This equity amount is a return of capital to the investor and is not deductible interest.

---

[13]   This property is located in a state (CA) which initially sets real estate taxes by the fair market value (typically the purchase price) and then limits annual increases to not more than 2% per year.

Cashflow After Taxes	Taxable Income
Net Operating Income	Net Operating Income
Less Interest	Less Interest
Less Loan Paydown (Equity) --->	(Equity is not tax deductible)
= Cashflow Before Taxes (CFBT)	Less Depreciation
Less Taxes Due and Payable	Less Amortization
= Cashflow After Tax (**CFAT**)	= Taxable Income
	x Marginal Tax Rate
	Taxes Due and Payable

The Depreciable Basis of the improvement is calculated in cell B9 by multiplying the total acquisition cost (not price) in cell B7 by the allocation factor in cell B8. Since this property is a residential property, the Depreciable Basis is recoverable over 27.5 years. Had this been a non-residential property,[14] the recovery period under current tax law[15] would have been 39 years.

This choice of depreciation schedules is controlled by the answer to the question in Cell A3. Entering a "Y" in cell B3 automatically adjusts the recovery period to 27.5 years. Cell C53 responds to this answer by selecting the appropriate recovery period and also adjusts for the mid-month convention: **=IF(B3="Y",11.5/12*B9/27.5,11.5/12*B9/39)**. The second year's depreciation should not include a mid-month adjustment. A simple correction is made in D53 by multiplying the result in C53 by 12/11.5: = **C53*12/11.5**.

Note that the last year's depreciation allowance will always be equal to the first since the investor is entitled to only 1/2 month's depreciation in both the month of acquisition and the month of disposition. Therefore cell **L53=C53**. If the model is broadened to include more years or shortened for fewer, the last year's depreciation allowance must be adjusted to equal the first.

Caveat

Bear in mind that the annual depreciation allowances are set by the MACRS schedule set out on p.3-23 and not by the more direct method used here. This program assumes that the property is purchased on the first day of the year and sold on the last day of the year. Therefore it should not be used as a substitute for determining current tax liabilities. No doubt that the MACRS table could be posted on a worksheet of this program and used to calculate the exact depreciation amounts for each year. But this program is designed to aid in buy-sell-hold decisions and is not a substitute for an accounting program.

Loan Costs Must Be Amortized

The points paid for the selected loan are entered in cell K17. Other loan costs are entered in cell K18 and the total is seen in cell K19: = **(K17* C23 + K18)**. This value is recovered ratably over the term (not the amortization schedule) of the loan. Therefore cell C54 contains: **=K19/H9**.

---

[14] Any property which is not residential is classified as non-residential for depreciation purposes.
[15] Year 2014

Computing Passive Loss Deductions

You will recall from Chapter 3 that losses from the operation of rental real estate are always classified as Passive Activity Losses and may be deducted only from Passive Activity Income. If the subject property produces Passive Activity Losses these losses may be deducted in the current tax year (under defined conditions) from income produced by other real estate rental properties which the taxpayer holds. But for the purposes of this model we assume that the taxpayer holds no other income property and that the deductibility of losses is constrained by the circumstances of this property alone.

In addition to the requirement for owning at least 10% of the property and meeting the tests for 'material participation,' there are three added conditions for the deductibility of PAL:

♦ The taxpayer must not have Adjusted Gross Income (AGI) greater than $150,000 in the current tax year.
♦ If the taxpayer has AGI greater than $100,000 but less than $150,000, he may deduct losses equal to ½ the difference between $150,000 and his AGI, up to a $25,000 limit.
♦ If the taxpayer has AGI less than $100,000 he may deduct actual losses up to $25,000 in PAL.

Any PAL which is not currently deductible must be 'suspended' and carried forward annually until it becomes deductible. Any suspended loss which remains at the time of sale is treated as an additional deductible *expense* in the current year. The total loss is then deducted from other Passive Activity Income from other rental property, if any, and then from the ordinary income from the subject property.

Because these losses are deductions from ordinary income, any suspended losses not used at the time of sale are converted to 'taxes saved' at the taxpayer's marginal tax rate and not at the long-term capital gains rate.

Since the deductibility of PAL is dependent upon the taxpayer's AGI in each year, we have inserted a range of AGIs on line 58. The values used may not be entirely realistic, but they are chosen to illustrate the program's ability to handle any combination of circumstances which enables or prevents the deduction of PAL. In actual use you will undoubtedly project more realistic values for future AGI.

Based on the entered AGI values on line 58, line 59 calculates the maximum allowable deductible PAL. The formula in Cell C59 is: **=IF(C58>150000, 0, IF(C58<100000, 25000, (150000-C59)/2)).** This formula contains an **IF** statement nested within an IF statement. The formula reads: **"If C58 is greater than $150,000, then use zero, but if C58 is less than 100000 then use 25000 else use ½ the difference between 150000 and C58."**[16]

On line 60 we have combined the taxable income for the current year (Line 56) with any suspended losses from the previous year. The formula in Cell C60 is: **=C56+B64.** We are aware that there is no value in B64 but when this formula is extended to the right (filled right) it will pick up any suspended losses from the cell on line 64. Line 61 compares lines 59 and 60 by use of the following formula: **=IF(C59>C60,C59,C60).**

---

[16] Notice that the Excel formula uses commas only to separate function variables. Do not use commas to separate the integers in dollar amounts.

Line 63 converts the taxable income on line 61 into taxes owed or <'dollars saved'> by multiplying it by the taxpayer's marginal tax bracket (B16). In the first year of this analysis the property generates negative taxable income (C56) which is not currently deductible because the AGI in cell C58 is $150,000. Taxable income in year 2 is also negative but still not <u>fully</u> deductible because the total of the taxable loss plus the suspended loss carried over from year 1 is in excess of the allowable deduction ($5,000). The non-deductible remainder (-$33,805),[17] is stored in Cell <u>D</u>64 as a suspended loss.

By the 4th year, taxable income (G56) has turned positive but there remains some suspended loss (-30,290) carried over from cell E64 in year 3.

In year 5, the taxable income (H56) is positive but there remains a carry-over loss from year 4 in the amount of -$18,796. The total of the income for the 5th year of $22,444 plus the suspended loss of -$18,796 results in net taxable income of $3,648. This taxable income results in a tax of $1,431 **G63= (G61* G62)**. From this point forward, there are no Passive Activity Losses and the Total Taxable Income (line 56) remains unaltered.

> Once the formulas are entered in Cells C58-C65, highlight this range and drag right through year 10.

Net Investment Income Tax Calculation

An additional 0.9% <u>Medicare Surtax</u> is required to be withheld by the employer on incomes over $200,000 but is not considered in this analysis since it is not property-related. The taxpayer has no control over the collection of this surtax. See p. 3-3 for additional details.

The Net Investment Income (NII) tax, however, must be calculated and paid by the taxpayer. Liability for this tax is both a function of the taxpayer's filing status and the amount of Modified Gross Adjusted Income (MAGI). Life would be made simpler if the AGI and MAGI were the same, but such is not the case. The difference between these types of income can be substantial but an explanation is beyond the scope of this text. In this program we assume that they are different and use different values for MAGI income (Line 68) as opposed to the AGI income amount (Line 58).

The calculation is relatively simple. If there is no NII income, there will never be a tax since the tax is always calculated on the *lesser* of the NII vs. the excess of the MAGI over the threshold amount. If NII income is greater then zero, there <u>may</u> be a tax due. When there is some NII **and** the MAGI is above the taxpayer's threshold amount, the tax due will be configured on the *lesser* of the NII vs. the amount by which the taxpayer's MAGI exceeds the threshold amount. When there is some NII **and** the MAGI is below the taxpayer's threshold amount, there will ne no tax.

Line 67 provides for entry of anticipated NII amounts. Line 68 also provides for forecasts of the annual MAGIs. Line 69 provides for the appropriate threshold amount per year, per taxpayer.[18]
Line 70 compares the estimated NII (Line 67) and the excess of Line 68 – Line 69, if any, and delivers the Taxable Amount. Line 70 cells contain the following *if* statement:
=IF(C67<=0,0,IF((C68-C69)<=0,0,IF(C67<(C68-C69),C67,(C68-C69)))).

This statement reads: **if C67 is less than or equal to zero,[19] then zero; else if C68 minus C69 is less than or equal to zero, then zero, else if C67 is less than C68 minus C69, then C67, else use C68 minus C69.**

---

[17] (-$22,291 -16,514+5000 = –$33,805) is the excess non-deductible loss total.
[18] In this case, married, filing jointly. See p.3-3 for applicable threshold amounts.

Line 71 multiplies the taxable amount on Line 70 times the NII rate (3.8%) to deliver the additional tax due.

Line 72 subtracts the additional tax on Line 71, if any, from the Cash Flow on Line 65. If no added tax is due, Line 72 remains equal to Line 65.

Determining the Adjusted Basis after Depreciation

The Adjusted **Basis** is an important number since it is the Net Sales Price less the Adjusted Basis at sale time that will determine the Recognized (taxable) gain. The major deduction from the total Acquisition Cost will be the depreciation taken each year. The major addition to the Basis will be the commission and costs of sale but other financial events may add to or subtract from the original Basis.[20] Additions to the Basis include major physical additions to the property or the cost of replacing a roof, new plumbing or electrical systems. Deductions from the Basis may include the sale of a portion of the original property, or cash paid to the owner for the use of an easement. These adjustments to the original Basis should be made and used here as the Adjusted Basis.

> During the period from April 2008 through 2014, interest rates declined to 50-year lows. Capitalization rates declined with them. As a result, investors paid higher prices relative to net operating income. These properties carry a very high Depreciable Basis and therefore are likely to extend the time of negative *taxable* income. Depreciation taken will eventually be taxed as Unrecaptured S.1250 Depreciation.

Calculation of Adjusted Basis, Gross Sales Price, Gain, (Loss)

The cost of Acquisition in Cell C74 is referenced from Cell B7 which remains the same for each year of the holding period.

The Total Depreciation Taken is calculated by adding each year's depreciation to the previous total. Therefore in the first year Cell C75 reads: = **C 53**. But in the second year, Cell D75 reads: = **D53+C75**.

The costs of disposition on Lines76 and 77 vary with the Gross Sales Price (Line 79). A commission cost equal to 3.00% of the Gross Sales Price has been entered in cell C76 but this commission is capped at $150,000.[21] The formula in C76 contains: **IF(($B$76*C79)>150000,150000, $B$76*C79)**. The dollar signs in B76 are inserted in order to render the value in cell B76 a fixed value. When cell C76 is filled right, cell B76 remains a constant and will calculate the estimated disposition costs for each year of the holding period. Other sales costs are estimated at 0.5% of the sales value. C77 contains =**$B$77*C79.**

The Total Adjusted Basis at the end of the first year is given in cell C78 and contains: =**C74– C75+C76+C77**. In this case we have added the costs of sale to the Total Acquisition Cost, but we could have subtracted them from the Gross Sales Price. In calculating the gain the net result would be the same. The Adjusted Basis at sale time is extended through the 10th year by filling right.

The Gross Sales Price at the end of each year **(Line 79)** is estimated by capitalizing the each year's Net Operating Income. A 0.25% margin was added (B18) to the capitalization rate at which the property was acquired (B17). This is a conservative measure which anticipates an increase in the capitalization rate. The result is an estimated sales price at the end of year 10 of $7,020,277. (**L44 ÷$B18**).

---

[19] Note the double operator (<=) which specifies that if C67 is either **less than** or **equal to** ... then...

[20] In the majority of cases the original Basis will be the total Acquisition Cost. But the Basis may be quite different depending upon how the property was acquired, e.g. as a gift or as an inheritance.

[21] Real estate commissions are negotiable.

When the Adjusted Basis (line 80) is subtracted from the Gross Sales Price (line 79) we have either an indicated gain or (loss) on line 81. In most cases this will be a loss if the property is sold after only one year.

Tax Computation on Sale

The Indicated Gain (Loss) on line 83 is referenced from Line 81 and the Total Depreciation Taken on Line 86 is referenced from Line 75. Whenever the Depreciation Taken exceeds the Indicated Gain, the Recapturable (taxable) Depreciation is limited to the Indicated Gain. If there is no gain (as in the case of Year 1) there is no recapturable S.1250 depreciation.

Current tax law requires that all unrecaptured depreciation taken[22] be taxed at 25%. The portion of any gain in excess of the deprecation taken is taxed as capital gain. Line 84 tests Line 83 for a taxable gain. If there is a negative or zero taxable gain on Line 83, the state tax is zero and entered on Line 84. If there is a state tax due, this amount is subtracted from any positive amount on Line 83 and the remainder of indicated gain is entered on Line 85.

In order to compare the remaining taxable gain with the amount of depreciation taken, the Total Depreciation Taken is retrieved from Line 75 and entered on Line 86. If the amount of indicated gain on Line 85 is equal to or less than the Total Depreciation Taken, the entire amount of remaining taxable gain on Line 85 is counted as recaptured depreciation and taxed at the 25% rate.

If the amount on Line 85 is greater than the Total Depreciation taken, the amount of the Depreciation is taxed @25% and the remainder (excess) is taxed as LTCG. Line 87 identifies which amount is less and posts this on Line 87 as Recapturable Depreciation. Line 89 determines the amount by which the Remaining LTCG (Line 89), if any, exceeds the amount of Depreciation taken. This excess is taxed as LTCG

The rate applicable to the LTCG depends upon the amount of Remaining Taxable gain shown on Line 89. When this amount is less than $450,000 the rate is 15%, but when the amount exceeds $450,000 the rate increases to 20%.[23] **=IF(D89>450000,0.2*D89,0.15*D89).** (Monitor future tax changes re this dollar amount and rate.)

Credit for Suspended Losses and Unamortized Loan Point

One last tax item remains: the ordinary tax credit which is due the taxpayer who has suspended losses or who was unable to recover all loan costs. These items are deductions from ordinary income, not from capital gains income. Therefore their tax value is credited to the taxpayer at his marginal tax rate (B16), and not at the LTCG rate (L6).

Cell C91 computes the unamortized loan points by subtracting the loan costs already taken (C54) from the original value in K19. Cell C91 contains: **=$K$19-(C22*($K$19/10)).** Cell C92 collects accumulated Suspended Losses from cell C64. Cell C93 adds these values together. Cell C94 holds the tax credit (negative tax) due the owner. This cell contains: **=C90*$B$91.**

---

22 Depreciation for properties acquired after 1986.
23 This assumes the taxpayer is married and filing a joint return.

The total tax (Line 95) is the sum of the tax on S.1250 unrecaptured depreciation (Line 88), the LTCG tax (Line 90) minus the ordinary tax credit from Line 94. Cell C92 contains:
=C85+C88-C94. This program assumes that the property is sold at the end of each year, 1-10. Otherwise, suspended losses would not be deductible. Note that there are no recoverable suspended losses in years 5-10.

Net Proceeds (Reversion Value) of Investment

The Sales Price on Line 100 is arrived at by capitalizing the ending NOI on Line 44. Cell C100 = **C44÷B18**. Cell C103 contains the proceeds from the sale, net of commissions, costs and loan balance but prior to payment of the tax on the gain: =**C100-C101-C102.** The amounts on Line 103 over the holding period would be the maximum amount available each year for a tax-deferred exchange in which no Boot was received.

Line105 tabulates the net cash amount from the investment after deductions of the Total Tax on Sale. C105 contains: = **C103-C104.** (1,843,879 – (–16,929) = 1,860,808.

Column L lists the comparable amounts for a sale in the 10th year. Note the amount of pre-tax cash available in Cell L013 (**$4,121,689**). If we were to construct a 10-year T-Bar to illustrate the cashflows from this property, the Internal Rate of Return could be determined using a calculator as follows:

> **Note:**
>
> Values shown on the spreadsheet have been calculated by underlining unchecking the option "Set precision as displayed" on the Excel Option menu. As a result the IRR calculated by the computer will be more accurate that the same metric using the calculator.
>
> *Excel Office Button/*
> *Excel Options/*
> *Advanced/*
> *When calculating this worksheet/*
> *Set precision as displayed.*

Computation of the IRR

Initial Investment (B20)	<$2,269,611>
CFAT Year 1	$78,214 (from Line 72)
Year 2	90,137
Year 3	100,810
Year 4	108,850
Year 5	117,329
Year 6	115,327
Year 7	120.840
Year 8	126,497
Year 9	132,300
Year 10	134,255 + $3,283,533 (Cell L105)
(HP-12C) IRR =	**7.89%**

In order to determine the IRR Excel requires that these cash values be arranged in a contiguous array. Values may be arranged either horizontally or vertically. This spreadsheet uses a horizontal array.

The cashflow for any year (1-10) is always the after-tax cashflows from operations, Line 72. If the property is sold before the 10th year, the last value for year **n** is the last cashflow from operations *plus* the reversion amount for year **n** on Line 105. When these values have been set, the IRR can be calculated for each year using the IRR function.

For example, the IRR formula for year 5 appears under the 5th year. Cell G119 reads Line 113 and contains: =**IRR(B113:G113)**. The IRR for year 10 appears in Cell L119 and reads: =**IRR(B118:L118).** It is mandatory that the first value in the array be a negative number. If it is not, you will get an error message (NUM) from the computer.[24]

---

[24] The first value entered into the calculator must also be a negative number.

The IRR expresses the annual yield from the investment when the investment is held for a stipulated number of periods.

Other Performance Indices

ROE

A few investors use the ROE (Return on Equity) metric to gauge the value of the investment. This measurement is fairly simple and an after-tax ROE value appears on Line 120 for each year of the holding period: **=C72/C105.**

Some investors use the Cash Flow < Taxes in Cell C49 as the numerator of a fraction of which the denominator is the amount of cash invested – in this case, $2,269,611 from B20: **=C49/B20** There is nothing wrong with this calculation if used for the first year only. But some promoters measure pre-tax cash flows for each future year divided by the *original* cash investment. In this way, the numerator value keeps growing but the original denominator-investment never changes. This variation is misleading and of no analytic value.

The Discount Rate

A market discount rate can be determined by adding to the current market capitalization rate[25] an allowance for inflation. It is not commonly understood that capitalization rates do not contain an allowance for inflation. The result is delivered in Cell B127, 8.39%.

Using this discount rate we can determine the Present Value (PV) of the after-tax cashflows which will accrue to the owner. Cell C128 contains the following formula:
=NPV(B128,C72:K72,L72+L105).
Note that the last cashflow is a combination of cash from final annual operations plus the reversion amount. The present value of this equity plus the amount of debt delivers the total present value of the property in Cell E128.

The Actual Net Present Value (NPV)

Given the Present Value of the Equity in Cell C128, the Net PV of the Equity is simply the Present Value less the initial investment (B20): $2,182,670 –2,269,611 = –$86,941.

> **Note:** The NPV (Net Present Value) function in Excel does not return the NPV of a cashflow series. It returns the PV of an uneven cashflow. In order to determine the actual NPV, withhold the first cashflow, i.e. the initial investment. Then determine the PV of the remaining series (using the NPV function if the values vary). Subtract the initial investment from the PV of the remaining series. The result will be the true NPV of the entire cashflow series
> The pull-down NPV menu function in Excel is also incorrect since it discounts all cashflows, even the initial cashflow, as occurring at the end of the period (EOP) whereas the initial cash flow occurs at BOP and is therefore never discounted.

An NPV greater than zero indicates that the yield on the investment will be greater than the discount rate used. A negative NPV, as in this case, does not necessarily mean that the investment will lose money; it does mean that the investment will achieve a yield lower than the 8.39% discount rate used. The computation of the NPV is not shown on the spreadsheet, but can easily be inserted.

An Internal Check

In cell C129 we have discounted the cashflows by the IRR value in cell L119 using the NPV function. The result is zero since this is one of two definitions of the IRR.[26] This procedure serves as an internal

---

[25] Derived from the current NOI and the value of this and other current sales.
[26] That discount rate which will deliver an NPV = 0.

check on the accuracy of the calculations. The formula in cell C129 is:
=NPV(B129,C72:K72,(L72+L105))-B20. If the result of this computation is not zero, there is an error in the program.

Constructing a Cap Rate

Capitalization rates are typically determined by gathering the NOI of similar, recently sold properties in the same general location and the price at which they sold: (NOI ÷ Price = Cap Rate). As such, their use is inherently retrospective and rests on the assumption that future interest rates will be the same as in the past. Because rates change there is a great advantage in constructing one's own capitalization rate.[27]

In cells B131:B134 we have constructed a capitalization rate using:

   1. the current safe rate for money[28]
   2. A rate for return of the investment (100%/C133) and
   3. A risk premium

The total is displayed in Cell B134.

The constructed capitalization rate is applied to the first year's NOI and shows a value of $5,008,565. The formula in B135 is: **=C44÷B134**. This compares with the asking price, referenced from cell B5, and suggests that the acquisition price specified in B5 is $521,435 greater than its financial value in B135 <u>to an investor who requires a 5.95% return</u>.

Determining Value Using a Constructed a Discount Rate,

Given the *constructed* cap rate of 5.95%, we need only add an estimated inflation factor to the cap rate to come up with a constructed discount rate, 8.95% in Cell B141. If the <u>PV</u> of the cashflows (Cells C118:L118) is added to original loan amount from C23, a significantly different value will be found. In order to do this, we will use the NPV function – not because we are seeking the Net Present Value but because the NPV function in Excel discounts uneven cashflows.

When the constructed discount rate is applied to the equity cashflows their PV is found to be $2,076,481. Cell C142 contains: = **NPV(B142, C118:L118).** This sum added to the original loan amount from B20 delivers a calculated value of $5,387,699. This value is $142,302 less than the asking price of $5,530,000 and much less than the value determined by capitalizing the NOI from year 1. The difference reflects the fact that the capitalization of the first year's NOI considers only the first year's income while the discounted cashflow technique takes into account increasing NOIs through year 10.

The Equity Dividend Rate

The term "equity dividend rate" is synonymous with Return on (Invested) Equity. The year-by-year ROEs for this investment are posted on Line 120. They are also charted.

Notice that the after-tax Cash-on-Cash return rate in Cell B123 is 3.45% while the Equity Dividend Rate (C120) for the first year is 4.20%. This discrepancy arises from the way these two indices are calculated: The Cash-on-Cash value is the CFAT (Cell C72) divided by the Initial Investment (Cell B20). The Equity

---

[27]   The value of income property is based on the Principle of Anticipation, not on Memory.

[28]   In normal times, the yield on a standard U.S. Treasury of similar maturity

Dividend Rate, however, is the quotient of the CFAT divided by the After Tax Proceeds (Cell C105) which is the net equity amount currently invested.

It is not uncommon to see properties offered for sale which boast a high ROE by dividing a future year's After Tax Proceeds by the Initial Investment. This is incorrect and very misleading. The term "Cash-on-Cash" is generally understood to mean the first year's pre-tax spendable income divided by the initial investment amount, while the ROE is a measure of the current year's after-tax income divided by the total net equity[29] currently invested in the property <u>at the end</u> of the reporting period.

Monitoring the ROE

The ROE is the best index of current investment performance: it measures the amount of after-tax income <u>currently delivered by the investment</u> in relation to the total net equity <u>currently invested</u>. Due to appreciation and equity buildup over time, the ROE will eventually fall below a rate which is equal to the current inflation rate. At this point the investor's real income (wealth) will begin to contract as the nominal income loses purchasing power. The chart on page 10, labeled **Return on Equity,** shows that the ROE begins a steady decline once the property begins to produce taxable income. The **IRR** is delayed in reflecting this turning point since it is a reflection of the Present Value of all income in comparison to the amount of initial investment. The investor must decide at what point the ROE has declined sufficiently to require some corrective action.

Utilizing the Spreadsheet in Decision Making

One of the Add-In tools provided in Excel is called 'Goal Seek.' This financial function can be used to determine the value of a variable required to obtain a specified result. Goal Seek will handle only one variable, while the other Excel Add-In, Solver, which is also located on the Data menu, is capable of handling a number of variables.
But because our model is so large, including many, many variables, you may not have sufficient memory in your machine to use Solver. You can however, use Goal Seek with this spreadsheet.

For example, we may ask what price would be required to produce a 10-year IRR of 10.0%?
To determine the price required, select the target cell L119, which is now 7.31%.
On the DATA Menu go to Data Tools and select What If Analysis. Click Goal Seek.
In the dialogue box which appears, enter these values:

Set Cell   L119
To Value   8.0% (**Note: Replace the formula in L119 with the value 10.0%**)
By changing cell   B5
Click O.K.
Goal Seek determines the required price and enters it in cell B5, $5,474,700. Notice that the capitalization rate (B17) has also changed from 5.34% to 5.44%. The IRR now reads 7.95% which is as close as Goal Seek can come to our requirement of 8.0%
Click *Control Z* to restore the original values.

Suppose, instead, that we want to buy at a capitalization rate of 7.00% and want to know what price is required.
Retrieve Goal Seek as before.

---

[29]   After all transaction costs, payment of taxes and repayment of mortgage.

In the dialogue box which appears, enter the following values:

Set Cell   B17
To Value   7.00%
By changing cell   B5
Click O.K.

The result in B5 is $4,286,933. B17, however, reads 6.96% - which is as close as it can come to 7.0%. Click *Control Z* to restore the original values.

Lastly, let's ask Goal Seek to determine the average percent increase in rents (B11) in order to produce an IRR of 8.5%.

Again, retrieve Goal Seek as before.
In the dialogue box which appears, enter these values:

Set Cell   L119
To Value   8.5%
By changing cell   B11
Click O.K.

The change in B11 is 3.32%, while the IRR shows 8.49%.

Note: Goal Seek may not work properly if you have your spreadsheet set to *Precision As Displayed*. Using the Excel Button, select Excel Options. Click *Advanced/When calculating...* and remove the check next to *Set Precision as Displayed*.
This Add-In is a powerful tool in conducting negotiations and may enable you to adjust a number of variables in order to reach your targeted goal.

This spreadsheet can be adapted to many different kinds of properties and situations. Once formed, any adaptation can be saved under a new file name and in this way the investor-analyst can accumulate a folder of ready-made formats which will facilitate important decisions in the acquisition and disposition of income properties.

O nce your analysis of the property and its environs has been completed and you have decided to submit a purchase offer, it is important that you move quickly and that negotiations, once begun, continue until you either have the property under contract or until you decide to pass.

Lapses of days between the initiation of an offer and a response from the seller may indicate that your offer is being "shopped" by the seller or his agent with other potential buyers to see if a better offer can be leveraged. We will discuss how to prevent this, but first there is the matter of an agent.

Working with a Broker

Most investment properties are brought to market by a broker acting as the agent of the seller. The agreement between the seller and the broker, a *listing* agreement, is a bi-lateral contract by which the seller accords the broker, for a defined period of time, the right to market the property as the owner's agent, to receive offers subject to the owner's approval, and to represent the owner's interests in a sale or exchange transaction.

There are a number of kinds of listing agreements, but the most common is the *Exclusive Right to Sell* agreement which accords the broker during the listing period the sole right to sell the property on the terms and conditions agreed to with the owner.

Sometimes the broker may be operating under an *Exclusive Agency* agreement by which the owner appoints the broker as his/her sole agent, but retains the right to sell the property and not be responsible to pay a commission. Much less frequently, the broker operates under an *Open Listing* by which the owner agrees to pay a commission or fee to whichever broker delivers a ready, willing and able buyer. If the agreement between the broker and the seller is either type of Exclusive listing, a termination date[1] is required. Open Listings do not require a termination date.

---

[1] Either a specific date or one which can be determined in reference to a future event.

It is almost immaterial to the buyer of investment property the type agreement the listing broker has with the seller – except for one very important point: the prospective buyer will invest a considerable amount of time, money and effort in performing *due diligence* on the property and it is very important that the broker has the ability to deliver the property. Brokers who operate under Exclusive Agency or Open Listing agreements do not have sufficient control of the property to assure the buyer of the ability to deliver the property to a binding agreement. Nothing is more wasteful for a buyer than to spend time and money investigating a property and preparing an offer only to be told that the property sold last week through another broker.

A direct question to the agent, "Do you have an exclusive representation agreement with the owner?" is both reasonable and prudent.

Who Represents Whom?

Many prospective buyers of real estate do not realize that the agent who introduces them to a property is frequently already under contract to represent its owner. He or she is the seller's *agent*. This relationship, known in law as a *fiduciary* relationship, requires the agent to be forthright and honest in all his/her dealings with the owner, to place the owner's interests above his/her own and to avoid any misrepresentations, actions, or failures to act, which would be prejudicial to the owner's legitimate interests. Beyond legal and ethical considerations which preclude misrepresentations to the buyer, the seller's agent has no fiduciary obligation to represent the best interests of the buyer and is under no obligation to advise the buyer regarding the best price and terms.

Many experienced investors rely instead on a broker of their own choosing. These brokers are selected according to their training and experience and are free to represent the buyer's interests with no fiduciary responsibility to the seller. Most states now require the agent to declare which party to a real estate transaction the agent represents. In some states, the agent can take the legal position of a neutral go-between, claiming that he or she represents the interests of neither party, but serves only as a *facilitator* in the transaction. Colorado, for example, defines a facilitator as a...

> "Transaction-Broker .... who assists one or more parties throughout a contemplated real estate transaction with communication, interposition, advisement, negotiation, contract terms, and the closing of such real estate transaction *without being an agent or advocate for the interests of any party to such transaction."* (Emphasis added).

Florida, Georgia and other states now have similar "facilitator" laws.

The *facilitator* status is designed to relieve the agent of a fiduciary responsibility to either party and thereby reduce the potential liability for litigation between the agent and the principals.[2] In most instances it leaves both buyer and seller with less than professional representation.

---

[2] It is impossible for the agent to be relieved of all responsibility simply by declaring that he/she does not have a fiduciary duty.

Dual Agency

In other states the agent may start out as the exclusive representative of the seller, but may later change that status to one of a *dual agency* in which he or she claims to represent the interests of both parties to the transaction. Many agents relish a dual agency because it places them in line to receive both shares (listing and selling) of the total fee or commission payable by the owner.

The practice of real estate is not an adversarial endeavor. It is unlike the practice of law in which attorneys adopt distinctly adversarial positions in a lawsuit. Nevertheless, there are so many instances in a real estate transaction in which the respective interests of seller and buyer are antithetic that an agent who attempts dual representation frequently provides inadequate and ineffective representation to one or both parties. In practice, dual agency simply does not work.

Who Pays the Broker?

Anyone can pay the broker but it is most often the seller who pays the broker the agreed upon commission or fee. If there are two or more brokers involved, one representing the seller and the other the buyer, they will have reached an agreement on how this fee is to be divided between or among them. But in reality, the seller only funds the commission or fee; it is the buyer's cash which is the source of all commission monies.

Since this is so, the buyer can make an offer to purchase a property through his own broker and to reduce the amount of the offering price by the amount the seller is obligated to pay to the broker who procures the buyer. By doing so the seller pays no more than he had agreed to, but the buyer achieves what he would ordinarily not have had: exclusive representation by someone not legally and ethically bound to represent the interests of someone else.

We have all known this for years: you cannot carry water on both shoulders.[3]

Hiring Your Broker

Your objective should be to acquire the real property of your choice at the best possible price and under the best possible terms and to do so without any legal complications or entanglements. To do so, you need a well-trained and experienced broker. An experienced and well-trained broker can save you thousands of dollars and can increase your effectiveness in negotiating with the seller. An inexperienced and untrained agent can cost you thousands of dollars and possibly involve you in a lawsuit which may take years and many dollars to resolve.

The best source of finding an ethical, competent and industrious agent to represent you is the recommendation of fellow investors who have themselves used the services of the agent or otherwise have first-hand knowledge of the agent's qualifications, experience and abilities.

Your agreement with the broker should always be in writing, signed and dated, and should outline the terms under which you are to pay a commission or fee for services rendered. If you are dealing with an experienced agent he or she will no doubt have a written agreement which you can review, negotiate and

---

[3]   Or, "No man can serve two masters."

change. **As you already know, real estate commissions are not set by law but are always open to negotiation.** Before finalizing the agreement, have it reviewed by your real estate attorney.

Preparing an Offer, Letter of Intent

Negotiations may be opened by preparing a formal, written offer to buy the property. This offer would contain all the terms, conditions and contingencies required by a buyer. If the offer is acceptable to the seller, he need only indicate his acceptance by executing the offer and notifying the buyer of this acceptance by returning a signed copy to the buyer or to the buyer's authorized agent. At that point, a formal, bilateral contract exists between buyer and seller.

Because preparing a formal offer takes a great deal of time and requires the buyer to focus on the details and minutiae of the offer before the broad terms have been agreed upon, many investors prefer to open negotiations by using a Letter of Intent (LOI). This letter need only recite the basic terms under which the buyer is willing to enter into contract negotiations. These terms would include a legal description of the property, the proposed acquisition price, method of payment (amount of cash plus a new or assumed loan), length of escrow period, requirement for seller's cooperation in a S.1031 exchange (if appropriate), contingencies for inspections and any other unusual or non-standard conditions of the offer.

The Letter of Intent should probably not extend beyond 1-3 printed pages. Long and overly-detailed LOIs defeat their purpose, which is to determine quickly whether or not a transaction is possible and, if so, to get contract negotiations started. Despite this, LOIs appear to be getting longer and longer in parallel with purchase/sale agreements which now often exceed 30-40 pages even for simple transactions. Their corresponding LOIs often reach 15-20 pages filled with minutiae which one would expect to find later in a purchase/sale agreement. Overly-detailed LOIs serve very little purpose other than to extend billable hours. A bit of irony is involved since *a well-written LOI will always stipulate that it is binding on neither the seller nor the buyer.*

LOI Caveat

The most important paragraph in the LOI is the one which should never be omitted since some LOIs have been interpreted by the courts as written, binding agreements to buy and/or sell the property. Since many of the details have not as yet been agreed upon, a one or two-page binding LOI will surely result in disagreements and disputes which may later devolve into protracted and expensive legal action once the details are addressed.

This important paragraph is the one which clearly and unambiguously states that the LOI does not represent an offer to purchase nor, if agreed to by the seller, an offer to sell the property. **It should state unequivocally that an offer to buy the property and the right to sell the property can only be established by a separate, written agreement and that no action or verbal communication by either party shall waive the requirement for a formal, written purchase/sale agreement.**

What you are asking for in the LOI is only an indication of the willingness of the seller to proceed to a binding agreement based on the broad terms outlined in the LOI. If these broad terms are acceptable to the seller, he can indicate his willingness to enter into negotiations on, but not limited to, the terms included in the LOI by signing the LOI and returning a copy to you.

If you are not comfortable with your LOI, have it reviewed by your real estate attorney and then keep a copy for future reference.

Making the Offer

Many a buyer wants to 'steal' the property at a very low price. There are bargains to be had, but if the seller of the property, or the property itself, is not under duress it is likely that the property is priced over the market. If your targeted acquisition price is more than 10-15% below a seller's asking price, and the seller is not under duress, the odds that you will be successful are greatly diminished because you may be dealing with an unrealistic or uninformed seller.

There are many reasons why sellers overprice their properties. One reason commonly heard is:

"...because that's how much I need to buy another property I am interested in."

If you encounter this reasoning your chances may be very slim since this reason bears no relationship to the property's market value. In effect, it requires that your agent convince the seller to accept a market value for his property that will not enable him to buy his new property.

The most frequent reason a property is overpriced is that the seller doesn't know its value in the present market. Therefore he overprices the property and hopes to 'back into' a market price by negotiating with a qualified buyer, like you. If a property has been on the market for a long time, it is probably overpriced, or it may have defects previous offerors did not want to remedy. Be circumspect about properties which have been marketed for a long time and have not sold, or, having sold, keep falling out of contract.

In the same way that you would like to buy at the very lowest price, the seller wants to sell at the very highest price. But deep in the heart of most – but not all – sellers is the secret that they would be happy to sell *at market*. They just don't want to sell below the market.

No Fax Please

The greatest disadvantage of allowing an agent to fax or e-mail your offer to the seller or his agent is that you lose control of your offer. Armed with the offer in hand, the seller's broker is free to contact other potential buyers – including his own – willing to pay just a bit more for the property. Your offer becomes a "stalking horse."[4] Faxes and e-mail may be very convenient for the escrow officer or the attorney, but faxing or e-mailing an offer to the seller does not afford your agent an opportunity to explain to the seller face-to-face who you are, your qualifications as a buyer, and what you are trying to accomplish. By making a personal presentation of your offer, the agent gains an opportunity to review the market, to cite recent comparable sales which support your offered price, and even to furnish the seller with information he may not have but needs in order to make an informed decision. Most importantly, an electronic presentation alone does not afford your agent the opportunity to obtain any verbal, non-verbal feedback or written response from the seller which can be important to you in continuing negotiations.

One safeguard here is to limit the time for a response to your offer. If the seller is not currently available delay the presentation of your offer to a time when you can reasonably expect a written response within 24-48 hours.. Make clear that your offer will expire at the end of this time period.

---

[4] This has become a significant problem for buyers who make offers on "short sale" properties. The listing agent obtains an exclusive listing from the current owner at a price below the current mortgage balance, and then collects offers which are presented to the lender for approval. In many cases a buyer may wait weeks for an answer only to learn that his offer was surpassed by someone else's.

How Low To Go

If your initial offer is too low, many sellers may turn to ice, rejecting the offer out-of-hand and refuse to make a counteroffer or to indicate an acceptable range. If this happens, and you still want to acquire the property, you have no choice but to adjust your bid and try again. But don't be surprised if your next bid is rejected as well. After all, with each new offer to buy you are conditioning the seller that by rejecting your bid he gets a better one. Very low offers do not strengthen a negotiating position.

Very low offers also tend to offend some sellers who perceive that the buyer is attempting to take "advantage" of them. Don't accept the assertion that commercial or investment real estate, unlike residential real estate, is devoid of passion and emotion. Sellers and buyers are people. Your offering price should be low enough to preserve your opportunity for a 'good buy,' but high enough to elicit a positive response or reasonable counteroffer from the seller.

In this regard, your own agent can be very helpful by first talking to the seller's agent, or if no agent is involved, directly to the seller himself. The objective should be to find out what the seller's objective is in selling, and whether or not his position requires special consideration in order to help the seller achieve his objective. This kind of information will prove invaluable in drafting an appealing LOI or purchase offer.

Solve the Seller's Problem

People are significantly motivated by the need to solve significant problems. A workable definition of a problem is the measure of the *recognized* gap between what is and what should be. The greater the gap, the greater the potential motivation. If the seller is a casual seller, doesn't need or want to sell, you will find negotiations difficult and even frustrating.[5] You must be dealing with a motivated seller in the same way you are a motivated buyer. If this is not the case, move on.

If you can uncover the seller's motivation for selling you should be able to adapt your offer to help fulfill his need. For example, if your seller is involved in an exchange and needs to sell this property to complete the exchange, your offer can indicate your willingness to cooperate in an exchange and to close within his required time frame. In personally presenting your offer, your agent has the opportunity to emphasize that – while it may not be everything (e.g. full price) the seller hoped for – your offer solves the seller's problem. If the cost of the solution is not too high, you will probably reach agreement.

About the Process

All negotiations are directed to the drawing of a bilateral, binding, written agreement under which you, the buyer, will furnish specified consideration in return for the seller's deed to the property. This agreement is the purchase/sale agreement executed by both the buyer and the seller.

Under the Statue of Frauds,[6] verbal offers to purchase real estate are – as Sam Goldwyn once said – "...not worth the paper they are printed on." If there are any parts of the agreement which are not included in the written contract, it is problematic that you will be able to add them after the contract has

---

[5]   "Do you need to receive an above-market price in order to sell?"
[6]   Universal throughout the U.S. with minor variations.

been formed. If an ancillary verbal agreement has been made, write it down and have it become a part of the written purchase contract by incorporation or amendment.

The Executory Cycle

When your offer is presented to the seller he has no legal obligation to respond. If the seller accepts your offer exactly as written, without any changes *of any kind*, indicates his acceptance by executing your offer and notifying you of his acceptance within the time allotted, a bilateral contract is immediately formed.

Up until the time that you are notified, in some verifiable fashion, that your offer has been accepted by the seller, you are free to withdraw the offer by notifying the seller, in a similar verifiable fashion, of the cancellation of your offer.

This pattern of *offer– acceptance– reconveyance of acceptance* constitutes the *executory cycle* and is essential for the establishment of an enforceable agreement.

The Counteroffer

If the seller does not accept your offer exactly as written, but instead alters your offer, even in the smallest detail, executes it and returns it to you, you do not have an agreement; you have a *counteroffer* to which you are not legally required to respond.

A counteroffer is considered a new[7] offer by the seller to sell on the modified terms and conditions presented in the counteroffer. For example, you may have indicated your willingness to arbitrate differences which may arise between you by checking the buyer's checkbox under the Arbitration clause in the contract form submitted to him. If he returns the offer properly executed, but with the seller's Arbitration checkbox left blank, his response is a counteroffer since it was clear that your intention was to arbitrate issues and his intention is not to arbitrate.

If the terms and conditions of the counteroffer are acceptable to you, you must indicate your acceptance of the counteroffer by signing it and by reconveying to the seller, by verifiable means, your acceptance of his new offer to sell: *counteroffer– acceptance– reconveyance of acceptance*. At any time until he receives notice of your acceptance of his counteroffer, the seller is free to withdraw the counteroffer by written and timely notification to you and to sell the property to someone else.

Requirements for a Contract

There are four basic requirements for a legal contract and five if real estate is involved. These are:

1. The object of the contract must be legal.
2. Both parties entering into the agreement must have the legal capacity to do so.
3. There must be mutual consent.
4. There must be good or valuable consideration.[8]
5. If the object is the transfer of title to real estate, the contract must be in writing.

---

[7]   The "new" terms consist of the original offer made, but modified by the terms of the counteroffer.
[8]   Good consideration is money; valuable consideration may be anything else, (e.g. love and affection)

The first requirement is fairly obvious and requires little comment.

The second requirement is important to the buyer since he must be assured that the seller of the property is the titled owner of the property (or property interest), or has the legal right to sell the property. It is not a pleasant experience to perform costly inspections only to find that the seller lacks the legal capacity to execute documents needed to transfer title to the property.

Capacity also refers to the ability of the seller to enter into valid contracts. Minors may own property but lack the legal capacity to enter into agreements to buy, sell, lease, exchange or option real property.

When the Seller Holds an Option

There are times when the seller is only the holder of an option to acquire the property and is not yet the legal owner. An option to buy real property is personal property and needs to be conveyed by means of an Assignment of the option or by a Bill of Sale for the option. If the option provides for the acquisition of the real property at current market value, the option has no apparent value but may still be valuable because the optionor is legally required to sell the property to the optionee. But most option holders offer to sell real property to which they do yet hold legal title and insert a clause in the resale agreement that states that their obligation to complete the sale is "subject to"[9] their obtaining title to the property. They do this by conducting two sales transactions,[10] the first at the option price with the current owner and the second, to you, at the resale price. Whenever possible, insist that the optionee first obtain legal title and then convey that title to you.

Many savvy optionees will prefer that you pay for the assignment of an existing option. They are motivated not only to avoid any potential problems in the actual transfer of title, but also seek to avoid the expenses of a sale. You will be far more secure in insisting on the transfer of title by a separate sale-purchase agreement to become effective when the optionee becomes the titled owner.

Note: If the individual who holds the option is also the agent of the seller, it is illegal for the agent to exercise the option and immediately sell the property to a third party without first revealing the selling price to the owner and without first obtaining the owner's written consent. Doing so is fraudulent and cause for revocation of the agent's license.

Assignment of Existing Agreement

Many real estate sale/purchase agreements contain language which permits the seller or the buyer to assign all the right, title and interest in the existing agreement to a third party. The assignment of an existing agreement is quite different from the assignment of an option by either the optionor or the optionee. When the assignment is that of an interest in an existing sale/purchase agreement the assignee stands in the legal shoes of the assignor and becomes responsible for carrying out all the obligations of the assignor.

Almost all real estate contracts are considered freely assignable except when there is a requirement for contract performance beyond the date of transfer. The most common limitation occurs when the seller has

---

[9]   Contingent upon.

[10]   A "double escrow."

agreed to finance all or part of the purchase price by accepting a promissory note or other consideration from the buyer, or when the agreement involves other future guarantees by the assignor.

The law frowns on any absolute limitation to the right to an assignment. Therefore contracts often contain language similar to the following:

> *"This agreement may not be assigned without the prior written approval of the seller, which approval shall not be unreasonably delayed or withheld."*

If the buyer is one acquiring a replacement property to complete a S.1031 exchange, he may be required to assign his interests in the contract to a Qualified Intermediary (facilitator) as part of his exchange agreement. The assignment of the contract may not, however, relieve the buyer or his assignee of the obligations pursuant to the contract. However, many Qualified Intermediaries no longer accept a deed to the exchangor's relinquished property: they accept only the **"Rights but not the Obligations"** of the Exchangor's agreement. (See Chapter 9 for additional information.)

Does the Seller Have the Right to Sell?

In other instances, the General Partner of a limited or general partnership, an Officer of a corporation or a Managing Member of a Limited Liability Company (LLC) must have the right to sell the partnership's property, the corporation's property or the LLC's property. Since this usually requires the consent of others, some written evidence must be furnished which documents this authority.

The same is true of property held in a trust: the Trustee must have the right to sell the property interest. If the individual who executes the sale-purchase contract does not have the legal capacity to sell the property, no valid contract can be formed and any contract so formed is invalid from the outset.

The preliminary title report which should be available will specify the legal description of the property and its titled owner, but you can ascertain ownership by pre-inspecting the deed recorded at the local Recording Office. If that is not convenient, call the customer service department of your favorite title company and ask them to verify current ownership.

Dealing with Minors

Minors are permitted to own real property[11] but persons who have not reached the legal age of majority lack the ability to enter into binding contracts to buy, sell or lease real property. This age is not always the customary age of majority since most states regard married (*emancipated*) minors as having the legal capacity to enter into contracts.[12]

Mutual Consent

The issue of mutual consent is extremely important to you as a real estate buyer. Mutual consent means that each party knows the terms and conditions of the contract, enters into the contract with the same understanding of its terms and conditions, and agrees to these. If it can be shown that there was no mutual consent, there was no contract.

---

[11] Most often they receive it as a gift or they inherit it.

[12] They already have.

The most frequent reason for the parties to a real estate contract to become embroiled in legal actions is ambiguity created by a poorly written agreement. In an effort to curtail misunderstandings and the consequences of poorly written contracts, many states now require the agent's use of very detailed, multi-paged forms which provide blanks for every conceivable provision. "Writing up an offer" by an agent in these states is nothing more than a process of assemblage of applicable forms and filling in the blanks. If your agent is not legally permitted to append minor clauses and amendments to a contract, or has poor writing skills, turn the matter over to your attorney, but avoid having the attorney become directly involved in negotiations with the seller. Use your attorney as a valuable resource, but not as a "deal maker."

Voidable Contracts

If any one of the requirements for a valid contract is missing, there is no contract *ab initio,* regardless of how far along you may be in the acquisition process. But once a contract comes into existence it may be void<u>able</u>, but only by the party who would be injured or harmed if the contract were to go to completion.

Existing legal contracts may be voided under five circumstances:
   ♦ Duress
   ♦ Undue influence
   ♦ Menace
   ♦ Fraud
   ♦ Mistake
The presence of any of these circumstances <u>does not</u> automatically void the contract.

Undue influence is self-explanatory. *Duress* pertains to the use of force to compel someone to do what he or she would ordinarily not do. *Menace* involves the threat of force (which coupled with the ability to carry out the threat constitutes *assault*).

Undue influence, duress and menace are not commonly involved in real estate contracts, but *Fraud* and *Mistake* sometimes are. Fraud may take the form of Fraud in the Inducement, which refers to a situation in which you were induced to enter into a contract on false or devious information. The contract arrived at may be perfectly legal, but it may also be voided by the party who would be injured if it were to proceed to completion. The party who potentially may be injured is under no obligation to void the contract; he/she simply has the right to do so.

Constructive fraud comprises all acts, omissions and concealments involving a breach of equitable or legal (fiduciary) duty. No *scienter*[13] is required; thus the party who makes a misrepresentation need not know it is false. This places a distinct duty on the part of an agent to be accurate in all representations, or to declare that he/she does not have the requested information.

There have been times when a buyer bought the wrong property, perhaps a lot or acreage in close proximity to the one he thought he was buying. This kind of mistake is grounds for voiding an executory contract. All these instances call for the services of an experienced real estate attorney.

---

[13]   Knowledge on the part of a person making a representation that the representation is false.

Consideration Required

In order to come into existence, every contract must involve good or valuable consideration. And that means to be legally binding your written offer must be accompanied by a deposit or 'earnest money,' or something else of value acceptable to the seller. If the seller accepts your offer and a deposit check is offered to him, he has the right to take the check immediately and cash it.[14] You do not want this to happen.

If you deliver a check payable to your agent he is required to deposit the check in his trust account on the next business day and to keep detailed records of the receipt and disposition of every check received. Upon acceptance of the offer the seller is entitled to demand and receive this legal consideration.

It is a very good rule to keep cash and negotiable checks out of the hands of the agent; in doing so you will be doing him/her a big favor. Instead, be certain that your sale-purchase agreement identifies the check as a deposit *and* stipulates that the check, which is made payable to the title company where you intend to hold the escrow, is to be held by your agent <u>uncashed</u> pending the opening of escrow.

Once a check is deposited into escrow[15] the escrow officer will not return a deposit without the written authorization of <u>both</u> parties even though the sale-purchase agreement may clearly give the buyer the right to recover the deposit. If there is a disagreement between the parties, the escrow officer will not release the cash and may, as an *interpleader*, turn the dispute and the cash over to a court to resolve the issue.

If you are required to sue the seller for return of the deposit, most of the deposit will go to legal fees.

Understanding Escrow

The term "escrow" derives from the French, *en escroue'*. In medieval times, when most of the populace were illiterate, laws and orders from the local authority were written on a scroll (escroue') which was delivered to a public area, read aloud to those assembled and then posted. Until the law was posted it was said to be *en escroue'* – in writing, but not yet law.

The modern escrow agreement is a <u>separate, second contract</u> which buyer and seller enter into in order to facilitate implementation of some, <u>but not all</u>, of the terms of their agreement. Because the escrow contract is not a duplicate of the sales/purchase agreement, it will not contain the entire agreement between the parties. Therefore suggestions that you "skip writing an offer and go directly to escrow" should be declined.

The escrow system is different from the systems in localities which use attorneys to close transactions in that the attorney represents the interest of only one party to the agreement, while the escrow officer represents *neither* party's interest. The escrow officer is truly a facilitator who must remain impartial and

---

[14] A currently dated check is a demand on funds already on deposit. A post-dated check is a promissory note. There is an important legal difference.

[15] Attorneys who do real estate closings provide a service similar to an escrow agent, except that an attorney will represent only one party while the escrow agent represents neither.

cannot act on behalf of, or at the direction of, either party alone. Escrow holders have been properly described as "neutral stakeholders."

The terms of the escrow contract are the written instructions which buyer and seller give to this facilitator. The major portion of these instructions will have been prepared as boilerplate in the escrow holder's 'standard' set of instructions. The escrow holder will incorporate the particular terms of the buyer-seller agreement but will rarely incorporate all. If there are conditions over which the escrow holder has no control or no role to play, the holder will either refuse to include these items or will include them as a Memo Only item *"... with which escrow holder is not to be concerned."*

For example, most contracts will call for a report on the presence or absence of hazardous and toxic wastes on or around the property. The escrow holder will not accept a direction to obtain such a report but will accept a direction to receive such a report from the seller for transmittal to the buyer for approval within a defined time period.

Conformed copies[16] of the escrow instructions will be presented to the buyer and seller for their individual approvals. Each identical set will be signed by buyer and seller separately, but taken together they stand as one document.

The Essence of the Escrow Contract

The essence of the escrow contract is that the escrow holder accepts a conditional deed of transfer executed by the seller. The escrow holder also accepts the buyer's cash. On the date agreed upon for the closing, and when the escrow has been *perfected*,[17] the escrow holder exchanges the seller's deed for the buyer's cash, delivering the cash to the seller and causing the buyer's deed to be recorded at the local recording office.

If a loan is involved, the escrow holder, acting also as an agent for the lender, will ensure that all the lender's conditions and requirements are met by the borrower. The escrow holder will obtain the borrower's signature on a promissory note (supplied by the lender) and on a Deed of Trust (or Mortgage). Loan funds are seldom delivered to the escrow officer but are held by the title company stipulated in the agreement.[18]

When the conditional deed has been executed by the seller and when all the buyer's cash is available, the transaction is ready to close. An early closing prior to the previously agreed date requires the written approval of both parties. It is important to define the close of escrow as the time at which the buyer's deed is recorded at the local recording office. This keeps the escrow holder involved up to the minute of recordation. If this definition of "closing date' is not contained in the escrow holder's standard boilerplate, ask that it be included.

---

[16] Copies which are legally the same as the originals and attested to by the escrow officer.

[17] All requirements satisfied.

[18] Other funds delivered to the escrow officer must be deposited in a segregated and dedicated account as "trust funds," which are not subject to confiscation or attachment by third parties.

Contingencies

Contingencies are conditions precedent. You cannot afford to enter into a contract to acquire property without the protection of certain contingencies. Contingencies render your obligation to complete the contract dependent upon an event happening or not happening prior to a defined period of time or prior to a certain date. Because the contingencies that will be meaningful to you will be largely under your control, the more contingencies you have the more uncomfortable a motivated seller becomes about your intentions.

If your offer contains contingencies which can only be satisfied once a contract has been entered into, the seller will probably go along. But if you insert contingencies which have no deadline, or which could have easily been satisfied prior to making an offer (e.g. area rent survey) the seller will negotiate to remove these or may not accept your offer.

Most sellers understand the need for contingencies, but they expect a serious buyer to act promptly to remove these contingencies at the earliest possible time. That's why an informed and motivated seller will insist on deadlines; unsatisfied contingencies keep his property off the market and if you are dealing with a motivated seller, as you should be, that will be very important. As a motivated buyer, you should keep contingencies to an absolute minimum and work quickly to satisfy and remove them.

The Escrow Holder and Contingencies

Once an agreement has been reached, many important contingencies can be satisfied before opening an escrow. It is notable that in Northern California, a state which uses *escrows* to close most transactions, an escrow account is frequently not opened until the last portion of the time allotted for closing. But in Southern California most transactions are delivered to the escrow holder within days of the seller's acceptance. In fact, some of these contracts specify that an escrow account must be opened within a certain number of days following final agreement, as though the agreement between buyer and seller has no legal force unless and until it is committed to escrow.

Contingencies Satisfied Early

There are a number of contingencies which may be satisfied following execution of a sale/purchase agreement but before opening escrow and before depositing cash into an escrow account.

For example, you need to receive and read a copy of every lease affecting the property and every contract which will survive the closing. Your agreement with the seller may require him to furnish these documents by a certain date and will require you to approve or disapprove of them, in writing, by a certain date. You may be asked to execute a Confidentiality Agreement.

You should also obtain *estoppel* certificates from every tenant in a multi-tenant property which verifies that the lease or rental agreement is in full and force effect, that the rent is correct, that there are or are no offsets[19] to the rent, the amount of security deposit held by the owner,[20] the existence of any options to

---

[19] Allowances to the tenant which reduce the amount of rent due.

[20] In most cases security deposits are not returned to the seller but rather debited to the seller and credited to the buyer at closing.

extend the lease, and their terms, and that the landlord is not in default on his obligations under the lease. All these verifications may be made prior to opening escrow.

You must also reserve the right to inspect the property and to have third-party specialists inspect the property. These inspections may include a physical 'walk-through' of the property as well as a professional inspection for infestation or damage by pests, termites and other wood-destroying organisms, for mold and for water damage. An inspection for the presence of hazardous (toxic) materials must be performed in order to get a loan. An inspection by a geologist or civil (structural) engineer may also be in order. Other specialists may be used to verify the current condition of plumbing and electrical systems, heating, ventilating and air conditioning (HVAC) systems.

These inspections, and others, can be performed prior to opening escrow. If any irreconcilable disagreement arises, you will be out your time and some money, but your deposit will not be at risk.

Contingencies Should Have Consequences

Every contingency in your offer to acquire should have both a time deadline *and* a consequence if the condition precedent is not met.

For example, if the roof inspection indicates the need for a new roof, and this eventuality is not covered in your agreement (as it should be), your release of the contingency will not happen. But then what? Unless the answer to the "so what?" question has been earlier provided for, the transaction may grind to a halt forcing a renegotiation of the contract.

You may also impose contingencies which need to be satisfied by the seller. For example, you may have a condition which requires the seller to furnish income and expenses statements for the operation of the property for the last three years. There should be a reasonable time frame within which the seller must comply. The consequence of his not meeting the deadline might be that   '... the buyer shall have the unilateral right to cancel this agreement, to receive back his deposit in full, and shall be under no further obligation and at no future liability of any kind to the seller..."

Key Conditions

Preliminary Title Report (PTR)

One of the most important contingencies is that of your approval of a current report on the condition of title. This report should be made available to you within five to seven working days following an initial order for title insurance.

Preliminary title reports are generally divided into two sections: Schedule A states the entity to be insured, the amount of the insurance, the legal description of the property, the interest conveyed (e.g. a fee interest, a leasehold interest, etc.) and the amount of any proposed mortgage. Schedule B recites the requirements and the exceptions to the coverage.

On receipt, verify that the titled owner is the same person or entity with whom you have entered into the sale-purchase agreement. Verify also that there are no previously unstated liens on the property which will survive the closing. Disregard liens representing current real estate taxes since these will be pro-rated, but pay particular attention to liens for past-due real property taxes or liens from federal or state income tax agencies since these <u>will transfer with the title</u> if not satisfied. Your contract should specify that <u>all liens</u> other than current real estate tax liens and other liens which you have agree to assume, must be removed at closing.[21]

Very often liens for the improvement of the property appear in the PTR. For example, a community improvement resulted in an assessment which could be paid in cash or could "go to bond." The periodic payment on this type debt is often collected by the tax collector as a convenience, even though it is not a tax and is not tax-deductible. In either case, the lien represents a deduction from the unencumbered market value of the property. If the property in question is encumbered by such a lien, while comparable properties in the same area are not so encumbered, there will be a measurable difference in value received.

Toxic and Hazardous Waste Inspection

Many land parcels contain hazardous or toxic chemicals caused by a prior use or proximity to a nearby source of toxic chemicals which have leached onto, under or around the property. Sources of contamination may be miles away from the property but borne there via the aquifer or leaching. This issue is of prime concern to the real estate buyer because the cost of removing this contamination may easily exceed the market value of the property. In addition, the owner of the property may be liable for the cost of remediation of other properties to which the contaminating materials have migrated.

The determination of any contamination in, on or around the site is accomplished by means of a Phase-I Environmental Site Assessment. (Phase-I ESA). A less intrusive inspection known as a Pre-Phase-I Inspection, or Transaction Screen, is intended for "low risk property" transactions where there is little concern about potential liability. But in general, a Phase-I inspection is the minimum requirement.

A Phase-I inspection consists of a review of all paper records concerning the property's present and past use. If this inspection indicates the possibility of contamination, a Phase -II inspection is required. A Phase-II inspection consists of collecting both surface and underground samples of the soil for testing. If tests reveal the presence of toxic or potentially toxic substances, a Phase-III operation is undertaken to remove or neutralize the substances.

If the buyer of the property seeks a commercial loan, the lender will most commonly require a Phase I inspection and report. Contaminated properties will become ineligible for an institutional loan. Needless to say, an offer to purchase should be contingent upon the receipt of a Phase-I Report showing that the property is not contaminated.

Easements as Encumbrances

All PTRs will list the existence of recorded easements on the property. *Easements-in-Gross* are for the benefit of utility and cable companies who need to service their lines; these easements cannot be removed. *Appurtenant easements* may permit a third party to use a portion of the property such as a common driveway or a strip of land to ingress and egress an adjacent parcel. This kind of easement will transfer with the transfer of the title with no mention of it in the transferring deed. If you are in doubt regarding the exact location of an appurtenant easement, ask the title officer to plot it out for you on a property (parcel) map.

If there are other covenants (agreements), conditions and restrictions (CC&Rs) referred to in the PTR, obtain and read each of these documents since they will affect your rights, duties and responsibilities connected with ownership. Be especially certain that no CC&R will interfere with your intended use of the property.

---

[21] This will include judgment liens.

Be mindful that the PTR will <u>not</u> verify the zoning of the property, required setbacks, height limitations, or the existence of additions, units or improvements which were added without a required permit. These facts can only be ascertained by a visit to city hall.

ADA Requirements

Provisions of Title II of the Americans with Disabilities Act ("ADA"), 42 U.S.C. §§ 12131-12134, and Section 504 of the Rehabilitation Act of 1973, 29 U.S.C § 794(a) impose important responsibilities on both landlords and tenants with regard to the compliance of properties accessible to individuals with disabilities. These regulations address a panoply of rules and design requirements intended to make properties accessible to those with disabilities. These regulations extend from the availability of handicap parking spaces to the height above the floor of bathroom tissue holders.

While the goals of ADA legislation are desirable, there has arisen in some states a cadre of attorneys and "disabled" individuals who have used the law to extort settlements from property owners and tenants for alleged violations. These suits are filed in Federal Court.

Although the property owner may agree to promptly remedy the violations, the minimum cost to resolve these suits ranges from $15,000 to $25,000. Buyers of a commercial and industrial property should consider a contingency that the property meets current ADA requirements upon closing. In those jurisdictions in which Certified Access Specialists are available, a Certificate of Compliance by a Certified Access Specialist (CASp) has a deterrent and defensive value in the event the owner or tenant is sued for an ADA violation.

Leases should assign to the tenant the responsibility to maintain the property in ADA compliance. Multifamily properties[22] and residences are exempt from ADA regs.

Loan Contingency

There are certain conditions precedent which should be preserved until the close of the escrow. Chief among these is a contingency for approval of a new loan or, if applicable, for assumption of an existing loan.

In order to protect his position the seller will probably insist that you apply for and obtain a loan commitment letter within a certain number of days for the amount stated in the contract and provide evidence of having done so to the escrow holder. This is common and reasonable.

But you need to have the extra protection of a contingency which states that the loan must not only be approved but that <u>it must also fund</u>. Almost all loans which are approved by the lender are approved <u>conditionally</u> and these conditions are delivered to the escrow holder who cannot close the transaction until the lender's conditions have been fully satisfied. This leaves lots of room for an 'approved' loan not to fund. Therefore your loan contingency should specify not only loan approval but *funding* as well.

Possession

A second contingency which should survive until the closing is the right of possession. You may be in contract to purchase an office or industrial building which you intend to occupy fully at closing. The seller may have leased this space to one or more tenants currently in possession. As you know, any tenant who occupies the property under a valid lease[23] which has not yet expired has the right to remain in

---

[22] A multifamily property which provides a separate sales office may be subject to ADA regulations
[23] Including options to extend

possession until the termination of the lease, despite a change in ownership. Some of the most famous words in real estate are,

> "…don't worry, I'll get them out."

If the terms of the contract call for the property to be vacant at closing, verbal reassurances that it will be should not be relied upon. You should have already examined any current lease and the estoppel certificate to determine whether the tenant has the right to remain in possession beyond the closing date. But even if the tenant does not, you must insist that the property be vacant at the time of closing.

If a tenant in possession decides not to cooperate by vacating the property before closing, you may find that it can take much money and many months to have the tenant evicted. The best way to assure yourself that the property is vacant is to inspect the property yourself on the day prior to closing, or have your agent do so. It is not something the escrow holder will do for you. If the property is not vacant, inform <u>all</u> parties and direct the escrow holder, *in writing*, not to close the escrow until it can be verified that the property is vacant.

New Leases and Service Contracts

If the property is an apartment building, retail center or multi-tenant industrial property, the seller may be faced with the task of leasing and releasing some spaces prior to the close of escrow. He may also face the need to initiate or renew certain service contracts, such as pest control, pool maintenance, landscaping, management and security agreements, and others.

Your obligation to buy the property should be absolutely contingent upon your right to approve or to reasonably disapprove any lease, rental agreement or service contract which is to be executed or renewed prior to the close of escrow and which will survive the closing. As with all contingencies, your approval and disapproval should have a time deadline. If a disagreement arises between you and the seller, you should have the unilateral right to terminate the escrow and to have your deposit money returned in full.

Arbitration Clause

Most contract forms in use today provide the buyer and seller the opportunity to agree that disputes arising between them shall be committed to neutral, binding arbitration, specifying a reputable arbitration service, such as a member of the American Arbitration Association, as arbiter. The intent has been to avoid lengthy and expensive litigation.

Recent experiences with the results of these provisions have begun to cast doubt on their advisability. An important aspect of these clauses is that they require the parties to give up their right to a court or jury trial and to an appeal of an unfavorable decision, and to be bound by the decisions of the arbitration panel alone. The difficulties which have arisen concern the qualifications of the arbiters; some cases have been decided in ways and by means which would not be permitted in a court trial.

Many lawyers will advise their clients not to initial such clauses in the contract and their reasons are quite apparent. But it appears that there must be some improvements in the arbitration agreement and process before the parties can be assured of consistently competent and reasoned decisions. In the meantime, we need to await such improvements.

Liquidated Damages

Most contract forms contain a clause pertaining to liquidated damages. These clauses propose that in the event of a <u>default</u> by the buyer, the seller agrees to liquidate all his claims against the buyer by accepting the amount specified in the clause. A default is not the equivalent of a failure to close because of an unsatisfied contingency. A default occurs when the buyer *could* close but *chooses* not to.

The amount of damages which the seller of a non-residential property, or 5 or more residential units, may claim upon default is not limited. But when the property is a residential property (1-4 units) the amount of the damages maybe limited by law. In most contracts intended for use in commercial/investment transactions there is no ceiling on the amount that can be agreed upon. If the proposed amount of the liquidated damages is reasonable, the buyer is probably well advised to agree to the liquidated damages provision since it sets a ceiling on potential liability. The alternative is to be prepared to defend against a suit for costs, attorney fees and damages.

Two considerations are important: 1) the seller may not be entitled to the full liquidated damage amount unless he can demonstrate that he has suffered the loss claimed. This may require a lawsuit to determine damages; 2) despite the liquidated damage agreement; the escrow holder will not release any funds to the seller without the buyer's consent and approval.

Therefore this clause tends to work in favor of the buyer. The portion of cash in escrow which is to be made subject to the liquidated damage provision is a matter of negotiation between seller and buyer. In order to be effective these clauses must be separately initialed by each party.

Time is of the Essence

Most contracts contain a clause which specifies that *Time is of the Essence*, meaning that in those contract matters containing a time deadline, the time limitation should be strictly interpreted. If, for example, your seller fails to deliver current copies of all leases within the 10-day period required, you have the legal right to cancel the agreement. But you can expect that if the seller delivers them on the 11th day, a court (of equity) will probably not uphold your right to cancel the agreement unless you can show that the one-day delay truly damaged you. If the seller fails to deliver within, say, 2 or 3 weeks, that would be another matter.

Fail-Safe Approval Clause

Almost all pre-printed sale-purchase agreements provide that if you fail to disapprove of some matter which requires your approval by a certain date and you neither approve nor disapprove it, the matter will be considered approved. Don't allow this clause to stand. It is better to have someone chase after you for your approval on a matter you have overlooked, or which became due when you were out of town, than to have the matter automatically approved. Either have the clause removed or have your failure to approve default to an automatic disapproval. Stay in charge. Ask your agent to draw up a time schedule for critical events. This is a great help in not missing important deadlines.

Security Deposits

Tenants are often required to render a security deposit to the landlord. The existence and amount of a security deposit in the hands of a landlord should be confirmed by the use of the estoppel certificate which the landlord has submitted to the tenant for your benefit. Your agreement should require the seller to verify these amounts and to resolve any discrepancy between his accounting and the tenant's signed certificate prior to the closing.

In the ordinary transaction the amount of the security deposit should transfer to the buyer since the buyer will have to refund these sums upon termination of the tenant's occupancy. Most escrow holders will accept a *security reconciliation statement* signed by both buyer and seller to be debited to the seller's account and credited to the buyer's account. There is no valid reason that these sums should transfer outside of escrow or after the close of escrow.

Disclosures and Physical Condition

In most states the seller is required to provide the buyer with a disclosure statement specifying, to the best of his knowledge, the condition of the property, enumerating any existing problems. The same disclosure is required of the seller's agent. The best disclosure, however, is obtained from an inspection of the property furnished by a certified or licensed, professional property inspector who is hired by the buyer. These inspections should cover both the structural and operating systems of the improvement including the roof, foundation, electrical, plumbing and sewer systems, as well as the heating, ventilation and air conditioning (HVAC) systems. These inspections are not the equivalent of inspections by a specialist in each of these systems, but they are very worthwhile in identifying latent problems not obvious to the untrained eye.

An inspection for the presence of hazardous waste materials on, under or around the property is essential and is usually an absolute requirement by the lender. If the property is to be acquired using all cash, this inspection should nevertheless be made since the cost of remediating contaminated property often exceeds its sales price.

Other Requirements

Depending upon the state and locality in which the property is located, there may be a number of other regulations and requirements which must be met upon the transfer of the property. These are in addition to federal regulations. Therefore you may wish to include an encompassing clause which states that "...*the property is to conform to all federal, state and local laws and regulations at the time of closing.*"

Preliminary Closing Statement

Approximately 1 week prior to the scheduled date of closing, direct the escrow holder to prepare and deliver to you a preliminary closing statement showing the amount to be credited and debited to your account. You do not need a statement showing the seller's position, and even if you did have it, it will not conform to your statement since there are debits and credits which will apply to the seller and not to you.

Take time to review your statement line by line. In the author's experience approximately 30-40% all escrow settlement statements contain significant financial errors. An error of more than $50,000 was once detected in an escrow for the sale of a $1,100,000 parcel of vacant land.[24] Any errors detected after the close of escrow become very difficult and costly to rectify.

Choosing the Escrow Holder

It goes almost without saying that you should be careful to choose an escrow holder (company) and officer (person) experienced in investment property transactions. Choosing an escrow service which is a part of, or a subsidiary of, a major title company has much to recommend it – although we hasten to add that there are many excellent independent escrow companies employing excellent escrow officers.

---

[24] The remaining loan balance submitted by the seller of the property who had carried back the entire first mortgage.

Title companies are always looking for more insurance business, and while they may be restricted in their ability to charge fees different from those filed with the insurance commission or supervising insurance department in the state in which they are located, they are free to negotiate their escrow fees. If you call for bids for both title and escrow services from the major title companies servicing your market, you will find that you can often save hundreds of dollars. Dealing directly with a major title company and its escrow department also provides you a ready resource for questions and problems which may arise in your transaction. That resource will be the title officer assigned to your account and policy. You will usually find these individuals very well-informed and most often quite anxious to help.

A final consideration in dealing with a major title company is that you don't have to worry about the safety of your funds. There are plenty of other things which will take your time and energy in closing the investment transaction. But the safety of your funds on deposit with an escrow holder ought not to be one of them.

W e all reach a point when the question of what to do with our assets is decided for us, but until that time we need to make decisions about what we should do with a real estate investment we hold: should it be sold, refinanced, exchanged or simply left for our heirs to enjoy?

For many investors, this decision point is reached when the ROE falls below the current inflation rate indicating that the real rate of return is negative. At this point the equity dollars in the property are losing purchasing power at a rate equal to the difference between the inflation rate and the ROE. This loss is not limited just to current earnings, but applies to <u>all</u> equity dollars currently in the investment. It indicates a contraction in real wealth.

Because this decision cannot be made in an economic vacuum, the answer to the question depends not only upon the individual investor's strategic goals but also upon the most probable future economic conditions.

Choices

Theoretically, there are only four courses of action available to the investor who has a very large equity position but now shows a diminishing ROE:

1. Sell the property, pay the tax and reinvest the proceeds.
2. Exchange the property for one capable of better performance.
3. Refinance the property.
4. Do nothing.

There was a time when the investor could obtain a reasonably reliable estimate of current inflation in order to help make this decision. If, for example, the ROE from the investment is 4.5% and inflation is proceeding at a 3.0% annual rate, the investor can see that his wealth is still growing, albeit at a very modest 1.5%. Recognition of this financial fact is the real value of monitoring the ROE: to be able to make changes when the ROE persistently falls below an acceptable rate. But the Sell/Re-invest decision is made difficult by the unprecedented interference by the federal government in both the reported inflation rate and market interest rates.

It is commonly known that the U.S. Department of Labor, Bureau of Labor Statistics,[1] manipulates the Consumer Price Index (CPI) to show inflation rates considerably below actual. The federal government has a vested interest in doing so; the CPI numbers are used in setting increases for government programs such as Social Security, Medicare and Medicaid, federal employee wages and pensions, and military pay adjustments.

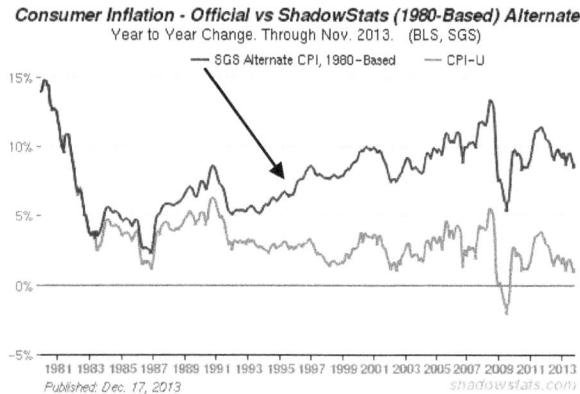

Consumer Inflation - Official vs ShadowStats (1980-Based) Alternate
Year to Year Change. Through Nov. 2013.   (BLS, SGS)
— SGS Alternate CPI, 1980-Based   — CPI-U
Published: Dec. 17, 2013
shadowstats.com

The U.S. federal debt, which in 2014 stands at $18+ Trillion, indicates that an increase of just 1.0% in the interest rate paid on the debt by the federal government would result in $180 Billion additional annual interest at a time when the annual budget deficit already exceeds $0.5 Trillion.

Dr. John Williams,[2] a well-trained and experienced economist who recalculates and reports government statistics as they were formerly measured, estimates that inflation in 2013 was 8-10% rather than as officially reported by the BLS's CPI index at 2.2% At an annual inflation rate of 8.0%, equity dollars accumulated in the investment lose 50% of their purchasing power within 9 years.

The Federal Reserve Bank employs stratagems such as *Quantitative Easing, Operation Twist*[3] and *Financial Repression* designed to suppress market interest rates. In 3Q2012, the FED announced plans to buy $85B per month of mortgages, indefinitely.[4]

The collateral damage associated with these stratagems is that an investor who would like to sell his/her property, reinvest the proceeds and settle into a secure retirement has difficulty in finding a conservative, passive investment to yield the true rate of inflation. For those who have already sold, chasing higher yield to keep up with inflation has led to higher risk- taking, which accounts, in part, for the rising rate of bankruptcies among seniors.

The way to crush the bourgeoisie is to grind them between the millstones of taxation and inflation.
V.I. Lenin

Unfortunately the individual investor has no defense against these tactics other than to transfer cash to non-dollar denominated assets or to "hard" assets whose nominal value will increase as the value of the dollar decreases.

The United States is not far from the point when other sovereignties will no longer accept the dollar as the reserve currency.[5] At that point, CDs, Money Market accounts, Bonds and other dollar-denominated passive investments will suffer a severe loss in value. The market will respond with severe price inflation.

---

1   www.bls.gov

2   See www.shadowstats.com

3   The practice by the Fed of selling short-term Treasuries (<3 yrs.) which it holds and buying longer-term (>5-10 yrs.) Treasuries. The increased demand for longer-term instruments forces prices up and interest rates down.

4   In March 2014 the Fed lowered the amount of bond purchases from $75B /month to $65B /month and forecasted the end of bond buying by EOY 2014.

As a result, a decision to sell real estate investments and reinvest in passive dollar-denominated investments is no longer an option for most investors, especially for owners of smaller income properties.

Should You Trade Your Investment?

The ability to trade real estate for other real estate is a very powerful estate-building tool. Because you will want to learn much more about it, we have devoted a separate chapter in great detail to the S.1031 tax-deferred exchange.

The Refinancing Option

If the future prospects for the property are good and you wish to keep it, you can remedy the low ROE by taking equity out of the property in the form of a new loan.

Refinancing is a very attractive option since it helps reestablish a healthy return on current equity and since the proceeds from a new loan are non-taxable. The proceeds can be used to acquire any other investment – REITs, stocks, or one or more new real estate properties. Refinancing always provides an opportunity for reinvestment to re-balance portfolios.

But take care. The property you refinance will still carry along the same low Adjusted Basis and unrecognized tax liability it did before the refinance. In fact, in the absence of new capital improvements or additions, the Adjusted Basis will continue to decline. (Adding a new loan will not affect the Basis.)

If you are required to sell, the unrecognized gain will become recognized and you may face a large tax liability with fewer funds to pay it. If you later decide to exchange this property for a replacement property the reduced amount of equity may not serve as a sufficiently large down payment to acquire a property whose maximum mortgage will cover the mortgage on the relinquished property. In this event, you may face *Net Mortgage Relief*, a form of Boot[6] which will expose at least part of your gain to immediate taxation. (See chapter 9 for additional details.)

If you had planned to sell the property and carry back a note to fund your retirement years, the excess of the high mortgage over Adjusted Basis would result in immediate tax recognition of the excess. This tax, together with the tax on unrecaptured S. 1250 depreciation, which is also recognized in the year of the installment sale, may amount to such a large tax liability that you could not follow your plan.

Many, many investors box themselves into a property by refinancing it for the highest loan possible and then not re-investing the proceeds. Sometimes the only way out is to die.[7]

Refinancing the Trust Property

If the property to be refinanced is held in a trust, it may be necessary to remove the property from the trust in order to refinance it. When a property is transferred into a trust, title to the property is bifurcated: the *naked legal title* is held by the trustee while the *equitable title* is held by the beneficiaries. Pledging both

---

[5]   A number of countries now pay for oil and commodity purchases in their native currencies while more and more press for a replacement of the dollar as the reserve currency.

[6]   Boot = unlike property received in an otherwise valid exchange.

[7]   In which case heirs will inherit the property with a stepped-up Basis.

these partial interests as security for a loan can be awkward. It is much simpler to remove the property from the trust placing it in the hands of one or more owners who can more easily pledge the title as security for the loan. Once the refinance has been completed the property can be returned to the trust.[8]

Do Nothing

A decision to do nothing is the financial equivalent of buying the property from yourself for the net equity currently invested in it. A detailed answer to this possible choice can be obtained by extending the Ten-Year After-Tax Analysis program developed in Chapter 6. But in general, if the ROE from the property is poor to begin with you can be certain that it will not improve with age.

---

[8]   It is a common happenstance that investors forget to return the property to the trust.

T he ability to exchange one real investment property for another without immediate tax consequences is one of the great advantages to investing in real estate. In almost every other kind of investment, the disposition of the investment triggers off the recognition of accumulated gains resulting in an immediate tax liability. Exchanging enables the investor to move untaxed equity into a replacement property, and by leveraging the same equity, acquire a property of much greater value. Exchanging is the most powerful tool available to the real estate investor to grow a real estate portfolio and increase wealth.

Because the rules governing real property exchanges are covered in Section 1031 of the Internal Revenue Code, these exchanges are popularly known as "1031 exchanges." The language of the Code is simple, straightforward and precise:

> *"No gain or loss shall be recognized on the exchange of property held for productive use in a trade or business or for investment if such property is exchanged solely for like-kind property which is to be held for use in a trade or business or for investment."*

This is one instance in which the distinction between real and personal property which we focused on in Chapter 1 becomes critical. Although we are primarily interested in real property exchanges, it should be noted that exchanges can also be made between certain kinds of personal property as well.

Realized vs. Recognized Gains

The meaning of the words *recognized*, *realized* and *indicated* is important. If you purchased a saleable article for $1,000 and its value over time increased to $2,000, your gain - for tax purposes - would be characterized as a *realized* or *indicated* gain. Your gain would not become *recognized*, however, until you sold the article. *Recognized* in this context means *taxable* in the current tax period.

The exchange - but not the sale - of real property may result in non-recognition of the indicated or realized gain thereby deferring the tax which would otherwise be due and payable; hence, *tax-deferred* exchanges. But exchanging does not eliminate the potential for tax later on; it only postpones it. Therefore casually referring to S.1031 exchanges as "tax-free exchanges" can be misleading.

Property Not Eligible for Exchange

There are certain kinds of property which are specifically excluded from the exchange option. These include:

- Stock in trade or other property held primarily for sale (inventory)
- Stocks, bonds or notes
- Other securities or evidence of indebtedness or interest
- Interests in a partnership
- Certificates of trust or beneficial interests[1]
- Choses in Action[2]
- Real property located in a foreign country
- Residences

The exclusion of trade property from the exchange privilege affects real property builders, developers and brokers who either build or acquire and hold real property primarily for sale to others (stock in trade). This does not mean that these individuals or companies cannot at times exchange property, but it does require them to segregate their investment properties from their inventory properties and to be prepared to prove that the investment properties have indeed been held primarily for investment and not as inventory for sale to others.

Except in those instances in which individuals have specifically qualified for exemption from treatment as a partnership,[3] neither a general nor a limited partnership interest is considered like-kind to real property. From a legal and tax point of view, property owned by a partnership is owned by a single entity, the partner*ship*, and not by the partners themselves who hold interests in the partnership. As such, a partnership, acting as a distinct entity, may exchange its real estate for other like-kind property, but the partners, both general and limited, who hold personal property in the form of partnership interests, are not eligible to exchange these interests.

The same principle applies to beneficial interests in trusts. If the need to exchange arises, partnership and trust interests may be converted, tax-free, to tenant-in-common interests, which converts an interest in personal property to a direct interest in real property.[4] Tenant-in-common interests are freely exchangeable.[5]

Residences Not Exchangeable

Residences, though real property, are not eligible for an exchange because they are not held primarily for investment or for use in a trade or business. But moving out of a residence and converting it to a rental property by treating it as a rental property[6] renders the property eligible for an exchange.

---

[1] Real property may be exchanged for units in a Delaware Statutory Trust if structured as in Rev.Rul. 2004-86.

[2] A claim or debt on which a recovery may be made in a lawsuit. Pronounced "showses."

[3] I.R.C Section 761(a) permits members of investment clubs to be treated as individuals rather than partners who would otherwise be ineligible to exchange.

[4] An experienced real estate attorney should be consulted.

[5] See page 9-23 for additional information re TICs.

[6] E.g., by offering it for rent, deducting operating expenses and depreciating it.

A house acquired via a S.1031 exchange must also be "held for investment or for use in a trade or business." Therefore converting a house into a personal residence shortly after acquiring it through an exchange may invalidate the exchange by demonstrating that the house was not *"...to be held for investment or for use in a trade or business"* as required by the Code.

There are no specific I.R.S. regulations which offer guidance as to how long a property must be held as an income property before it can be converted into a residence. A very aggressive stance would be 6 months; a more conservative stance would be at least one year, or a sufficient time which would allow the taxpayer to report the income from the rental over at least two consecutive tax years. Competent tax guidance should be sought.

Taxpayers should be aware of HR 4520 which was passed into law on Oct. 22, 2004. This bill requires that a property that was acquired as the result of a S.1031 exchange and later occupied as a residence will not be eligible for the long term capital gains exclusions under S.121 until that date which is 5 years following the date of acquisition. Occupancy for at least 2 years out of the last 5 years remains a requirement.

Although the residents of a home may qualify for a long term capital gain exclusion of either $250,000 (single individuals) or $500,000 (married) at the time the home is sold, this exclusion does not extend to the recapture of depreciation taken by the owners during the years the property was used as a rental. Any depreciation taken by the owners of the property during their period of ownership will be treated at the time of sale as *Unrecaptured S.1250 Depreciation* subject to taxation at the prevailing rate.[7]

Like-Kind Property

Like-kind property refers to property of the same nature or character, and not to its quality or grade. "Like-kind" means real estate for real estate, without regard to whether the real properties exchanged are improved or unimproved, or whether they are retail, office, residential income, industrial properties, or vacant land.

In the case of improved real estate which has been subject to depreciation, the exchange of this kind of property for unimproved real property carrying no depreciable element, or for property with insufficient depreciable value, may result in recapture of all or some of the depreciation taken on the relinquished property. Exchanging from an improved parcel into an unimproved parcel will not invalidate the exchange, but it will result in recapture of depreciation. Consult S.1250 and experienced tax counsel.

For federal tax purposes - to which most state laws conform - a leasehold interest in real property with thirty (30) or more years to run, including options, is considered to be like-kind to real property and may be freely exchanged for real property. A leasehold interest with less than 30 years remaining may be exchanged only for another leasehold interest with less than 30 years remaining.

Transaction Must Be an Exchange

It is important that the exchange be structured as an exchange and not as a sale followed by a purchase. For example, if a property owner seeks to exchange his property he may not be the actual or constructive[8]

---

[7] Twenty-five percent as of 2015.
[8] If he could take the cash, even though he does not, or if he benefits from the cash, he is deemed to be in constructive receipt.

recipient of the proceeds from a sale, even if the proceeds are immediately used to acquire a replacement property. Leaving the funds in escrow, or with a third party (lacking an agreement with the third party to exchange), will <u>not</u> cover the requirements of S.1031. The I.R.S. considers the unfettered ability to take the funds, pledge the funds, borrow the funds, benefit from the funds or the right to demand and receive the funds before a suitable replacement is acquired to be equivalent to receipt of unlike-property. This limitation extends to agents of the owner as well.

It is also important to declare one's intent to deliver title to the property to be relinquished via a qualified S.1031 exchange. This intent of the exchangor should be threaded through all the appropriate sale and exchange documents, including agreements for the disposition of the relinquished property and for the acquisition of the replacement property.

Boot

In a real property exchange it is rare that the accounts between the exchangors balance out evenly. In almost all cases one of the parties to the exchange gets more than he gives, or gives more than he gets. In order to "balance the equities," cash, or other personal property, is usually added or "thrown in *to Boot*." *Boot* is defined as unlike property given or received in an otherwise valid tax-deferred exchange. Perhaps an example will help to illustrate:

> Jones owns Parcel A worth $50,000 which is free and clear of debt.
> Smith owns Parcel B worth $45,000, also free of debt.
> Jones and Smith agree to exchange their parcels.
> Smith agrees to add $5,000 in cash to be paid to Jones to "balance the equities."

Here's how this looks on paper:

Jones' Account		Smith's Account	
Gives Deed A worth	−$50,000	Gives Deed B worth	−$45,000
Gets Deed B worth	+$45,000	Gets Deed A worth	+$50,000
Gets Cash (taxable Boot)	+$5,000	Gives Cash	−$5,000
Net Position	0	Net Position	0

The $5,000 which Smith gave to Jones to balance equities, in this otherwise valid 1031 exchange, is characterized as unlike property, or <u>Boot</u>.

Boot is taxable to the receiver, but never to the giver. Therefore if we assume that Jones had a realized or indicated gain in Property A of, say, $15,000, $5,000 of this gain would be recognized for tax purposes in the year of the exchange. If Jones had only a $3,000 realized gain in his property at the time of this exchange, only $3,000 would be recognized as taxable Boot. This is so because Boot is taxable to the receiver only up to the limit of his gain at the time of the exchange. The remaining $2,000 which Jones would have received would be counted as a return of Basis and would not be taxable.

Smith would have a completely tax-deferred exchange regardless of any realized gain he may have in Property B because he received only like-kind property and did not receive Boot.

Exchange of Mortgaged Properties

The phrase "to balance equities" is used because the guideline for settling accounts in exchanging is not the agreed-upon fair market value of the respective properties, but rather the amount of equity each owner has in the property he contributes to the exchange. By *equity* we mean the fair market value less the total of all liens[9] against the title at the time of the exchange and which will remain on the property after the exchange. These liens may include one or more mortgages or trust deeds, tax liens, bonds, assessments or any other money-encumbrances which reduce the owner's financial stake in his property.

We can build on our previous example by placing a mortgage on Jones' property:

Property A (Jones)		Property B (Smith)
$50,000	Fair Market Value	$45,000
–$10,000	Mortgage	0
$40,000	Net Equity	$45,000

When properties are mortgaged, the equities to be balanced are the net equities which each owner has in the relinquished property. In this case, Jones would receive Smith's property with a net equity of $45,000 in exchange for a relinquished property with a net equity of only $40,000. Jones would be required to offset the $5,000 which he lacks in equity by conveying something worth $5,000 to Smith.

Adding Real Property to Balance Equities

If Jones has a parcel worth $5,000 which Smith is willing to accept, he could convey this to Smith along with his deed to property A. Since the parcel is also real property, Smith would receive nothing but like-kind properties for the real estate he relinquished and would experience no tax recognition of any gain.

If Jones made up the deficiency by adding any personal property (e.g. cash, a promissory note, automobile, etc.), Smith would be a receiver of Boot and would have tax recognition up to the limit of $5,000, provided he has a realized gain of at least that amount. If Jones has $5,000 in cash, he may be able to reduce the mortgage on his property from $10,000 to $5,000 rendering his equity equal to Smith's thereby eliminating the issue of Boot.

Net Mortgage Relief

The most overlooked form of Boot is Net Mortgage Relief (NMR). NMR occurs when a party to the exchange relinquishes a property which has total mortgage balances greater than the total amount of mortgages which will be on the replacement property at the time it is received. In the example described above, note that Jones transfers a property subject to a $10,000 mortgage and receives a free and clear property. Therefore Jones experiences NMR in the amount of $10,000.

In most cases, Boot received may be offset with Boot given (and vice versa). But this is not true of NMR. NMR may only be offset with cash. In this case, Jones did contribute cash in the amount of $5,000 and may offset part of his NMR by this amount on the theory that he could have used the cash to reduce his mortgage balance prior to the transfer. Smith, on the other hand, gave up a property with no mortgage and received one with a $10,000 mortgage in place. Smith experienced no NMR

---

[9]   L$ens are encumbrances against the title which always involve money, and therefore reduce owner equity.

NMR is a particularly insidious trap. It occurs frequently to taxpayers who have held a property for a number of years, have seen it rise in value and have extracted part of the equity by refinancing the property. The cash received from the refinance is non-taxable. But when they subsequently attempt to exchange the property, they find that the equity remaining will not enable them to acquire a replacement property of a market value sufficient to support a mortgage as large or larger than that on the relinquished property. Either they must pony up additional cash to pay down the mortgage on the relinquished property, or acquire a more valuable property which will support a larger mortgage, or - lacking the cash - they must pay the tax on the difference between the relinquished property's mortgage and the replacement property's mortgage up to the amount of their gain.

Change in Basis

Basis refers to the value of a property for the purpose of calculating taxable gains and losses. In its simplest form, the Basis of a property acquired in an exchange is equal to the Basis of the relinquished property. In other words, the Basis of the relinquished property carries over to the replacement property and is referred to as "*Substituted Basis.*" But in most cases there will be a change in Basis as the result of the addition of cash to the transaction, an increase in mortgage liability, or the receipt of Boot, including Net Mortgage Relief, which triggers the recognition of some gain.

It is important to measure the Basis in the replacement property because the deprecation account set up for the replacement property will be determined with reference to its Substituted Basis and not to its agreed-upon acquisition value. When and if the replacement property is eventually sold, the amount of taxable gain will also be determined with reference to the adjusted Substituted Basis, and not with reference to a Basis determined by its contracted acquisition value.

The most convenient method of calculating the Basis of the replacement property is:

- Total Acquisition Cost of Replacement Property
- Less Unrecognized Gain Carried Over from Relinquished Property
- Equals Basis of Replacement Property

We can apply this to each owner's position in the table above. Assume that at the time of the exchange Jones had a $10,000 adjusted Basis in his property. Smith had a $15,000 adjusted Basis.

Jones' Position

Value of Property Conveyed $50,000
Less Adjusted Basis .... -10,000
Equals Realized (Indicated) Gain 40,000
Less Recognized Gain [10] .... -5,000   (NMR minus cash Boot given)
Unrecognized Gain Carried Over $35,000

Acquisition Value of Replacement ... $45,000
Less Amt. of Unrecognized Gain .... -35,000
New Basis in Replacement $10,000

---

[10]   Net of the Mortgage relief of $10,000 offset by cash Boot given in the amount of $5,000

Smith's Position

```
Value of property conveyed ............. $45,000
Adjusted Basis.................................... 15,000
Realized (Indicated) Gain................... 30,000
Less Recognized Gain  ........................ -5,000    (Cash Boot received)
Unrecognized Gain Carried Over     $25,000
Acquisition Value of Replacement... $50,000
Less Amt. of Unrecognized Gain ...... -25,000
New Basis in Replacement.............. $25,000
```

Jones benefits from the exchange by deferring the tax on $35,000 of his $40,000 realized gain. Smith also benefits by deferring the tax on $25,000 of his $30,000 realized gain. This is true despite the fact that both parties to the exchange received some Boot and paid some tax. Most 1031 exchanges are not completely "tax-free."

If Jones were to sell his new property soon after the exchange, he would pay tax on the difference between its value ($45,000) and his adjusted substituted basis ($10,000) which is the $35,000 of unrecognized gain.

If Smith were to sell his new property soon after the exchange, he would pay tax on the difference between its value ($50,000) and his adjusted substituted basis ($25,000) which is the $25,000 of unrecognized gain.[11] Jones neither lost nor gained Basis in the exchange while Smith, who exchanged up in value, increased his Basis even though it is not as high as it would have been had he acquired Jones' property by purchase.

Continued Depreciation of Carry-Over Basis

That portion of the adjusted Basis in the relinquished property which is carried over into a like-kind depreciable property may continue to be depreciated over the years remaining in the original depreciation schedule of the relinquished property. That portion of the substituted Basis of the replacement property which is in excess of the Basis of the relinquished property is treated as newly acquired property and depreciated under the conventional MACRS schedule. Therefore in some circumstances, the depreciation account of the replacement property *may* contain two sub-accounts: one representing the remaining un-depreciated Basis of the relinquished property and the other a depreciation amount representing the excess (if any) of the Basis of the newly acquired property over the relinquished property. However, if the replacement property represents a different recovery period,[12] the replacement property *must* be depreciated over the recovery period applicable to the relinquished or replacement property, whichever is longer.

In constructing the exchange analysis spreadsheet (see below) we have not established two separate depreciation accounts, principally in the interests of simplicity.[13] In practice, however, the un-depreciated Basis of the Dartmouth Apartments (Chapter 6) would continue to be depreciated under the same schedule as originally established. The amount by which the depreciable Basis of the replacement property, the Cambridge Apartments, exceeds the un-depreciated Basis of the Dartmouth property would

---

[11] These gains would be reduced by the costs of sale.

[12] As in the acquisition of a non-residential property for a residential property.

[13] For additional information see IRS Publication 544, *Sale and Disposition of Assets* as well as *Instructions for IRS Form 8824.*

be treated as a new property.[14] The applicable percentage from the MACRS schedule, the mid-month convention and the applicable fraction for the first year would apply to this new portion.

There are, however, two circumstances in which this consolidation would not be insignificant.

1. If the remaining depreciation schedule on the relinquished property had only a few years to run, it would be important to separate the two accounts since long term gains accrued after the end of the depreciation period would be taxed at the LTCG rate and not at the S.1250 depreciation recapture rate. (No further depreciation could be taken.)

2. If the exchange is one in which a residential property is exchanged for a non-residential property (or vice-versa), it would be necessary to segregate the depreciation accounts since they would continue on different schedules: the residential over 27.5 years and the non-residential over 39 years.

Exchanging Results in a Loss of Depreciable Basis

The exchange of property with a realized gain typically results in some loss of Basis. In most cases (e.g. Smith) this loss is offset by acquiring a more valuable property. If the property acquired includes a depreciable improvement, this loss in Basis will result in some loss of deductible depreciation allowances as well. Nevertheless, this loss may be overshadowed by the greater depreciation provided by a higher-priced, improved property. The loss of depreciation is still present, but not readily discernible.

Simultaneous Three-Party Exchanges

It is quite unusual to find an exchange conducted between two parties each of whom wants the other's property. In terms of our Jones-Smith scenario, Jones may not want to "trade down" and thereby expose himself to immediate taxation. Or he may wish simply to sell and receive cash, not property. Enter the three-party exchange, now the typical format of the great majority of S.1031 exchanges.

Let's assume that Jones does not want to exchange; he wants to sell his property, pay his tax and move on. Smith, however, remains interested in exchanging his property for Jones' property.

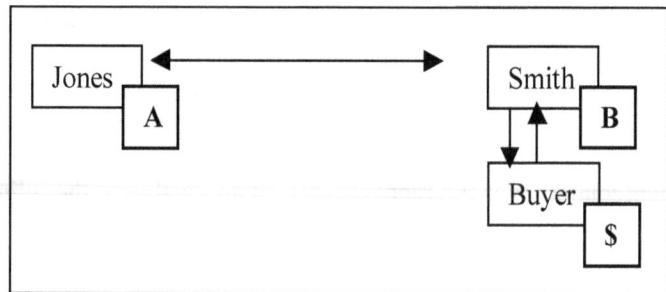

Step 1.
Smith places his property on the market, specifying that he retains the right to deliver title to Property B through a S.1031 exchange. The sale/purchase agreement notifies the Buyer of this intent and also commits the Buyer to cooperate in accomplishing the exchange by promptly executing all required documents. His sale/purchase contract with the Buyer also allows Smith to assign the sales contract to another party (who will be Jones).[15]

---

[14] Alternate methods are available. Consult your tax specialist.

[15] Unless specifically prohibited, most contracts in which the seller is not involved in financing the acquired property are freely assignable: e.g. a seller carry-back note as part of the purchase price.

Step 2.
Once the Buyer is under contract to purchase Property B and all contingencies have been satisfied, Smith enters into an exchange agreement with Jones whereby Jones agrees to accept title to Property B <u>in exchange for</u> title to Property A (Jones' property). This contract, however, contains a condition that Jones' obligation to accept Property B is dependent upon a *simultaneous* sale of Property B to the Buyer whom Smith has placed under contract.

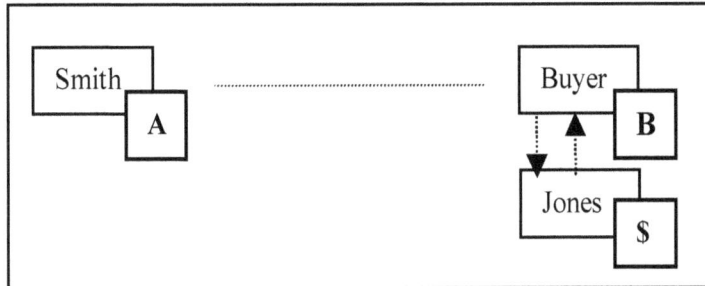

Step 3.
When the conditions of the three-party exchange have been satisfied, Jones exchanges title to Property A with Smith in return for title to Property B. <u>In the next legal instant</u>[16] Jones sells Property B to the Buyer to complete the exchange.

At the completion of the transaction, Smith owns Property A, the Buyer owns Property B and Jones has cashed out. Notice that Smith was never a seller, only an exchangor. The sale of Smith's Property B was accomplished by Jones, who, by virtue of the sale, becomes a taxpayer. As a result, all the realized gain which Jones had in Property A is recognized. As described above, Jones' Basis in Property B immediately after the exchange with Smith was $10,000. Following the sale of Property B to the Buyer for $45,000, all of Jones' unrecognized gain, $35,000, becomes recognized. Jones is the only taxpayer in this three-party exchange.

Costs and Potential Liabilities of the Exchange

There are no rules regarding the payment of costs for an exchange. Each party to the exchange usually agrees to pay transaction costs[17] of the property conveyed. Generally, the total costs of a simultaneous exchange are not significantly greater than if Jones and Smith had sold their properties.

The Buyer should experience no greater costs by reason of his cooperation with Smith's exchange. It is customary that Smith's sale/purchase agreement with the Buyer specifies that Smith will be responsible for any extra expenses incurred by the Buyer as the result of his cooperation in the exchange.

But there is also a legal instant in which Jones becomes the owner of Smith's property which is sold to the Buyer. Jones, therefore, is introduced into the chain of title and could be held liable for any undisclosed defects or the presence of hazardous substances on, under or about Smith's property.[18] As a result, it is customary that Smith also agrees to indemnify and hold harmless Jones for any defects or liabilities arising out of Jones' sale of Smith's property to the Buyer.

Simultaneous vs. Deferred Exchanges

The three-party exchange described above is a simultaneous exchange because the deeds to all properties passed in the same (linked) transaction on the same day. Jones agreed to the exchange with Smith only on the condition that the sale of Smith's property by Jones to the Buyer occurs simultaneously.

---

[16] Completed simultaneously, preferably – but not necessarily -- in the same escrow.

[17] Title, escrow, commissions and other closing costs

[18] Single Family Residential properties are seldom involved with toxic substances, but non-residential properties should always be suspect.

As you might expect, the Buyer of Smith's property will want to close the purchase within a reasonable time period. Unless he can be assured of a closing, the Buyer will not agree to cooperate in the exchange and will certainly not incur the costs of inspecting Smith's property and arranging for a loan. But if Smith has not yet located his replacement property, he may be contractually obligated to sell Property B to the Buyer. If Smith were to become a seller, however, he would become a taxpayer.

The Starker Cases

An analogous situation developed with the Starker family and resulted in a series of legal decisions which have eventually become the foundation for deferred, or delayed, exchanges.

The Starker Decisions actually involved two separate actions by the I.R.S. in an attempt to upset non-simultaneous exchanges structured by Bruce and Elizabeth Starker and, separately, by Bruce's father, T.J. Starker. Briefly, here's what happened...

The younger Starkers agreed to convey to Crown Zellerbach Corp. (CZ) timberland in Columbia County, Oregon, in exchange for the transfer to them of similar properties in the future. Since CZ had no properties for immediate transfer to the Starkers it entered a credit on its books for the market value of the property, and agreed to increase this "Exchange Value" by a 6% "growth factor" per year.

Within months, the younger Starkers located three suitable replacement properties whose value totaled the amount of credit on CZ's books, and directed CZ to acquire the properties for transfer to their ownership to complete the exchange. No cash or Boot was involved because the total value of the replacement properties equaled the credit on CZ's books.

T. J. Starker

When the Starkers filed their current tax return they treated the transfer of the timberland as a tax-deferred exchange under S.1031. The I.R.S., however, asserted that the transfer did not qualify for non-recognition under S.1031 because it was not simultaneous, and assessed a tax deficiency against the Starkers, who paid the assessment and then filed a claim for a refund, which the I.R.S. disallowed. The Starkers filed a lawsuit which has since become known as Starker I.

The issue, as defined by the court, was whether Section 1031 of the Code covers transactions in which a taxpayer disposes of all his rights in property (in exchange) for a promise from the transferee to convey like-kind properties in the future.[19] The District Court judge opined that it did, and ruled in favor of the Starkers.

Meanwhile Bruce's father, T.J. Starker,[20] also entered an agreement with CZ under virtually identical terms. The Exchange Value of the parcels conveyed by T.J., however, was $1,500,000. T.J.'s agreement also called for an annual increase, or "growth factor," in the Exchange Value. Because of the larger amounts involved, CZ required a number of years to complete the exchange.

In all, CZ eventually located 12 parcels acceptable to T.J. Starker. Of these, nine parcels were acquired by CZ and deeded to T.J. Two other parcels, identified as the Timian and Bi-Mart parcels, were deeded, at T.J.'s request, directly to his daughter.

---

[19] 75-1 U.S.T.C. para 9443 (D.C. Ore. 1975)

[20] Upon his death in 1983, T.J. Starker left an estate including more than 65,000 acres of timberland in Oregon and Washington. He was a professional forester and a generous community member.

The 12th property, known as the Booth property, involved an interesting real estate issue.. In this case, CZ had acquired, by assignment from a third party, contractual rights to acquire the Booth property. One of the original owners of the Booth property had retained a life estate in the property and it was only on this individual's death that the fee-simple interest (title) was free to pass. CZ acquired these rights and re-assigned them to T.J. Starker to satisfy their exchange agreement.

Therefore what were conveyed to T.J. Starker were the contractual rights to the fee interest and not the fee itself. Again, the I.R.S. denied the exchange, the same scenario ensued, and T.J. Starker filed suit.

This time the I.R.S. argued not only that the exchange was not simultaneous, but also that, in the case of Timian and Bi-Mart properties, no exchange had occurred since CZ had deeded the properties directly to Starker's daughter and Starker had never received any property ownership himself. Furthermore, the I.R.S. contended, the Booth property involved a complete failure to transfer a deed so the nature of what was received by Starker, the rights to real property, was not like-kind property.

The "growth factor," contended the I.R.S., was nothing more than disguised interest and should be taxed not as long-term capital gains income but as income subject to tax at the Ordinary rate.

In a startling turnabout the same judge, Gus Solomon,[21] who had rendered the decision in favor of Bruce and Elizabeth Starker concluded first, that he had erred in the Starker I decision and secondly, that the exchange of T.J. Starker's properties did not qualify for non-recognition treatment under Section 1031. Furthermore, he ruled that the cash which had accumulated on CZ's books as a "growth factor" was indeed interest which should be taxed as ordinary income.

These decisions by the lower court were appealed to the Ninth Circuit Court of Appeals[22] which reversed the lower court's ruling regarding the nine parcels declaring that, despite the lack of simultaneity, they did qualify under Section 1031. Therefore, declared the Court of Appeals, exchanges need not be simultaneous. This ruling established an important precedent.

The Appeals Court affirmed the lower court's ruling that the Timian and Bi-Mart properties were not qualified exchanges since T.J. Starker, by virtue of CZ's direct deeding to his daughter, never took title to these properties. This part of the ruling established that the exchangor must take title to the replacement properties in order to complete a qualified exchange. We can also say that the entity relinquishing a property in an exchange must also be the same entity that acquires the replacement property.

With respect to the Booth property, the Appeals Court ruled that the property rights, received under the circumstance of this case, were equivalent to the fee interest itself for the purpose of Section 1031. This established that the right to receive real property in an exchange is tantamount to the receipt of the property itself.

Lastly, the Court of Appeals agreed with the lower court that the 6% "growth factor" was indeed a disguised interest payment subject to taxation at ordinary rates.

---

21 "My opinion in Starker I has been given wide publicity. I believe that it is desirable that my opinion in this case be published to prevent the mischief that I believe Starker I has caused."

22 Starker v. U.S., 602 F. 2d 1341 9th Cir. 1979).

We recite the particulars of the Starker decisions because, with one exception, they form the legal basis for today's deferred, or non-simultaneous, exchanges. The one exception is the matter of direct deeding, which will be covered subsequently.

It was many years[23] before the I.R.S. succeeded in influencing the Congress to establish certain time limits governing non-simultaneous exchanges. The I.R.S. also added a number of restrictions and conditions to these exchanges which were formalized as regulations in 1991 and since amended.

Requirements of the Deferred Exchange

In order to accomplish a deferred exchange the exchangor must abide by strict time constraints and adhere to carefully proscribed procedures.

The first of these is to declare to all parties the exchangor's intent to deliver the relinquished property and to acquire the replacement property through a qualified S.1031 exchange. With respect to the property being relinquished, this exchange clause might say:

> *"The sale of the subject property is part of an I.R.C. Section 1031 tax-deferred exchange. Buyer agrees to an assignment of Seller's interest in this agreement to a Qualified Intermediary of Seller's choice and to cooperate in the exchange by promptly executing all necessary documents to accomplish the exchange. Buyer to be at no additional expense or liability by reason of Buyer's cooperation in the exchange."*

The exchangor will typically negotiate with the owner of the replacement property and enter into a contract for its acquisition. This contract will be assigned to a third-party "accommodator." Therefore a similar statement should be inserted in the acquisition contract for the replacement property.

Time Restraints

The exchangor must properly and unambiguously identify the potential replacement property or properties within 45 days beginning on the day following the day on which he transfers his relinquished property. This 45-day period is known as the *Identification Period*. If the relinquished property is transferred on June 15, for example, the replacement property or properties must be identified not later than midnight on July 30th.

If he is transferring out of more than one property, and all properties will be involved in the same exchange for one or more replacement properties, the 45-day period begins on the first day following the day on which he relinquishes the deed to the first of the properties to be included in the same exchange.

All replacement properties must be acquired not later than 180 days following the day on which he transfers his first relinquished property, OR, by the due-date of his next tax return (including extensions). The 180-day period is referred to as the *Exchange Period*.

> Therefore any transaction in which an exchange property is relinquished after October 17 of a given year will not afford the individual taxpayer the full 180 days, unless he/she files for an automatic 4-month extension for the tax return.

---

[23]   From 1975 to 1984

No Extensions Because of Holidays

If the deadline for the performance of any act falls on a Saturday, Sunday or legal holiday, I.R.C. Section 7503 permits the deadline to be extended to the next business day. Such is not the case, however, with regard to either the 45-day deadline or the 180-day deadline.

If a deadline date falls on a Saturday, Sunday or holiday – days on which most attorneys, accommodators, title companies and escrow offices are usually closed – then the deadline, for all practical purposes, must be moved to a preceding business day.

Identification of Potential Replacement Properties

Although the Starker cases laid the legal foundation for deferred exchanges, today's exchangor is saddled with many more regulations and restrictions than were the Starkers. One of these is the method of identification of potential replacement properties and the number of such properties which may be identified. The exchangor must unambiguously identify *in writing* all potential replacement properties as replacement properties. Acceptable descriptions favor a legal description or a street address, but a distinguishable name, such as the "Moore Apartments on State Street" would be acceptable.

The description must be signed by the exchangor and may be hand-delivered, mailed, telecopied, or *"otherwise sent,"* before the end of the identification period to the person obligated to transfer the replacement property to the taxpayer or to any party to the exchange other than the taxpayer or a disqualified person. An exchange agreement specifying the replacement property and signed by all parties to the exchange prior to the end of the 45-day identification period will suffice to satisfy the identification requirement.

During the 45-day identification period the exchangor may identify more than one potential replacement property. However, the maximum number of properties is:

♦ Three properties without regard to their fair market value (the **3-Property Rule**), or
♦ Any number of properties as long as their aggregate fair market value at the end of the identification period does not exceed 200% of the aggregate fair market value of all the relinquished properties as of the date the relinquished properties were transferred by the taxpayer (the **200% Rule**), or
♦ Any identified property the fair market value of which is at least 95% of the fair market value of all identified properties (the **95% Rule**), or
♦ Any replacement property received before the end of the *identification* period.

In many cases the exchangor will find that he is limited to the nomination of not more than 3 replacement properties. He may, however, revoke and replace any nominated property before the end of the identification period provided the revocation and re-identification of the substitute property is *in writing* and follows the same rules as for identification. Oral identifications and revocations are not valid.

Properties to Be Constructed

Nothing in the Code bars the identification of a replacement property which is either under construction or to be built. In this situation the exchangor must adequately and unambiguously identify the legal parcel on which the new construction is to be built and, to the extent which is *"practical,"* describe the structure which is to be placed on the land. The exchange period will still end not later than 180 days following the date of identification even if the structure is not completed. The nature of the property to be received is considered to be like-kind only if the property to be received is "substantially" equal to the property earlier described:

"It will be considered like-kind only if, had production been completed on or before the date the taxpayer receives the replacement property; the property received would have been considered to be substantially the same property as identified."[24]

The value of any construction received by the exchangor after the exchange period will not be included in the exchange, and therefore will be considered taxable Boot.

Required Use of an Accommodator

In our previous example, if the exchangor, Smith, has not yet located or is not yet ready to close on the replacement property, but is now contractually required to sell his property to the Buyer, he must avoid being the seller, since sellers become taxpayers.

Therefore, using a deferred exchange, Smith enters into an exchange agreement, the Qualified Exchange Accommodation Agreement (QEAA), with a Qualified Intermediary (a.k.a *accommodator*) whereby the accommodator accepts Smith's property in exchange for a *promise* (Starker reprised) by the accommodator to acquire and transfer to Smith at a later date a replacement property.

In this case, an accommodator takes the place of "Jones," who has not yet been located by Smith. Once the accommodator becomes the owner of property B, he sells it to the Buyer. Since the acquisition price and the sales price are the same, the accommodator experiences neither a taxable gain nor loss. When a suitable replacement property has been found by Smith,[25] he will place it under contract and again assign the purchase contract to the accommodator, who will acquire the property using the cash proceeds from the sale of Property B. The subsequent conveyance by the accommodator of the replacement property to Smith completes the deferred exchange.

The Qualified Intermediary

It takes two to tango and at least as many to exchange. Unless the exchangor has someone with whom to exchange his property, there can be no exchange. Some investors have sold their property and directed the escrow agent to retain the cash pending the identification and acquisition of a replacement property.[26] Much to their chagrin, these investors learned that this strategy does not qualify for non-recognition of gain under Section 1031.

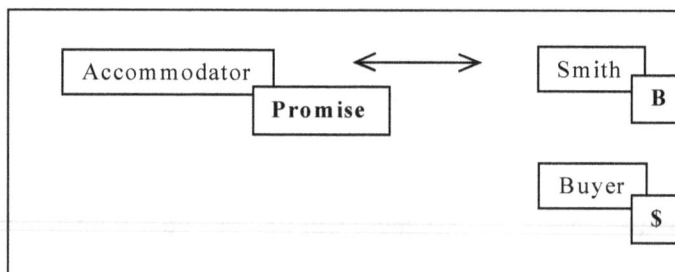

If the exchangor has not been able to find a replacement property by the time he is required to deliver title to a buyer, he has no choice but to enter into an agreement with a third-party, whom we have referred to as the *accommodator* or Qualified Intermediary; *Qualified*, because not everyone is permitted to act as an intermediary.

---

[24] Title 26, CFR, Part 1, Sec. 1.1031 (k-1) (e)(3)(iii)
[25] Accommodators will not locate a replacement property.
[26] Klein vs. Comm. 66-TCM, 1115 1993

Qualified Intermediary Defined

A Qualified Intermediary is a person who:

♦ Is not the taxpayer (exchangor) or a disqualified person (as defined above) and

♦ Enters into a written agreement (the exchange agreement) with the taxpayer and, as required by the agreement, acquires the relinquished property from the taxpayer (exchangor), transfers the relinquished property to one or more third parties, acquires the replacement property and transfers the replacement property to the taxpayer (exchangor).

The most conspicuous non-qualified person is anyone who is or who has been an agent of the exchangor within two years prior to the date of the transfer of the relinquished property. These ineligible persons may include the exchangor's attorney, accountant, real estate broker or agent, financial planner, investment banker or employee. Related persons are also excluded: brothers and sisters,[27] spouse, ancestors and lineal descendents. But if an individual or entity has provided services to the exchangor which have solely to do with prior exchanges of property intended to qualify for non-recognition under Section 1031, then these individuals or entities will not be regarded as disqualified. These may include escrow agents, attorneys, accountants, trust services and title insurance companies. Because there are additional entities belonging to a controlled group which may be disqualified, the investor is advised to consult with an experienced real estate attorney prior to selecting the intermediary.

Exchanges between Related Parties

While a related party may not act as the Qualified Intermediary, an exchange of property with a related party is valid. If, however, either related party disposes of the property within two years after the trade, both parties must report the unrecognized gain in the year in which the property is later disposed. This does not include a disposition as the result of the death of a party, or an involuntary conversion (e.g. eminent domain).

Safety of Funds

If the need for a deferred exchange arises, the foremost consideration in the selection of a Qualified Intermediary should be the ability of the Intermediary to guarantee the safety of the funds. In many exchanges the amount of cash entrusted to the Intermediary is measured in the millions of dollars. There have been instances in which the Qualified Intermediary simply disappeared with the exchangor's cash, never to be seen again. In other instances, the Intermediary converted taxpayer funds for personal use.[28] This is a very painful experience, not only because of the loss of funds but also because the inability to complete the exchange triggers the recognition of any tax due on the accumulated gain. At the present time only CA, NV, WA, ID and CO, have any regulatory control over who may or may not act as a Qualified Intermediary. Even in these states, the bonding requirements are quite low.

Funds in the hands of an accommodator may be securitized in either of three ways:

♦ By a mortgage, deed of trust or other security interest in property other than cash or cash equivalent,

---

[27] Including half-brothers and half-sisters.

[28] U.S. v. Okun, 3:08-cr-132, U.S. District Court, Eastern District of Virginia (Richmond).

♦ By a standby letter of credit which may not be drawn upon in the absence of a default of the transferee's obligation to transfer like-kind property to the taxpayer, or

♦ By a guarantee by a third party.

Experience has shown that deferred exchanges are best placed in the hands of a major title company or its corporate subsidiary that offers both escrow and accommodation services and whose financial statement is adequate to guarantee the exchange funds.[29]

Nevertheless, the Qualified Exchange Accommodation Agreement (QEAA) which is offered to the exchangor should not be accepted prior to a thorough vetting by a competent and exchange-experienced real estate attorney. For this reason, any decision to enter into a QEAA should be made well in advance of the required date. If any other entity is to be considered as a Qualified Intermediary, the entity should be adequately vetted, insured and bonded.[30]

Who Owns the Exchange Funds?

In addition to a number of QIs who have either absconded with the exchange funds or simply converted them to personal use, a recent case involves a QI which accepted property whose equity amounted to $28.2 million. In *Millard Refrigerated Services Inc. vs. LandAmerica Exchange Services* (LES), the equity was conveyed in October 2008 to LES in three identical exchange agreements which gave LES *"right, title and interest"* in the Exchange Funds and *"dominion, control and use of all exchange funds including interest, if any, earned on the Exchange Funds."*

The cash was held in three segregated sub-accounts[31] under a master control account that LES maintained at Citibank. Each segregated account was associated with Millard and referred to Millard's taxpayer ID number, but were titled in the name of, and controlled by, LES. Given full control and use of the funds, LES used them to acquire auction-rate securities. When the market for these securities became frozen LES was unable to retrieve the funds to acquire replacement properties. LES then declared bankruptcy.

The U.S. Bankruptcy Court[32] in two successive decisions ruled that the funds were the property of LES and that Millard had no equitable title to the funds. Therefore all the funds became subject to the claims of 85 other claimants. Although Millard argued that LES acted as a trustee of the funds, the court could find no language or evidence that a trust had been intended or created.

There are multiple safe harbors which can be employed by an exchangor to secure the transferee's obligation to deliver the replacement property including the use of a separate qualified trust or qualified escrow.[33] In the absence of such agreements, funds in the hands of a Qualified Intermediary may be regarded as the QI's separate funds, subject to disposition through a bankruptcy proceeding.

---

[29]   Based on a verifiable Balance Statement

[30]   Consider members of the Federation of Exchange Accommodators (FEA) but do not rely on membership alone.

[31]   Funds in excess of $2 million which are not held in a segregated account are considered a loan to the Qualified Intermediary.

[32]   Eastern Division of Virginia

[33]   Treasury Reg. 1.1031 (k)-1(g)

When the QI Declares Bankruptcy

The IRS has provided for a safe harbor method of reporting the gain (or loss) when the QI defaults on its obligation to acquire and transfer to the exchangor a suitable replacement property by reason of the QI's bankruptcy or receivership. In most cases the bankruptcy or receivership proceedings will extend beyond the exchangor's Exchange Period deadline,[34] thereby invalidating the exchange and exposing the exchangor to recognition of the realized gain on the relinquished property. Once the Exchange Period has elapsed, the exchange is invalidated.

The IRS has taken the position, however, that under these circumstances tax on the gain shall not be payable until the exchangor receives whatever repayment is ordered by the court. The conditions and terms for calculating the tax due (or reportable loss) are contained in Revenue Proceedings 2010-14. In those cases in which the exchangor receives less than the funds transferred to the QI, the amount of the gain taxable is determined by a *safe harbor gross profit ratio*, in which the nominator of the fraction is the profit from the sale of the property and the denominator is the selling price. The profit is the total amount of reimbursement scheduled to be made to the taxpayer less the Adjusted Basis, plus any Net Mortgage Relief. The selling price is the total amount of the payments scheduled to be received by the taxpayer and not necessarily the value at which the property was transferred to the QI.

This safe harbor permits the taxpayer to pay taxes due as payments are received rather than in one lump sum. If the repayment schedule exceeds 6 months beyond the date of the court's order (*safe harbor sale date*), imputed interest may be involved. Because the determination of the tax due may also be complicated by mortgage relief in excess of Basis, a competent tax advisor should be consulted. This safe harbor is available to taxpayers whose like-kind exchange failed due to a QI default on or after January 1, 2009.

When the Exchange Fails

Not every exchange proceeds to a successful conclusion. There are occasions when the nominated replacement property or properties fail to survive the due diligence period. If the exchangor has engaged the services of a qualified intermediator and has transferred the relinquished property to the QI but is unable to find and close on a suitable replacement property, the funds derived from the sale of the relinquished property by the QI will not be available for return to the exchangor until the end of the exchange period which will be 180 days following the date of sale of the relinquished property. See Treas. S. 1.1031(k)-1(k).

Direct Deeding

Many states impose a tax on the transfer of real property. The transfer of the replacement property from its owner to the Qualified Intermediary, and again from the Qualified Intermediary to the exchangor to complete an exchange causes two transfer taxes to be incurred. Similarly, the transfer of a property by the exchangor to an accommodator, and then the sale of the exchangor's property by the accommodator to the Buyer (*Smith → Accommodator → Buyer*) also results in two tax levies.

---

[34] 180 days following the date of transfer to the QI

The I.R.S. has stated in Revenue Ruling 90-34[35] that the owner of the replacement property may deed the replacement property directly to the exchangor thus avoiding the double transfer tax.
The exchangor (e.g. Smith) may also deed his property directly to the Buyer of the relinquished property.

In concert with this Ruling, many QIs no longer accept a deed from the exchangor but rather accept only an Assignment of the "Rights but not the Obligations" of the exchangor's agreements.[36]

Direct deeding without non-recognition of a gain is possible only when there is an assignment of the exchangor's deed (or "Rights and Obligation") and when there is a written agreement with a Qualified Intermediary to receive the relinquished property and to convey the replacement property to the exchangor.

Interest Earned and Earnest Deposits

The funds received by an accommodator may be in his possession for as long as 6 months. Many QEAAs specify that the accommodator has the right to place these funds in a safe investment[37] to earn interest during this time. If $2 million is invested @ 3% for 6 months, interest earned will be approximately $30,000. Some unscrupulous accommodators assert that the exchangor may not receive this interest without invalidating the exchange. One accommodator who had negotiated the right to keep the interest purposefully delayed the closing of the exchange in order to continue to receive the considerable interest earned on exchange funds he had invested.

Interest earned on exchange funds does not necessarily belong to the accommodator. But interest paid to the exchangor <u>during</u> the exchange period, or prior to the receipt of the replacement property by the exchangor, will conclusively demonstrate that the exchangor benefited from these funds <u>during</u> the exchange period, and therefore had *constructive receipt* of these funds. This will invalidate the exchange. The prohibition is not against the exchangor's receipt of interest but rather against his receipt of interest <u>during the exchange period</u> or prior to the receipt of the replacement property (which event should define the close of the exchange escrow).

You will recall that the Starkers were unsuccessful in having interest on their money on deposit with Crown Zellerbach classified as capital gains. The receipt of interest by the Starkers did not invalidate their exchange, but it did require them to pay tax on the interest as Ordinary income.

A deposit (earnest money) made by the Buyer of an exchangor's property may or may not invalidate an exchange. If the deposit is made by a party to the exchange to the taxpayer prior to his assignment to an accommodator of the contract to sell the property, this deposit will not invalidate the exchange. It will, however, be regarded as Boot which will expose to taxation the exchangor's gain on the relinquished property. If the deposit is paid to the taxpayer after the assignment to an accommodator of the contract to sell the property, then this cash will demonstrate constructive receipt of the funds in the exchange escrow and may invalidate the exchange. To avoid recognition, any deposit held by the exchangor should be transferred to the Qualified Intermediary at the time of the assignment of the purchase agreement.

---

[35] Rev. Rul. 90-34, 1990-1 C.B. 154, 1990-16, I.R.B. 6.

[36] The function of these QIs is reduced to holding and transferring the cash from the sale of the exchangor's property to the seller of the replacement property.

[37] Such as U.S. Treasury securities.

Safe Harbor Rules re Constructive Receipt

The Code of Federal Regulations[38] has set out 4 "safe harbors" which, if observed, will result in a determination that the exchangor is not in actual or constructive receipt of money or other property. These safe harbors, which require the use of a Qualified Intermediary and a written Qualified Exchange Accommodation Agreement, pertain to: 1) security and guarantee arrangements, 2) qualified escrows and qualified trusts, 3) qualified intermediaries, and 4) interest and growth factors.

In each of the safe harbors, the exchangor is prohibited from actual or constructive receipt of funds in the escrow or trust, or from receiving any benefit from these funds during the exchange period. If the terms of these safe harbors are adhered to, the exchangor will not be at risk for invalidating the exchange other than by failing to identify properly and failing to close on time.

Reverse Exchanges

Now and then an investor espies an attractive investment property which is currently on the market, but whose owner is not interested in exchanging directly for the investor's property. Waiting to sell a current investment property in order to use the funds to acquire a new property can cause the opportunity to be lost. In this case, a "reverse" exchange may be carried out.

The reverse exchange is what it sounds like: an exchange in which the replacement property is acquired by an accommodator before the property to be relinquished has been placed under a sales contract. Some investors have used a third party to "park" the new investment property until one or more of the properties to be relinquished could be marketed and placed under a sales contract. The difficulty is that the early disposition of the acquired property by the entity used to hold the new property may demonstrate a lack of intent to hold the property for investment of for use in a trade or business, as required under the Code. As such, reverse exchanges have been considered risky. However the I.R.S. has issued Revenue Procedure 2000-37 providing a safe harbor for qualifying exchanges in which the replacement property is "parked" with an "Exchange Accommodator Titleholder" (EAT) until the investor's current property can be placed into an exchange escrow. This safe harbor is available for transactions entered into on or after September 15, 2000.

If the property is held in a QEAA the I.R.S. will not challenge the qualification of the property either as "replacement property" or "relinquished property," or the treatment of the Exchange Accommodator Titleholder as the beneficial owner of the property for federal tax purposes.

There are six conditions to be met:

1. Qualified indicia of ownership of the property is held by the Exchange Accommodator Titleholder (EAT) who is not the taxpayer (exchangor) nor a disqualified person, and the EAT is subject to federal income tax. If the EAT is treated as a partnership, or S corporation, more than 90% of the partners or shareholders must be subject to federal taxation. The qualified indicia of ownership means legal title or other evidence of beneficial interest, such as a contract for deed, or interests in an entity that is disregarded as an entity separate from its owner for federal income tax purposes - such as a single member of a limited liability company. This indicia of ownership must be held continuously by the EAT from the date of acquisition to the transfer to the taxpayer (exchangor) as a replacement property.

---

[38] Title 26, Vol. II, Part 1 (1.1001 to 1.1400) as revised April 1, 2000.

2. At the time the qualified indicia of ownership is transferred to the EAT, it is the taxpayer's (exchangor's) bona fide intent that the property held by the EAT represents either the replacement or relinquished property in an exchange that is intended to qualify for non-recognition under S.1031.
3. No later than five business days after the transfer of the qualified indicia to the EAT, the taxpayer (exchangor) and the EAT enter into a written QEAA which provides that the EAT is holding the property for the benefit of the taxpayer in order to facilitate an exchange under S.1031, and under Revenue Procedure 2000-37, and that both parties agree to report the acquisition, holding and disposition of the property under the provisions of 2000-37. The QEAA must specify that the EAT will be treated as the beneficial owner of the property for all federal income tax purposes. Both parties must report the federal income tax attributes of their property on their federal income tax returns in a manner consistent with the QEAA agreement.
4. No later than 45 days after the transfer to the EAT of the qualified indicia of ownership of the replacement property, the relinquished property or properties must be identified. (The method of identification must follow rules previous described.)
5. Not later than 180 days after the transfer of the qualified indicia of ownership to the EAT, the property must be transferred either directly or indirectly through a Qualified Intermediary to the taxpayer as a replacement property, or to a person who is not the taxpayer or a disqualified person as relinquished property.
6. The combined time that the relinquished property and the replacement property are held in the QEAA may not exceed 180 days.

The following agreements or arrangements are also permitted:

1. The EAT may also serve as the exchange accommodator.
2. Either the taxpayer or a disqualified person may lend or guarantee funds to the EAT for the acquisition of the property.
3. Either the taxpayer or a disqualified person may reimburse the EAT for costs and expenses.
4. The EAT may lease the property either to the taxpayer or to a disqualified person.
5. Either the taxpayer or a disqualified person may manage the property, supervise improvements to the property, or provide services to the property while title is in the hands of the EAT.
6. The taxpayer and the EAT may enter into an agreement for the purchase or sale of the property including the rights to sell or buy at a predetermined price, or as the result of a formula, for a period not in excess of 185 days from the date the property is acquired by the EAT.
7. The taxpayer and the EAT may enter into agreements or arrangements to adjust any change in the price of the relinquished property between the date of acquisition by the EAT and the receipt or delivery by the exchange accommodator. The taxpayer may receive or remit funds to the exchange accommodator for this purpose.

Revenue Procedure 2000-37 takes care of most reverse exchanges in which the replacement property is "parked" with a third party. The I.R.S., in its preamble to 2000-37, acknowledges that there may be some reverse exchanges which are outside the safe harbor rules, but nonetheless may be legal. An exchange involving a property to be constructed may be one of these.

Exchanging Tenant-in-Common Interests

In recent years interest has arisen in acquiring Tenant-in-Common (TIC) interests as replacement properties. You will recall from Chapter 1 that a TIC owner holds a direct interest in real property which is therefore eligible for an exchange under S.1031. This is in contrast to interests in a Limited Liability Company (LLC), Trust or Partnership which are interests in personal property and are not exchangeable.[39]

Many TIC sponsors promote the acquisition of a TIC interest as a replacement property in S.1031 exchange situations. These offerings are often made in connection with properties net-leased to tenants such as Arby's, Sherwin Williams Paint, Staples, Walgreens, Applebees, Taco Bell and other occupying, single-tenant, credit-worthy businesses which are concerned about their pubic image and therefore take good care of their properties. Other TIC sponsors, however, acquire properties which are distressed in one way or another but which offer the potential for gains following remediation of a particular problem. These kinds of properties may include retail, office or industrial properties with significant vacancy problems, or older apartments in need of renovation.

Some investors are attracted to TIC replacement properties because they are virtually management-free to the investor and because they offer the advantage of diversifying from one property into several, potentially mitigating investment risk. Since the exchange investor can acquire a partial interest which utilizes all the cash flowing from the relinquished property the investor can also avoid Boot and any immediate recognition of gain.

But there are caveats. In Code Section 761(a) the IRS defines a partnership as "a syndicate, group, pool, joint venture or other unincorporated organization through or by means of which any business, financial operation or venture is carried on, and which is not, within the meaning of this title, a corporation, a trust or estate." The danger is that a group of TIC owners may be classified by the IRS as a partnership even though no partnership has been intended or formed. Therefore the transfer of a partnership interest into a fee interest (TIC) would constitute a non-like-kind exchange and the exchange would be invalidated.

There are also those occasions in which some members of an existing partnership seek to exchange while others prefer to cash out. To resolve the problem, the partnership's attorney often arranges to dissolve the partnership and to deliver the interests to each owner as a TIC interest equal to his pro-rata share in the partnership. This title transformation often occurs only weeks before the exchange. The IRS subsequently claims that the interests now held by the TIC owners who seek to exchange were not ".. held for investment or for use in a trade or business..." and therefore the exchange is invalid. A parallel situation exists when, following an exchange, a TIC owner places his interest in a Trust, LLC or Partnership.

One determining factor is whether or not the TIC owners in a contractual arrangement provide a service and are therefore engaged in a business, trade, financial operation or venture to create and divide the profits. The IRS has ruled that co-ownership of property that is maintained, kept in repair, and rented or leased does not constitute a separate entity for federal tax purposes. But if the same owners provide other services or engage in other business activities by which they generate and divide a profit, the association may be classified for tax purposes as a partnership. This helps explain the preference for net-leased properties since these TIC owners provide no services of any kind.

For this reason many sponsors of TIC investments once requested an *advanced ruling* or *determination letter* on the question of whether an undivided fractional interest in real property is or is not an interest in an entity which is eligible for exchange. Initially the IRS refused to deliver such determinations. But in March 2002, the service released Revenue Procedure[40] 2002-22 which outlines 15 conditions under

---

[39]   Although the LLC, Trust or Partnership, acting as a single entity, may exchange property.

[40]   Not a Revenue Ruling

which the IRS will accept a Request for a Ruling. Since that time many TIC sponsors have followed the conditions set forth in RP 2002-22 and have regarded the RP as a "safe harbor." The IRS appears to have acquiesced since no actions have been brought against a TIC sponsor who follows these guidelines. Nevertheless there are many unanswered questions regarding TICs. The investor should be alert to potential problems and should consult an informed real estate attorney familiar with this particular type of transaction.

Simultaneous or Deferred Exchange ?

Experience has demonstrated that most investors who open an exchange escrow with an accommodator immediately upon finding a qualified buyer expose themselves to unnecessary anxiety and stress. Some Qualified Intermediaries, whose services are not required in a simultaneous exchange, fail to point out that simultaneous exchanges are still very much legal. The 45-day period afforded the investor to identify a potential replacement property following the relinquishment of the property to an accommodator is often a very inadequate time to locate and investigate one, let alone three (or more) investment properties.

Experienced investors are very aware that quality properties are hard to find and that many properties offered for sale (or exchange) turn out to resemble only faintly the advertised product. Other properties, on closer inspection, reveal serious deficiencies and issues[41] that are best avoided. But if these defects are discovered after the close of the identification period, the remaining identified replacement properties may have been sold by the time the investor concludes that his first choice is not acceptable. It is at this point that some investors accept a less desirable property simply to save taxes, however large. This is the worst of investment decisions.

A better strategy is to negotiate for a longer escrow period – 90 or 120 days – and postpone the use of the deferred exchange until needed. If the replacement property has been located, the sale/purchase agreement for the relinquished property may contain a negotiated clause which gives the exchangor the unilateral right to extend the escrow for an additional 30-60 days, perhaps sufficient to close the transaction as a simultaneous exchange.

If, toward the end of the escrow period, the investor has not yet located a suitable property, the sale/purchase contract for the relinquished property can be assigned to a Qualified Intermediary under a QEAA. From that point onward, the exchangor has an additional 45 days in which to identify one or more suitable replacements, and up to 180 days following the date of relinquishment to acquire a quality replacement. Hopefully, that should be sufficient.

The exchangor needs to be mindful, however, that the Safe Harbor rules are only available to the taxpayer who has a written exchange agreement with a Qualified Intermediary. In a great many cases, the extra cost of a QI is quite minimal, especially when the QI has the right to all or some of the interest earned on funds held during the Exchange Period.

Stepping Through a Three-Party Exchange

Life would not be quite complete without an example of a three-party exchange in which all the steps are described. At the end, we will draw an Exchange Equity Balance Sheet in which all costs of the exchange

---

41 E.g. the presence of toxic or hazardous substances, title difficulties such as unrecorded easements, rights of tenants in possession, etc.

are included and all equities among the three players are balanced. We will continue with our usual players, Jones, Smith and Brown, the Buyer.

Here are the facts:

Jones   owns an office building with a fair market value (FMV) of $1,050,000. This property is currently subject to a non-assumable loan in the amount of $375,000. Jones' Adjusted Basis in the property is now $448,000. Jones has placed the property on the market for sale and is not interested either in carrying the mortgage or in an exchange. He <u>does not have any free cash</u> to pay for commissions (6% of the FMV of his property) and transaction costs (estimated to be $21,000), but is willing to cooperate with a buyer of his property in carrying out a S.1031 exchange.

Smith   has owned a retail center which he acquired for $150,000. The center now has a loan balance of $75,000 and a FMV of $500,000. Adjusted Basis is $90,000. Smith has extra cash to pay for commissions (6% of FMV), new loan costs of $9,375 and normal transaction costs (estimated at $10,000.). He expresses a desire to move out of retail and into an office property. He specifies that he must obtain a replacement property via a qualified S.1031 exchange which minimizes his immediate tax exposure.

Brown,   a Buyer, seeks to acquire a retail center with a FMV of approximately $500,000. Brown will put 35% cash down and obtain a new mortgage for the balance of the purchase price. Brown has cash to cover his loan costs (2% of loan amount), and transaction costs estimated to be 1.5% of the purchase price. As a buyer, he owes no commission.

The following dates and actions describe the steps taken by each participant in the order taken.

Step	Date	Action by	Action	Comment
1	Sept. 1	Smith	Places his property on market subject to buyer's cooperation in S.1031 exchange. Smith reserves the right to specify escrow and title providers.	Intent to exchange should be documented throughout the transaction, beginning with the listing.
2	Nov.10	Smith	Accepts an offer from Brown to acquire retail center for $500,000. Brown agrees to cooperate in the exchange, but insists on not more than a 90-day escrow. Escrow to close not later than Feb. 8 of following year. Contract gives Smith right to assign contract to third party for the purposes of the exchange.	Smith accepts deposit of $35,000 from Brown but directs check to be made payable to Acme Escrow. Smith directs broker to hold check, uncashed pending the opening of escrow. Brown insists on clause to relieve him of extra costs and liability. Smith concurs in writing.
3	Nov. 15	Smith & Brown	Open escrow with Acme Title Escrow Service. Orders preliminary report of condition of title for Brown's approval.	Smith's broker conveys cashier's check for deposit to escrow holder in compliance with Smith's direction.
4	Nov.25	Brown	Completes review of report of condition of title, physical inspection and Phase I Hazardous Material Report.	Relieves relevant contingencies in writing. Property is free of hazardous substances as defined in purchase contract.

Step	Date	Action by	Action	Comment
5	Dec.10	Brown	Receives loan approval for the retail center. Loan \must close in 60 days (Feb 8th).	Brown removes loan approval contingency but retains condition that loan must also fund.
6	Jan. 15	Smith	Unable to locate suitable replacement property. Requests Acme Exchange Service to furnish his attorney with Acme's QEAA for review.	Attorney reviews Acme's QEAA, makes minor changes and obtains Acme's approval of changes.
7	Feb. 5	Smith	Assigns contract with Brown (and deposits Brown's check) to Qualified Intermediary (Acme) in return for a written promise to acquire a replacement property for conveyance to Smith under S.1031. The assignment documents Smith's intention to exchange and provides that Smith shall have no access to, or use of, funds on deposit, proceeds from sale of property to Brown, or interest earned on funds retained until receipt of replacement property, or anytime after August 4th.	This date begins Smith's identification period. Must now locate one or more replacement properties not later than March 22 and complete the exchange not later than Aug. 5th (180 days).[42] Assignment again repeats Smith's intention to exchange. QEAA bars Smith from actual or constructive receipt of funds prior to receiving replacement property or end of exchange period. Note that exchange period extends beyond April 15th.
8	Feb. 5	Smith	Notifies accountant to file automatic 4-month extension for tax return due April 15th.	Extends the reporting period from April 15th to Aug 15th but not the exchange period.
9	Feb. 8	Q.I.	Closes sale of Smith's property to Brown, receives cash and invests proceeds in short-term T-Bills. Smith executes direct deed to Brown.	Direct deeding to Brown by Smith avoids double transfer tax under Revenue Ruling 90-34. Closes out responsibility to Brown.
10	Mar. 1	Smith	Locates and identifies suitable replacement property #1 held by Jones. Identifies property by legal description and forwards notice to Acme Escrow Service by registered mail, return receipt requested.	Smith decides to limit himself to three identified properties. Begins inspection of area surrounding Jones's property, including public files at City hall and County Building department.
11	Mar. 4	Smith	Locates and identifies potential replacement property #2.	Continues Public records inspection of both properties.
12	Mar. 8	Smith	Enters into sale/purchase agreement with Jones to acquire retail center for $1,050,000. Agreement commits Jones to cooperate in S.1031 exchange by promptly executing all necessary documents. Issues $35,000 deposit check payable to Acme Escrow Service but directs broker to retain check uncashed pending opening of escrow. Escrow to open in 10 days.	Uses time to continue to inspect the property and reviews preliminary report of condition of title of Jones' property. Submits copies of agreement to attorney and accountant for review and comments.

---

[42] The 180-day exchange period begins on the day following the date of relinquishment.

Step	Date	Action by	Action	Comment
13	Mar.13	Smith	Receives notice from broker that replacement property #2 has been sold. Revokes identification of property #2 by written notice to Acme. Advises attorney. Applies for loan on Jones' office building	Any oral revocation of selected replacement property #2 is invalid. Revocations must be in writing.
14	Mar.25	Smith	Identifies new replacement properties #2 & #3. Notifies Acme Escrow Service in writing as before.	Maximum number of replacement properties has now been identified under the "3-Property Rule." Smith must close on one of these by Aug.5 to qualify for non-recognition
15	April 27	Smith	Loan is approved and Smith removes loan approval contingency but retains condition that loan must fund. Loan to fund in 45 days	Smith is safeguarded against premature end of exchange period on April 15th by having previously filed for automatic extension.
16	May 8	Lender	All physical and hazardous materials inspections are completed and approved. Jones' property is ready to close upon loan funding.	Smith notifies escrow of satisfaction of all contingencies except funding of loan .
17	May 10	Smith & Jones	Assigns interest in purchase contract with Jones to Q.I. under existing QEAA. and transfers deposit check to escrow.	At this point Smith owns no property except right to receive identified replacement property from Q.I.
18	June 12	Lender	Funds Loan	Funding contingency satisfied
19	June 14	Jones	Direct-deeds title to office property to Smith, not to Q.I.	Saves expense of double deeding. Jones pays fo transfer tax. Q.I. has no tax to pay. Smith avoid this charge by Q.I.
20	June 15	Escrow	Records deed to office property in Smith's name and closes exchange escrow.	Formal end of exchange period.
21	June 16	Q.I.	Remits any remaining cash, together with interes earned on invested funds to Smith to conclude QEAA.	End of exchange.

Three points are noteworthy:
- Had Smith been able to locate and close on Jones' property within the 90-day escrow period afforded by the Brown agreement, he could have avoided the necessity and extra cost of an accommodator. *However, the cost of an accommodator may be minimal and affords the taxpayer the protection of Safe Harbor Regulations.*
- Had Smith been able to close the Jones escrow within the 45-day exchange identification period, the documents provided to escrow would have served as adequate identification.
- Had Smith not revoked the potential replacement property that was sold, and still nominated an additional 2 properties, he would not have been protected by the safe harbor of the 3-Property Rule. Because the value of the replacement property was greater than 200% of the value of the property relinquished, Smith would have also exceeded the safe harbor of the 200% Rule.
- (200% * $500,000 = $1,000,000 vs. $1,050,000 for the Jones property.) The only safe harbor left to Smith would have been to acquire at least 95% of the value of all 4 properties which he had identified (the 95% Rule). If Smith were unable to do this, the Jones property acquired by Smith would be deemed unlike property resulting in non-recognition under S.1031. Smith would become a taxpayer.

Let's proceed to balancing out the equities among these parties.

The Exchange Equity Balance Worksheet

This Exchange Worksheet has great practical value to the individual who must arrange the exchange. It's greatest value, aside from being a guideline to settling the accounts, is that it provides a template to conduct negotiations between and among the parties. It provides a visualization of the exchange which may suggest a number of potential solutions to structural problems which at first glance may appear to be irresolvable.

In working with the Exchange Worksheet, do not be overly concerned about whether any one party has adequate cash to cover his/her costs. What is important is whether or not there is sufficient total cash, regardless of source, to cover those costs which must be paid in cash. When the exchange involves a Buyer for one of the properties, adequate cash is typically not a problem. But when the exchange takes place between two or more owners who want only to exchange, they may not contribute sufficient cash to cover the transaction costs. In this case, determining if sufficient cash is available is the first order of business.

The amount of cash required to complete the exchange is usually the total of:
1. Transaction costs, as defined below
2. Loan origination costs
3. Brokers' commissions

In general, transaction costs such as escrow fees, title fees, loan fees, appraisals, property inspections and recordation fees must be paid in cash. Occasionally, the brokers involved in the transaction may be willing to take a part of their fees in the form of a promissory note secured by a Mortgage or Trust Deed on one or more of the involved properties. For this reason, the cash required to compensate the brokers is listed separately in column L. The total cash required may also be reduced if the seller of the relinquished property is willing to take part of the selling price in the form of a promissory note. This note may be secured by a lien on the replacement property or on any other property acceptable to the seller. Quite frequently, small parcels of land may also be used to help compensate the seller.

Costs are tabulated in columns K, L and M of the Exchange Worksheet. Their total is listed in Cell J21. The amount of available cash is summarized in the Escrow Cash Position box under columns B- D on lines 22 through 28. This sum includes the net proceeds from new financing. If the total cash required in Cell J23 is greater than Cell I23 the exchange is not financially feasible unless the a seller is willing to carry back a promissory note as part of the purchase price or the brokers are willing to take part of their fees in the form of a note. In the example given, there is more than adequate cash available even though Jones is a party to the exchange but contributes no cash to offset his costs of $84,000.

When "Paper" is Involved

Paper refers to promissory notes either contributed to or received in the exchange. In this example exchange, Smith contributed a promissory note with a negotiated fair market value of $15,000. It is more often the rule than the exception that promissory notes are not valued at their nominal amount, nor at their remaining balance. In most cases the reversionary amount, together with payments remaining until term, are discounted at a negotiated rate. This pre-discounted note was assigned to Jones to help satisfy his Net Trade Equity requirement of $591,000.

 The party that is to receive the promissory note needs to exercise the same precautions and follow the same due diligence as would be followed in the purchase of any note. Paramount is the credit worthiness of the maker of the note.[43] Since the note may have changed hands more than once, consideration should be given to requiring the party contributing the note to guarantee it.

Configuring the Equity Balance Worksheet

Here is a sequence you may wish to follow in completing this format:[44]

Begin on the HAS Line

1. Begin by inventorying the properties that each party will contribute to the exchange.
2. Enter the agreed-upon FMV under column D on Line 7 and the total liens under column E.
3. Under column F, calculate the gross equity contributed to the exchange. (D – E).
4. Under columns K, L and M enter the costs for which the party will be responsible.
5. If the party wishes to pass a promissory note, enter its agreed-upon value (discounted value) in Cell G7 on the HAS line.
6. If the party will cover all costs for the property conveyed, add the total and enter the result under column I (eye) on the HAS line.
7. Calculate the amount of Net Trade Equity: (Gross Equity plus paper or cash added, less all costs.) Enter the total under column N.
8. Under column O enter the amounts of the <u>new</u> loans which will be on this property at the close of escrow. Under column P enter the balance of the existing loans which will be paid off. Subtract from the new loan the balance of the old loan and enter the remainder under column Q, Net Proceeds. The balance of the old loan should include any required pre-penalty payment. Observe signs.

Move to the GETS Line

1. Enter the agreed-upon FMV of the property to be received (if any) under column D.
2. Enter the amount of mortgage which will be on each property at close of escrow under column E
3. Duplicate the amount of Net Trade Equity (Col. N) and place on the GETS line (Col... N). Each party must leave the exchange with the same NTE with which he entered the exchange. Add the total of Net Loan Proceeds to the total of Cash In and compare this to the total of all costs. If total costs exceed total cash, the exchange cannot proceed unless brokers are willing to take some paper (promissory notes) as part of their commission or a seller is willing to accept a promissory note as part payment. Title and escrow will usually not take promissory notes. If available cash exceeds total costs, the exchange is feasible.
4. Calculate the gross equity which each party will receive and compare this to the Net Trade Equity. If the gross equity received is greater than the Net Trade Equity, that party must apply for a larger loan, add cash, or write a promissory note secured by their new property to reduce this equity.
5. If the Gross Equity to be received is less than the Net Trade Equity, that party must receive cash, paper or a combination of the two.

The exchange is balanced when each party receives the same net equity from the exchange as the net equity contributed and when all **Paper In = Paper Out**, and all **Cash In = Cash Out.**

---

[43]   See Chapter 12 for additional information re promissory notes.
[44]   If this format is constructed on an Excel spreadsheet, much of the addition drudgery is eliminated.

EXCHANGE EQUITY BALANCE SHEET

	A	B	C	D	E	F	G	H	I	J	K	L	M	N	O	P	Q
			Property	FMV	Total Liens $	Gross Equity	Paper In	Paper Out	Cash In	Cash Out	Less Transaction Costs	Less Commission Costs	Less Loan Costs	Net Trade Equity	New Loan Acquired	Old Loan Payoff	Net Loan Proceeds
1																	
2																	
3																	
4																	
5	Party																
6		Jones															
7		Has	Office Bldg.	$1,050,000	375,000	675,000			0		21,000	63,000	0	591,000	$0	$375,000	-$375,000
8		Gets	Cash	0				15,000		576,000				591,000			
9																	
10	Party																
11		Smith															
12		Has	Retail	$500,000	75,000	425,000	15,000		34,375		10,000	30,000	9,375	425,000	$625,000	$75,000	$550,000
13		Gets	Office Bldg	$1,050,000	625,000	425,000								425,000			
14																	
15	Party																
16		Brown															
17		Has	0	0	0	0	0		189,000		7,500	0	6,500	175,000			
18		Gets	Retail	500,000	325,000	175,000								175,000	$325,000	$0	$325,000
19																	
20																	
21		**Escrow Cash Position**					$15,000	$15,000	$223,375	$147,375	38,500	93,000	15,875		Total New Cash		$500,000
22			Loan Proceeds	$500,000					$500,000								
23			Deposits	223,375					$723,375	$723,375							
24			Less Trans.Csts	-38,500													
25			Less Comms	-93,000													
26			Less Loan Fees	-15,875													
27																	
28			Required Cash	$576,000													
29			Adequate Cash ?	Yes													
30																	

Results for Each Participant

As the result of this exchange Smith (the only exchangor) moves gross equity of $425,000 from the retail center with a fair market value of $500,000 into a property worth $1,050,000, dramatically changing his leverage position and Return on Equity (ROE). His total debt is now $625,000. The entire amount of Smith's realized gain in the retail center will qualify for non-recognition under S.1031 since he received no Boot. Smith also benefits from additional depreciation benefits, despite a loss of some Depreciable Basis equal to the untaxed gain he has carried over from the retail center to the office building. Smith's loan costs of $9,375 must be capitalized and amortized separately over the effective term of the loan. Smith's Basis in the office building becomes:

Acq. Price of New Property	$1,050,000.
Plus Transaction Costs[45]	+$40,000.
Total Acquisition Costs	$1,090,000
Less Unrecognized Gain Carry Over	-$410,000
New (Substituted) Basis	$680,000

This new Basis must be allocated between land and building value. Had Smith purchased the building, he would have had a new Basis of $1,090,000.

Jones, who did not exchange but sold his office property to the Qualified Intermediary,[46] realizes $518,000 ($1,050,000 – $84,000 – $448,000[47]) in long-term capital gains. The $15,000 note which he accepted as partial payment is taxable Boot but will qualify for the installment method of reporting the gain. All future interest paid on the note will be taxed as Ordinary income while the principal portion of each installment payment will be treated partly as recovery of Basis (we do not have Jones' original Basis) and partly as capital gains. Depreciation taken will be taxed as Unrecovered S.1250 depreciation at 25%.

Brown has no tax liabilities since he was a buyer, and neither an exchangor nor a seller. His Basis in the property is equal to all the costs proper and necessary to place title in his hands: $500,000 in price plus $7,500 in transaction costs, $507,500. The costs of his loan, $6,500, must also be capitalized and amortized separately over the term of the loan. Loan costs are not added to Basis.

More Complex Exchanges

There are occasions when exchanges involving more than two properties are required. The Exchange Equity Balance Worksheet can be a great help in sorting out all the Has and Gets to a multi-party exchange. But it is the better part of valor not to attempt exchanges which involve too many properties and too many people. The failure of one property to sell, or the failure of one party to perform, may bring down the entire structure with serious tax consequences. Excluding the Buyer, exchanges involving more than 4 properties are best simplified.

Modifying the Analysis Spreadsheet for Exchanges

The analysis spreadsheet constructed in Chapter 6 for the Dartmouth Apartments can readily be adapted to reflect the results of acquiring a new property by exchange rather than by purchase.. Of these one of the

---

[45] Note that transaction costs for an exchangor are added to Basis and not usually expensed in the year of the exchange. But any transaction costs may be deducted from cash Boot paid, but not below zero.

[46] Following Smith's assignment of his purchase contract with Jones to the QI.

[47] His Adjusted Basis

most important is the determination of a new depreciable Basis. Once modified, the resulting program can be saved under a different file name to provide a convenient template for future exchange analyses.

Bypassing IRS Form 8824

IRS Form 8824 may be used for this computation. This form is regarded by many CPAs and tax preparers as one of the most complicated and time-consuming forms to complete.[48] The method of arriving at the new (Substituted) Basis, however, can be simpler. To illustrate, we will use the same facts given in the example presented in I.R.S. Instructions for Form 8824.

> A and B carry out a 2-way exchange between themselves. A relinquishes a property with a fair market value of $220,000, subject to an $80,000 mortgage. At the time of the exchange, A's Adjusted Basis in the relinquished property is $100,000.
> B relinquishes a property with a fair market value of $250,000, subject to a $150,000 mortgage. B's Adjusted Basis in the relinquished property is $175,000. Each party assumes the other's mortgage.[49]

> The new Basis of a property received in an exchange is simply the total acquisition cost of the replacement (new) property <u>less</u> any <u>Un</u>recognized gain carried over from the relinquished property.

You will need to make four determinations:

1. the Indicated Gain in the relinquished property.
2. the amount of Boot received by the exchanging party.
3. the Unrecognized gain (if any) remaining at completion of the exchange
4. the Basis (substituted) of the replacement property.

The amount of indicated gain for each party is easily calculated:

Exchangor A		Exchangor B
$220,000	Fair Market Value	$250,000
−100,000	Less Adjusted Basis	−175,000
$120,000	Indicated Gain	$75,000

The amount of equity held by each party is only a short step away:

Exchangor A		Exchangor B
$220,000	Fair Market Value	$250,000
−80,000	**Less Mortgage Bal.**	**−150,000**
$140,000	Equity	$100,000

The table above shows that A must receive $40,000 in Boot from B (cash, notes or valuables) in order to balance equities. It also shows that B will also be a receiver of Boot in the form of Net Mortgage Relief

---

[48] On p.4 of the Instructions to Form 8824, the IRS estimates that understanding and completing the form will require an average of 4 hours, 13 min.

[49] No transaction costs are given in the IRS Instructions to Form 8824.

($150,000 – $80,000) = $70,000. As we already know, the amount of cash paid by B to A can be deducted from the amount of Net Mortgage Relief (NMR) received by B on the theory that B could have used the $40,000 to reduce the mortgage on his property to $110,000 prior to the exchange.[50] In this example, B has NMR equal to $70,000 less $40,000 in cash paid to A, or $30,000 NMR.

Treatment of Transaction Expenses

Regulations specify that transaction costs incurred in an exchange must be added to Basis and recovered through depreciation. When, however, Boot is received transaction costs may be deducted from Boot, but not below zero. If the deduction of these costs results in a remainder below zero, the amount below zero must be added to Basis.[51]

Transactions costs of an exchange can be considered Boot paid. As such, Boot can reduce Boot received. In this example, both Parties, A & B, have received Boot.

Assume that Party A has incurred $15,000 in costs while B has incurred $18,000. Therefore Party A who received $40,000 in Boot realizes a reduction in Boot by $15,000 to $25,000. Party B who receives $30,000 ($70,000-40,000) of net Boot deducts costs of $18,000 a for a remainder of $12,000. Both these remaining Boot amounts are deducted from Indicate Gain to deliver Unrecognized gain:

Exchangor A		Exchangor B
$120,000	Indicated Gain	$75,000
-25,000	Less net Boot	-18,000
$95,000	**Unrecog. Gain**	$57,000

The new Basis for each replacement property will be its acquisition price minus the Unrecognized gain carried over from the relinquished property.

Exchangor A		Exchangor B
$250,000	New Acquis. Price	$220,000
-95,000	Less Unrecog.gain	-57,000
$155,000	**New Basis**	$163,000

The new *Substituted Basis* in each property must be allocated between the land and the value of the improvements in order to establish a Depreciable Basis.

The need to deduct Unrecognized gain (untaxed gain) from the acquisition cost of the new property is that Uncle Sam will not allow you to re-depreciate a gain on which you have not yet paid a tax. This is the less-than-obvious disadvantage of exchanging: it results in a loss of some Depreciable Basis. For the most part, this disadvantage is usually offset because the Unrecognized gain carried over is leveraged as additional down payment to acquire a more valuable property which contributes to a higher Depreciable Basis. The loss of Depreciable Basis is real but less evident.

---

[50] Remember that only cash paid can offset Net Mortgage Relief. Other forms of Boot paid cannot offset NMR received.

[51] If an exchangor receives no Boot in the exchange, all transaction costs must be added to Basis.

A pro-forma exchange analysis based on transferring equity from the Dartmouth Apartments (Chap. 6, pp.8-10) into the Cambridge Apartments using a S.1031 exchange is provided on pages 34-36.

Determining Cash Required to Complete Exchange

Reference to cell L103, of the Dartmouth Analysis in Chapter 6 shows that the Proceeds Before Tax is $4,121,486. This is the untaxed cash available for acquiring a replacement (upleg) property using S.1031.

At this point the taxpayer can decide whether to take a cash sum at closing which will result in some taxable Boot, or to limit the amount of the new loan so that no Boot is received, no gain is recognized and no tax is currently paid. In this example, the taxpayer elects to receive $250,000 in cash.[52]

Cash Out Adjustments

Extracting cash at closing not only creates a taxable event but also changes new mortgage requirements and alters the Adjusted Basis of the property. A fragment of the Cambridge spreadsheet appears at the right.

The amount of mortgage required for Cambridge is equal to the total acquisition costs (**L9**) less the amount of pre-tax cash carried over from the Dartmouth transaction. But in this case, the exchangor elects to have $250,000 withdrawn from the transaction. This amount, which will be paid at the close of the exchange escrow – and not before, will be taxable as Boot. Therefore the amount of required mortgage in Cell L12, $4,087,911, = (**L9 – L10 + L11**).

The amount of mortgage that may be obtained from a lender may be determined using any of the three methods described earlier. These results appear in Cells H5 through H17. But it is also necessary to test whether the required mortgage does not exceed the lowest mortgage obtainable. This selection can again be made by using Excel's =**Min** function. Cell H18 contains the following statement. =**Min(H5, H14, H17, L12).**

I	J	K	L
1			
2	Fed. Capital Gains Rate		20.0%
3		CA Max Tax	9.3%
4	Depreciation Recapture rate		25.0%
5		Fed. Ord. Tax Rate	33.0%
6	Combined Ca+Fed Tax (Ord. Inc.)		39.23%
7		NII Tax Rate	3.8%
8	**Mortgage Required**		
9	Acq. Cost Replacement Prop.		7,959,600
10	Less Pre-tax Carry-over Proceeds		4,121,689
11		Plus Cash Out	250,000
12	**Total Mortgage Required**		4,087,911
13	**Amt. of Tax Deferred**		
14	Gain on Relinquished Prop.		2,780,617
15	Less Recognized Gain (Boot)		250,000
16	Total Remain.Unrecognized Gain		2,530,617
17	Unrecog. Depreciation Carryover		1,503,092
18	Remaining LTCG Carryover		1,027,525
19	Tax on unrecog. Depreciation		375,773
20	Tax on Unrecog. LTCG		205,505
21	Total Deferred Tax		581,278

If the amount in L12 is higher than the lender-amounts, then the taxpayer may be limited to the lowest lender amount *or* would also have to contribute cash to the transaction *or* lower his Boot requirement. In this example in which the required mortgage amount is less than either of the lender- amounts, the amount in L12 is used. Loan fees are estimated in H21 and are recovered ratably on Line 57.

The Exchange Investment Base

It is apparent that the exchangor is using cash which would ordinarily be paid in taxes as additional funds to control this investment. Therefore the investor's cash investment is less than it would be without the

---

[52] The exchangor is willing to pay the tax on the Boot received.

use of deferred taxes. But what is the amount of deferred taxes? This amount is determined by the calculations in Cells L14:L21.

The amount of the pre-tax gain, $2,780,617, is found in Dartmouth Cell L81 and entered in Cambridge L14. The amount of the taxable Boot ($250,000) is subtracted to leave $2,530,617 in unrecognized gain carried over. Of this amount $1,503,092 is unrecognized <u>depreciation</u> which would otherwise be taxed @25%, or $375,773. The remainder of the unrecognized gain, $1,027,525, is taxable as <u>LTCG</u>, or $205,505. The total tax <u>not</u> paid is the sum of these unpaid taxes; $375,773 + 205,505 = $581,278

The adjusted Investment Base, $3,291 690,, is given in Cell B23: (**B7-C26 + H21 – L21**). This lower Investment Base accounts for the relatively high IRR achieved (13.22%) because a higher discount rate is required to reach a lower Present Value.

The Ten-Year Exchange Analysis which appears on pages 34-36 of this chapter can be developed from the Dartmouth workbook in Chapter 6 with only modest modifications. The Exchange workbook will prove very helpful in verifying the accounting used by the exchangor's tax accountants. .

S. 1033 Exchanges

When a property is involuntarily or compulsorily converted, perhaps as the result of destruction, theft, seizure or an eminent domain action by which an authorized governmental unit takes the property for public use, the holder of the property is entitled to exchange the equity in the property for another property of *similar use*. This type of exchange does not permit the exchange of simply *like-kind* properties.

For example, an office building taken by eminent domain must be replaced with a similar office building; a retail center must be replaced with a retail center, etc.

In addition, the time constraints for replacement are much different: the owner has until the end of the second year following the year in which the transfer took place to acquire a replacement.

This type of involuntary 'exchange' is covered in Section 1033 of the Code. Because this type conversion is not common and because the rules are so dissimilar they have not been covered here. The services of an attorney experienced in involuntary conversions are essential.

Ten Year Exchange Analysis

#	A	B	C	D	E	F	G	H	I	J	K	L
1	Multi-Family Real Estate Analysis											
2	Property Ident.	Cambridge Exchange					Date	Today			Fed. Capital Gains Rate	20.0%
3	Residential (Y/N)	Y									CA Max Tax	9.3%
4	Number of Units	36					**Loan by Leverage**				Depreciation Recapture rate	25.0%
5	Acquisition Price	7,920,000	$220,000	cost per unit			1st TD Loan	5,544,000			Fed. Ord. Tax Rate	33.0%
6	Acquisition Costs @ 0.5%	39,600					Int. Rate	0.05			Combined Ca+Fed Tax(Ord. Inc.)	39.23%
7	Acquisition Cost	7,959,600				Amortization Schedule (Yrs.)		30.00			NII Tax Rate	3.8%
8	Less Unrecognized Gain Carryover	4,121,689					Term (Yrs.)	10.00			**Mortgage Required**	
9	Plus Recognized Gain (Boot)	250,000					Pmt	30614.17			Acq. Cost Replacement Prop.	7,959,600
10	Substituted New Basis	4,087,911					**Loan by DCR**				Less Pre-tax Carry-over Proceeds	4,121,689
11	% To Improvement	70.00%					NOI	512496.00			Plus Cash Out	250,000
12	New Depreciable Basis	2,861,538					DCR	1.25			Total Mortgage Required	4,087,911
13	Estimated Expenses/Unit/Yr	6,500					Annual Loan Cost	409996.80			**Amt. of Tax Deferred**	
14	Rent Inflator/Yr	4.00%					1st TD Loan	6,187,282			Gain on Relinquished Prop.	2,780,617
15	Expense Inflator/Yr	3.00%					**Loan by DYRatio**				Less Recognized Gain (Boot)	250,000
16	Vacancy & Credit Loss Rate	4.00%					DYR	0.10			Total Remain. Unrecognized Gain	2,530,617
17	Tax Area Code Rate	1.20%					Loan Amount	5,124,960			Unrecog. Depreciation Carryover	1,503,092
18	Annual Tax Inflator	2.00%					Lowest Loan Amt.	4,087,911			Remaining LTCG Carryover	1,027,525
19	Owner's Incr. Tax Bracket	39.2%									Tax on unrecog. Depreciation	375,773
20	Capitalization Rate In	6.47%					Loan Points	1.0%			Tax on Unrecog. LTCG	205,505
21	Capitalization Rate Out	6.72%					Loan Fees	40,879			Total Deferred Tax	581,278
22	Leverage (vs. Acq. Price)	70.0%										
23	Total Investment Base	3,291,690										
24												
25		Year	1	2	3	4	5	6	7	8	9	10
26	Loan Progress	Beg. Bal.	4,087,911	4,030,269	3,969,528	3,905,519	3,838,068	3,766,989	3,692,088	3,613,158	3,529,983	3,442,335
27		Rate	5.25%	5.25%	5.25%	5.25%	5.25%	5.25%	5.25%	5.25%	5.25%	5.25%
28		Ann. Debt Serv.	270,883	270,883	270,883	270,883	270,883	270,883	270,883	270,883	270,883	270,883
29		Interest	213,241	210,141	206,875	203,432	199,804	195,982	191,953	187,708	183,235	178,521
30		Equity	57,642	60,742	64,009	67,451	71,079	74,901	78,930	83,175	87,648	92,362
31		Remain. Bal.	4,030,269	3,969,528	3,905,519	3,838,068	3,766,989	3,692,088	3,613,158	3,529,983	3,442,335	3,349,973
32		DCRatio	1.89	1.98	2.07	2.17	2.27	2.37	2.48	2.59	2.71	2.83
33	Income											
34	Potential Rental Income	Annual	777,600	808,704	841,052	874,694	909,682	946,069	983,912	1,023,269	1,064,199	1,106,767
35	Other Occ. Depend Income		0	0	0	0	0	0	0	0	0	0
36	Total Potential Income		777,600	808,704	841,052	874,694	909,682	946,069	983,912	1,023,269	1,064,199	1,106,767
37	Vacancy / Credit Loss	4.0%	31,104	32,348	33,642	34,988	36,387	37,843	39,356	40,931	42,568	44,271
38	Effective Rental Income		746,496	776,356	807,410	839,706	873,295	908,227	944,556	982,338	1,021,631	1,062,497
39	Non Vacancy-depend. Income		0	0	0	0	0	0	0	0	0	0
40	Total Gross Operating Income		746,496	776,356	807,410	839,706	873,295	908,227	944,556	982,338	1,021,631	1,062,497
41	Expenses											
42	Operating Expenses < Taxes		138,960	143,129	147,423	151,845	156,401	161,093	165,926	170,903	176,030	181,311
43	RE Taxes		95,040	96,941	98,880	100,857	102,874	104,932	107,030	109,171	111,355	113,582
44	Total Operating Expenses		234,000	240,070	246,302	252,703	259,275	266,025	272,956	280,074	287,385	294,893
45	% Increase Expenses/Year		NA	2.59%	2.60%	2.60%	2.60%	2.60%	2.61%	2.61%	2.61%	
46	Percent Expenses to GOI		31.35%	30.92%	30.51%	30.09%	29.69%	29.29%	28.90%	28.51%	28.13%	
47	Net Operating Income		512,496	536,286	561,108	587,004	614,020	642,202	671,600	702,263	734,246	767,604

Ten Year Exchange Analysis

	A	B	C	D	E	F	G	H	I	J	K	L
48												
49	Spendable Income											
50	Net Operating Income		512,496	536,286	561,108	587,004	614,020	642,202	671,600	702,263	734,246	767,604
51	Annual Debt Service		270,883	270,883	270,883	270,883	270,883	270,883	270,883	270,883	270,883	270,883
52	Cash Flow < Taxes		241,613	265,403	290,225	316,121	343,137	371,319	400,716	431,380	463,363	496,721
53	Taxable Income, CFAT											
54	Net Operating Income		512,496	536,286	561,108	587,004	614,020	642,202	671,600	702,263	734,246	767,604
55	Less Interest		213,241	210,141	206,875	203,432	199,804	195,982	191,953	187,708	183,235	178,521
56	Less Depreciation		99,720	104,056	104,056	104,056	104,056	104,056	104,056	104,056	99,720	104,056
57	Less Amortization of Points		4,088	4,088	4,088	4,088	4,088	4,088	4,088	4,088	4,088	4,088
58	Total Deductibles		317,050	318,285	315,018	311,576	307,948	304,125	300,097	295,852	287,043	286,665
59	Total Taxable Income		195,446	218,001	246,089	275,428	306,071	338,076	371,502	406,411	447,203	480,939
60	Passive Losses/Taxable Inc.											
61	Estimate AGI		150,000	120,000	160,000	140,000	130,000	130,000	125,000	90,000	140,000	125,000
62	Maximum Allowable Passive Loss		0	15,000	0	5,000	10,000	10,000	12,500	25,000	5,000	12,500
63	Total Suspnd + Taxable Inc		195,446	218,001	246,089	275,428	306,071	338,076	371,502	406,411	447,203	480,939
64	Net Taxable Income		195,446	218,001	246,089	275,428	306,071	338,076	371,502	406,411	447,203	480,939
65	Incremental Tax Bracket		39.23%	39.23%	39.23%	39.23%	39.23%	39.23%	39.23%	39.23%	39.23%	39.23%
66	Ordinary Tax		76,676	85,524	96,543	108,053	120,075	132,631	145,744	159,439	175,442	188,677
67	Total Suspended Losses		0	0	0	0	0	0	0	0	0	0
68	Net Investment Income Tax											
69	Estimated NII		20,000	30,000	45,000	55,000	25,000	35,000	35,000	35,000	35,000	35,000
70	Estimated MAGI		260,000	250,000	300,000	265,000	270,000	275,000	275,000	275,000	275,000	275,000
71	Threshold		250,000	250,000	250,000	250,000	250,000	250,000	250,000	250,000	250,000	250,000
72	Taxable Amt		10,000	0	45,000	15,000	20,000	25,000	25,000	25,000	25,000	25,000
73	NII Tax	3.8%	380	0	1,710	570	760	950	950	950	950	950
74	Total (NII + Ordinary Tax)		77,056	85,524	98,253	108,623	120,835	133,581	146,694	160,389	176,392	189,627
75	Cashflow > Tax		164,557	179,879	191,971	207,498	222,302	237,738	254,022	270,991	286,971	307,093
76	Adjusted Basis											
77	Total Acquisition Cost		7,959,600	7,959,600	7,959,600	7,959,600	7,959,600	7,959,600	7,959,600	7,959,600	7,959,600	7,959,600
78	Less Total Depreciation Taken	9.3%	99,720	203,776	307,832	411,888	515,944	620,000	724,056	828,112	927,832	1,031,888
79	Plus Real Estate Commission	3.0%	200,000	200,000	200,000	200,000	200,000	200,000	200,000	200,000	200,000	200,000
80	Plus Other Costs of Disposition	0.5%	38,127	39,897	41,743	43,670	45,680	47,776	49,963	52,245	54,624	57,106
81	Total Adjusted Basis		8,098,007	7,995,721	7,893,511	7,791,382	7,689,336	7,587,377	7,485,508	7,383,733	7,286,392	7,184,818
82	Indicated Pre-Tax Gain		-138,407	-36,121	66,089	168,218	270,264	372,223	474,092	575,867	673,208	774,782
83	Tax Computation on Gain											
84	Indicated Gain		-138,407	-36,121	66,089	168,218	270,264	372,223	474,092	575,867	673,208	774,782
85	CA State Tax Payable	9.3%	0.00	0	6,146	15,644	25,135	34,617	44,091	53,556	62,608	72,055
86	Remaining Fed Taxable Gain		0	0	59,942	152,574	245,130	337,607	430,002	522,311	610,600	702,727
87	Total Depreciation Taken		99,720	203,776	307,832	411,888	515,944	620,000	724,056	828,112	927,832	1,031,888
88	Recapturable Depreciation		0	0	59,942	152,574	245,130	337,607	430,002	522,311	610,600	702,727
89	Depreciation Recapture Tax @	25.0%	0	0	14,986	38,143	61,282	84,402	107,500	130,578	152,650	175,682
90	Remaining Fed. LTCG		0	0	0	0	0	0	0	0	0	0
91	Federal LTCG Tax @	20.0%	36,791	32,703	28,615	24,527	20,440	16,352	12,264	8,176	4,088	0
92	Unamortized Loan Points		36,791	32,703	28,615	24,527	20,440	16,352	12,264	8,176	4,088	0
93	Total Suspended Losses		0	0	0	0	0	0	0	0	0	0
94	Total Susp. Losses + Points		36,791	32,703	28,615	24,527	20,440	16,352	12,264	8,176	4,088	0
95	Ord. Tax Credit from Points	39.2%	14,434	12,830	11,226	9,622	8,019	6,415	4,811	3,207	1,604	0
96	Total Tax on Sale		62,622	72,694	108,159	152,789	199,233	246,184	293,474	341,315	390,047	437,364

Ten Year Exchange Analysis

	A	B	C	D	E	F	G	H	I	J	K	L
97												
98	Sales Price		7,625,397	7,979,371	8,348,689	8,733,996	9,135,962	9,555,284	9,992,690	10,448,935	10,924,808	11,421,129
99	Less Costs of Sales		238,127	239,897	241,743	243,670	245,680	247,776	249,963	252,245	254,624	257,106
100	Less Mortgage Balance		4,030,269	3,969,528	3,905,519	3,838,068	3,766,989	3,692,088	3,613,158	3,529,983	3,442,335	3,349,973
101	Pre-Tax Proceeds		3,357,001	3,769,946	4,201,427	4,652,258	5,123,293	5,615,420	6,129,569	6,666,708	7,227,850	7,814,051
102	Less Total Tax on Sale		62,622	72,694	108,159	152,789	199,233	246,184	293,474	341,315	390,047	437,364
103	After Tax Proceeds		3,294,379	3,697,252	4,093,268	4,499,470	4,924,060	5,369,236	5,836,095	6,325,393	6,837,803	7,376,687
104	IRR Calculation											
105		Init. Investmt.	1	2	3	4	5	6	7	8	9	10
106	Year 1	-3,291,690	3,458,936									
107	2	-3,291,690	164,557	3,877,131								
108	3	-3,291,690	164,557	179,879	4,285,239							
109	4	-3,291,690	164,557	179,879	191,971	4,706,967						
110	5	-3,291,690	164,557	179,879	191,971	207,498	5,146,361					
111	6	-3,291,690	164,557	179,879	191,971	207,498	222,302	5,606,974				
112	7	-3,291,690	164,557	179,879	191,971	207,498	222,302	237,738	6,090,117			
113	8	-3,291,690	164,557	179,879	191,971	207,498	222,302	237,738	254,022	6,596,384		
114	9	-3,291,690	164,557	179,879	191,971	207,498	222,302	237,738	254,022	270,991	7,124,774	
115	10	-3,291,690	164,557	179,879	191,971	207,498	222,302	237,738	254,022	270,991	286,971	7,683,780
116	IRR =		5.1%	11.1%	12.6%	13.1%	13.4%	13.4%	13.4%	13.4%	13.3%	13.2%
117	ROE=		5.0%	4.9%	4.7%	4.6%	4.5%	4.4%	4.4%	4.3%	4.2%	4.2%
118	Performance Indices											
119	Capitalization Rate In	6.47%										
120	Cash-on-Cash > Tax	5.00%										
121	Discount Rate											
122	Calculated Capitalization Rate	6.47%										
123	Inflation Rate	3.00%										
124	Discount Rate	9.47%	Equity Value	Total Value								
125	Present Value @	9.47%	6,562,084	10,649,995								
126	Net Present Value @	9.47%	7,358,305									
127	NPV @ IRR	13.2%	0									
128	Constructed Cap Rate											
129	Current Safe Rate	3.5%										
130	Return of Investment	2.0%	← 50	years estimated remaining economic life								
131	Risk Premium	1.0%										
132	Constructed Cap Rate	6.50%										
133												
134	Value @ Constr. Cap Rate	7,884,554										
135	Listed Price	7,920,000										
136	Premium	35,446										
137												

IRR

15.0%
10.0%
5.0%
0.0%
1 2 3 4 5 6 7 8 9 10

AFTER-TAX ROE

5.5%
5.0%
4.5%
4.0%
3.5%
1 2 3 4 5 6 7 8 9 10

O f all the documents affecting the value of an income-producing real property, the lease is the most important. The lease stipulates the responsibilities of both landlord and tenant, determines the income obtainable from the property, specifies the rights and duties of the parties to the contract and figures predominately in the valuation and financeability of the asset.

Chapter 10
Occupancy
Leases

A Lease is a Legally Binding Document

You already know from Chapter 1 that when the owner of real property sells the rights to use and possess the property for a limited time, he creates two different estates: the leasehold interest and the leased-fee interest. The leasehold interest is held by the tenant or lessee, while the fee owner, now the *lessor*, holds the leased-fee interest.

It is not unusual that someone will refer to a rental agreement as a 'lease.' But the two are not the same and it is important to the investor to determine which tenants are bound by leases and which by rental agreements since the rights and obligations of both tenant and landlord differ under each arrangement.

A lease is a particular type of bilateral contract which creates an *estate for years* in which the owner of a property agrees to deliver the rights to use and possess the property for a determinable period of time in return for the payment of rent. Leases are different from rental agreements in two important ways. In contrast to a rental agreement, a lease:

♦ is for a specified period of time with a definite (or determinable) ending date, and
♦ the lessee's obligation for rent payable is for the whole of the rent due <u>under the entire term of the lease contract</u> despite the fact that the rent may be payable periodically (/month /quarter, etc.).

Rental Agreements, on the other hand, are used to represent an *estate from period-to-period* and do not bind the lessee for a specific period.[1] Therefore a tenant who occupies a property under a rental agreement is not obligated for the payment of rent for an extended period of time. In most jurisdictions, the tenant is responsible only for the rent for a period equal to the period for which the rent is paid, typically one month, but could be some other agreed-upon period of time (e.g. a quarter or year).

---

[1] Although the month-month tenant is usually contractually required to give advance notice to terminate.

Page 10-1

Many agreements between lessor and lessee start out as leases, but any 'holding over'[2] by the tenant at the end of the lease converts the contract to a month-to-month or *Periodic Tenancy* agreement. These 'holding over' clauses are commonly found in residential leases but may be present in any lease. When found in non-residential leases, however, the rent during any holdover period is usually much greater than the rent most recently paid.[3] The aim is to require the commercial tenant either to negotiate a new lease or to vacate the property.

The downside of a month-to-month agreement for the tenant is that the landlord is free to lease the property to any newcomer with as little as a 30-day Notice to Quit served on the tenant. Most commercial tenants cannot operate without the assurance of a stable location. Therefore month-to month arrangements beyond residential properties are quite rare.

The importance of the lease to the value of the income property cannot be overemphasized. The lease determines the rent and the rent determines property value. Since a transfer of ownership will not usually cancel a lease, a prospective buyer needs to be diligent in examining each lease which will survive a transfer of ownership. Leases in place, as well as those entered into during the period of the sales contract, will either enhance or detract from the market value of the investment. For this reason, any agreement to acquire an income property with tenants in place should be absolutely conditioned upon the buyer's receipt and approval of all existing and proposed leases and/or rental agreements, together with all amendments, additions and modifications which will survive the closing date.

Quality, Quantity and Duration of Rent

The value of the lease is a function of: 1) who pays the rent, 2) the amount of rent to be paid and 3) the length of the lease: the quality, quantity and duration of the rental stream.

Who pays the rent refers to the *quality* or financial creditworthiness of the tenant. A tenant whose resources and credit rating assure the lessor that the entire amount of rent payable under the lease will be paid is a '*credit-tenant*,' and is highly prized. A credit-tenant also improves the attractiveness of the property to lenders and may enable the owner to obtain a lower debt coverage ratio and a lower interest rate because of the diminished risk. This reduced risk is reflected in a lower risk premium in both the capitalization and discount rates and these lower rates applied to net operating income result a higher market value for the property.

Ability of Tenant to Pay Market Rent

Not all tenants have the ability to pay the market rent in upscale locations. Although a prospective new tenant may present a sound balance sheet, the ability of the tenant to pay the on-going rent in a highly desirable location maybe limited by the class of products and services which the tenant intends to provide. In many popular seaside or littoral locations main streets which were once populated by butchers, bakers and candlestick makers are now occupied by art collectors, jewelry shop, antiques shops, high-end fashion clothing shops, restaurants and other retail businesses engaged in the sale of products with relatively high gross margins.[4] Over time these high-end shops crowd out merchants operating on much smaller margins and downtown Main Street quickly become a tourist Mecca.

---

[2]   A continued occupancy by the tenant beyond the expiration date of the lease.
[3]   Increases of 10% - 25% are not uncommon.
[4]   Profit as a percent of Revenue

The *quantity* or amount of rent entails not only the initial amount of rent, but also the periodic increases provided for over the entire term of the lease agreement. If these increases permit the lessor to keep pace with operating expenses and/or inflation, the lease becomes more valuable because it supports the market value of the property. If the lease fails to deliver adequate periodic increases in rent, the purchasing power of the collected dollar will deteriorate, as will the market value of the investment for as long as it is encumbered by such a lease. Individual retail locations in many new shopping centers experience a 33% mortality rate in the first 3 years of operation which underscores the value of a center with long-established tenants.

The *duration* of the rent pertains to the length of the lease. A long-term lease with a credit-tenant may be highly desirable. But if the increases provided for in the lease are unable to keep pace with market rents, or - in the least - with inflation, the lessor has an encumbrance on his title which will actually diminish the market value of his property.

Negotiations with a Credit-tenant

In many negotiations with a credit-tenant the landlord is presented with trade-offs between a market rent vs. a diminished rent and oftentimes less than adequate periodic increases.

For example, a credit-tenant may seek to limit its rent increases to adjustments every 5 years, and even then to adjustments which are less than the compounded inflation rate. If inflation over a 5-year period averages 3% per year, each $1.00 of rent today should be increased in 5 years to $1.16 just to maintain the purchasing power of the rent dollar. A lease which increases rents by only 10% every 5 years is the equivalent of a 1.9% increase per year - significantly below the average historic 3% rate of inflation.[5] Even a lease which increases the rent 16% every 5 years deprives the landlord of the purchasing power of annual increases.

In negotiations with a credit-tenant, these two issues need to be addressed: 1) the rental rate of the lease and 2) the frequency and amount of the periodic increases. While the credit-tenant has cause to seek a lower rent because he reduces the risk of non-collection, there is no economic justification for demanding a lower increase or a longer interval between rent increases. The first concession compensates the tenant for the fact that it will remain responsible for the lease throughout the term of the lease, but the second concession often demanded functions to reduce the purchasing power of future rent.

Landlords value credit-tenants and while a slightly lower rent may be required to secure such a tenant, every effort should be made to negotiate adequate increases on, if possible, an annual or bi-annual basis.

Nomenclature of Leases

In this chapter we are talking about *occupancy* leases in which the tenant takes *possession* and *use* of the property for a limited time. In a following chapter we will discuss *ground leases* whereby the tenant obtains not only the rights to possess and use the land but also the right to *develop* it.

In an attempt to classify occupancy leases, a number of short-hand descriptions have evolved which, though handy, sometimes become murky.

---

[5]   Current (2014) estimates of inflation as published by the Bureau of Labor Statistics are purely fictional.

Net, Net-Net and NNN Leases

A Net Lease properly refers to an agreement under which the lessor passes to the lessee <u>all</u> the costs of operating and maintaining the property. These costs include the real estate taxes, insurance, maintenance, utilities, assessments and all other potential costs of ownership other than personal income taxes, money judgments against the title and liens made against the lessor's leased fee-interest. The rent paid to the lessor is absolutely net of any and all other costs which are to be borne by the tenant. But various sellers mean various things by 'Net' leases.[6]

A triple-net lease (NNN) usually refers to a lease in which the tenant is responsible for the real estate taxes, insurance and complete maintenance of the property. Yet many properties which are offered for sale with leases described as 'net,' 'triple-net' or 'NNN' are not truly net leases. Many 'triple net leases' assign to the owner responsibility for the integrity and maintenance of the structural walls, the foundation and the roof.[7] References to a double-net (NN) lease suggest that the tenant is responsible for two of the three expenses: taxes, maintenance and insurance. But we can never be absolutely certain as to which two costs are the tenant's responsibility without a thorough reading of the lease.

The Gross Lease

A Gross Lease, on the other hand, commits the lessee to pay a stipulated rent while the lessor retains responsibility for all expenses of operation and maintenance. Between these two extremes (Net vs. Gross) are rafts of *modified* net and *modified* gross lease arrangements.

Modified gross leases are those in which the tenant is asked to pay one or more of the costs of operation, typically one or more utilities or cleaning services. The term *industrial gross lease,* for example, is commonly understood to mean that the tenant pays the insurance and maintenance costs. But, again, as to which expenses are to be borne by the tenant, we can never be certain without reading the lease.

Expenses Stops

Many 'gross leases' are 'gross' only for the first year, which means that the owner assumes all operating expenses for the first year. Beginning in the second and each subsequent year, however, the tenant becomes responsible for any increases in expenses in excess of the first year. A lease provision which calls for the tenant later to assume one or all of the costs of operation over a base amount equates to a *"stop"* on expenses payable by the owner, hence *expense stop*. Most expense stops apply to the first year only, but it is not uncommon to see the owner held for the total of certain expenses (e.g. real estate taxes) for a number of years.

Real Estate Tax Increases

Many states have followed California's lead (Proposition XIII) and reassess property upon a transfer of title. Therefore tenants who have agreed to pay real estate taxes become exposed to a significant increase in operating expenses if a landlord of long standing should sell the property thereby triggering a

---

[6] Efforts by professional real estate groups to standardize lease nomenclature have not been very successful.

[7] The term "roof" can mean the supporting structure of the roof while "roofing" can mean the covering of the supporting structure.

reappraisal. In these states it is quite common for the tenant to negotiate to pay the usual and ordinary increases in property taxes excepting those that arise from a transfer of title.

Landlords are generally quite resistant to these provisions. If taxes increase from, say, $10,000 to $20,000 per year, the reduction of $10,000 in net operating income (NOI) when capitalized at , say 7.0%, results in a loss of market value of $142,857 ($10,000 ÷ 0.07). If the landlord negotiates to limit any increases in taxes for 3-5 years, he commits to a loss of only $30,000 or $50,000, not $142,857.

In dealing with ground leased properties the situation becomes somewhat more complicated. In California the taxing authority[8] regards the fee interest to vest with the tenant when the lease has at least 35 or more years (including options) remaining. A transfer of the leasehold interest would trigger a reassessment, whereas a transfer of the underlying leased-fee interest would not. But if the lease has fewer than 35 years remaining the same taxing authority regards the fee title to vest with the land owner (leased-fee interest). A transfer of the leasehold interest will not cause a reappraisal but a transfer of the leased-fee interest will.

Investors acquiring long-term leases, especially those promoted as net leases, need to be careful to investigate local law regarding the method and timing of tax reappraisal.

Read the Leases

As you can see, there is great variation in the nomenclature of leases: a 'net' lease may not be 'net' at all and a 'gross' lease may be modified in some way or another. Don't be misled by the printed title of a lease form which proclaims it to be a *Standard....... Lease*. There is no such thing as a 'Standard Lease' and if you could obtain a copy of every different 'Standard Lease' form in current use, they would fill a courtroom.

If an investor is contemplating the acquisition of a property subject to one or more leases, it is absolutely imperative that the investor obtain a copy of every lease, together with all amendments, options and modifications and to read each lease carefully. This is a chore, but it is a chore which cannot and should not be avoided by accepting the assertion that "if you've read one, you've read them all."

Most landlords and management companies make a determined effort to use one form of a lease for all tenants, but you can rely on the fact that each lease has been separately negotiated by each tenant and what is contained in one lease may not be contained in every lease. In other circumstances, a different form of a "Standard Lease" may have been brought to the landlord by a leasing broker and its acceptance, however modified, results in one or more different leases encumbering the property. It is for this reason that landlords typically insist on using their own version of a lease in order to avoid, as much as possible, future confusion.

Lease summaries or abstracts are only a convenient way to summarize the key features of every lease but they are never a substitute for <u>reading each lease</u>. Do not rely on them.

Measuring Leasable Space

Since office, retail and industrial spaces are usually rented on the basis of the number of square feet provided, it is important to understand how these footages are to be measured. The guidelines of the Building Owners and Managers Association (BOMA) are the generally accepted method for measurement

---

[8]   California Franchise Tax Board

and can be applied to any architectural configuration. BOMA guidelines define both the *Usable Area* and the *Rentable Area*. Guidelines are available for office, industrial, retail and residential properties. See **www.boma.com**

The **Useable Area** is a measure of all the 'occupiable' area of a floor or individual office space. Useable Area may expand or contract depending on the size of corridors or re-configurations of space. It is measured from the finished side of the (office) corridor and other permanent walls to the midpoint of the partitions which separate one Useable Area from an adjoining Useable Area to the inside finished surface of the dominant portions of the permanent outer building walls. No deductions are made for columns and other projections necessary to the building.

The **Rentable Area** measures the tenant's pro-rata share of the entire Floor Area (the sum of all Useable Area on that floor), excluding elements of the building that penetrate through the floor to the floor below. The Rentable Area is measured from the inner finished surface of the dominant portions of the permanent outer building walls, excluding any vertical penetrations of the floor. The Rentable Area is fixed for the life of the building and is not affected by changes in corridors and configurations excluding any major vertical penetrations of the floor. No deductions are made for columns and projections necessary to the building.

The definition of "major vertical penetrations" includes stairs, elevator shafts, flues, pipe shafts, vertical ducts and their enclosing walls which serve more than one floor of the building. Any such areas which are devoted to a single tenant's use are not excluded.[9]

The Rentable Area for a particular office is the product of the Useable Area for that office x the quotient of the $\frac{\text{Rentable Area for Floor}}{\text{Useable Area for the Floor}}$.

Since the Rental Area is larger than the Useable Area the ratio is always larger than 1 and is called the R/U Ratio. The Rental Area is used in computing a tenant's share of the area of a building for the purpose of rent escalation and the apportionment of Common Area Maintenance charges for which the tenant may be responsible.

Load Factor	R/U Ratio – 1
Useable Area x R/U	Rentable Area
Rentable Area ÷ R/U Factor	Useable Area
Useable Area x (1+Load Factor)	Rentable Area

The *Load Factor* is the percentage of space on a floor that is not useable, expressed as a percentage of the total Useable Area. It is equal to the R/U Ratio minus 1.

Common Area Maintenance (CAM) Charges

When a property is shared by more than one tenant, it is usual that the actual expenses of maintaining the common areas are shared by the tenants on a pro-rata basis according to the Rentable Area of the space occupied.

These 'CAM' charges are in addition to any base rate to be paid. It is not unheard of that some owners will include in CAM charges expenses which are properly *capital expenses*,[10] such as for the replacement of HVAC units[11], re-roofing, or replacements of electrical or plumbing systems which under the lease are

---

[9] Such as a stairway connecting two floors occupied by the same tenant.
[10] "Capex" expenses
[11] Heating, Ventilating, Air-Condition units.

the responsibility of the landlord. Therefore in examining the books of the owner in connection with a purchase, the buyer should review the charges transferred to the tenants as CAM charges since any errors may be recoverable by the tenants from the owner.

A well-drawn lease will afford a tenant the right to inspect the landlord's books to confirm the validity and application of CAM charges. The tenant should be required to submit a written request for audit at least 24-48 hours before the date of the requested audit.[12] This request should also specify the particular areas of concern to the tenant. Material furnished to the tenant for review should be limited to the areas specified.

Since most CAM charges for the coming year are estimated based on expenses for the prior year, it is reasonable to confine tenant audits to a period of 90-120 days following the close of the prior year's books. These restrictions are not meant to impede legitimate inquiry but they are intended to forestall harassing audits by a disgruntled tenant.

Estoppel Certificates

A well-drawn lease will contain a clause which requires the tenant to complete an *Estoppel Certificate* within *x* number of days following a written request by the landlord.

An *estoppel* is a bar to the exercise of a right which an individual once had but failed to exercise when the opportunity to exercise the right was offered. The right is later denied because to exercise the right at a later time would work an injustice against another. In plainer language, an estoppel says:

> '*You had a right and were offered the chance to exercise that right but did not act. To exercise that right now would work an injustice against the party who offered you the opportunity. Therefore you have lost the opportunity to exercise that right.*'

Estoppel certificates should be obtained from each tenant. The receipt and approval of these certificates should be a condition precedent (contingency) to the buyer's obligation to complete the purchase agreement and therefore should be obtained early in the due diligence period.

If the buyer intends to obtain a new loan on the property, the lender will undoubtedly request estoppel certificates from each tenant; a buyer may legally rely on these same certificates provided that they expressly state that they are to be completed for the benefit of both the (named) lender and the (named) buyer.

Estoppel Certificates are important documents for the buyer to obtain and to keep since the buyer will rely on these documents to confirm the identity of the tenant in possession, the amount of rent, the duration of the lease, the terms of any options to renew, modifications, amendments and extensions of the lease, and the status of the landlord's obligations under the lease. If, for example, a tenant declares in the estoppel certificate that the rent to be paid is $5,000 per month and that there are no offsets to the rent, the tenant would be estopped (barred) from later claiming the right to deduct an amount from the rent to compensate for some service (such as bookkeeping or property maintenance) performed by the tenant for the landlord. Courts have ruled that the facts declared by the tenant in an estoppel certificate are binding, even when they may vary from the terms stated in the lease. If the estoppel certificates can be obtained before a physical 'walk-through' of the property is scheduled to take place, they afford the buyer an opportunity to

---

[12] Most leases will specify the required lead time for conducting an audit; 7 to 14 days is not uncommon.

'match' the tenant with the occupant. Obvious as it may seem, there should be one registered tenant for each estoppel certificate received and the occupant should be the tenant. But this is not always the case. Caveat emptor.

Contents of Estoppel Certificate

The estoppel certificate, furnished by the buyer to the seller for completion by each tenant, should provide for:

- the identity of both tenant and landlord
- a description of the property or premise subject to the lease
- the commencement and termination dates of the lease
- the existence of any options to extend the lease, their number and length[13]
- the amount of rent as of a specified date
- the amount of any pass-through expenses to be paid by the tenant
- the date through which pass-through expenses have been paid
- the amount of any prepaid rent and the date to which the rent is prepaid
- the amount of any offsets (e.g. deductions from rent due for services rendered)
- the amount of security deposit held by the landlord
- the status of the landlord's performance under the lease (e.g. are there any unfulfilled obligations).

The estoppel certificate should be dated and signed by each tenant on the rent roll, and the tenant's name on the rent roll should correspond to the name on the lease or rental agreement. Do not accept an estoppel certificate from anyone other than the registered tenant unless that individual presents evidence of legal representation such as a notarized Power of Attorney.

Lenders Require Estoppel Certificates

In those cases in which a number of non-residential tenants occupy a property, the lender will invariably require copies of all leases and estoppel certificates signed by each tenant. Some lenders will accept an estoppel certificate signed by the tenant for the benefit of a prospective buyer but most lenders will require a certificate of their own design which specifically states that the estoppel is for the lender's benefit. In these cases, the buyer should request an amendment to the certificate to include his own name. In executing a new lease, it's a good practice to attach to the lease the Estoppel Form which is to be used and to specify that the failure of the tenant to return the executed Estoppel Certificate within the proscribed time (10-30 days) shall be considered a default under the lease. Doing so will obviate the landlord's obligation to provide two separate Notices of Default under the lease.

---

[13] If options exist, it is important to obtain the language of the option.

ESTOPPEL CERTIFICATE

For the Benefit of John Jones and

_____

Property Identification: _____

Address: _____

City, State, Zip _____

Suite/Unit No.: _____

Tenant's Business or Trade Name:_____

Address of Tenant: _____

_____

_____

Tenant's Phone Number_____

Authorized Agent/Officer _____

Date of Current Lease: ____/____/_____

Name of Landlord: _____

Address of Landlord: _____

_____

The lease is presently in full force and effect and unmodified, except as follows: (If no exceptions,

so state)_____

_____

Tenant has accepted possession of premises and all improvements required to be completed by Landlord under the terms of the Lease have been completed

The term of the lease commenced on: _____

There are no uncured defaults in the Landlord's performance of its obligations under the Lease.

Tenant has no offset, counterclaim, or defense under the Lease or otherwise against rent or any other charges due or to become due to Landlord and there exists no event which would constitute a basis for any such offset, claim or defense upon the lapse of time or the giving of notice, or both, except as follows: (if there are no exceptions, so state)

_____

_____

Monthly installments of Minimum Annual Rental have been paid to: _____

(date)

All additional Rent due as of this date has been paid.

Tenant has prepaid no rent or other sum whatsoever to Landlord, other than the current month's installment of Minimum Annual Rental, except as follows: (if there are no exceptions, so state)

_____

Tenant acknowledges that no payment to Landlord of rent or other sums more than 30 days in advance of the due date under this Lease will be recognized by a beneficiary under a Deed of Trust which takes possession of the property under such Deed of Trust.

The amount of Security Deposit or other deposit held by Landlord is $_____
The undersigned Tenant acknowledges that it has been given notice that you are or may become the purchaser of the Property under an agreement with the Landlord and that said agreement of purchase and sale contains an assignment of Lease.

The undersigned Tenant acknowledges that it has been given notice that you are or may become the Trustor under a Deed of Trust encumbering the Property and that said Deed of Trust contains an assignment of rents due under the Lease.

Dated _____   Tenant: _____

By: _____

Rent Escalations

From the vantage point of the investor, rent increases are needed to cover increasing expenses and to maintain the purchasing power of the rent dollar. From the vantage point of the commercial tenant, income going to rent is less income going to operating profit, so it is understandable that each party will diligently negotiate increases in rent. Initially the question may appear to be "what is a fair and equitable increase?" but as time goes by the question becomes "what is the current fair market rent for the occupied space?"

The concept that rent increases should only match rising expenses or match the current rate of inflation deprives the owner of a fair market rent when rents in his locale are rising faster than inflation. There are other times when the lessor will be unable to increase rents by the current inflation factor either because the rate of inflation is very high or because of a surfeit of vacant space in the immediate market area.

Some landlords are reluctant to schedule rents far in advance. If the occasion to sell the property arises at a time when fair market rents exceed current contract rents, the property will have a diminished market value. Therefore an owner may attempt to negotiate a schedule of rents for a shorter term and then call for an increase in rents as determined by "current rents for comparable space."

Using the Consumer Price Index as an Escalator

The Consumer Price Index (CPI), which is often used to determine the rent increase, is cited as the rationale for the amount of the rent increase. The fact is that the CPI has very little to do with real estate and much less to do with fair market rents. The data which are gathered by the Bureau of Labor Statistics pertain to the section of the CPI labeled *Shelter*. Rents collected in this section reflect a home owner's estimate of the fair market value of the rent for his residence and, separately, the rent paid by renters. These rents do not reflect rent paid for industrial, commercial or office properties.

The widespread use of the CPI is rooted in its simplicity and ready acceptance by most tenants as a fair and impartial arbiter of inflation[14] but is in no way an index to the fair market rent.

Data for using the CPI to adjust rents can be obtained monthly from the U.S. Department of Labor which maintains a website at **www.bls.gov**. Information on how to use the various indices and the particular data for each metropolitan statistical area (MSA) in the country are available at this website, but the calculation is simplicity itself.

A lease whose rent increases are to be determined by the CPI should clearly specify the exact index and sub-index to be used. The most common index is the All Urban Consumers Index (CPI-U). Under this category are a number of sub-indices, one of which is more specific to the particular geographic area in which the property is located. It's a good idea to make the base index month at least three months earlier than the inception date of the lease. Otherwise a new rent will not be determinable until the index is published, which is always a month or two in arrears.

To determine the factor by which the rent is to increase, divide the new index by the base index and multiply the result times the starting rent. Alternately, you may divide the new index value by the index value used for the last increase; in this case multiply the result times the last rent applied.

For example, if the new index is 174.2 and the old index (applying to the last increase) is 154.8, the increase factor is 174.2/154.8 = 1.1253. If the current rent is $3,000 per month, the new rent will be ($3,000 *1.1253) = $3,375.90 per month.

It is very good practice to include an example of the calculation in the lease itself. This eliminates ambiguity and any future discussion about the correct method of applying the CPI.

Specifying Future Rents

When the CPI is used, it is common that owners and tenants will negotiate *floors and caps* to the percent increase in rent. The floors assure the owner-investor of a minimum rent increase regardless of the change in the CPI; the caps protect the tenant from exaggerated CPI increases during an acute bout of inflation. This is important because almost all leases do not permit the rent to decline, even in the face of an economic recession.

Future rents may also be *stipulated* in the lease. Apartment rents are generally specified in total dollars of new rent while rents applicable to office, retail and industrial properties are most often expressed in the price per square foot of gross leasable area (GLA). Scheduled rents work fine for short-term leases but should be avoided in longer term leases because of the uncertainty of future fair market rents.

---

[14] The CPI has become highly politicized because it serves as the basis for many labor contracts and COLA increases, such as Social Security.

Percentage Rents

In some situations, rent payable may be expressed as a percentage of gross income. Percentage rents are quite common in retail leases, especially in shopping malls. The percentage applied to the gross receipts varies according to the kind of retail business involved. Percentages in low margin retail sales, such as food, are often 0.5% – 1.0% while high-margin items such as jewelry and art may be 8–12%. As you might expect, these percentages are negotiable.

In some instances the total rent to be paid is the percentage rent. A few very large retailers balk at paying a minimum rent until the new center has established itself. But this creates problems with potential lenders who rely on the minimum rent in any percentage rent situation.

More common is the percentage rent against a minimum rent. For example, rent may be specified as 4% of gross sales against a minimum rent of $120,000 per year. In this instance, the tenant is obligated to pay a minimum of $120,000 + 4% of gross sales over $3,000,000 ($120,000 ÷ .04). In a few cases a lease may call for a minimum rent plus a percentage of gross sales. For example a tenant may be required to pay a minimum rent of $60,000 plus 2% of gross sales. If gross sales amounted to $3,000,000 per year, the total rent would be $120,000.

Whenever a lease is subject to percentage rent it is extremely important to define precisely which items of sale are to be included and which are to be omitted from the definition of "gross sales." In some states the seller of a lottery ticket is paid 3% per dollar of ticket value, but may be subject to a 4% percentage of gross ticket sales. Therefore certain items can be identified, excepted or assigned a separate percentage charge.

Internet Sales Complicate Percentage Rents

A complicating factor associated with percentage rents is the rapidly growing amount of sales derived from the internet. Many retail shops now enjoy gross sales derived from e-marketing equal to or surpassing the amount of gross sales from walk-in trade. Landlords usually insist on a monthly report of gross sales verified by a sales system which records sales with sequential serial numbers. Internet sales to local zip code addresses may be included in the total. The percentage rent is payable together with the report.

A 'percentage' lease must provide for the landlord's right to periodically audit the tenant's record of gross sales. The cost of these audits is typically borne by the landlord except in those cases in which an audit reveals an underage of more than 1-3%. In this instance, the lease may require the tenant to pay the unreported percentage rent as well as the cost of the present audit and the cost of future audits. In extreme cases a lease may permit the landlord to cancel the lease when a number of audits result in significant shortfalls within a certain period of time.

Extensions and Options

There are times when a business owned by a tenant is offered for sale. If the remaining time on an existing lease is insufficient to permit a prospective owner to continue business long enough to recover the cost of the business, a sale will be seriously impeded. In these circumstances the offer to purchase the business will usually be made contingent upon an extension of the lease term. Once the lease is opened to renegotiation, any clause in the lease may be renegotiated.

Most tenants seek options to renew a lease in order to provide stability to their business, to amortize the cost of tenant improvements to the property and to avoid the expenses and disruption of moving. This is true of all commercial tenants including office, industrial and retail tenants. Relocation costs money, disturbs the business and may even result in a loss of clients and customers. So it is to be expected that the tenant will negotiate for any number of options in order to remain in a good location.

As you already know, an option grants to the tenant the right to extend the lease but not the obligation to do so. It is binding upon the landlord (the optionor) but not upon the tenant (the optionee).

Landlords are happy to continue to lease a property to a good tenant, but the difficult issue is the rent to be applied for any future option period. You can be sure that if rents have declined and vacancies have increased at the time of lease expiration the tenant will attempt to re-negotiate a new lease at a lower rent rather than exercise an existing option to renew. But if market rents have risen substantially, the tenant will exercise a favorable option. Since rents generally rise and the option is binding only upon the lessor, the option advantage is most often to the tenant.

Options are Calls on Future Income

The landlord must consider an option for what it is: a 'call' on the landlord's future income. It may be necessary to grant an option to a tenant in order to attract the tenant initially, but after the tenant has become established in a location that fits its needs, options should be avoided.

A middle ground often taken is to grant the tenant the right to extend the lease but to leave the matter of rent open to future negotiation. This is a kind of 'agreement to agree in the future' and may be difficult to enforce without legal action unless the option clearly defines the method by which the future rent is to be determined. Many poorly written leases fail in this regard.

Language in options which specifies future rent as the 'fair market rent,' or 'prevailing market rent' is a lot less specific than one might believe. A resolution to the problem may be to require a determination of the fair market rent by qualified *rental appraisers*: generally the tenant and landlord each secure an appraisal. If they cannot resolve the difference between the two estimates, a third appraiser is hired whose expenses are shared by both principals. The final rent is the average of the third appraiser's estimate and the estimate of one of the other two appraisers whose estimate of fair market rent is closest to the third appraiser's estimate.[15]

Care must be taken to specify a window of time during which an option may be exercised. The date at which the tenant may serve notice that it will exercise the option varies from 3-12 months prior to expiry but the time-window does not last beyond 30-45 days. The option period should be close enough to the scheduled expiration date to allow the tenant to make a measured decision, but early enough to allow the owner to pre-arrange for the renovation and re-marketing of the space if the option is not exercised.

If the tenant fails to exercise the option during the designated time-window, the landlord is freed[16] from the obligation to continue the lease. Many a favorable lease has been lost because the tenant forgot to exercise the option within the specified time-window.

When all is said and done, most landlords will grant an option with future rent which is either stipulated or to be determined by application of an independent inflation factor, such as the CPI, using floors and caps. But the number of options granted should be held to a minimum.

---

[15] Sometimes known as the "baseball clause."

[16] In the absence of any mitigating language in the lease.

Lease with Option to Buy

There are a number of instances which may cause the owner of a property to be unwilling to sell, but willing to lease a property and grant the tenant an option to buy at a later date. In these cases the prospective tenant needs to include in the body of the lease an option clause which specifies the right of the tenant to buy the property at a later date under stipulated terms and conditions.

The option should be exercisable during an Option Notification Period which should not be later or earlier than a reasonable time prior to the expiration date of the lease. If the tenant fails to exercise the option during the period provided, the option expires and the landlord is under no further obligation to sell the property.

The simplest method of specifying the terms and conditions of the purchase is to prepare a purchase/sales agreement as though the property were to be purchased immediately. The sales/purchase agreement should contain all the terms of the sale <u>except the date and the buyer's signature</u>. <u>It must contain the seller's signature.</u> This agreement is attached to and becomes a part of the lease. When the time comes for the buyer to exercise his right to purchase, he need only sign the purchase agreement, deliver a signed copy to the seller and open a sales escrow.

As is true with all options, the most difficult task is to agree upon a purchase price. The farther in the future the option is exercisable the more difficult is the task of agreeing upon the price. "Agreements to agree" in the future are likely not to be enforceable unless a method is clearly described for the determination of the future price: e.g. by third party appraisal(s) which shall be binding.

Assignment and Sub-Leasing

There is an important difference between the assignment of a lease and the sub-letting of a property.

In the case of an assignment, the present tenant transfers all the interest, rights and obligations under the lease to a third-party. The assignee *attorns*[17] to the landlord and the landlord is required to look to the assignee for the full performance of all terms of the lease.

Landlords have a legitimate concern with the assignment of a lease since it may relieve a credit-tenant of the obligation to pay the rent and substitute a less creditworthy tenant. Landlords attempt to maintain control over the assignment by requiring that any assignment be first approved in writing. But the courts have a distaste for unreasonable restrictions on the right of a tenant to alienate an interest in property and have consistently voided clauses which unconditionally bar this tenant right. Therefore these clauses generally append verbiage to the effect that the landlord's approval is required for an assignment but *..."which (assignment) approval shall not be unreasonably withheld."*

Even in those cases in which the landlord approves the assignment, this assignment need not be absolute. The landlord may approve the transfer subject to the current tenant's guaranty of the lease. In the event of a default by the assignee, the landlord must first look to the assignee for full performance of all terms of the lease, but in the absence of such performance the landlord may look to the assignor, the former tenant. This guaranty typically expires at the end of the original term of the lease, including options, if any, or in the event the lease is novated[18] by the landlord.

---

[17]   Agrees to honor the rights of the landlord as previously contracted by the current tenant.

[18]   Replaced by a new lease

The Sublease

The legal rights and obligations under a sub-lease are quite different. If the landlord reasonably refuses to approve an assignment, the tenant may be able to sub-let the property to a third party. In the event of a default - for any reason - the landlord will look first to the original tenant and not to the sub-tenant. The original tenant will be held primarily responsible for keeping all the terms of the lease, including the payment of rent. It will then be up to the original tenant to enforce the lease against the sub-tenant or to evict him.

Subleases are often prevalent during recessionary times when large-space users decide to downsize. This is particularly true for office and industrial properties. Many of these subleases are made by a credit-tenant for less than the contract rent in the original lease. The new sub-tenant enjoys a lower rent, but one which is usually near current market rent. The sub-tenant pays the sub-lease rent directly to the lessee who makes up any shortfall and forwards it on to the lessor. The sublease expires on the date on which the original lease expires and a new lease must be re-negotiated by the landlord with any sub-tenant who wishes to remain. For this reason a buyer of property containing tenants who occupy under a sublease needs to be more cautious in price paid since it may be very difficult to replace the sub-tenant with one willing to pay the original contract rent. In 2014 an estimated 30-35% of workers were working from home. As a result, a growing number of companies are now much more willing to lease space for shorter periods of time even though the rent/sq.ft. may be higher.

Leases which give to the tenant the unrestricted right to sublet the property also offer the tenant the potential to profit from a rise in rental rates. Consider the situation in which a tenant leases 10,000 s.f. at $18.00/ s.f./year. If market rent rises to $20.00/s.f./year and if there are 10 years remaining on the lease, the premium to be earned by a sublessor is $20,000/year, or $200,000 over the remaining term. Discounting this annual premium at 7.0%, results in a present value of $140,472.

In those instances in which the lessee has the unrestricted right to sublet, the lessor's lease very frequently requires that if the property is sublet for a rent which exceeds the contract rent paid to the lessor, the lessor shall be entitled to a percent by which the sublessees's rent exceeds the lessee's rent. A 50% share is not uncommon.

Recordation of Leases

A recorded lease is an encumbrance against the owner's title since it limits what the owner may do with his property. Most short-term[19] occupancy leases prohibit the recordation of the lease against the title of the property for good reason - primarily because it is much easier to record a lease than it is to remove one from the record of title. A tenant who has recorded his lease against the owner's title may move away, go out of business[20] or simply disappear, presenting the owner with the pesky task of clearing the lease from the title in order to be able to sell, re-lease or re-finance the property. In these cases the landlord must initiate a *Quiet Title* action to remove the lease from future legal consideration. This can be an expensive and time-consuming task.

Very often an abstract of a long lease, rather than the lease document itself, is recorded.[21] It is important to verify that the abstract conforms to the lease document and includes any amendments or modifications

---

[19]   Three to 5 years.
[20]   Approximately 50% of new small businesses do not survive a 3-year lease.
[21]   Reduces costs in large multi-unit buildings.

which may have been made. Reading the abstract, however, is not a substitute for reading the unabridged lease.

Subordination, Non-Disturbance and Attornment Agreements

'Attornment' is a legal step by which a right is transferred from one party to another. Almost all commercial leases contain an attornment clause by which the tenant agrees to regard a new owner, or a lender who becomes the owner, as the landlord and to fulfill all its obligations under the lease to the new owner as it did to the original owner. The attornment provision maintains the tenant's lease obligations thereby preserving the cashflow necessary to service the existing debt. It also preserves the lease for a new owner to whom a foreclosing lender is likely to transfer the property. In those instances in which the lease is recorded earlier than the date of recordation of the lender's lien a subordination agreement in a lease moves the tenant's senior rights under a recorded lease to a position subordinate to the rights of a new lender.

The shortcoming of a subordination agreement is that while it safeguards the lender's rights it does not always assure the tenant's rights under the lease. In some states, a foreclosure by a lender whose lien is recorded senior to (dated earlier than) a tenant's lease affords the lender the right to cancel the tenant's lease. This exposes the tenant to the cost and disruption of moving its business.

In other states, known as 'option' states, a foreclosing lender may either maintain or cancel the tenant's lease. Therefore most tenants who are asked to sign leases containing subordination and attornment provisions will also require a *Non-Disturbance* clause by which the new owner (or lender) agrees to respect the rights of the tenant under the existing lease and not to undertake any actions which would interfere with the tenant's quiet enjoyment of the premises.

These SNDA[22] clauses should be present in all commercial leases, protecting the rights of a new lender as well as the rights of the tenant. Without these assurances, the property may be difficult to lease and next to impossible to re-finance.

Breach, Eviction and Re-Possession

A well-drawn lease will enumerate the tenant's obligations under the contract. These obligations will include, but not be limited to, the timely payment of rent. But the tenant may also default under the lease agreement by failing to pay taxes, by failing to maintain the property or by using the property illegally or for a purpose which is legal but which is not permitted by the lease. There are many other acts and failures to act which could constitute a default, or breach, of the agreement.

In addition to enumerating the events which will constitute a default, the lease will also post a time given to the tenant to cure the breach. In the case of non-payment of rent, this could be a *Notice to Pay or Quit* within three days. In the case of other defaults the time period may for a number of weeks or months, depending on the nature of the default and a reasonable time to cure. These time periods are negotiable. Upon discovery of a breach, the landlord should formally notify the tenant of the default and enter a demand for the default to be cured. This should be done in writing by certified mail, return-receipt requested. In many states a 3-10 day period is set aside for delivery but the lease may require a different period. The tenant's cure period begins upon service of the notice.

---

[22]   SNDA = Subordination, Non-Disturbance and Attornment

If the tenant fails to timely cure the breach the landlord must file an action to recover Use and Possession of his property.[23] Notice of this action must be legally served on the tenant. This action is known as a UD action (Unlawful Detainer) and refers to the fact that the landlord is being unlawfully detained from regaining his rights to his property. UDs receive preferential treatment on the court calendar and move to the top of the court's docket for an early hearing. The tenant has a right to appear at the court on the designated day of the hearing and may oppose the UD on a variety of grounds.

The process of evicting any tenant must be conducted with scrupulous attention to the legal requirements. Although the landlord may anticipate fair and equal treatment, experience shows that courts tend to favor the tenant in any instance in which the letter of the law is not carried out. Therefore it is money well spent to hire an experienced attorney who conducts evictions and UDs in your community.

If a judgment is rendered in the landlord's favor, a time is set for a legal deputy (sheriff), accompanied by the landlord, to go to the site and physically remove the tenant and the tenant's belongings from the property. A physical lock-out of the tenant must ensue. If the tenant attempts to reenter the premises, he will be subject to the penalties for unlawful entry and trespassing.

Restrictive Covenants

Covenants are contractual agreements that appear in both deeds and leases. Restrictive covenants in deeds and leases limit what the owner or landlord can do with the property. (See p.1- 6).

It is extremely important for an investor, who is contemplating the acquisition or lease of a commercial property which is adjacent to or proximate to other properties, to determine if the property is subject to a restrictive covenant. The question of whether or not the intended property has a restrictive clause which limits others from engaging in a similar business can be uncovered by a thorough reading of the CC&Rs. But equally important is the question of whether or not the owner of the subject property will be limited or prohibited from accepting a replacement tenant whose business would violate a restrictive clause held by a nearby owner or tenant. Again, this information should be contained in the CC&Rs for the tract or in a Reciprocal Easement Agreement (REA). These documents "run with the land" and bind successors –in-interest.

The law regarding Reciprocal Covenants is quite complex. An experienced real estate attorney should be consulted as needed.

Finally…This chapter barely scratches the surface of what you should know about leasing real property. The reader is referred to a more comprehensive source of additional information.[24] But perhaps what has been covered will serve as a beginning point for more study and evaluation. We hope so.

---

[23] This Notice (Unlawful Detainer) may be filed concurrently with the Notice to Pay or Quit.
[24] "Negotiating Commercial Real Estate Leases, " Zankel, Martin I, ISBN 0-940352-14-1

Chapter 11
Investments Subject to a Ground Lease

I n Chapter One we established that leasing involves the rental of two important property rights: the right to use and the right to possess the property for a determinable period of time.

Most of the leases encountered in real estate convey the right to use and possess space in an apartment, in an industrial building, in an office building or in a retail center in return for the payment of rent. These leases are *occupancy leases.*

But there is another kind of lease which involves the leasing of land: the *ground lease*. Under a ground lease, the tenant receives not only the rights to use and possess the land, but also the right to develop it.

Partial Interests Created

When the fee interest in a property is divided by any kind of lease, two derivative estates[1] are created: the *leased-fee estate* and the *leasehold estate.* The landowner, or landlord, retains the leased-fee interest consisting of the land and appurtenances, while the tenant owns the leasehold interest.

Most ground leases originate when a developer contracts to lease unimproved land for a long period of years. His lease also gives him the right to construct an improvement on the land and the right to sell or sublease the improvement to a third party, subject to the terms of the ground lease and the lessor's approval of the type of improvement to be built.[2] Not all ground leases originate this way. There are

---

[1] Recall that an *estate* represents an interest in property. An interest refers to the ownership of any of the rights listed in the Bundle of Rights (p.1-4)

[2] The ground lessor has a vested interest in what will be built on his land since the improvement will be the source of his ground rent.

times when the owner of an improved, fee-simple property divides the two interests and sells the improvements subject to a long-term ground lease. This "splitting the fee," however, is not common.

Because ground leases usually specify that ownership of improvements built on the land by the ground tenant will become the property of (revert to) the landowner at the termination of the Lease, the landlord is said to hold a *reversionary* interest in the improvements during the term of the ground lease.

Naming Names

The terminology of ground leases is sometimes confusing because many ground leases (especially retail leases) involve not just a single ground lease but a number of sub-leases.

The primary ground lease is the lease which exists between the landowner and his tenant who has title to the leasehold interest; the tenant may also be the original builder and/or owner of the improvements. The land owner is usually referred to as the lessor or ground-lessor and the tenant as the lessee or ground-lessee. If the property is sublet, the ground-lessee becomes a sub-lessor and his tenant becomes the sub-tenant or sub-lessee.

The lease which is held by the ground-lessee and a *non-operating* sub-tenant is a 'sandwich' lease. Some properties are subject not only to a ground lease but to a number of sandwich or sub-leases. The last lease in the chain is the *operating lease*. The operating tenant is the tenant whose business activities generate the primary rent.

> *So naturalists observe..*
> *A flea hath smaller fleas that on him prey;*
> *and these have smaller still to bite 'em,*
> *and so proceed ad infinitum.*
> Jonathan Swift

CAVEAT: It is quite common to see leasehold interests offered for sale as, **"*Groundlease (fee-simple interest).*"** Ownership of the "fee-simple interest," as has already been described, refers to the ownership of all the rights in the Bundle of Rights. Advertising a property as one subject to a ground lease doesn't adequately identify what is for sale; it could be either the leased-fee interest or the leasehold interest. It can't be both. Investors who respond to these advertisements should take special care to establish exactly what is for sale. The exact nature of what is for sale will eventually be revealed in the Preliminary Title Report, but a buyer ought not to have to wait that far into the transaction to learn what is being offered for sale. Insist on a clarification before expending any time, effort or money. The title officer at the title company is your most reliable source and is only a phone call away.

Most ground leases are written for a term of 50-60 years, although some parcels are leased for periods up to 99 years and a few for as little as 35 years.[3] In those states which permit it - and not all do - some parcels are leased forever, *in perpetuity*. The State of Hawaii, for example, is replete with properties which are leased in perpetuity.

The tenant, or ground-lessee, almost always has the right to sub-lease to occupying sub-tenants without the specific prior approval of the lessor provided the sub-tenants also agree to observe and be bound by

---

[3]   Some municipalities are restricted in the length of a ground lease which they may offer.

the terms of the ground lease. For this reason, sub-leases are drawn to closely parallel most of the provisions and conditions of the underlying ground lease.

The tenant invariably has the right to assign the remaining term of the ground lease to a successor-in-interest, subject to the prior approval of the land owner. Because the law frowns on clauses which prevent or restrict an owner of real estate, or of an interest in real estate, from alienating himself from his property, the right of the landlord to approve the assignment is typically qualified with a phrase such as *".... which (approval) shall not unreasonably be delayed or withheld."*

The ground lessor, however, always has the unfettered right to transfer his interest in the land, but this *leased-fee interest* will transfer subject to the existing ground lease and any encumbrances which act as security devices.[4]

Why Owners Lease Land

The primary motivation for most landowners to lease land is to retain control and ownership in land which they believe will continue to increase in value and to put into economic use an unimproved or under-improved[5] parcel which currently delivers little or no income. A strong second reason is that the owner of the land either lacks the capacity and/or experience to develop the land, or simply does not wish to do so. By leasing land the landowner creates for himself a long-term annuity which he may enjoy during his own lifetime and still pass on to heirs upon his demise.

A third reason, which is quite common, is that the land has been held in the same hands for a long period of time and has appreciated substantially. Selling the land would cause recognition of a large capital gain and trigger the tax on that gain. Leasing land does not cause recognition of a gain and therefore there is no tax penalty associated with leasing.

Lastly, perhaps, is the fact that the ground rent to be realized from leasing land is often greater than the income which could be realized by selling the land, paying the tax and reinvesting the net proceeds.

For example, consider a parcel of vacant land presently worth $1,000,000 in the hands of an owner whose Adjusted Basis is only $150,000.[6] The sale of the land would result in a federal long-term capital gains tax plus state taxes. If we assume total costs of sale equal to 6%, a state tax of 5% and a federal LTCG tax of 20.0%, the net proceeds become:

---

4   The owner may arrange a loan secured by the leased-fee interest only.
5   *Under-improved* because its improvement fails to justify rent sufficient to deliver a market yield on the value of the underlying land, let alone a satisfactory return on the value of the improvements.
6   Most of the gain is due to inflation, but taxed nonetheless since capital gains are not adjusted for inflation.

Fair Market Value	**$1,000,000**	Taxes & Costs
Costs of Sale @6%		$60,000
Net Sales Price	$940,000	
Less Adjusted Basis	$150,000	
Taxable LTC Gain	$790,000	
Less State Tax @ 5%		$39,500
Net Gain Subject to Federal Tax	$750,500	
Less federal tax @ 20.0%		$150.100[7]
Total Costs		**$249,600**
Net Proceeds	**$750,400**	

In order to match the pre-tax annual income from a ground lease on this property delivering $80,000 in rent (8.0% lease rate), the ground owner would need to find an investment for his remaining after-tax funds yielding 10.6% per year.[8]

Therefore ground leases can provide a very profitable use of vacant or under-developed land by returning ground rent which is based on the *pre-tax value* of the land and by avoiding the tax penalties of a sale.

Owner Retains Right to Encumber the Leased-Fee Interest

Unless specifically prohibited in the ground lease, the land owner is free to borrow money pledging the leased-fee interest (only) as security. In the event of a default by the land owner, his lender would take title to the leased-fee interest *subject to* the ground lease. To ensure that this is the case, the ground lease should contain one or more clauses which specify that the ground tenant's interest will not be terminated by a transfer of the leased-fee interest. In the absence of such a clause(s) a foreclosure by the lender on the leased-fee (land-owner's) interest could expunge the ground lease.

Why Tenants Lease Land

Tenants lease land in order to use the land for agricultural purposes or to develop an improvement in a favorable location without the need to buy the underlying land. Oftentimes the fee-simple land at the desired location is simply not available and leasing is the only alternative. But most tenants who lease land also seem to understand that it is not necessary to own land to profit from it; it is necessary only to control it.

Ground leasing is sometimes described as a "financing device" because it enables a developer to construct the improvement without the need to buy the land. Rent on the land is paid in lieu of an increased mortgage payment which would have represented the additional cost of financing the land. This concept

---

[7] The sale of the property may also expose the seller to the Alternate Minimum Tax.

[8] $750,400 * 10.6% ≈ $80,000

of a ground lease as a financing device is harmless as long as it is not relied upon: a loan is not a lease, nor is a lease a loan.

An Unexpected Benefit

Because the tenant does not own the underlying land, there is no need to allocate the value of the property between the land and the depreciable improvement. Therefore the entire cost of construction/acquisition of a leasehold interest under current law is depreciable by the tenant.

Income from Two Sources

Some investors are unaware that the income from an improved income-producing property is really the sum of the income from two separate sources: income from the land plus the income from the improvement on the land. The rate at which the improvement returns income is different from the rate at which the land returns income. This difference is accounted for by the risk premium attached to each interest.

The ground lessee is exposed to all the risks of operating the property, including the risks of credit and vacancy losses, escalating operating expenses, reassessments, the threat of increased competition, management and labor issues, and losses due to natural disasters such as fire, floods and earthquakes, etc. Management of the improvement is also a more time-consuming and specialized task than is management of the underlying land. Therefore it is the lessee who bears the greatest burden and the greatest risk and is entitled to the greatest return.

The risk borne by the landowner depends upon whether the ground lease is subordinate to a mortgage on the improvement or whether the lease remains unsubordinated. At this point, we need to digress for just a moment...

Subordinated and Unsubordinated Ground Leases

If the ground lease is subordinated, it means that the mortgage on the improvement has priority over the landowner's ground lease. A foreclosure on the mortgage secured by the improvement imperils the leased-fee interest since the land owner has effectively offered his interest in the land as additional security for the loan. This is so because a foreclosure under the primary mortgage would erase all junior liens, including the landowner's lease.[9]

When the lease is <u>un</u>subordinated, however, the ground lease is recorded senior to the mortgage on the improvement. In the event the tenant defaults on the mortgage and on the ground lease, it is the lender who must "step-up" to cure the default on the ground lease, a senior lien. The lender does this by curing all deficiencies and continuing the payments on the ground lease in order to protect its security interest in the improvement. The lender will assume all the obligations of the tenant under the lease. If it did not do this, a foreclosure by the landowner under the ground lease would expunge the mortgage lender's security interest and the landowner would take title to the improvement free of all mortgages.

---

[9]   Landowners are often asked to subordinate their lease to a construction loan.

Therefore, while subordinated ground leases are risky for the landowner, unsubordinated ground leases are considered to be quite safe, especially when the improvement is mortgaged since the ground lessor has the lender standing between him and a loss of income.[10] Because of this extra safety margin, the ground lessor is often willing to accept a lease rate[11] equal to or somewhat less than the rate on the improvement's mortgage.

Two Incomes, Two Sources

The fact that an improved property delivers cashflows from two sources is obscured when the two interests - the leasehold interest and unsubordinated leased-fee interest - are held in the same set of hands.[12] But when the interests are held in different hands, the difference is readily apparent.

Consider the following allocation of these two interests and the rate of return earned on each interest:

Component	Value	Return Rate	Annual Income
Improvement	$675,000	8.0%	$54,000
Land	$325,000	5.0%	$16,250
Total Value	$1,000,000	-	$70,250
Capitalization Rate =	Income ÷ Value =	7.025%	

When the property is held as a fee-simple property, the owner recognizes that his overall capitalization rate is 7.025%, but is often unmindful that this rate is the weighted yield on the capital invested in the improvement plus the weighted yield on capital invested in the land. It is common for some investors to see only the improvement on the land when they look at "property" and fail to appreciate that the economic value of the land is also contributing to total income.

When these interests are held in separate hands, the rates applied to the interests are separately negotiable. This is one of the principal reasons why leasehold interests typically sell at capitalization rates and discount rates which are higher than comparable fee-simple properties and why unsubordinated leased-fee interests may even sell at rates which are below those of a fee-simple property.

Adequacy of the Constructed Improvement

In order to benefit from the lease, the developer must construct an improvement capable of delivering sufficient income to cover the economic rent for the land over the expected economic life of the improvement. Failure to do so means that as time passes an increasing share of total property income will divert to the landowner as ground rent and less and less to the owner of the improvement. It is for this

---

10 In fact, the larger the mortgage the more likely it is that the lender will assume the lease if the lessee defaults.
11 Lease rate x land value = ground rent.
12 A fee owner actually cannot hold these two interests separately because one cannot lease from or to oneself.

reason that the landowner reserves the right to approve the original improvement and most subsequent modifications to be constructed on the land.

Important Clauses in Ground leases

Every clause in a well-drawn ground lease, as in every lease, is important and has financial value. But there are three that are vital: the Use clause, the Rent clause and the clause which identifies the improvement lender's rights in the event of a default. Of these, the most important is the Use clause.

Use Clauses

Ground leases may contain a type of Use clause which permits the lessee to develop the property for any legal purpose, or it may restrict the property to a range of uses, or even to a single use. In some cases, the ground lessor may own adjacent or nearby property which he wishes to develop for a special use and will bar or restrict the use of the ground-leased property to prevent the nearby development of a competitive improvement. He does this by adding a *restrictive condition* in the deed.

The consequences of these limitations depend upon how a potential lender for the improvement will view the limitations. If the intended economic use of the property fails and the lender is unable to use or sell the property for an alternate use, it is highly unlikely that the lender will accept this risk and will probably decline the loan. Therefore there is a balance to be struck between restrictions which may protect the ground lessor and the future financeability and marketability of the project.

Another important consequence of placing restrictions and limitations on the use of the property is that reappraisals of the land, for the purpose of readjusting the ground rent, may require the land to be appraised for its current use and not for its highest and best use. Case law supports the position that if the ground lessor participated in determining or limiting the use of the property, then its reappraisal must be for the specified use (or range of uses) and not for its highest and best use. If, on the other hand, the land was leased for "any legal purpose,[13] the courts have regarded the use to which the property has been improved to be the result of the lessee's sole decision and that the land may be re-appraised for its highest and best use.

The highest and best use, however, is not necessarily a unique use to which a particular future tenant may put the property. The American Institute of Real Estate Appraisers defines highest and best use as:

> "The use, from *among reasonably probable and legal alternative uses*, found to be physically possible, appropriately supported, financially feasible and that results in the highest present land value." (emphasis added)

This definition is easily applied to vacant land, but once the land has been improved, the highest and best use may refer either to the highest and best use *as presently improved* or to the highest and best use *as though vacant*. If the present use is not the highest and best use as though vacant, the ground lessor may receive a lower appraised value and therefore lower rent.

---

[13] Subject only to local zoning codes

It is of such stuff that nettlesome and expensive lawsuits are made. Legal entanglements can be avoided by unambiguous and well thought-out ground lease contracts.

Rent Clauses and Rent Escalation Clauses

Since ground leases extend over many years during which time the value of the land usually increases, it is important that the ground lessor provide for a clearly stated method of periodically re-pricing the ground rent to reflect the economic value of the land. Five methods are used:

1. The rent is scheduled over the term of the lease, or more likely, initially over an interim term of the lease combined with periodic reappraisals of the land.
2. The rent is specified for the first year (the base rent) with periodic adjustments made later with reference to an inflation index, such as the Consumer Price Index (CPI).
3. The rent is determined as a *percentage of the gross income* derived from the improvement.
4. The rent is level until determined by a reappraisal of the land and a readjustment of the lease rate using an outside indicator, such as the five-year or ten-year U.S. Treasury note rate.
5. The rent is specified for the first year, then made subject to CPI adjustments and periodically (10-15 years) reappraised. In most cases the lease *rate* is specified in the lease and is not subject to change.

Each of these methods has its advantages and disadvantages to both parties, a discussion of which could fill a book. But the investor should be careful that the method of rent adjustment is clearly defined, ideally by a written example placed within the lease and that the method of appraisal also be precisely defined. Obtaining the services of a competent attorney, experienced in the language and matters affecting ground leases, is advisable.

Adjusting the Ground Rent to Preserve Purchasing Power

The amount and pattern of the rent increases will affect the value of the leased-fee interest held by the ground lessor. Since the leased-fee interest may also be mortgaged (subject to a non-disturbance clause executed by the tenant and tenant's lender) it is important that the ground rent be kept as close to market as is feasible. Failure to do so will diminish both the market and loan value of the leased-fee interest for as long as the ground lease encumbers the property.

Of particular concern is the need to maintain the purchasing power of the ground rent. It is not uncommon to see ground leases that schedule rent for, say, 5-10 years and then provide for an adjustment of rent which is insufficient to maintain the purchasing power of the lessor's rental income.

For example, consider a long-term lease which schedules rent for each 5-year period of a 20-year lease. The lease provides that rent will increase 10% every 5 years. A 10% increase in rent each 5 years equates to an annually compounded rental increase of only 1.92% per year.

n	i	PV	PMT	FV
5	?	-$1.00	0	1.10
Solving...	**1.92%**			

But the historic rate of inflation in the United States (measured over many years) is about 3.0% per year, compounded. If the rental dollar kept up with inflation, the rent at the end of 5 years would be:

n	i	PV	PMT	FV
5	3.00	-$1.00		?
			Solving..	**1.159**

A land owner collecting a rate increase of 10% every 5 years will experience a 5.9% loss in the purchasing power of the 5th year rent. Periodic rent increases less than 10% and adjustments in the schedule longer than 5 years exacerbate the problem.

The situation assumes grave proportions when the lease term is set for 15-20 years and options are granted which call for the same pattern of rent increases (5 years) over a total of, say, 40 years. Using the same assumptions, the rental dollar at the end of the 40th year will have lost 43% of its purchasing power.

As time goes by, it is very common that the rent payable to the ground lessor falls well below the current fair rental value of the land. In this case, the ground-lessee is said to have acquired a *financial interest in the land.* This unearned premium may be passed along by the tenant by assignment of the leasehold interest to a creditworthy successor-in-interest.

All this argues for a periodic reassessment of the land value and an adjustment in ground rent consistent with its value. It also underscores the land owner's interest in the right to approve the size and quality of the improvement to be placed on the land. If the rent is to be increased as the land value improves, the improvement must have the economic potential to keep pace.

Subordinated Leases

Lenders would much prefer that the ground lessor subordinate his lease to its mortgage on the improvement. This form of subordination pledges the value of the land as additional security for the loan on the improvement. Oftentimes the ground lessor joins in the mortgage but usually obtains a waiver for personal liability for the debt. A recent case, however, indicates that the ground lessor may assert a defense on the grounds that he is a guarantor of the mortgage by virtue of his offering his land as additional security for the loan. The ground lessor thereby avails himself, in most states, of all the defenses available to a guarantor. Therefore, in the case of a subordinated lease the lender will obtain a waiver from the ground lessor waiving all rights which the lessor may have as a guarantor of the loan.

A second issue of importance to the lender is that the occupancy (operating) leases have an attornment provision which requires that in the event of termination of the ground lease the operating tenants will recognize the new leased-fee owner of the property as the landlord. This provision obviates the need to have the lender maintain the fiction of the ground lease.[14]

---

[14] By holding the leased-fee interest and the leasehold interest in separate legal hands.

Unsubordinated Leases

The overwhelming majority of modern ground leases are <u>un</u>subordinated leases under which the lender's security interest is limited to the lessee's leasehold interest and does not involve the lessor's land as additional security.[15] In the event of a default under the lease,[16] the lender must have the right to cure the default and to assume the legal position of the former ground tenant. Unless the lender can do this, he cannot protect his loan and he will usually not lend on the leasehold interest.

Financing Clause

For want of a better term, we have referred to the clause or clauses which define the rights of the lender on the improvement as the 'financing clause.' There may be, in fact, a number of these clauses written into or later appended to the ground lease in order to make the leasehold interest financeable. The 'financeable' ground lease needs to address and resolve these lender issues:

1. No Notice of Default under the ground lease should be valid unless the lender receives a copy.
2. Any Notice of Default under the ground lease must be delivered simultaneously to the lender at the time it is delivered to the tenant.
3. If the tenant fails to cure the default within the time granted in the lease, the lender is accorded an extended period of time (e.g. 60-90 days) following the tenant's time in which to cure the default before the lessor may take steps to terminate the lease.
4. Upon termination of the ground lease, or in the event of a bankruptcy by the tenant in which the tenant rejects the lease,[17] the lender should have the right to obtain a ground lease from the lessor under the same terms and conditions which the former tenant enjoyed.
5. In the event of a destruction or partial destruction of the property, the lease should provide for the proceeds from the tenant's insurance to be held by the lender or by a neutral third party and used for the repair of the property.
6. If the proceeds from an insurance policy are not to be used for repairs, then the proceeds should be payable first to the lender up to the limit of the mortgage balance any unpaid charges and then to the ground lessor to protect his reversionary interest in the improvements and only then to the ground-lessee.
7. If the lender extends a mortgage to the tenant whose full amortization period extends beyond the date of the termination of the lease, then the ground lease should be extendable by the number of years required to completely amortize the balance of the loan at the time of scheduled termination.
   Most landowners will not agree to this provision and therefore most lenders will lend only that amount of loan which can be amortized over the remaining period of the

---

[15] A lender may require a security interest in other assets owned by the prospective tenant.
[16] The lender always has the right to foreclose under the mortgage.
[17] Under a bankruptcy proceeding, a tenant generally has 60 days in which to agree to continue or to abandon a lease.

lease, less five years, or so, as a safety margin. This foreshortened amortization period limits the amount of the loan as the lease matures.

8. The ground lease in the hands of the lender should be freely assignable without the need for the lessor's prior approval. If this were not so, the ground lessor could always refuse to approve the assignment on the grounds that the proposed assignee does not have the financial creditworthiness equal to the assignor. The assignor would, of course, remain responsible for the lease.

9. The lender should have the right to deal directly with the operating tenants and to lease sub-space without the lessor's prior approval.

If the investor experiences difficulty in financing a leasehold improvement which affords these protections to the lender, it may be that the underwriter is not sufficiently experienced in crafting this type loan, or that the lender's legal staff will not take the time to alter or amend its standard security document (mortgage or trust deed) to adequately safeguard the lender.

The solution is to find another lender.

Valuation of Separate Interests under a Ground lease

Both the leasehold interest and the leased-fee interest have value proportionate to the quality, quantity and duration of the cashflows which the ground lessor and ground-lessee can hope to realize over the term of the lease.

The value of the leased-fee interest is equal to the discounted value of all the ground rent payments the lessor can expect to receive, plus the discounted value of the fair market value of the land at reversion, plus the discounted value of the reversion value (if any) of the improvements.

The value of the leasehold interest is the discounted value of all the future operating income (net of ground lease payments) which the tenant can expect to receive - without regard to any reversion value. This is so because the typical ground lease provides that at the termination of the ground lease title to the improvements invariably reverts to the land (fee) owner.

Valuing the Leasehold Interest

It is quite common to see many leasehold interests priced to market by "adding a point of two to the prevailing capitalization rate" for comparable fee-simple properties. This is a serious error and can result in significant misstatements of value.

Consider a leasehold interest which will generate $80,000 in NOI during the first year of operation. Assume that the NOI will increase an average of 3.5% per year over a 60-year lease term. Similar fee-simple properties are currently discounted @12%/year or capitalized @ 8.5%/ year.

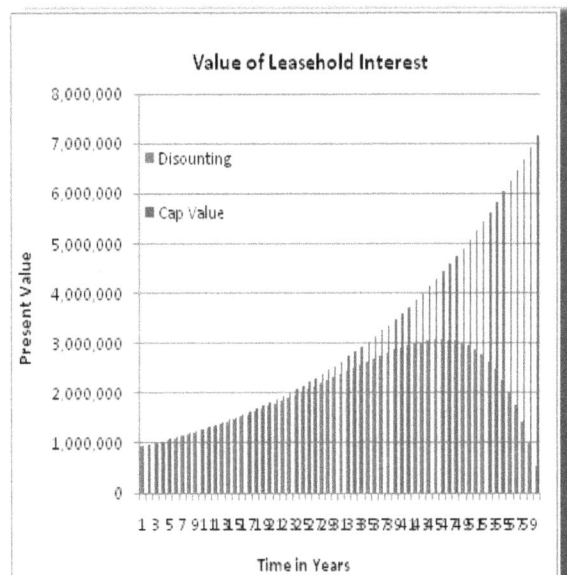

Value of Leasehold Interest

The adjacent graph depicts the difference in the Present Value of the leasehold interest obtained by 1) discounting the remaining NOI over the years remaining on the lease and 2) by capitalizing current Net Operating Income. The graph shows that the value of the property, determined by discounting the future income (darker bars), continues to increase until the 46th year,[18] when it reaches a peak value of $3,071,116. From that point on, the value declines despite rising NOI.

The lighter shaded bars in the graph depict the market value arrived at by capitalizing NOI for each year. Although it is difficult to detect on this compacted graph, the estimate of value arrived at by capitalizing the NOI overstates the value by 0.9% in the very first year. This error continues to grow; by the 20th year the value is overstated more than 4.0% and by the 40th year by more than 23%.

So it is clear that the common practice of capitalizing the NOI of a leasehold interest is an inappropriate method of determining investment value. This is especially so when the remaining years under the ground lease are limited. Value should always be arrived at by using Discounted Cashflow techniques.

Financing the Leasehold Interest

It is interesting to note that even in the last year of the lease this leasehold property has a value of $543,692, which is the discounted value of the last year's NOI in the amount of $608,935.[19] As this partial interest ages, however, its finance-ability declines because the time remaining over which a loan can be fully amortized also declines. In order to amortize a significant loan over the time remaining under the lease the payments would be set so high as to exceed the property's NOI.

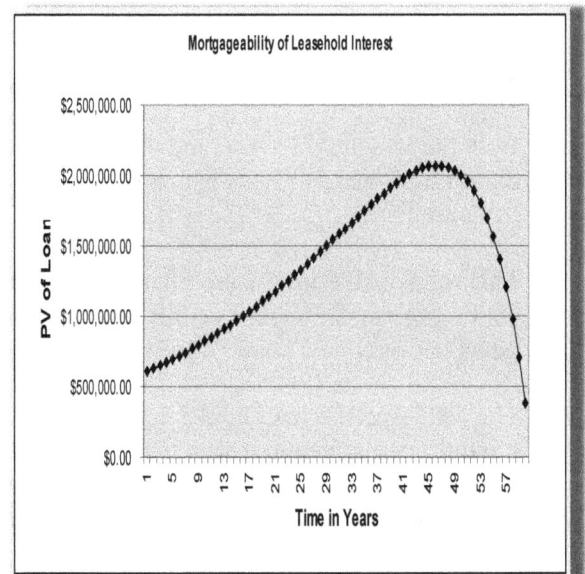

This graph also shows that the amount which can be borrowed as a percent of market value declines sharply after the 53rd year. Nevertheless, a leasehold interest at that time remains financeable for approximately 65% of its current market value if the market value is determined by discounting the remaining income stream.

Valuing the Leased-fee Interest

The valuation of the leased-fee interest is accomplished in exactly the same way with the important difference that in addition to the Present Value of future rents, the lessor will reclaim the financial value of the land at the end of the lease as reversionary income.

---

[18] The length of the ground lease will affect this turning point.
[19] Discounted @ 12.0%

Since the lessor will receive the reversionary value of the improvements, their present value could also be added to the value of this interest. But the value of the depreciating improvements, unlike the value of the land, will likely decline significantly in 60 years. Therefore their present value is often disregarded or heavily discounted.[20]

The Present Value of the land is initially insignificant but becomes more valuable as the lease draws closer to expiry. (The value of a $1 million parcel which can be recovered in 60 years has a present value when discounted @ 8.5% of only $7,485; at 10% only a value of $3,284.) As the Present Value of the remaining ground rent diminishes, the Present Value of the reversionary interest in the land increases until, finally, the ground rent contributes little to the Present Value of the property, the value of which is represented almost entirely by the market value of the land.[21]

A Word or Two about NNN Leased-fee Interests

Many large retailers such as Walgreens, Home Depot, Dollar General, CVS and RiteAid Drugstores and others, offer "triple-net" leased properties for sale. These companies offer free-standing buildings in prime locations and are attractive to many investors because of the perceived credit worthiness of the tenant[22] and the fact that the investor-owner has little to do in the way of maintenance.

In the typical case, the retailer (or developer-affiliate) finds and acquires a fee-simple interest in a vacant or re-developable parcel in a desirable location. The affiliate designs and constructs a highly branded building to the retailer's unique specifications. When completed, the retailer "splits the fee" by drafting a long-term NNN ground lease to its own lease specifications and offers the NNN leasehold interest <u>for sale</u> to an investor.

As owner of the improvements, the investor acquires a virtual maintenance/management-free investment with a long-term NNN lease in-place guaranteed by a strong financial statement. As owner of the improvement, the leasehold owner enjoys the depreciation rights to the property. As owner of the leased-fee interest, the retailer-ground lessor retains ownership of the underlying land and the reversionary rights to the improvement at the expiry of the ground lease.

Walgreens, a prototypical example, offers a 25-year lease (the *prime term*) with beginning rent equal to 6.0-7.5% of the purchase price and with as many as 5-10 five-year options to renew. The options are controlled by the tenant – in this example, Walgreens – which can exercise this control for as long as 50 years following the prime term with an occupancy commitment not longer than 5 years. Walgreen has also offered a 25-year prime term lease with the right to cancel each year thereafter, but this variation has proved to be difficult to finance.

---

20 In those case in which an improvement of very high value is constructed on the land, the lessee will require a very long lease.

21 If the improvement is to be demolished, the cost of the demolition is subtracted from the market value of the unimproved land.

22 Credit worthiness varies however.

Follow the Money

It should come as no surprise that large-box retailers are highly in favor of selling a self-designed and self-constructed, branded building while enjoying not only a flat rent for as many as 25 years but also an immediate construction profit to help finance future expansion.

It is noteworthy that promotional ads for properties leased to big-box retailers and chain-store retailers emphasize the safety of the investment, the advantages of a NNN lease and the stability of income for the length of the prime term. What is less emphasized is that the prime term offers no increase in rent for 25 years and the consequences of this on current and future value. As a result, the investor collects unadjusted rent which declines steadily in purchasing power each year. The accompanying chart illustrates the loss of purchasing power over 25 years in an inflation environment of 3.0% p.a.: 24% in 10 years; 44% in 20 years; 52% in 25 years.[23]

PURCHASING POWER OF FLAT RENT OVER 25 YEARS

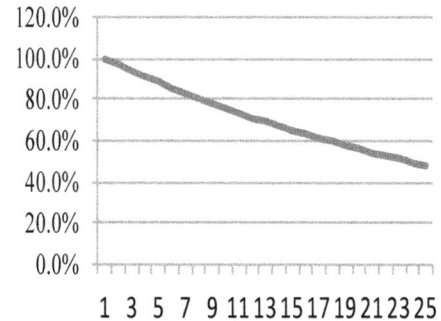

Perhaps the most untoward aspect of this particular kind of NNN lease becomes evident when the owner of the leasehold interest decides to sell. As is true for all leases, the Present Value of the lease[24] after 5 years is equal to the discounted value of all the lease payments remaining under the contract. An investor who has held a similar lease for 5 years has 20 years remaining with an unknown likelihood of an extension of the prime term to accommodate a sale.[25]

Assume that the lease was purchased for $4,000,000 and delivers $240,000 Net per year during the prime term of 25 years. This lease will behave as a fixed annuity for the remaining 20 years. Its Present Value, discounted at 6.0% is:

$$PV = \frac{\$240,000}{(.06)} \times \left[1 - \left(\frac{1}{1+.06}\right)^{20} \right] = \$2,542,781.$$

No doubt this lease was initially priced to the retail investor by capitalizing its annual income @ 6.0%:

$$\frac{\$240,000}{(.06)} = \$4,000,000.$$

Had it been originally priced by discounting the fixed income stream @ 6% for 25 years it value would have been:

---

[23] The real rate of inflation in recent years has been much greater than that reported by the Bureau of Labor Statistics.

[24] Assume that the Present Value is close to the Market Value.

[25] Including income from future option periods is pure speculation.

$$PV = \frac{\$240,000}{(.06)} \times \left[1 - \left(\frac{1}{1+.06}\right)^{25}\right] = \$3,068,005.$$

Using the capitalization approach to value, the investor assumes (implicitly) that the income, $240,000 p.a., will continue beyond the 25th year to infinity. It may not.[26] But yield capitalization (DCF) takes into account only the first 25 years of tenancy. The value of the capitalized income beyond the 25th year, still $4,000,000, is ignored.[27] The Present Value of $4,000,000 at the end of the 25th year has a PV today of: $PV_0 = \$4,000,000/(1.06)^{25} = \$931,995$. Therefore the PV of the initial term of 25 years is ($4,000,000 − 931,995) = $3,068,005. A buyer who accepts the valuation using the direct capitalization of income method will overpay by $931,995.

This example illustrates the valuation of these particular NNN leases. It also calls attention to the professional responsibility of the commercial brokerage community to provide better information and counsel to less well-informed investors who are likely to overpay for this kind of investment.

Marketability of Partial Interests

There is a continuing strong demand for unsubordinated leased-fee interests under ground leases occupied by quality tenants. These real property interests require little management time or expertise, are low in risk, are usually structured to keep pace with inflation and represent a future payoff in the ownership of the appreciated land (and possibly in the improvements). They are also quite financeable since lenders like them for the same reasons.

Leasehold interests, on the other hand, are more difficult to market, probably because they are not well understood by the average private investor. As a result they generally sell at a discount to their true investment values as measured by prevailing discount rates for similar fee-simple properties.
Some investors are also basically uncomfortable about not owning the land, even though they acknowledge that they could invest the cash representing the land's value in a separate land investment with greater potential for appreciation. Investors who are comfortable with leasehold properties are similar in their methods of valuing investments to investors who buy discounted trust deed and mortgage notes.

Exchangeability of Interests

Leased-fee interests are interests in real property and are exchangeable under S.1031 to the same extent and under the same regulations applicable to a fee-simple property, without exception.

Leasehold interests, however, may or may not be exchangeable. The federal government regards a leasehold interest with at least 30 or more years remaining on the lease to be equivalent to ownership of the fee-interest, and therefore *like-kind* to other fee-interest properties. Most states conform to the federal position. The measurement of "30 or more years remaining" includes any options which are available to

---

[26] A perpetual ground lease may be an exception.
[27] As it should be. The tenant controls the renewal after the prime term.

the ground-lessee. Therefore a lease with only 20 years remaining, but which has two 5-years options to extend the lease, will be considered 'like-kind' to other fee-interest properties for a tax-deferred exchange under S.1031.

But the exchange of real property, or real property interests, under S.1031 is not restricted to fee-interests. While it is true that a leasehold interest with less than 30 years remaining on the lease is not "like-kind" in the eyes of the IRS to a fee-interest, a leasehold interest is "like-kind" to other leasehold interests, and is therefore exchangeable with other leasehold interests.

Summary

It is apparent that an investment in a leasehold or leased-fee interest in real estate requires a very careful evaluation of the proposed or existing lease and the services of competent real estate professionals and attorneys specifically experienced in this subject.

Chapter 12
Investments
In Promissory
Notes

This chapter is a departure from the others since it deals with an item of personal property, the promissory note, rather than with real property. But the information and experience acquired by the real estate investor can also be well applied to profitable investments in mortgage and trust deed notes.

Investments in promissory notes provide the informed investor yields which are generally much higher than yields on stocks and bonds. For example, second-mortgage promissory notes returning a 12% yield will double the investor's pre-tax capital in just 6 years. They are especially attractive for inclusion in tax-deferred accounts where both the interest and returned principal can be rolled over every 3-5 years.

Promissory notes are frequently used in S.1031 exchanges to balance equities. Sometimes they are original notes created by one of the parties to the exchange but frequently are third-party notes which a participant in the exchange acquired elsewhere but desires to pass along as additional equity. In either case, it is important that the investor understand these instruments and how to value them.

Source of Promissory Notes

Many promissory notes which you may encounter will be notes created in a real estate transaction in which the seller takes back part of the purchase price from the buyer in the form of a note secured by the real property which is transferred.[1] (Under these circumstances the note is technically not considered a loan but rather an extension of credit.)

The seller typically accepts the note but does not wish to retain it and offers it for sale to a third party. You may also encounter an opportunity to acquire a note from an owner who wishes to access some of the accumulated equity in a real property. Most equity borrowers are unaware that private investors are willing to lend on established equity and do not usually require points and origination fees as does a lending institution.

---

[1]   "Purchase money trust deeds."

Safety First

The safety of these investments is paramount. The arena of the secondary note market is strewn with the financial corpses of investors who bought either a note or an interest in a note with insufficient knowledge of how they behave and what needs to be done to limit investment risk. So while we are advocates of investments in promissory notes, our first concern is to emphasize the basics of these investments and how to arrange purchases which minimize risk.

The Note vs. the Security

Many individuals refer to a mortgage or trust deed when they really mean the promissory note. It is very important to distinguish between the note and its security instrument, whether the security instrument is a trust deed or a mortgage.

The promissory note is *legal evidence* of a debt, while the mortgage or trust deed acts as *security* for the debt. Separating the whites from the yolks is important since it emphasizes that a promissory note may be collateralized by other assets acceptable to the holder of the note, not simply by the property related to the real estate transaction from which the note originates.

Therefore in this chapter we will take special care not to use the terms *mortgage* or *trust deed* interchangeably with the term promissory note, or note. They are not the same.

> As an aside...
>
> It is interesting that many investors carefully retain a copy of the mortgage or trust deed but are less careful about the promissory note itself. Since a mortgage or trust deed usually is recorded, a legal copy of the mortgage or trust deed is readily obtainable from the county recorder's office. But if a promissory note, which is not recordable, is misplaced or lost it may become a difficult problem to reestablish the existence of the debt.

Types of Promissory Notes

A note is an I.O.U. and states the amount of the debt, the interest rate to be paid, the period and amount of the payments, its due date and perhaps a specified late charge if a payment is not received by a required date. If the note is collateralized, it is said to be a *secured* note, otherwise it is an *unsecured* note. When the security is a parcel of real estate, or an interest in real estate, the secured note is either a mortgage note or a trust deed note, depending upon the security device used. The term *chattel mortgage* once referred to notes secured by personal property, but the term is now obsolete. I.O.U.s secured by personal property are now typically secured by UCC-1 (Uniform Commercial Code) Agreements. Auto loans, for instance, are usually secured by UCC-1 Agreements.

Basically, there are <u>5</u> types of promissory notes:

- A *straight* note is a note calling only for payments of interest during its term. No payment of principal is made until the due date of the note.
- An *installment* note is one which requires periodic payments of principal, separate from interest payments; e.g. the payor may be required to make interest payments monthly but separate quarterly payments to reduce the principal.
- An *amortizing* note is one which calls for periodic payments each of which contains a sum earmarked for the reduction of the principal. The length of time required for the note balance to come to zero is the amortization *schedule* of the note. Amortizing notes may become all due and payable on a *call date* before the end of their amortization schedule.
- *Adjustable* rate notes are those in which the interest rate is periodically changed in response to changes in some agreed-upon, arms-length index.

♦ *Demand* notes are those which do not become payable except on the demand of the holder of the note.

Negotiability of Notes

If you are to invest in promissory notes it is important that you invest in *negotiable* notes. In order for a note to be negotiable 4 conditions must be met:

1. The note must be signed by the maker.
2. The note must be an unconditional promise to pay a certain sum in lawful money and by no other promise, order, offset or obligation.
3. The note must be payable at a definite time, or on demand.
4. The note must be "payable to order,"[2] or to the bearer.

Holder-in-due-course

If a note is not a negotiable note it may still be legal but the assignee (payee/transferee) will not enjoy status as a *holder-in-due-course*. In this case the assignee enjoys no more legal benefits than the seller (assignor) had. Acquiring the promissory note as a *holder-in-due-course*, however, frees you from any *personal defenses* which the maker of the note can assert against you. You may acquire the note as a holder-in-due-course even if the party from whom you acquire it is not a holder-in-due-course.

A holder-in-due course is one who:

1. Acquires the note for value,
2. Takes it in good faith and without notice of any defect in the note (such as the fact that it is overdue), and without any notice of defense against the note by the maker or claim by any third party. If this is so, the maker of the note is barred from invoking certain personal defenses against a holder-in-due-course.

Personal defenses may include breach of contract, lack of consideration, fraud in the inducement, incapacity (other than minority[3]), unauthorized completion of the note and non-delivery. The note maker may still invoke certain *real defenses* such as forgery, fraud in the execution of the note, duress, legal incapacity, illegality, minority, misrepresentation, discharge in bankruptcy and material alteration (e.g. kiting).

Although regulations of the Federal Trade Commission[4] regarding holders-in-due-course preserve the personal defenses of a consumer who has entered into a consumer credit contract, these regulations have very limited applicability to real estate, save, perhaps, for a note secured by a trust deed or mortgage in favor of a contractor who has installed some home improvement.

Transferability

A promissory note may be transferred to a new holder either by endorsement or, if the note is payable to the bearer, simply by delivery. The types of endorsements include:

1. *Blank*: the holder simply signs his or her name on the back of the note

---

[2] *Payable to order* enables the creditor to designate the receiver of the payments.
[3] Failure of maker to be of legal age
[4] Code 16, Part 433 "Preservation of Consumers Claims…."

2. *Special*: the holder endorses the note by writing "Pay to the order of…(transferee)" and then signs the note
3. *Restrictive*: a type endorsement which restricts the future transferability of the note. For example, "Payable to the order of (xyz Bank) for deposit only."
4. *Qualified*: the transferor adds the words "without recourse" to what otherwise would be a Blank endorsement. The effect of this addition is to insulate the endorser from any defenses which may be raised by the maker. If a problem arises, the holder (transferee) must seek redress from the maker of the note and not from the transferor. This 'protection' is attenuated, however, by certain implied warranties that a) the note is genuine, b) the transferor has good title to the instrument, c) all prior parties had the legal capacity to contract for the debt, and d) the transferor knows of no impediments to the validity of the note.

Ordinarily it is unnecessary to arrange for a transfer of the recorded security instrument since it transfers, by operation of law,[5] with the note.

Significance of Priority

It is important to note that promissory notes are not recordable. But mortgages and trust deeds (security instruments) are recordable and the exact time, date, hour and minute of the recording determines their ranking or *priority*.

For example, suppose that a seller takes back a promissory note as part of the purchase price. The buyer obtains a new loan from a lender who requires that its security device (let's call it a trust deed) be recorded in first position. Therefore the trust deed which is to secure the seller's promissory note will be recorded after – or junior to – the lender's lien.

This recording position makes the seller's trust deed a 'second deed of trust' recorded behind (later in time than) the lender's trust deed.

If you examine the second trust deed document you will not find any pre-printed language on its face which indicates that the document is a second (or third, or fourth, etc.) trust deed. The priority is established by the date and time of recording and not by the date on which the security device may have been drafted, signed or notarized. In the event of a foreclosure by the primary lender, the proceeds of a sale would be deliverable, first to the holder of the senior T.D. and then (if any proceeds remain) to the holder(s) of the junior T.D.s in the order in which they were recorded. After all liens are satisfied, any remaining cash is payable to the owner of the property.

But this is a textbook explanation almost always at variance with the actual proceedings.

When the Lender Forecloses

When a primary lender forecloses, its demand is for the balance of its first trust deed note, together with accrued interest and costs. This demand will not include sums necessary to pay off junior liens. If the property is foreclosed by a 'power of sale' clause in either a trust deed or a mortgage, the property is auctioned off to the highest bidder. If the amount of the bid is only equal to the demand of the first trust deed holder, the property is conveyed to the successful bidder free of all subsequent or junior liens.[6] All

---

5   Without any further legal action
6   With the exception of tax liens which, regardless of the time of recording, always assume first priority.

junior liens are extinguished. If a lien holder forecloses on a junior lien, the foreclosure does not affect any senior liens. These remain on the property and the successful bidder takes title 'subject to' them.

Therefore the priority of recording establishes the order in which each lien holders gets paid and consequently assigns to each lien holder a degree of risk of <u>not</u> getting paid, which is reflected in the interest rate charged in its corresponding promissory note. The lower the priority of the securing lien, the greater the risk and the greater the risk the higher the interest rate charged.

The Junior Lienholder's Defense & Recourse

All mortgages and trust deed documents contain a clause which, in effect, says:

> *...the trustor (mortgagor) agrees to keep this trust deed (or mortgage) current*
> *and all **senior** obligations current...*

Therefore when the trustor defaults on any senior lien he automatically defaults on the junior lien, <u>even if he continues to make timely payments on the junior promissory note</u>.

This legal default on the junior lien enables the junior lien holder to initiate a foreclosure under his junior lien. In order to do so he must first cure the default on the senior lien. Unless he is able to do this the senior lien holder may foreclose on its lien earlier thereby expunging the junior lien from the title record. This does not invalidate the junior promissory note but it does convert it from a secured to an unsecured note and reduces its market value to near zero.

In view of this, it is vital that the purchaser of any promissory note secured by a junior mortgage or trust deed be able to 'step up' to make the payments necessary to cure the default on any and all senior liens which are in default. These payments will vary according to the amount of the payments on each prior lien, as well as attendant costs. Since most foreclosures are not begun until the debtor has missed at least two payments, it is essential that the junior trust deed investor maintain sufficient liquidity to cure defaults which may have been in progress for many months. Remember to include amounts necessary to pay delinquent taxes. If cash reserves are not sufficient to cover the payments on the senior loan(s) for <u>at least</u> two months plus the time required for foreclosure, <u>don't make the loan</u> regardless of the amount of owner-equity in the property.

The amount to cure a default will vary according to the time required for the foreclosure action. In some states this may be up to 10 months while in others the first lienholder may complete a foreclosure in as little as 60 days following initiation of the foreclosure proceeding. The table at the end of this chapter lists the approximate number of months required to effect a foreclosure in each state.

Method of Foreclosure

The method by which a lien holder may initiate a foreclosure action varies from state to state. In states which rely principally on the mortgage as the securing device, a foreclosure is generally initiated by the filing of a *complaint*, similar to the complaint which is filed in a civil suit. This type of foreclosure is termed a *judicial foreclosure*. If the state is one which uses a trust deed as the security, the foreclosure is initiated by the publication and recordation of a *Notice of Default*. This type of foreclosure is termed *non-judicial* since it does not require involvement of the court.

The time required to complete the foreclosure varies from as few as 60 days in Texas, which uses trust deeds, to as many as 10 months in New Jersey, Illinois and Wisconsin which use mortgages. Most lenders would prefer a non-judicial foreclosure because it is less expensive, requires a shorter time for completion and does not provide for a period of redemption - as does a mortgage. But many states bar non-judicial foreclosures. Others, which permit judicial foreclosures, also allow the mortgage instrument to contain a 'power of sale' clause which allows the lender the option of choosing a judicial or a non-judicial foreclosure.

Deficiency Judgments, Power of Redemption

If a mortgage or trust deed is foreclosed and the available cash is insufficient to pay off the balance of the promissory note, the lienholder may or may not be able to obtain a deficiency judgment. In some states in which the note is foreclosed by a non-judicial proceeding under a power of sale clause, deficiency judgments are prohibited, but in others the lienholder may attempt recovery of the shortfall by suing the debtor.

Some states, such as California which offers both a judicial and non-judicial foreclosure remedy, absolutely prohibit deficiency judgments if the loan was a 'purchase money' loan: i.e. a loan the proceeds of which were used to <u>acquire</u> title to the property.

Period of Redemption

An important difference between a trust deed and a mortgage is that trust deed sales do not provide a period following foreclosure during which the debtor may regain his property by paying all costs and amounts past due. Some states which use mortgages and provide for judicial foreclosures permit the debtor to remain in possession of the property and to redeem it for periods varying from 10 days (New Jersey) up to 12 months (Alabama).

Creditworthiness of the Borrower

Although the amount of equity which the borrower has in the property is among the most important of the lending criteria, it is not the most important for the trust deed investor. The most important criterion is the creditworthiness of the borrower. Borrowers who have a history of paying their debts - and paying their debts on time - are the best insurance the trust deed investor can have against potential loss. Fortunately the investor has a number of resources to call upon to ascertain the borrower's creditworthiness.

FICO Score	Odds of 90-Day Delinquency
595	2.25 to 1
600	4.5 to 1
615	9 to 1
630	18 to 1
645	36 to 1
660	72 to 1
680	144 to 1
700	288 to 1
780	576 to 1

The first of these is a merged credit report which shows the borrower's credit history as compiled by the three principal credit reporting agencies: Experian (formerly TRW), Equifax (formerly CBI) and Trans-Union. These reports are available on the Web for a nominal sum. This report should include the borrower's FICO® score. A FICO score is created by a rating model developed by Fair, Isaac Company and furnished to the credit reporting agency. Using this model, the agency develops the score which estimates the borrower's likelihood of <u>not</u> repaying the loan or not making payments on time. It examines 5 credit-score indicators:

1. Payment history (approx. 35% weighting)
2. Amounts owed (30%)
3. Length of Credit History (15%)
4. New Credit (10%)
5. Types of Credit in Use (10%

Institutional lenders will generally not make a loan to an applicant whose FICO score is less than 620. A score between 640 and 680 is an indication for a thorough risk evaluation, while 680 justifies a basic review only. Applicants who have scores ranging from 700-725 generally can obtain a rate reduction of 1/8 point in the interest rate, while those with scores in excess of 725 may qualify for a 1/4 point reduction.

While these guidelines are used by major lenders they do vary from lender to lender and are subject to individual interpretation. But for the private trust deed investor, these FICO scores can be very helpful in assessing creditworthiness.

The accompanying table shows the likelihood of a 90-day delinquency based on the FICO score.

Equity Criterion for Purchasing Notes

A second important criterion for the purchase of a note is the amount of equity which the owner of the securing property has in the property net of all senior liens.

During the late 1980s, the early 1990s and mid-2000 years more than 90% of all mortgages that went into foreclosure were loans made to borrowers who had less than 10% equity in the property. Many had less than 5% equity and some had none. When the value of the securing real estate dropped 5 or 10 percent, the homeowner simply walked away from the obligation reasoning that by continuing to make payments he was defending only the lender's financial interest in the property and none of his own.

In recent years lenders have resumed extending loans to borrowers who have as little as 3-5% equity, but this time with an important variation. When the borrower has less than a 20% down payment the lender on the first mortgage (or deed of trust) will require mortgage insurance. Since the cost of this insurance is not tax deductible, lenders encourage the 80-15-5% or 80-10-10% mortgage plans under which the borrower qualifies for an 80% first mortgage and thereby avoids the requirement for insurance. The lender also issues a second, fully-amortizing 15-year mortgage for either 10% or 15% of the purchase price, emphasizing to the borrower that the interest on the junior lien is tax deductible. The balance, 5% or 10%, represents the purchaser's equity. The second trust deed or mortgage loans usually carry an interest rate of from 10 to 15% enabling the primary lender to dispose of these loans in the secondary market by sale to promissory note investors.

For example, consider the financing of a $250,000 home using the 80-15-5% percent plan. The amount of the first mortgage is $200,000; the amount of the second mortgage is $37,500 and the balance, $12,500 represents the owner's 5% down payment. This property would have to lose 20% of its value before the holder of the first mortgage became at risk for a loss. But it would have to lose only 5% before the holder of the 15% junior lien is at risk of losing money. A 5% decline in value would completely eradicate the owner's equity.

It is a prudent rule to follow that you will not lend money on a property in which the borrower does not have as much (equity) to lose as you do.

Other Safeguard Requirements

Every purchase of a note secured by real property should be subject to your receipt and approval of a current Preliminary Title Report by which you can verify not only the property's ownership but also the rate and amount of all liens recorded against the title. If the note which you will buy is, or is to be, in second priority position there should be only one lien[7] recorded on the title with an earlier date.

> **Don't** be concerned if there is a current real property tax lien against the property. In most states there are only a few weeks during the year in which the property is not subject to a lien for property taxes. In some states the unpaid real property tax becomes a lien against the title even before the amount of the tax has been determined by the tax assessor.

> **Do** be concerned if real property taxes are overdue or unpaid for prior years.
> Be especially concerned if there is a lien for unpaid income taxes due either the I.R.S. or the state. Unless you are willing to dabble in purchasing tax liens, avoid these properties since the government liens may result in a tax foreclosure requiring you to pay the taxes to preserve the safety of your junior lien. If the I.R.S. has a tax lien on a property and has not received the required 25-day advance notice of a pending foreclosure, it reserves the right for a period of 120 days following foreclosure to acquire the property for the same amount paid to the lienholder. It is not required to reimburse the lienholder for any repairs or improvements made to the property following foreclosure.

It is also vital that the owner carries insurance naming you as 'additionally insured' on these policies. In reviewing the insurance policies in effect take care to determine that in the event of total or partial destruction the holder of the first mortgage or trust deed is bound to make the proceeds of insurance available for the reconstruction or repair of the property and does not have the option simply to reduce the balance on the first-position outstanding note. A lender who uses these funds to reduce a loan balance leaves you, the junior lienholder, with an impaired security.

Valuing the Promissory Note

Like all investments, promissory notes derive their value from the present value of all remaining payments due under the note, discounted at a rate acceptable to the buyer of the note.

Consider, for example, a note held by a seller in the amount of $25,000, payable monthly including interest at the annual rate of 10%, fully amortized over 30 years but all due and payable in 3 years. Suppose further that the owner of the note has held the note exactly 3 months and now wishes to sell it to you. The correct payment on the note can be determined with the aid of Excel or any financial calculator:

n	i	PV	PMT	FV
360	10/12	-$25,000	?	0
		Solving...	$219.39	

The balance of the note that will be due in 3 years can be determined by inserting 36 (months) into the
$\boxed{\text{n}}$ register and solving for FV.[8]

---

[7] Liens involve only *money* encumbrances on the title. An easement, for example, is not a lien.

[8] The balance of any amortizing loan of equal payments is equal to the FV of all the *made* payments.

n	i	PV	PMT	FV
36	10/12	-$25,000	$219.39	?
			Solving..	**$24,537.91**

> Values in FV are <u>always</u> received or paid at the end of the nth period.

Therefore if you were to acquire this note you would be entitled to 3<u>3</u> remaining payments of $219.39 plus a final payment of $24,537.91. The *balloon payment* [9] will be due together with the last monthly payment since mortgage payments are always made in arrears.

The value of these payments depends upon the discount rate which you choose to apply. <u>The discount rate will become the yield on your investment.</u> For, example, if you elect to discount these remaining payments at an annual rate of 15%, but applied monthly (since the payments are monthly), the present value of the note becomes:

n	i	PV	PMT	FV
33	**15**/12	?	$219.39	$24,537.91
	Solving....	**$22,188.27**		

If you pay exactly $22,188.27 for this note your yield will be 15% per year. If you pay more than this amount, your yield will be less and if you pay less for the note your yield will be greater.

Calculating the Yield Given a Price

It may be that the holder of the note offers the note for (say) a 10% discount from face value. What then would be your yield?

A 10% discount from face value of $25,000 indicates an asking price (PV) of $22,500. The amount of the monthly payments and the amount of the balloon payment will not change.

Solving for the yield is simple:

n	i	PV	PMT	FV
33	?	-$22,500	$219.39	$24,537.91
Solving...	**1.20**			

---

9   Any payment in the schedule which is at least twice as large as any other payment in the previous 6 months,

This value, 1.20 %, is the monthly yield which, when annualized,[10] equates to:

n	i	PV	PMT	FV
12	1.20	-1.00	-	?
			Solving...	**1.1539**

Subtracting the $1.00 leaves 0.1539 or 15.4%.

Be aware that the price of a note offered at a discount from face value may be substantially higher than the calculated Present Value of all future payments when discounted at your desired yield. This is especially true of notes that have seasoned for some time because the payor has demonstrated some degree of credit worthiness reducing some risk.

Yield after Costs

If your costs of acquiring this note total $500, this amount must be added to the purchase price of the note:

n	i	PV	PMT	FV
33	?	-$23,000	$219.39	$24,537.91
Solving...	**1.12**...			

The annualized value of the yield is 14.3%.

[The calculator carries over extra mills even though the display shows only 2 decimal places. This may account for small differences which you observe in your answers. The ellipsis (...) after 1.12% indicates that extra mills (1.12**2404**) are used in determining the answer.]

When the Payments are Not Equal

If a note in which you are interested calls for payments which change from time to time, then you must use a calculator which can determine the Present Value of an uneven cashflow. Most financial calculators can handle this kind of series. It is also easy to use a spreadsheet.

Suppose, for example, that a note calls for payments as follows: Year 1, $200; Year 2, $225; Year 3, $250. The term and interest rate will remain the same, but the final balance of the note will not be the same as a fully amortizing note with level payments. In order to determine the remaining balance of this note your must develop an amortization table for a loan with varying payments.

---

10   Multiplying by 12 to annualize ignores that the rate is compounded monthly.

An Amortization Schedule for a Loan of Uneven Payments

Consider these elements of the first two months of the note's schedule.

	A	B	C	D	E	F
3		Begin				Remain
4	Month	Balance	Payment	Interest	Paydown	Balance
5	1	25,000.00	200	208.33	-8.33	25,008.33
6	2	25,008.33	200	208.40	-8.40	25,016.74

> Copied from Excel

The interest for the first month in D5 is $1/12^{th}$ the annual interest (10%) of the Beginning Balance ($25,000 * 0.10/12). The Paydown is the amount of the Payment (C5) less the Interest due (D5). Since the interest due is greater than the stipulated Payment, the shortfall is added to the Beginning Balance of the loan to determine the Remaining Balance at the end of the month. (Remaining Balance = Beginning Balance – Paydown), or (25,000 – (–8.33)) = 25,008.33.

The Beginning Balance for the second month in cell B6 is equal to the Remaining Balance of the previous month (= F5). Once this entry is made, highlight cells C5:F5 and drag down one row. Then highlight cells B6:F6 and drag down to fill 36 rows. Then change the Payment for months 13 through 24 to $225.00; change the Payment for months 25 through 36 to $250.00. The program will automatically calculate the Remaining Balance for each month of the 36-month term.

You can see that this note involves **12** payments of $200, **12** payments of $225, **11** payments of $250 and a final payment of $24,622.87 ($24,372.87 + $250.00) since the balloon payment is due simultaneously with the last monthly payment.

How you enter these uneven payments into your financial calculator depends on the calculator you are using. But since you already have all the payments on the spreadsheet, alter the payment in cell C40 from $250.00 to $24,622.87. In cell C41 use this formula: **=NPV (rate, C8:C40)** where **rate** is your desired yield from the investment. Use the monthly rate if payments are monthly.

A	B	C	D	E	F
34	24,511.24	250.00	204.26	45.74	24,465.50
35	24,465.50	250.00	203.88	46.12	24,419.37
36	24,419.37	24,622.87	203.49	24,419.38	0.00
		22,231.42			

Don't forget that you will not receive the first three payments. If your desired discount rate is 15% per year, then the formula in C41 will becomes: **=NPV(15/12,C8:C40)**. This function will discount all the values in the array C8:C40 at the monthly rate of 1.25% and deliver the PV [11] of the series. Therefore this note, involving uneven payments, has a present value of $22,231.46 to an investor requiring a 15% annual yield.

---

[11]   The NPV function in Excel delivers the PV of an uneven cashflow series.

Determining a Yield When a Price is Quoted

If a price is quoted for this note and you wish to determine the yield using the quoted price, you need to use the IRR function. Excel's IRR function requires that all the values in the spreadsheet be contiguous. Therefore open up the spreadsheet by inserting a row after the third payment and insert the value –22,000, the quoted price.

Modify Cell C41 by adding together the final balance of the loan ($24,372.87) and the last payment ($250), since these cashflows will occur together at the end of the 36th month. Enter the result ($24,622.87) in Cell C41.

	A	B	C	D	E	F
7	3	25,016.74	200.00	208.47	-8.47	25,025.21
8			**-22,000.00**			
9	4	25,025.21	200.00	208.54	-8.54	25,033.75
10	5	25,033.75	200.00	208.61	-8.61	25,042.37

In Cell C42 enter the formula for the IRR: **= IRR (C8:C42).** Note that <u>C8</u> is negative.

	A	B	C	D	E	F
40	35	24,465.50	250	203.88	46.12	24,419.97
41	36	24,419.37	24,622.87	203.49	24,419.38	0
			=IRR(C8:C41)			

The result may be #NUM., indicating that Excel needs a little help in solving the problem. Let's assume that the IRR on a monthly basis will be about 10%/12, or 0.0083 per month. Alter the IRR formula by adding a comma after the last value and adding your guess rate as a decimal: **= IRR (C8:C41, 0.0083).** Excel responds with a value of 1.29% = 15.4% per year.

About Balloon Payments

A balloon payment in a note is defined as any payment which is at least twice as large as any other payment in the schedule of the loan. If the loan is an adjustable rate loan (ARM), a balloon payment is defined as any payment which is as least twice as large as any payment in the last 6 months.

In some states the holder of the note is required to notify the debtor if a balloon payment is about to become due. This requirement is generally limited to loans secured by residential properties (1-4 units), one unit of which is occupied by the owner. Generally this requirement does not apply to residential properties great than 4 units even if one of the units is owner-occupied, nor does is usually apply to any commercial (non-residential) property. If the note represents a seller carry-back loan, 60 days advance notice is typically required; if the note represents a 'hard money loan'[12] 90 days advance notice may be required[13]

---

[12] Cash was actually extended

[13] A *hard money* loan is one in which cash was actually advanced to the borrower, as opposed to an extension of credit as in the case of a seller carry-back note.

The notice must be in writing and contain the following:

1. The date the balloon payment is due.
2. The amount which is due. If the holder is unable to calculate the exact amount due, a 'good faith' estimate must be rendered.
3. The name and address of the person to whom the balloon payment must be made.
4. A description of the payor's right to refinance the loan (if such right exists) and the terms of the refinance.

The notices are required to be in writing and may not be made too far in advance – most regulations specify not more than 150 days before the due date. In the event that proper notice is not served, the holder of the note may not foreclose on the property nor demand payment until it has been properly served. Check your local state regulations regarding these notices.

In some states hard-money loans with a due date less than 3 years may not contain a balloon payment. If one of the units is owner-occupied, a hard-money note of 6 years or less may not contain a balloon payment, which is to say that the note must be fully amortized in 6 years.

These limitations do not usually apply to seller-carry-back notes which do not involve an actual extension of cash.[14]

Reconveyance of Security Device

When the debt has been satisfied the lienholder is required to clear the owner's title of the lien by causing a Reconveyance of Mortgage or Trust Deed to be recorded in the jurisdiction in which the security document was first recorded. Most jurisdictions provide substantial penalties, including fines and imprisonment, for lien holders who do not timely fulfill this responsibility. The lienholder is also required to return the note to the borrower. Check with the county recorder or a title company for the requirements in your state.

Reconveyance is usually accomplished through a title company or an escrow holder. In some cases the security instrument will have been made in favor of a prior owner of the note.[15] The title company will notify the party named in the mortgage or trust deed of the impending reconveyance. If the necessary documents are not forthcoming within a statutory period of time, the title company may prepare and record a *Release of Obligation*. Provided the title company has complied with the requirements for notification to the original trustee, beneficiary or mortgagee, the Release will be deemed equivalent to a reconveyance.

Lastly...

This chapter does not purport to give you legal advice, but rather to alert you to some of the important considerations which may affect an investment in promissory notes. When in doubt, consult a competent real estate attorney and an experienced Realtor.® Additional information is available at **http://www.realtytrac.com/real-estate-guides/foreclosure-laws/**

---

[14] Technically, seller-carry back notes are not loans but rather extensions of credit.

[15] In the case of a seller-carry-back note, the original seller of the property. In the case of a 'hard money' mortgage or trust deed, the original lender.

AMORTIZATION OF NOTE WITH UNEVEN PAYMENTS

	A	B	C	D	E	F
3		Begin				Remain
4	Month	Balance	Payment	Interest	Paydown	Balance
5	1	25,000.00	200	208.33	-8.33	25,008.33
6	2	25,008.33	200	208.40	-8.40	25,016.74
7	3	25,016.74	200	208.47	-8.47	25,025.21
8	4	25,025.21	200	208.54	-8.54	25,033.75
9	5	25,033.75	200	208.61	-8.61	25,042.37
10	6	25,042.37	200	208.69	-8.69	25,051.05
11	7	25,051.05	200	208.76	-8.76	25,059.81
12	8	25,059.81	200	208.83	-8.83	25,068.64
13	9	25,068.64	200	208.91	-8.91	25,077.55
14	10	25,077.55	200	208.98	-8.98	25,086.53
15	11	25,086.53	200	209.05	-9.05	25,095.58
16	12	25,095.58	200	209.13	-9.13	25,104.71
17	13	25,104.71	225	209.21	15.79	25,088.92
18	14	25,088.92	225	209.07	15.93	25,072.99
19	15	25,072.99	225	208.94	16.06	25,056.93
20	16	25,056.93	225	208.81	16.19	25,040.74
21	17	25,040.74	225	208.67	16.33	25,024.42
22	18	25,024.42	225	208.54	16.46	25,007.95
23	19	25,007.95	225	208.40	16.60	24,991.35
24	20	24,991.35	225	208.26	16.74	24,974.61
25	21	24,974.61	225	208.12	16.88	24,957.74
26	22	24,957.74	225	207.98	17.02	24,940.72
27	23	24,940.72	225	207.84	17.16	24,923.56
28	24	24,923.56	225	207.70	17.30	24,906.25
29	25	24,906.25	250	207.55	42.45	24,863.80
30	26	24,863.80	250	207.20	42.80	24,821.00
31	27	24,821.00	250	206.84	43.16	24,777.84
32	28	24,777.84	250	206.48	43.52	24,734.33
33	29	24,734.33	250	206.12	43.88	24,690.45
34	30	24,690.45	250	205.75	44.25	24,646.20
35	31	24,646.20	250	205.38	44.62	24,601.58
36	32	24,601.58	250	205.01	44.99	24,556.60
37	33	24,556.60	250	204.64	45.36	24,511.24
38	34	24,511.24	250	204.26	45.74	24,465.50
39	35	24,465.50	250	203.88	46.12	24,419.37
40	36	24,419.37	250	203.49	46.51	24,372.87

FORECLOSURE DATA BY STATE

	State	Security	Type	Initiated by	Time mos.	Redemption	Deficicency
1	Alabama	Mortgage	Non-Judicial	Publication	3	12 mos.	Allowed
2	Alaska	Trust Deed	Non-Judicial	N. of Default	4	None	Allowed
3	Arizona	Trust Deed	Non-Judicial	N. of Sale	3	None	Allowed
4	Arkansas	Mortgage	Judicial	Complaint	3	None	Allowed
5	California	Trust Deed	Non-Judicial	N. of Default	4	None	Prohibited*
6	Colorado	Trust Deed	Strict	N. of Default	5	75 days	Allowed
7	Connecticut	Mortgage	Non-Judicial	Complaint	6	None	Allowed
8	Delaware	Mortgage	Judicial	Complaint	7	None	Allowed
9	Dist. Of Col.	Trust Deed	Non-Judicial	N. of Default	4	None	Allowed
10	Florida	Mortgage	Judicial	Compliant	7	None	Allowed
11	Georgia	Security	Non-Judicial	Publication	3	None	Allowed
12	Hawaii	Mortgage	Non-Judicial	Publication	7	None	Allowed
13	Idaho	Trust Deed	Non-Judicial	N. of Default	9	None	Allowed
14	Illinois	Mortgage	Judicial	Complaint	10	None	Allowed
15	Indiana	Mortgage	Judicial	Complaint	9	3 mos.	Allowed
16	Iowa	Mortgage	Judicial	Petition	7	6 mos.	Allowed
17	Kansas	Mortgage	Judicial	Complaint	4	None	Allowed
18	Kentucky	Mortgage	Judicial	Complaint	7	None	Allowed
19	Louisiana	Mortgage	Exec. Process	Petition	6	None	Allowed
20	Maine	Mortgage	Non-Judicial	Complaint	10	None	Allowed
21	Maryland	Trust Deed	Non-Judicial	N. of Default	5	None	Allowed
22	Mass.	Mortgage	Judicial	Complaint	5	None	Allowed
23	Michigan	Mortgage	Non-Judicial	Publication	3	6 mos.	Allowed
24	Minnesota	Mortgage	Non-Judicial	Publication	4	6 mos.	Prohibited
25	Mississsippi	Trust Deed	Non-Judicial	Publication	4	None	Prohibited
26	Missouri	Trust Deed	Non-Judicial	Publication	3	None	Allowed
27	Montana	Trust Deed	Non-Judicial	N. of Default	6	None	Prohibited
28	Nebraska	Mortgage	Judicial	Petition	4	None	Allowed
29	Nevada	Trust Deed	Non-Judicial	N. of Default	4	None	Allowed
30	New Hamp.	Mortgage	Non-Judicial	N. of Sale	3	None	Allowed
31	New Jersey	Mortgage	Judicial	Complaint	10	10 days	Allowed
32	New Mexico	Mortgage	Judicial	Complaint	5	None	Allowed
33	New York	Mortgage	Judicial	Complaint	10	None	Allowed
34	N. Carolina	Trust Deed	Non-Judicial	N. of Hearing	3	None	Allowed
35	N. Dakota	Mortgage	Judical	Complaint	4	60 days	Prohibited
36	Ohio	Mortgage	Judical	Complaint	8	None	Allowed
37	Oklahoma	Mortgage	Judical	Complaint	7	None	Allowed
38	Oregon	Trust Deed	Non-Judicial	N. of Default	5	None	Allowed
39	Penn.	Mortgage	Judicial	Complaint	8	None	Allowed
40	Rhode. Is.	Mortgage	Non-Judicial	Publication	3	None	Allowed
41	S. Carolina	Mortgage	Judicial	Complaint	6	None	Allowed
42	S. Dakota	Mortgage	Judicial	Complaint	4	180 days	Allowed
43	Tenn.	Trust Deed	Non-Judicial	Publication	3	None	Allowed
44	Texas	Trust Deed	Non-Judicial	Publication	2	None	Allowed
45	Utah	Trust Deed	Non-Judicial	N. of Default	5	None	Allowed
46	Vermont	Mortgage	Judicial	Complaint	10	None	Allowed
47	Virginia	Trust Deed	Non-Judicial	Publication	4	None	Allowed
48	Washington	Trust Deed	Non-Judicial	N. of Default	5	None	Allowed
49	W. Virginia	Trust Deed	Non-Judicial	Publication	4	None	Prohibited
50	Wisconsin	Mortgage	Judicial	Complaint	10	None	Allowed
51	Wyoming	Mortgage	Non-Judicial	Publication	3	3 mos.	Allowed

GLOSSARY OF COMMON INVESTMENT TERMS

3-Property Rule: A rule governing the number of properties which an exchangor may nominate for acquisition in a delayed S.1031 exchange.

200% Rule: A rule which limits the total value of replacement properties in an exchange to not more than twice the value of the relinquished property or properties.

ABS: Asset Backed Security

Accession: A means by which real property may be acquired by the physical addition of land, as by a landslide.

Accommodator: A financial entity used to carry out an exchange.

Adjustable Rate Mortgage (ARM): A loan in which the interest rate is changed periodically to reflect changes in market rate interest.

Adjusted Basis: *Tax Basis* with adjustments made for additions, divestments, depreciation and amortization of certain expenses.

Adverse Possession: A means of obtaining title to a property which is hostile to the true owner's interests by possessing the property and paying its taxes.

After-tax Cashflow: Spendable Income after payment of current taxes.

AITD: An acronym for All-Inclusive Deed of Trust. Also knows as a *wraparound mortgage*.

Allocation of Basis: Apportioning the value of a property between the value of the non-depreciable land and its depreciable improvement.

Amortizing Loan: A loan whose regular payments will eventually reduce the balance to zero.

Appurtenance: A non-tangible asset associated with property ownership: e.g. an easement.

Assessed Value: An estimate of the value of a property usually for tax and loan purposes.

Assumption of loan: Assuming from another legal responsibility for a loan.

Attorn: Recognition by a tenant of a new landlord.

Balloon Payment: A loan payment at least twice as large as any other payment in the schedule or, in the case of an ARM, in the last 6 mos.

Basis: Value of a property for the purpose of computing gains and losses.

Beneficiary: One who benefits from a trust or agreement.

Boot: Unlike property given or received in a S.1031 exchange.

Bundle of Rights: A land theory which equates property ownership to the ownership of a collection of property rights.

CAM Charges: Common Area Maintenance charges incurred in the upkeep of areas used by more then one tenant.

Capital Asset: Property held which is not used in a trade or business.

Capital Gain: A gain from the disposition of a capital asset.

Capitalization rate: The rate at which an investment property delivers Net Operating Income in relation to (divided by) its fair market value.

Capital Structure: The amounts and sources of cash used to acquire a property.

Cash-on-Cash: The ratio of the cash received from property operations in relation to the cash invested.

CDO: Collateralized Debt Obligation.

CLO: Collateralized Loan Obligation

CMBS: Collateralized Mortgage-Backed Security.

Conduit lender: A lender whose mortgages are used as collateral for securities.

Contingencies: Provisions in a contract or agreement which qualify the obligation to complete the agreement.

Contract for Deed: An agreement which conveys only possession and use but not legal title until a future stipulated payment is made.

Counteroffer: The response to an offer to buy or sell which changes some terms or conditions.

Covenant: A contractual agreement to do or not to a certain thing.

CPI: Acronym for Consumer Price Index. An index published by the Federal Bureau of Labor Statistics intended to measure the cost of a basketful of goods purchased by the average household. A measure of inflation.

Credit Tenant: A tenant whose balance sheet virtually guarantees the ability to continue lease payments.

Debt Coverage Ratio: The ratio of the Net Operating Income to the annual cost of servicing the loan. Same as **Debt Service Ratio.**

Debt Yield Ratio: The ratio of the Net Operating Income to the total loan amount.

Deed: A recordable legal instrument which evidences ownership of a real property.

Deed of Reconveyance: A deed used to return a security interest in real property upon satisfaction of the loan.

Defeasance clause: A kind of pre-payment clause found in mortgages issued by conduit lenders.

Deficiency Judgment: A court order to pay a creditor the balance of a secured loan when the sale of the security is insufficient to discharge the debt.

Delayed Exchange: An exchange in which the relinquished property and the replacement property transfer on different dates.

Depreciation: A loss of value from any cause.

Depreciation Allowance: An annual deduction from income to compensate for the diminution of property value.

Depreciation Recapture S. 1250: The recapture (taxation) of depreciation allowances already taken.

Discounting: A process of converting a future value to a present value.

Discount Rate: a rate used to convert the value of a future sum to a present value.

Due-on-Sale Clause: A clause in a mortgage or deed of trust which permits the lender to call in a loan upon transfer (alienation) of title.

Easement: the right to use but not possess another's property.

Easement by Prescription: An easement obtained against the will of the property owner.

EBITDA: Earnings before interest, taxes, depreciation and amortization deductions from operating income. Commonly understood to be equal to cashflow.

Economic Obsolescence: Loss of real property value as the result of a deterioration in the physical surroundings. See Functional Obsolescence.

Escrow Account: the type account held by an escrow agent (officer).

Escrow Agent: A neutral stakeholder who holds assigned assets of the parties to a contract pending completion of the contract.

Estate: an interest in property.

Estate-in-Remainder: The interest which exists at the end of a life-estate which passes to a third party.

Estate-in-Reversion: The interest which exists at the end of a life-estate which passes to the grantor or to the grantor's heirs.

Estate for Years: An interest in real property for a determinable period of time.

Estoppel Certificate: A certificate used to elicit and record the rights of a party at a particular moment in time. The party would later be legally barred (estopped) from exercising that right to the detriment of others.

Exchange Period: The period which is 180 days following the relinquishment of an exchange property in a delayed exchange: a period which runs parallel to but longer than the Identification Period.

Executory Cycle: The cycle of the offer: presentation, acceptance of the offer and reconveyance of the acceptance to the original offeror in the formation of a binding contract

Expense Stop: A limitation to the landlord's responsibility for the payment of operating expenses above a specified dollar amount.

Fee Simple: Unqualified ownership of all the rights to a real property.

Fee Simple Absolute: Same as above.

Fixture: Once an article of personal property which has since become a part of real property. A *fixture* is real property.

Functional Obsolescence: A loss in value as the result of outdated features or design.

Future Value: The monetary value of a present sum or series of payments to be received in the future.

Grant Deed: A deed used to convey real property but with only limited warranties.

Green Building: A commercial or residential property built, adapted or managed to lessen adverse effects on the environment.

Gross Lease: A lease in which the landlord pays all expenses of operating and maintaining the property.

Gross Rent Multiplier: The ratio of the price of a property to its scheduled rent.

Ground Lease: A lease which conveys the rights to use, possess and develop real property.

Holder in Due Course: A legal status of a receiver of a promissory note which bars the maker of the note from exercising certain *real defenses* against repayment of the note.

Holding Period: The length of time an asset is owned.

HVAC Systems: An acronym for Heating, Ventilating and Air Conditioning systems.

Identification Period: The period in a delayed exchange which is 45 days *following* the date of the transfer of the relinquished property.

Installment Sale: A sale in which a portion of the sales price is received in the year or years following the year of the sale.

Internal Rate of Return (IRR): The yield on an investment measured over the entire holding period. That single discount rate that will deliver a Net Present Value of zero.

Investment Value: The financial value of an investment in contrast to its current market value.

Junior Lien: A lien recorded at a time following the recordation of another lien. Does not refer to the dollar value of the lien.

Land Contract: A contract between a vendor and vendee which conveys the rights of use and possession but not the deed to a property. See Contract for Deed

Lease: A legal contract conveying use and possessory interests to a tenant for a defined or definable period of time.

Leased-fee Interest: The remaining interest held by the owner of a property who has leased the property.

Leasehold Interest: The real property interest held by a tenant.

Letter of Intent: A letter outlining some of the proposed terms for the acquisition or rental of a property.

Leverage: The amount of borrowed funds in relation to property value used to control an investment.

Lien: An encumbrance against the title which involves money.

Life Estate: A fee interest whose duration is tied to the life of a living person and whose duration is therefore indeterminable.

Liquidated Damages: The amount of monetary damages which is accepted by a party to an agreement to satisfy all future potential claims in the event of a contract default.

Littoral: Bordering water as coastal, lakeside or riverside property

Lock-in Clause: A clause barring the prepayment of a loan.

MACRS: An acronym for Modified Accelerated Cost Recovery System. A federal depreciation schedule.

Mid-Month Convention: A required accounting convention which regards the date of purchase or disposition of an investment real property to be at mid-month regardless of the actual day of transfer.

Modified Gross Lease: A lease in which the tenant pays some, but not all, of the costs of property maintenance and repair.

Mortgage Over Basis: In an installment sale, the amount by which the balance of an existing mortgage exceeds the taxpayer's current Basis in the property.

Net Investment Income: A surtax of 3.8% levied on Mod. Gross Adjusted Income derived from interest, investments, dividends, rents, royalties, and trading activities.

Net Mortgage Relief: The incremental amount by which an exchanging party is relieved of mortgage on a relinquished property over the mortgage on an acquired property. A form of taxable Boot.

Net Operating Income: Income received from operations net of operating expenses. Does not include income from one-time dispositions or passive investments.

Net Present Value: The present value or worth of a sum or series of sums minus the original investment amount.

Non-Disturbance Clause: A clause in a lease which permits the tenant to continue quiet enjoyment following a transfer of ownership.

Occupancy Lease: A lease which delivers the rights to use and possess real property.

Offset Statement: A statement showing the current balance of an account after any allowances due either party.

Option: A right, but not the obligation, to do or not to do something in the future. An option is binding on the grantor of the option but not on the optionee.

Ownership in Severalty: Single ownership apart from all others.

Passive Activity: A tax classification applied to persons who do not materially participate in the management of an asset. Used to determine the deductibility of operating losses.

Periodic Tenancy: A rental agreement which extends from one period to the next with no definite ending time. Also, Tenancy from Period to Period

Preliminary Title Report: A report on the condition of the title to real property issued by a title company preliminary to the issuance of a title insurance policy.

Present Value: The discounted worth of sums to be received in the future.

Pro-forma: An estimate of the income and expenses of a property over a number of future periods of operation.

Qualified Intermediary: An entity which acts to implement a delayed exchange. An accommodator or "strawman."

Quiet Title Action: A legal procedure taken to remove a cloud from title to real property.

Quitclaim Deed: A deed which conveys an interest which may be owned but which offers no representations or warranties that any interest is actually owned.

Realized Gain: The excess of net selling price over Adjusted Basis but which is not yet taxable. Same as Indicated Gain.

Recognized Gain: A realized or indicated gain which becomes currently taxable.

Recourse Loan: A loan in which the lender has recourse to other assets of the borrower in the event of a default.

Relinquished Property: The property given up in an exchange.

Replacement Property: The property acquired in an exchange.

Restrictive Covenant: An enforceable clause in a deed or lease which limits what the owner or tenant may do with the property.

Return on Equity (ROE): The yield (percent return) on the owner's equity invested in a property.

Return on Investment (ROI): The yield on all invested funds (equity + debt).

Reverse Exchange: An exchange in which the replacement property is acquired by the Qualified Intermediary before the relinquished property is delivered to the Intermediary.

Reversionary Interest: The residual value of the investment at the end of the investment or lease period.

Safe Harbor Rules: Rules outlined by the IRS which if followed will safeguard the taxpayer from violations.

Senior Lien: A lien recorded earlier in time to another lien.

Spendable Income: The amount of operating income left after the payment of all operating expenses and loan costs but before income taxes.

Simultaneous Exchange: An exchange in which the relinquished and replacement properties transfer on the same date.

Starker Exchange: A now-obsolete reference to a delayed exchange patterned after exchanges by B.J. Starker whose I.R.S. cases first validated the concept of non-simultaneous exchanges.

Straight-line Depreciation. Depreciation which is equal in amount in each tax reporting period.

Straight Note: A promissory note which provides no payment on the principal during the term of the loan.

Subordination: The act of moving an earlier recorded instrument to a junior priority position.

Tenants-in-Common: A distinct form of ownership in which multiple owners may hold equal or unequal direct interests in real property.

Triple Net Lease (NNN): A lease under which the tenant pays all costs of maintenance and operation of the property.

Trust: Property, real or personal, held by one party for the benefit of another.

Trustee: An individual who manages the assets of a trust for the trust's beneficiaries.

Trust Deed: A deed which conveys to a beneficiary the non-judicial right to sell the security in the event of a default. No other property rights are conveyed.

Trustor: One who creates a trust. A settlor. A person or entity who conveys assets to a trust.

Unlawful Detainer Action: An action in law taken to regain use and possession of real property following a default by a tenant.

Unrecaptured S.1250 Depreciation: Depreciation taken by the taxpayer on which taxes have not been paid at the time of sale.

Warranty Deed: A deed which conveys title to real property and also makes certain express representations concerning the condition of the title.

Wrap-Around Mortgage: Same as an AITD. A junior note whose principal and payments wrap around or encompass the principal and payments due on one of more senior notes.

Yield Capitalization: A synonym for Discounted Cash Flow

Yield Maintenance Clause: A kind of pre-payment clause used by conduit lenders to maintain the original yield contemplated by the lender.

INDEX

INDEX

INDEX

NOTES

www.ingramcontent.com/pod-product-compliance
Lightning Source LLC
Chambersburg PA
CBHW080524220326

41599CB00032B/6189